W9-CQF-366

This is an annual. That is to say, it is substantially revised each year, the new edition appearing each November. Those wishing to submit additions, corrections, or suggestions for the 1999 edition should submit them prior to February 1, 1998, using the form provided in the back of this book. (Forms reaching us after that date will, unfortunately, have to wait for the 2000 edition.)

What Color Is Your Parachute?

Other Books by Richard N. Bolles

The Three Boxes of Life,
And How to Get Out of Them

Where Do I Go from Here with My Life?
(co-authored with John C. Crystal)

Job Hunting on the Internet

Job-Hunting Tips for the So-Called Handicapped

How to Find Your Mission in Life

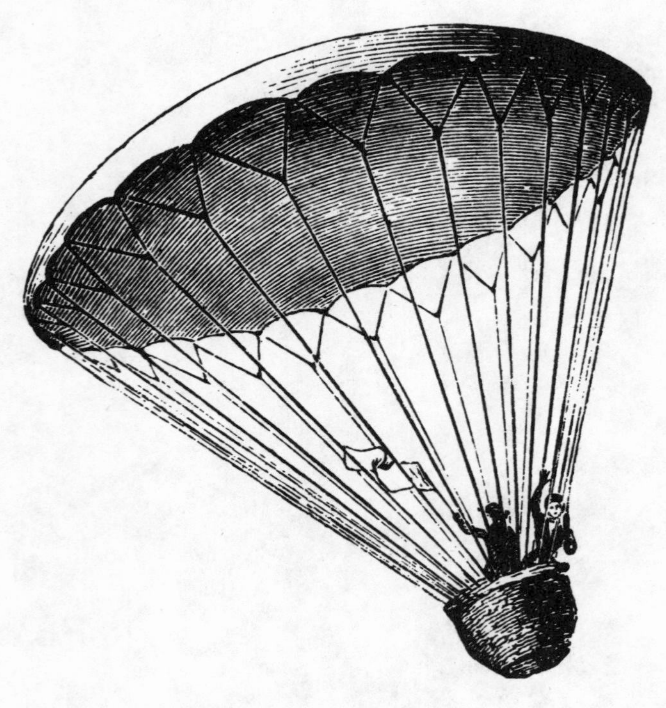

1998 Edition

What Color Is Your Parachute?

A Practical Manual for Job-Hunters & Career-Changers

by

Richard Nelson Bolles

Ten Speed Press

PUBLISHER'S NOTE

This publication is designed to provide accurate and authoritative information in regard to the subject matter covered. It is sold with the understanding that the publisher is not engaged in rendering professional career services. If expert assistance is required, the service of the appropriate professional should be sought.

Photograph of parachutist on book divider © Bernard Parker. Used with permission.

The drawings on pages 104, 116, 117, 119, 148–149, and *Workbook 8–9* are by Steven M. Johnson, author of *What The World Needs Now.*

Library of Congress Catalog Card Information on file with the publisher.
ISBN 0-89815-931-8, paper
ISBN 0-89815-932-6, cloth

Published by Ten Speed Press, P.O. Box 7123, Berkeley, California 94707

Typesetting by Star Type, Berkeley
Printed in the United States of America

3 4 5 6 7 8 9

Contents

Parachute Workbook and Resource Guide

This is dedicated to the one I love
(my wife, Carol)

Preface to the 1998 Edition

This is the 28th annual edition of this book.

It is the most popular job-hunting book in the world, existing in ten languages currently, and more to come.

Six million people have used this book, and twenty thousand people a month go into a bookstore to buy it. Many, in fact, buy the new edition each year. So, it is a book many people are quite familiar with.

Nonetheless, for new and old readers alike, it is occasionally worth summarizing what the book is all about.

Its history is: first published December 1, 1970; revised every year since 1975 -- and sometimes completely rewritten *(as, last year).* It has contributed to our culture such original concepts as *informational interviewing, trioing, The Party Exercise (of John Holland's work), and -- ugh -- "golden parachutes."* It was the first to popularize for a broader public the ideas of Sidney Fine, John Holland, John Crystal, Arthur Miller, Bernard Haldane, Dick Lathrop, and numerous other original thinkers in this field. It has been much honored. In fact, *by some fluke,* it even appeared on the Library of Congress' 1995–1996 list, called "25 Books That Have Shaped Readers' Lives."

Its motto is: "Give me a fish, and I will eat for today; teach me to fish, and I will eat for the rest of my life." We want to teach you not only how to do *this* job-hunt or career-change that currently faces you, but how to do every job-hunt for the rest of your life. In a word, we want to *empower* you. *These words were in the very first edition of this book, back in 1970.*

Its purpose is: to save job-hunters from lowered self-esteem. The unfortunate characteristic of the job-hunt is that if you use a method *(like resumes)* that you think works for everyone else, but it doesn't work for you, you don't just fail to find a job; you feel there's something really wrong with you. The purpose of this book is to tell you how often a particular method fails, so you don't take it *personally.*

Its attitude is: iconoclastic. It is not only willing, but anxious, to tell *the truth* about *everything* -- ads, agencies, resumes, counseling, testing, the Internet, and other methods that everyone swears by.

Its style is: that of a friendly uncle (with a playful sense of humor) giving you advice on a subject he knows well, using informal writing, amusing cartoons, and helpful graphics.

Its target is: every kind of job-hunter or career-changer, both those who want to spend the least amount of time possible on their job-hunt, and only want some quick tips (the impatient job-hunter), and those who are willing to roll up their sleeves and put in a lot of time and work on their job-hunt, or career-change (the determined job-hunter).

Its structure is: What. Where. How. The aim of *Parachute* is to teach a simple method that everyone can understand. Hence, for twenty-seven years, its structure has been: What do you most enjoy doing? Where would you most like to do that? *And,* How do you identify and then secure such a job, or career?

Its method is: a careful inventory of yourself, by writing and analyzing stories about yourself, then filling out a pictorial diagram of A Flower (which represents both You, and your desired job or career).

Its content is: two volumes in one, two books in one -- the first (this one) containing the essential stuff that *every* reader needs to know; the second volume or book behind this one, but in the same binding (called *The Parachute Workbook and Resource Guide*) containing stuff that only *some* readers need to know.

Its design is: created by a genius called Bev Anderson, who from the first -- and for twenty-five years thus far -- has shaped each year's new edition of this book, together with the author (*Ye Humble Author,* let us emphasize) -- who pastes up much of this book with his own hands, using scissors, paper, galleys, graphics, hot wax, and playfulness.

Its publisher is: Phil Wood, owner of Ten Speed Press in Berkeley, California. For twenty-five years *(the first two years of its life, this book was self-published)* I have watched large publishers go through whole battalions of editors, and executives, while all these years I have been able to deal with the same man, the same publisher, the same friend. We have travelled together, lunched together, argued together, and supported one another through thick and thin. That kind of long-lasting friendship has inevitably put its stamp also on this book and its success.

Well, here endeth the summary.

In addition to this summary, I need to add a little bit about what has been going on in my own life. My annual readers (of whom there are *many*) always want to know -- for, this book has also made us friends.

To keep this brief: this past year I put a great deal of time and work into setting up a website, dealing with job-hunting on the Internet (`www.washingtonpost.com/parachute`) -- with the help and kindness and support of (as you may guess) *The Washington Post.* The contents of this site are summarized in one of the chapters of the Workbook here, and also are available (in an expanded form) as a separate booklet -- available from Ten Speed Press or your local bookstore.

I also have been working on helping to produce a CD-ROM of *The Quick Job-Hunting Map,* featuring lots of video instruction from me, which will be out by the time you read this.

Also, a beloved colleague and friend of mine, Howard Figler, and I have been working on producing together a training manual for career counselors, which should be out by mid-1998.

An audiotape of *The Art of Living,* by Epictetus, is now out; with me as the reader.

And -- on the health front -- I turned 70, had two uneventful but miraculous cataract surgeries -- and now can *see* what I'm talking about.

I conclude this Preface, with my annual bunch of heartfelt thank you's:

• My thanks first of all to all my readers, and most especially to the two thousand or so, who write me each year. I deeply regret I can no longer answer each individual correspondent. I think authors should answer their mail, and I did so for twenty-five years, sometimes staying up late at night to do so, answering every single letter I ever received; but now at the age of 70, I can no longer keep this up. I trust you will understand, and forgive.

I still *read* every one of the letters that come in, and feel that no author could possibly ask for more loving, and appreciative readers -- not in a million years. So if you write me, you can be assured that I will read what you have to say, and ponder it well. But if you have job-hunting problems, or other questions, I strongly recommend that rather than writing to me, you contact instead one of the counselors near you, who are listed on pp. 243 ff in *The Parachute Workbook and Resource Guide.*

• My thanks to my beloved publisher, Phil Wood, as I mentioned, and to all the folks over at Ten Speed Press who help get this book out, each year: Kirsty Melville, Mariah Bear, Jackie Wan, the folks at Fifth Street Design, Hal Hershey, and Linda Davis, our caring typesetter.

• My thanks to my family -- my dear, dear wife, Carol, for her wit, wisdom, and wonderful love over many years; my four grown children, Stephen, Mark, Gary, and Sharon, and my dear stepdaughter, Serena; my dear sister, Ann Johnson, and last but hardly least, my ninety-four-year-old aunt, Sister Esther Mary, of the Community of the Transfiguration (Episcopal) in

Glendale, Ohio, who has taught me to serve the Lord, from my youth up.

- Indeed, no litany of thanks would be complete without my thanking The Great Lord God, Father of our Lord Jesus Christ, and source of all grace, wisdom, and compassion, Who has given me this work of helping so many people of different faiths, tongues, and nations, with their job-hunt, and the meaning of their life. I am grateful beyond measure for such a life, such a mission, and such a privilege.

Dick Bolles
P. O. Box 379
Walnut Creek
California 94597-0379
7/13/97

My Annual Grammar & Language Footnote

I want to explain three points of grammar, in this book: pronouns, commas, and italics. My unorthodox use of them invariably offends unemployed English teachers so much that they write me to apply for a job as my editor.

To save us unnecessary correspondence, let me explain. Throughout this book, I often use the apparently plural pronoun "they," "them," or "their" after *singular* antecedents -- such as, "You must approach *someone* for a job and tell *them* what you can do." This sounds strange and even *wrong* to those who know English well. To be sure, we all know there is another pronoun -- "you" -- that may be either singular or plural, but few of us realize that the pronouns "they," "them," or "their" were also once treated as both plural and singular in the English language. This changed, at a time in English history when agreement in *number* became more important than agreement as to sexual *gender.* Today, however, our priorities have shifted once again. Now, the distinguishing of sexual *gender* is considered by many to be more important than agreement in *number.*

The common artifices used for this new priority, such as "s/he," or "he and she," are -- to my mind -- tortured and inelegant. Casey Miller and Kate Swift, in their classic, *The Handbook of Nonsexist Writing,* agree, and argue that it is time to bring back the earlier usage of "they," "them," and "their" as both singular and plural -- just as "you" is/are. They further argue that this return to the earlier historical usage has already become quite common *out on the street* -- witness a typical sign by the ocean which reads:

"*Anyone* using this beach after 5 p.m. does so at *their* own risk." I have followed Casey and Kate's wise recommendations in all of this.

As for my commas, they are deliberately used according to my own rules -- rather than according to the rules of historic grammar (which I did learn -- I hastily add, to reassure my old Harvard professors, who despaired of me during English class, weekly). In spite of those rules, I follow my own, which are: I write conversationally, and put in a comma wherever I would normally stop for a breath, were I speaking the same line.

The same conversational rule applies to my use of *italics*. I use *italics* wherever, were I speaking the sentence, I would put *emphasis* on that word or phrase. Rarely, I also use italics where there is a digression of thought, and I want to maintain the main thought and flow of the sentence. All in all, I write as I speak.

P.S. Over the last twenty-five years, a few critics (very few) have claimed that *Parachute* is too complicated in its vocabulary and grammar for anyone except a college graduate. An Englishman wrote me this year with a different view. He said there is an index that analyzes a book to tell you what grade in school you must have finished, in order to understand it. My book's index, he said, turned out to be 6.1, which means you need only have finished sixth grade in a U.S. school in order to understand it.

Here in the U.S., a college instructor came up with a similar finding. He phoned me to tell me that my book was rejected by the authorities as a proposed text for his college course, because the book's language/grammar was not up to college level. "What level was it?" I asked. "Well," he replied, "when they analyzed it, it turned out to be written on an eighth-grade level."

Sixth or eighth -- that seems just about right to me. Why make things complicated, when they can be expressed simply?

R.N.B.

"I don't have a parachute of any color."

Well, yes, you do have
great big teeth; but, never mind
that. You were great to at least
grant me this interview.

Little Red Riding Hood

CHAPTER ONE

A Job-Hunting We Will Go

Okay, this is it.
The moment of truth has arrived
For You. It's time
To go out, and look for a job,
Out there in *the job-market,*
Which all your friends speak of
In hushed tones, as though it were
A battlefield, littered with the bodies
Of the unemployed,
Who tried and failed to find a job
Before you.

You've heard of course
Their stories:
Of graduates
With shiny MBA degrees
Who cannot find
The simplest kind of work.
Of friends who
Studied all the occupational trends,
And then went back to school
To learn the *hot* trade of the moment, but
Can find no work in that *hot* trade,
And two years later are still
Unemployed, angry, or depressed
Beyond all measure.
You've heard
Of people who worked for thirty-five years
For just one place,
And then got downsized
And now are only able
To find temporary work.
You've heard
Of former college profs with two degrees
Working now at the local deli;
Of union workers who went out on strike
Only to find, this time,
Their jobs were not waiting for them, when
They wanted to return,

And now they wander, lost,
And bewildered,
For no one told them that if they strike
They might strike out
In this *new world.*
Such sad and tragic stories
As these
Are in the papers, everyday;
And so, we know,
How well we know,
What lies in store
For us, out there
On the job-market battlefield
Littered with bodies --
Eight million of them
By last count.

So, now it is our turn,
And what is it we do,
When our job-hunting time has come?
We procrastinate,
That's what we do.
We're *busy winding things up*, we say.
Or, just waiting until we feel a little less
'Burnt-out,' and more 'up' for the task
Ahead, we say; though actually,
If the truth were known,
We're hoping for *a miracle*,
You know the one I mean:
A rescuer, suddenly appearing
On a white horse,
Coming, coming to save us
We don't know
His name: is it
Our former employer,
Or the government,
Our union,
Our relatives or friends?
We are unclear; we only know

The world owes us
A job.
It shouldn't be up to us
To have to go hunting for it,
So hard, ourselves,
Although of course we know
It is precisely up to
Us.

So, we make up a glorious resume
By ourselves or with some help.
How it sparkles, how it shines,
How quickly it will get us
A job.
We send it out
By the hundreds,
By the bushels,
And then we sit by the phone
Waiting for that inevitable
Call,
From some bright-eyed employer-type
Who, seeing our glorious history,
Will cry out "*This is exactly the person*
That we have been looking for!"

But there is one small problem: the call
Never comes.
And we are left to wait
And wait
And wait
While the world goes out of its way,
It seems,
To tell us how little
It cares
Whether we find work,
Or not.

We seek out family and friends' advice,
And the first thing

That they say to us, is,
"Have you tried employment agencies?"
"Why, no," we say,
So down we go.
Down, down, down
To the ante-room, and all those hopeful
Haunted faces.
Our first bout, here,
With *The Dreaded Application Form.*
"Previous jobs held.
List in reverse chronological order."
We answer the questions, then we sit
And wait.
The interviewer, at last, calls us in;
She (or he) of the over-cheerful countenance,
Who we know will give us good advice.
"*Let's see, Mr. or Ms.,*
What kind of a job are you looking for?"
"Well," say we,
"You can see, there, what I've done.
What do you think?"
She studies, again, our application form;
"*It seems to me,*" she says, "*that with your background*
-- It is a bit unusual --
You might do very well in sales."
"Oh sales," say we. "*Yes, sales,*" says she, "*in fact*
I think I could place you almost immediately.
We'll be in touch. Is this your phone?
I'll call you tomorrow night, at home."
We nod, and shake her hand, and that
Is the last time we ever hear
From her.

We're reduced to the want ads,
By our miserable plight,
But we are dumbfounded
Right there, at the sight
Of those little boxes
Describing jobs that are built

As little boxes
For the soul.
We call on the employers,
We tell them, of course, that we're job-hunting now,
"*And your ad looked just right for me . . .*" O wow!
Look at that face change, are we in the soup!
As we wait for the heave-ho, the ol' Alley-oop!
Overqualified you say?
Two hundred before me
Have been here already,
And you have only five
Vacancies? No,
Of course I understand."

It is the end of paper, for us.
We know now that our feet
Must be pressed
Into service; so
Out we go,
Pounding the pavements,
Knocking on doors,
Visiting companies,
Getting rejected
At place after place,
Getting discouraged,
Day after day,
Getting depressed --
How pathetic, this is,
How crushing to
Our self-esteem.

Weeks drag by,
Months drag by,
And we are reeling
From rejection shock,
And ever we are thinking:
The job-hunt seems the loneliest task in the world.
Is it this difficult for other job-hunters
Or career-changers?

Well, friend, the answer is YES.

Are other people this discouraged,
And desperate and depressed,
And frustrated, and so low in self-esteem after
A spell of job-hunting?

The answer, again -- unhappily -- is

YES.

YES.

YES.

But now, it's time to tell you,
There is something you can do
To change all this.

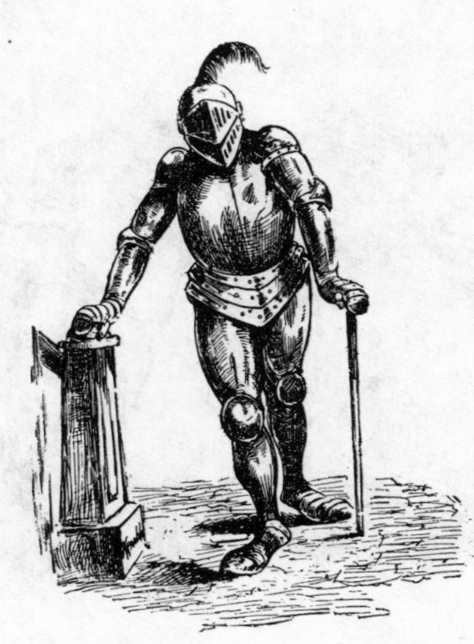

It was the best of times,
It was the worst of times,
It was the age of wisdom,
It was the age of foolishness,
It was the epoch of belief,
It was the epoch of incredulity,
It was the season of light,
It was the season of darkness,
It was the spring of hope,
It was the winter of despair,
We had everything before us,
We had nothing before us,
We were all going direct to heaven,
We were all going direct the other way . . .

Charles Dickens
A Tale of Two Cities

CHAPTER TWO

FOR THE IMPATIENT JOB-HUNTER

THERE ARE ALWAYS JOBS OUT THERE

Table of Contents

Chapter 2

Now I know you're patient. *Really.* Normally.

It's just that *time* has become the big issue, for you.

You're out of work, you're running out of money, and the sheriff is closing in. You've *got* to find work -- like: *yesterday.*

You want tips, hints, quick strategies. Briefly described.

You haven't got time for a lot of reading.

You want to get charged up, motivated, filled with hope and optimism.

And then, you want to find a job within two weeks. Or yesterday.

In any event, the question is, what should you do?

Where should you begin?

You must begin by understanding this simple truth:

THE WORKPLACE IS ALWAYS CHANGING

The workplace is always changing, always in turmoil, always in flux.

Fields rise, fall, and all but disappear. Look at farming. In 1890, 43% of all the workers in the U.S. were farmers. By 1920, that was down to 27%. By 1950, 12.2%. By 1970, 4.6%. And in 1995, only 1.9%.[1] The number of farms currently (1,925,000) is at a level not seen since 1850. Of course, at the same time new occupational fields arise, such as computing, and we begin the process all over again.

Occupations rise, fall, and all but disappear. Look at the blacksmith, the buggy-whip maker, and others. Of course, at the same time new occupations arise, such as computer animator, and we begin the process all over again.

Companies rise, fall, and often disappear. Remember Gimbels, Wanamakers, The New York Sun, I. Magnin's, the *Saturday*

1. *U.S.A. Today*, April 8, 1996.

Review, Kresge's, any number of steel companies, and others? Gone. Of course, at the same time new companies arise, such as Netscape, and older companies redesign and reshape themselves, with new strategies, new technology, and new products or services, and thus we begin the process all over again.

It follows from all of this that *jobs* also rise, fall, and often disappear. Look at the hostile takeovers, mergers, downsizing, and other trends which have caused so many jobs to disappear in the last few years. Of course, at the same time new jobs are born, at least two million of them a year (on average) in the U.S., often in other fields, and we begin the process all over again.

Yes, the workplace is always in flux, always in transition, always in turmoil -- it always has been, and it always will be.

So, in the '90s the workplace is just doing what it has always done. But there *are* six things that are different about the '90s:

First of all, this normal process of change and flux has been greatly speeded up, much like the 'time-lapse' photography you sometimes see on TV, where the clouds seem to race across the sky. They've thought of a dozen names for this *speeded-up process*: merging, downsizing, restructuring, rightsizing, reengineering, delayering, reorganizing, consolidating etc. They all refer to the speeding up of a normal process in the job-market.

Secondly, what is different about the '90s is that a larger number of workers than normal have been affected by this more rapid change. *And,* these workers come from all different classes -- even those classes which, in the *old days* seemed immune to the changes affecting everyone else -- particularly

white-collar workers, and middle to upper management. In the U.S. alone almost three million people are laid off annually, which means more than 43 million U.S. jobs have been erased since 1979. This is beyond normal. In fact, seven out of ten U.S. households have had some kind of 'close encounter' with layoffs since 1979; four out of every ten households know a relative, friend, or neighbor who was laid off; and one out of every three U.S. households has had a family member laid off.[2]

Thirdly, what is different about the '90s is that there is much less warning of anything. When the changes occur, when jobs are terminated or disappear in this decade, there may in fact be no warning at all. Some workers have learned they had no job by listening to the radio while driving to work that morning. This has greatly increased people's jitters and anxiety, in the workplace. Every new layoff causes more anxiety among those who are left.

Fourth, what is different about the '90s is that there is a great deal more injustice in the workplace. While admittedly mergers or downsizings are used by employers to get rid of employees they wished to fire anyway, it is also true that loyal, effective employees, with ten, twenty years' devoted service, are getting unjustly discharged. In too many places, these include those employees who helped make the place run well, gave it heart, and caring. They are let go because downsizings demand every employee justify his or her existence, and their contribution was hard to measure *according to the bottom line.* Thus more than one U.S. business is unwittingly, by its downsizing, turning into a machine without a heart, because it unjustly discharged the 'heart people' that every organization needs if it is to bless the earth, and be a humane workplace.

Fifth, what is different about the '90s is that we are now in a global market, and the new jobs being born in the U.S. and elsewhere are under great pressure to stay competitive with the lower wages paid elsewhere in the world. Hence, many of the new jobs being born offer lower wages than job-hunters have been accustomed to -- resulting in lower living standards for many.

---

2. *The New York Times,* March 3, 1996.

Finally, what is different about the '90s is that the workforce is increasingly dividing into a two-class society: *those who are well off,* due to inheritance, or stockholdings, or savings in their younger years, or the fact that they are currently high-skill, high-wage, high-in-demand workers; versus *those who are having trouble keeping their head above water,* due to their having no savings, or being low-skill, low-wage workers in today's economy.

The interests of these two classes often are diametrically opposed, as when one part of the society weeps at the news of higher unemployment, while another part of the society -- namely stockholders -- rejoices at the news, since this means interest rates will stay level or come down, *that they might flourish.*

Dickens put it best, for the words he once used to describe two cities now describe the workplace of the nineties: *it was the best of times, it was the worst of times.*

Best for the many corporations and other organizations now recording record profits.

Worst for the workers who have no job security anymore, because life-long jobs are almost unheard of, and, nobody's job is safe.

That's what is different about the '90s.

MUSIC TO GET DEPRESSED BY

You may already know all of this, from vivid personal experience. Your job may have been wiped out from under you without any warning whatsoever. Your boss may have told you that you were absolutely indispensable. But, that didn't save you, because your boss lost his or her job too, at the same time you lost yours -- in that merger, that takeover, that downsizing. Your job was *gone.*

And now that you face the job-hunt, *everyone* is giving you advice.

Magazines and newspapers are.

The books in the bookstore are.

The newscaster on the TV is, in a special report.

Even your friends are, and especially those who were laid off before you, and have had a very difficult time making ends meet, ever since. They will recount their detailed history to you, of what happened to them, as a depressing prophecy of what is going to happen to you as well.

Yes, you will get advice from every side, and what it will all add up to is: *you don't stand a chance. Give up . . . now! That isn't a kind world waiting for you out there, anymore. There isn't a single job out there for you to find . . . trust us, we've looked. And even if there is, it will be at a vastly reduced income for you. Take our advice, and just retreat to your bed, pull the covers over your head, and turn the electric blanket up to nine.*

All in all, a sort of *music to get depressed by.*

You will be left with the impression that you're going to be lucky in the future if you can just manage to keep body and soul together.

PAY NO ATTENTION

You must pay no attention to this advice, of course.

And you must not give up hope.

Even if you already began your job-search -- have sent out resumes (or curricula vitae[3]) by the bushel, searched want ads by the hour, and visited federal/state, and private employment agencies from A to Z, all without turning up a single thing.

This says nothing about whether or not you can find a job.

3. Curricula vitae (plural) or curriculum vitae (singular) is a term used in academia and in other countries than the U.S., as a synonym for *resumes.* It's abbreviated, often, to c.v.

There *is* a way. You *can* find a job, and a job which you love. You *can* flourish.

In order to understand how, let us look together at:

TWO FUNDAMENTAL TRUTHS ABOUT THE JOB-MARKET

You may know people trapped by their inability to find anything like the work they used to have, losing their home, breaking up their marriage, never recovering the standard of living they formerly enjoyed. And if you have kindness and compassion within you, you will feel deeply the pain of these lives, wrecked by their inability to survive in today's job market.

Yet, beyond your compassion for them you of course want also to have compassion for yourself. You want to know if there is anything you can do to avoid their fate. And perhaps even help them, once you've turned your own life around.

You want to know if it is possible to conduct a job-hunt victoriously in today's vastly-changed job-market.

The answer is, *Yes, it is.* But only if you first learn, and memorize, two fundamental truths about the job-market.

These have always been true. These will always be true. They are:

1. There are always jobs out there.

2. Whether you can find them or not, depends on what methods of job-hunting you are using.

Let's begin with the first.

THERE ARE ALWAYS JOBS OUT THERE

I will illustrate my points with U.S. statistics, but the same truths obtain, in countries around the world.

As I write, there are currently 125,163,000 people holding jobs in the U.S. One out of every 8.5 of those is self-employed.[4] That leaves 110,466,000 who work for somebody else. Now, even if the number of jobs in the U.S. were frozen at that number, and not another single job were created for some time to come, there would still be jobs available. Why?

Because people presently holding jobs get **promoted**, thus leaving vacant the job they had.

And because people get **fired** due to unsatisfactory performance on the job, thus creating vacancies.

And because people presently holding jobs **quit**, thus creating vacancies.

And because people presently holding jobs get seriously **injured**, on the job or on the road or at home, and are no longer able to come to work, thus creating vacancies.

And because people presently holding jobs develop **illnesses** requiring long hospitalizations, thus creating vacancies.

And because people presently holding jobs have to **move**, in order to be near a sick or dying relative, thus creating vacancies.

And because people reach the age where they decide to **retire**, thus creating vacancies.

And because people **die** suddenly, while still in the workforce, thus creating vacancies.

And because some of those jobs are actually **limited contracts**, and when they run out, there will be monies available for new contracts, often in those same companies.

Vacancies, then, are *always* being created -- simply because we are human. And that will never change.

4. According to the U.S. Department of Labor, *Monthly Labor Review*, January/February 1996, p. 3. The Department claims that only one out of every 11 workers is self-employed, but this is because they exclude all self-employed who have incorporated their business (the Department's reasoning here is *legal:* technically self-employed people who incorporate their business thus become employees of their own businesses). However, totaling all self-employed persons, whether they have incorporated their business or not, yields the conclusion that one out of every 8.5 workers in the U.S. is self-employed.

VACANCIES EVEN DURING RECESSIONS

These 'revolving chairs' in the workforce occur even during recessions or other economic 'hard times.'

In the U.S., there have been nine recessions since World War II. During a recent recession, the National Federation of Independent Business conducted a survey to discover how many vacancies there were among small businesses. They discovered there were one and a half million, *during that recession.* And that was just for *small* businesses, never mind *large* businesses.

Sometimes, these vacancies take a *long* time to be filled. Our job-hunting system is Neanderthal. And employers are just as baffled about how to find good workers, as the unemployed are about how to find good employers.

If you can find one of these jobs while it is vacant, and you are qualified to perform it, and if you stand out in the job interview, you have as much chance as anyone of winning that job.

Whether you *can* find it, or not, depends of course on what methods you are using to search for it -- point #2 above, which we shall get to shortly. But, for now, my point: there are always jobs out there, even during recessions.

NEW JOBS BEING CREATED

All of this is true, as I said, even if no new jobs were ever created. But new jobs are always being created. Jobs that never existed previously. As I write, a net of 624,000 new jobs were created in the U.S. *last month alone,* despite over 300,000 layoffs.[5]

---

5. It should be emphasized that this figure, which the U.S. government publishes on the first Friday in each month, is a *net gain.* To illustrate, suppose in a given month 1,300,000 jobs were downsized and eliminated, but in that same month some 1,250,000 new jobs were created and successfully filled. The government will subtract 1,300,000 (lost) from 1,250,000 (gained) and report that the *net figure* for that month was 50,000 jobs lost -- implying that *no* job-hunters found a job that month -- or, as the average reader, interprets it, "there are no jobs out there." This is wrong. With my rich skills at overkill, let me repeat: there were 1,250,000 jobs found that month. From this you can see that in those months which report a large increase -- say, a *net gain* of 624,000 jobs as above -- there is actually a much larger number of job-hunters successfully finding jobs *that month* than even the figure of 624,000 would suggest.

If you want the yearly statistic, it is: during the twelve months ending February 1996, 2,566,000 new jobs were created in the U.S. (This is, I remind you, the *net* figure.)

That's a lot of new jobs. And you have as much chance as anyone of winning one of these jobs, *if* you can find them, and *if* you are qualified to perform them, and *if* you stand out in the job interview.

Whether you *can* find them, or not, depends on what methods you are using to search for them -- which we shall get to shortly. For now, my point: there are always jobs out there.

Write it on your bathroom mirror, hum it, sing it, repeat it like a litany, this refrain: there are always jobs out there. There are always jobs out there.

HOW MANY JOBS ARE THERE FOR ME TO GO AFTER?

That's a natural curiosity. It takes a little figuring, so follow this step by step *(or just skip over this section, and take my word for it):* U.S. studies have repeatedly turned up the fact that during a typical year as many as twenty percent[6] of the workforce are out of work *at some time* during that year. That would currently work out to 25 million workers who are unemployed at some time during the year. Now, the monthly unemployment rate is never around 25 million. It's around 8 million.

So, obviously, sometime during the year, 17 million unemployed people were able *to find a new job before the year ended.*[7]

To be sure, some of these jobs are new jobs in places and fields that the job-hunters-in-question would have preferred to turn down, so that they could go find some new place which would let them do their old jobs again.

---

6. The first source of this figure is The Conference Board, 1991. A Time/CNN poll put it even higher, at 23% ("23% of American workers were unemployed, not by their own choice, at some time in 1991" *Time,* January 13, 1992). The yearly count has been taken by the U.S. government over a number of years, and in good times or bad it seems to always work out that approximately one out of every five people in the workforce is unemployed *sometime* during any given year.

7. The figure of 17 is arrived at by subtracting 8 from 25.

Also, some of those jobs are part-time, when the job-hunters-in-question would have preferred them to be full-time.

And some of those jobs pay lower wages when they would have liked them to pay higher wages.

And some of these jobs are temporary, when the job-hunters-in-question would have liked them to be -- *I dare not say* permanent, *because I believe hardly any jobs are permanent anymore, in this new world economy* -- but, yes, they would have liked them to last at least a few years, maybe more. That's 'permanent' in today's economy.

Well, you get my point. The quality of the work found isn't always up to snuff; nonetheless, each year *millions* of people become unemployed, and then successfully find jobs.

There is no reason why you should not be among them. And no reason why you should not aim to find the very best job you can imagine, even if it later turns out that you have to get to it in two or three steps. In good times or bad, there are *always* jobs out there. *Say it again, Sam.*

THEY'RE OUT THERE, BUT CAN YOU FIND THEM?

> 2. Whether you can find them or not, depends on what methods of job-hunting you are using.

We come now to our second fundamental truth about the job market.

How do you find the jobs that are out there, waiting for you to find them?

Well, you say, *if they're out there, it should be easy to find them.* No, no, no, mon ami. That is not the case.

To illustrate this, let us step outside the world of work for a moment, and let us take an example from personal life.

Suppose you moved to a big city, and found a really nice apartment to rent, but you decided you didn't want (or need) a telephone. And now let us suppose that some months later someone over on the other side of that city is asked if you live there. They've never heard of you, so their first response is, "I dunno." *(An English major, obviously.)* Being resourceful, they go and look in the telephone book, because they assume that *anyone* who lives in the big city *must* have a telephone. But when they look, there is no mention of you. They call information to ask if you have an unlisted number. Nope.

So, what do they conclude? They conclude you don't exist -- at least not in that city. And why did they reach this conclusion? Because they thought the way to find you was through the telephone book, and in that, they were quite wrong.[8]

Mark the main point of my little illustration. The fact that you exist does not automatically mean you are easy to find. Normal methods for locating you may not work.

And so it is with the job-hunt. The fact that a job exists does not automatically mean it is easy to find. Normal methods for locating it may not work.

You know what I mean by *normal methods,* of course: the ones we all turn to -- resumes, want-ads, and employment agencies.

The job you most want to find may be out there, waiting for you to come find it; yet resumes, want-ads, and employment agencies cannot turn it up. You need to know about other methods. I have listed them all, here, together with their estimated success rate, based on studies of actual job-hunters after they found -- or didn't find -- a job.[9]

---

8. Now, lest you think I am downplaying the phone book in general, let me mention that in job-hunting the telephone book is a lifesaver, particularly The Yellow Pages, as you will see, later. Don't let such details make you forget the overarching point of my parable, which is: choose one method to try to find somebody, and you may strike out . . . even though they're *there.*

9. Since my tips and suggestions rest heavily on what successful job-hunters did, you may have an idle curiosity to know where these studies are to be found. Their sources are:

Steven M. Bortnick and Michelle Harrison Ports, "Job search methods and results: tracking the unemployed, 1991," *Monthly Labor Review,* December 1992. Studied the success of job-seekers who had been looking for a job, over a period of 8 weeks.

THE FIVE WORST WAYS TO TRY TO FIND THOSE JOBS THAT ARE OUT THERE

1. Mailing out **resumes** to employers at random. *This method has a 7% success rate -- that is, out of every 100 job-hunters who use this method, 7 will find a job thereby.*

93 job-hunters out of 100 will not find the jobs that *are* out there -- if they use only this method.

(*One study revealed there is only one job-offer for every 1470 resumes floating around out there; another study puts the figure even higher -- one job offer for every 1700 resumes floating around out there. Would you take an airplane, if you knew only one out of 1700 got through, to their destination?*)

2. Answering **ads in professional or trade journals**, appropriate to your field. *This method also has a 7% success rate -- that is, out of every 100 job-hunters who use this method, 7 will find a job thereby.*

93 job-hunters out of 100 will not find the jobs that *are* out there -- if they use only this method.

3. Answering **non-local newspaper ads**, in other parts of the state or country. *This method has a 10% success rate -- that is, out of every 100 job-hunters who use this method, 10 will find a job thereby.*

90 job-hunters out of 100 will not find the jobs that *are* out there -- if they use only this method.

John Bishop, John Barron and Kevin Hollenbeck, *Recruiting Workers: How recruitment policies affect the flow of applicants and quality of new workers.* The Ohio State University, The National Center for Research in Vocational Education, Sept. 1983. They discovered that "informal search methods" (such as described here in *Parachute*) are more effective than "formal search methods," such as employment agencies.

Carl Rosenfeld, "Job Search of the Unemployed, May 1976," *Monthly Labor Review,* November 1977. A Bureau of Labor Statistics study, which - - unlike the first study cited above - - interviewed job-hunters at only one moment in time.

Bureau of the Census, "Use and Effectiveness of Job Search Methods," *Occupational Outlook Quarterly,* Winter, 1976. A study of ten million job-seekers.

4. Answering local newspaper ads. *This method has a 5–24% success rate -- that is, out of every 100 job-hunters who use this method, between 5 and 24 will find a job thereby.*

76–95 job-hunters out of 100 will not find the jobs that *are* out there -- if they use only this method.

(The fluctuation in range is due to the level of salary that is being sought; the higher the salary being sought, the fewer job-hunters who are able to find a job using this method).

5. Going to private employment agencies for help. *This method also has a 5–24% success rate, again, depending on the level of salary that is being sought -- which is to say, out of every 100 job-hunters who use this method, between 5 and 24 will find a job thereby.*

76–95 job-hunters out of 100 will not find the jobs that *are* out there -- if they use only this method.

(*It should be noted that the success rate of this method has risen slightly in recent years, in the case of women but not of men: in a recent study, 27.8% of female job-hunters found a job within two months, by going to private employment agencies.)*[10]

Well, as we noted earlier, there are always jobs out there, waiting to be found. But, the methods just described are the five *least* effective ways of locating them.

10. There are at least four other methods for trying to find the jobs that are out there, which fall neither into the "Five Least Effective" category, nor into the "Five Most Effective" category. These are:

a. Going to places where employers pick out workers. This has an 8% success rate -- that is, out of every 100 people who use this method, 8 will find a job thereby. 92 will not. (15% of U.S. workers are union members, and it is claimed that those among them who have access to a union hiring hall, have a 22% success rate -- that is, 22 out of every 100 find a job using this method. What is not stated, however, is how long it takes to get a job at the hall, and how long a job typically lasts-- in the trades, that may be for just a few days.)

b. Taking a Civil Service examination. This has a 12% success rate -- that is, out of every 100 people who use this method, 12 will find a job thereby. 88 will not.

c. Asking a former teacher or professor for job-leads. This also has a 12% success rate -- that is, out of every 100 people who use this method, 12 will find a job thereby. 88 will not.

d. Going to the state/Federal employment service office. This has a 14% success rate -- that is, out of every 100 people who use this method, 14 will find a job thereby. 86 will not.

I'm sure you noticed that our old friends -- resumes, ads, and agencies -- all appear on this Five *Worst* List.

So, if you use resumes, ads, and agencies to find a job, but they turn up *nothing*, it doesn't mean there are no jobs out there. It only means *those methods* can't find them. Sorry about that.

It's time to learn some new ways of finding the jobs that are out there. This brings us to:

THE FIVE BEST WAYS TO TRY TO FIND THOSE JOBS THAT ARE OUT THERE

1. **Asking for job-leads** from family members, friends, people in the community, staff at career centers -- especially at your local community college or the high-school or college where you graduated. You ask them one simple question: do you know of any jobs where you work -- or elsewhere? *This method has a 33% success rate -- that is, out of every 100 people who use this method, 33 will find a job thereby.*

67 job-hunters out of 100 will not find the jobs that *are* out there -- if they use only this method.

2. **Knocking on the door of any employer, factory, or office that interests you**, whether they are known to have a vacancy

or not. *This method has a 47% success rate -- that is, out of every 100 people who use this method, 47 will find a job thereby.*

53 job-hunters out of 100 will not find the jobs that *are* out there -- if they use only this method.

3. **By yourself, using the phone book's Yellow Pages** to identify subjects or fields of interest to you in the town or city where you are, and then calling up the employers listed in that field, to ask if they are hiring for the type of position you can do, and do well. *This method has a 69% success rate that is, out of every 100 job-hunters or career-changers who use this method, 69 will find a job thereby.*

31 job-hunters out of 100 will not find the jobs that *are* out there -- if they use only this method.

4. **In a group with other job-hunters, using the phone book's Yellow Pages** to identify subjects or fields of interest to you in the town or city where you are, and then calling up the employers listed in that field, to ask if they are hiring for the type of position you can do, and do well. *This method has an 84% success rate -- that is, out of every 100 people who use this method, 84 will find a job thereby.*

16 job-hunters out of 100 will not find the jobs that *are* out there -- if they use only this method.

5. ***The Creative Approach to Job-Hunting or Career-Change***. This can be done by individuals, or in groups. The characteristics of this system, in general, are: *Do thorough homework, and inventory, upon yourself. Know your favorite skills, in their order of priority. Know in what kinds of fields you want to use those skills. Talk to people who are in those kind of jobs. Find out if they like their job, and how they found their job. Then choose organizations where you want to work, rather than just those* known *to have vacancies. Do research on the organizations, thoroughly, before approaching them. Seek out the person who actually has the power to hire you for the job you want; use your personal contacts and friends to get in to see him or her. Show them how you can help them with their problems.* Cut no corners, take no shortcuts. This method is explained completely in the chapters entitled, *For the Determined Job-Hunter. This method has an 86% success rate -- that is, out of every 100 job-hunters*

or career-changers who use this method, 86 will find a job or new career thereby.

14 job-hunters out of 100 will not find the jobs that *are* out there -- if they use only this method.

"WHILE YOU'RE WAITING FOR YOUR SHIP TO COME IN, WHY DON'T YOU DO SOME MAINTENANCE WORK ON THE PIER?"

WHAT IF YOU USE MORE THAN ONE METHOD?

Ah, how brilliant you are, to have thought of that! Thanks to the studies that have been done, we happen to know the answer. In general, as you might suspect, the answer is that the greater the number of job-hunting methods any job-hunter uses, the greater his or her success at finding a job. That fact was uncovered in a study that was done over 25 years ago.[11] Makes sense, doesn't it?

But, a more recent study, published four years ago, uncovered this strange twist: it is true that the likelihood of your uncovering those jobs that are always out there *increases* with each additional method that you use, but only *up to four.* If you use

11. The study was made a number of years ago, in Erie Pennsylvania, by A. Harvey Belitsky and Harold L. Sheppard. It was published under the title *The Job Hunt: Job-Seeking Behavior of Unemployed Workers in a Local Economy* (now out of print). A summary of it was published by The W.E. Upjohn Institute for Employment Research, 300 South Westnedge Ave., Kalamazoo MI 49007, called *Promoting Jobfinding Success for the Unemployed* (now also out of print). Originally, I did much of my own research on job-hunting when this Institute kindly gave me an office at their Washington D.C. offices. What remains of that Institute is now located only in Kalamazoo.

more than four methods, your likelihood of uncovering those jobs that are out there, starts to *decrease.*[12]

I have pondered this bizarre finding, and concluded that the explanation may lie in the fact that if you try to do more than four methods you will end up not doing any of them very well. You will give each method less time than it deserves and needs, if it is to be effective.

DON'T JUST USE ONE METHOD

Well, then, why not use just one job-hunting method, and do it exceptionally well?

The answer lies in the fact that in the U.S. as well as other countries the job-hunt typically lasts two to four months, *and* one-third of all job-hunters never find a job because they *give up* during that time. Often, of course, the job-hunt lasts far longer -- from six months to two years or more -- and many more job-hunters don't find a job, simply because they abandon their job-hunt.[13] Job-hunting demands persistence, and stick-to-it-ive-ness.

So, why do we give up? I mean, we need that income, don't we? Why do we give up?

It turns out the 'why' is related to the number of methods you use. For example, studies have discovered that out of every 100 job-hunters who use only one method of job-search, 51 of them abandon their search, by the second month.

On the other hand, out of every 100 job-hunters who use *several* job-search methods, only 31 abandon their search, by the second month.[14] The logic seems to be that if you use only one method -- say, resumes -- and it doesn't turn up anything rather quickly, you tend to give up hope. But if you are using two, three, or four methods, your hope tends to stay alive --

12. Steven M. Bortnick and Michelle Harrison Ports, "Job search methods and results: tracking the unemployed, 1991," *Monthly Labor Review,* December 1992, p. 33.

13. "How Long Does Unemployment Last?" by the late Robert G. Wegmann, *The Career Development Quarterly,* September 1991. The median for unemployed workers in the U.S. was 13.7 weeks in 1994; currently as I write, 1,300,000 U.S. job-hunters have been unemployed for 27 weeks or longer.

14. Steven M. Bortnick and Michelle Harrison Ports, "Job search methods and results: tracking the unemployed, 1991," *Monthly Labor Review,* December 1992.

surely, one of these will pay off -- and so, you keep on looking.

The moral of our tale, then, is this: avoid using just one job-search method, because it will lead quickly to discouragement, if it doesn't pay off almost immediately. The experience of successful job-hunters is that you should use more than one method, though not more than four.

Beyond numbers, you want of course to choose one or more of these from the Five *Best* List, above -- and not pick *all* of them from the Five *Worst* List. *(Among the Five* Worst, *stand resumes -- and I am assuming you will not give up that misplaced faith in their effectiveness, no matter what I tell you. Okay, okay. Just be sure to supplement them with one or more methods from the Five* Best *List.)*

SUMMARY

Most job-hunters, and career-changers, believe that whatever job-hunting method they use, if there are jobs out there, they will find them.

But in fact, studies of successful and unsuccessful job-hunters have revealed that *everything* depends on what method or methods you are using.

> There are always jobs, waiting to be filled. The successful job-hunter is the one who knows how to find them.
>
> Successful job-hunting is a learned skill. It can be studied. It can be mastered. By You.
>
> This book is dedicated to teaching you that skill.

If you use a relatively ineffective method, and it turns up nothing, you will, of course, say to yourself, Well, there are no jobs. But the truth is: yes there are; you are simply using the wrong method for finding them *(hint: resumes don't cut it!)*.

You must use an effective method, and in fact, if you are to stick with your job-hunt, you should consider using at least two effective methods, though not more than four, for thus you keep hope alive. With hope, you can persist until you find what you are looking for.

*"It ain't what you don't know
that gets you in trouble;
it's what you know for sure
that ain't so."*

Mark Twain

CHAPTER THREE

FOR THE IMPATIENT JOB-HUNTER

QUICK STRATEGIES

47 TIPS, HINTS, SHORTCUTS

Chapter 3

Table of Contents

What makes us become impatient with the job-hunt?

Well, for one thing, it lasts too long. Many years, the U.S. job-hunt typically lasts around 100 days. It can be much shorter than that, but alas! it can also be much longer -- many times longer. Six months. A year. Two years.

And . . . one-third of all job-hunters never find a job because they *give up* during the first months -- especially if they were using only one method, such as resumes, to locate the jobs that are out there.[1]

No wonder we so easily become The Impatient Job-Hunter. "Let's get this over with!"

And then our grumpiness grows. We know the jobs are out there, but why do we have to go *hunting* for them? Why doesn't somebody just hand us one of them?

We wish someone would save us from this hunt. We want someone to *rescue* us, come after us, offer us work: *"Here, here's a job; take it. It's for you!"* Save us all that *huntin'*, and blood, sweat, and tears.

We're a little vague about who that someone should be: the government perhaps, or our previous employer (who, after

1. "How Long Does Unemployment Last?" by the late Robert G. Wegmann, *The Career Development Quarterly,* September 1991. The median for unemployed workers in the U.S. was 13.7 weeks in 1994; currently as I write, 1,300,000 U.S. job-hunters have been unemployed for 27 weeks or longer.

all, *owes* us), or the unions. But we expect rescue. We wait for rescue.

And it does not come.

The hard truth is this: no one owes you a job, no matter what your family or friends may have told you; if you want a job, it is you who is going to have to go out, and work hard to find it.

WHO ARE THE JOB-HUNTING EXPERTS?

If you don't know how to find a job, there is a simple remedy to accelerate and speed up your learning: go talk to *successful* job-hunters among your family, friends, and acquaintances -- people who *were* out of work, and since then have found a job they really love -- and learn what *they* did. Then go imitate it. If you do that, you can probably throw away this book.

This is, after all, how you master *anything.* If you play tennis, and you want to learn how to improve your game, you go talk to, or train with, *good* tennis players, to learn how they do it. If you run, and want to improve your running, you would go talk to, or train with, *good* runners, and learn how they do it. If you paint, and want to learn how to paint better, you would go study under *master* painters, to see how they do it.

It is the same with job-hunting. If you are job-hunting, and you want to learn how to do it better, talk to people who are good at it.

Of course, you may not know that many successful job-hunters, in your circle of acquaintances. Which is why you have this book in your hand. You are hoping that I do. Ah yes. I know *thousands* and *thousands* of them. And, in the remainder of this chapter, I want to share with you a number of hints, tips, shortcuts, and quick strategies for the impatient job-hunter, that I have learned from them, during the last twenty-five years and more.

Needless to say *(but I'll say it, anyway)*, none of these tips can *guarantee* you a job. Life can never be so mechanized. There is always so much in life that depends on luck and chance and serendipity. But if faithfully followed, these ideas should at least dramatically *improve* your chances of finding a job more quickly, as so many successful job-hunters have discovered, before you.

Tips
About the Job-Hunt In General

★ You will have to job-hunt many times in your life.

★ It will be an average of eight times, in each U.S. worker's lifetime.

★ It may be as often as every three years.

★ You must master the job-hunt for yourself, this time, so that the next time you go about it, you will know how to do it.

★ Most people make career decisions on the flimsiest of grounds, justifying the root meaning of the word *career*, which comes from *careen* -- to go around the ancient Roman race-track at top speed, in a precipitous headlong rush.

★ There are three parts to every job-hunt or career-change: What, Where, and How. You need to learn techniques, to help you do each part.

★ More important than techniques, however, is your attitude toward your job-hunt. Attitude is *everything!*

> "We who lived in concentration camps can remember the men who walked through the huts comforting others, giving away their last piece of bread. They may have been few in number, but they offer sufficient proof that everything can be taken from a man but one thing: the last of the human freedoms -- to choose one's attitude in any given set of circumstances . . . "
>
> Victor Frankl

Attitude is a matter of: Your attitude toward the job-hunt. Your attitude toward the employer. Your attitude toward the job. Believe me, your attitude is the first (and last) thing everyone notices about you.

It is hardly any surprise, therefore, that when asked why they didn't hire *so and so*, employers invariably reply, "He had a real *attitude* problem." *Or* "I didn't like her attitude." *Or* "I thought he had a lousy attitude."

For the impatient job-hunter, anxious to find a job as quickly as possible, attitude is the first thing that must be looked at and (if necessary) fixed.

GENERAL ATTITUDE

Attitude is, first of all a matter of how you come across to people, in your personality. It is the first thing that every employer notices about you, during a job-interview, *or even earlier -- in telephone contact, or resume.*

Attitude is the killer question about you, that dances like sugarplums in every employer's head.[2] They notice, immediately, whether you would be a pleasant person to be around, or not. They notice, immediately, whether you are interested in other people, their interests and needs, or totally absorbed with yourself. Whether you project energy and enthusiasm, or minimal effort and sullenness. Whether you are angry, or at peace with yourself and the world. Outgoing, or turned in on yourself. Communicative, or monosyllabic. Interested in giving, or only in taking. Anxious to do the best job possible, going the extra mile, or anxious to 'just go through the motions.'

Employers will hire someone with lesser skills, who has the right attitude, rather than a more-skilled person with a bad attitude. They have had enough experience with bad attitudes in the past, to know that if they were foolish enough to hire you, and you turn out to have a bad attitude, they will soon ache to get rid of you. That is why they are supersensitive to your attitude, from the first moment they lay eyes on you.

YOUR ATTITUDE TOWARD TODAY'S JOB MARKET

From general attitude, we progress to *specific.* Employers are sensitive to how you are dealing with the world as it is, today . . . not the world you wish existed.

---

2. Or, if you are self-employed, this dances in every one of your potential clients' heads.

If you have been unjustly let go at your previous job, your first great need is to let go of your righteous anger at how different the world of work is from what you thought it would be; otherwise, that anger will cripple your job-hunting efforts. You will reek of it to every employer you go see, even as a drunk reeks of strong drink.

You may love or hate what's happened to the job market in the '90s, and what it's done to your life. But you've got to make your peace with it. In this arena, as in others, your attitude is *crucial,* and every employer will notice it.

Okay, so, how should you mentally prepare yourself for today's job market? There are four attitudes I think are crucial to the success of your job-hunt:

• **1. Every job you get is temporary**. *That is, 'of uncertain length.' 90% of the workforce in the U.S. is* not *self-employed; so, you are probably going to end up working for someone else. And how long that job lasts will be up to them, and not just you. If they so will it, your job may end at any time, and without warning.* You are always 'on probation,' as is the company you are working for. The question is: are you ready for the next job when this one fails?

This is the *nature of today's job market. So, when you go job-hunting, you must think to yourself, "I am hunting for a job that is basically a temporary job, whose length I do not know. Therefore, this is not going to be my last job-hunt, in all likelihood. I'm going to have to be mentally prepared to start job-hunting again, at any time."*

It is helpful for you to have the attitude, before you start your job-hunt, that whatever job you find is going to be treated by you as a temporary job, which may end at any time. This has always been true to some degree, but now it is even more true than ever.

As a preparation for this attitude in the future, write down, on a separate piece of paper, how long each job has lasted, throughout your work history.

• **2. Every job you get is essentially a seminar**. The question is: what are you learning there?

Of course you want this job to put bread on the table, clothes on your back, and a roof over your head. And, you want it to give you a sense of satisfaction and accomplishment. But. Almost every job today is moving and changing so fast, in its very nature, that you must think of this job you are looking for, as one that will inevitably be a learning experience for you. Think of it as enrolling in a seminar. There is a lot you will have to learn . . . when you begin . . . and throughout the time you are there. You must not only be ready to learn, but eager to learn. You must emphasize to every would-be employer how much you love to learn new tasks and procedures, and how fast you learn.

It is helpful for you to have the attitude, before you start your job-hunt, that whatever job you find is going to be treated by you as a seminar, and learning experience. This has always been true to some degree, but now it is even more true than ever.

As a preparation for this attitude in the future, write down, on a separate piece of paper, what you have learned at your present or most recent job/seminar.

• **3. Every job you get is essentially an adventure.** *Most of us love adventures. An adventure is a series of unfolding events that were unpredictable. That's today's jobs, all right! You never know what's going to happen next. If you end up working in an organization of any size, it is very likely that the dramas which will be played out there, monthly, will rival any soap opera that is on television today. Power plays! Ambition! Rumors! Poor decisions! Strange alliances! Betrayals!*

Rewards! Sudden twists and turns that no one could have predicted ahead of time, will unfold before your very eyes. Sometimes you'll love the way it is turning out; sometimes you'll hate it!

But, it is helpful for you to have the attitude, before you start your job-hunt, that whatever job you find is going to be treated by you as an adventure. This has always been true to some degree, but now it is even more true than ever.

> As a preparation for this attitude in the future, write down, on a separate piece of paper, what were the adventures -- unpredictable turns of events -- that happened to you in your present or most recent job.

• **4. Every job you get is one where the satisfaction must lie in the work itself.** *In the old days, most of us hoped we would find not only work we enjoyed, but also appreciation and recognition for that work. In other words, we looked for a kind of love at our place of work. Well, there are indeed such places still out there, where you can be appreciated, saluted, singled-out and praised to the skies* -- but *they are not as common or as easy to find, as they used to be -- particularly if the organization has over 50 employees.*

Despite your best research during your job-hunt, you may end up in a job where your bosses fail to recognize or acknowledge the fine contribution that you make, leaving you feeling unloved and unappreciated -- and finally, even after many months or years, they may let you go, and without warning, citing a business turn-down, the need for 'new blood,' bankruptcy, merger, or the full-moon.

So consider how urgent it is, in today's job market, that your attitude should be: "I am going to choose a job which feeds my self-esteem by the very doing of it, rather than settling for work which has no satisfaction unless I receive praise from my supervisors."

It has always been true, but now it is more true than ever: before you start job-hunting, you *must* spend as much care as you possibly can, on defining carefully for yourself what kind of job(s) would give you great pleasure in the very doing of it; pleasure because:

you get to use the skills you most love to use,
in the field you most love to work in,

toward those goals you would most love to accomplish,

knowing that God knows what an asset you are to that place, even when your employers don't.

As a preparation for this attitude in the future, write down, on a separate piece of paper, what were the satisfactions that you got out of your present or most recent job.

MORE THAN JUST A JOB-HUNT

You can choose to go reluctantly, or gladly, into today's job market. If you go reluctantly -- if you demand that your next job should give you permanence, predictability, and no need to learn anything new -- then your job-hunt may turn out to be very difficult indeed, where you end up settling for just the most boring of jobs.

But if you love learning, if you love adventure, if you love finding satisfaction in the work itself, and if you can handle a job's uncertain length, then you can go job-hunting gladly, as this will be more than just a job-hunt.

It will be a hunt for new ways to learn. It will be a hunt for adventure. And it will be a hunt for the skills you most love to use, in the field where you most love to use them. And it will be a full-time job, in itself.

And now, we move on, from *attitude*, to 47 tips, hints, and shortcuts dealing with the three parts of a job-hunt:

Tips
About Deciding WHAT You Would Like to Do

1

☆ Do not expect that you will necessarily be able to find exactly the same kind of work that you used to be doing. Oh, I know what you're thinking. If you enjoyed your last job, you're thinking: *"I would like to look for exactly the kind of work I used to do, in the past, with the same exact job-title."*

And maybe you can. *But,* be prepared for the fact that in this changing life, and changing world, jobs do vanish. You must not necessarily expect that you will be able to find exactly the same kind of work that you did in the past. So, you need to take the job-label off yourself *("I am an auto-worker," etc.)* and define yourself instead as *"I am a person who . . . "*

Define some other line (or lines) of work that you could do, can do, and would enjoy doing.

☆ Forget about "vacancies." Go after the job you really want the most.

☆ Maybe you already know what that is. Ask yourself this question: *what is it in the world that I'd love to do more than anything else?* Whose job that you see *out there* -- among all the people you've met, know, or read about -- would you most love to be able to do? You may be able to describe this right off the top of your head; perhaps something you've already done, in your spare time (*like: make dresses, repair sailboats, etc.)*

4

Maybe you don't know what the job is, that you'd most love to do. In that case, there is a simple rule: **don't decide on your future, until you have first inventoried your past** (get out a pad of paper, and a pencil -- or, go to your computer, and list some answers to these questions):

"What have I done in the past that I really loved doing?" (Hobbies, spare time activities, and volunteer work?)

"What *did* I like about these things? What do I *still* like doing?"

"What am I good at? What does everyone tell me?"

"What would I love to sell, if I *had to* make a living as a salesperson?"

5

Ask yourself simple questions, for example, whether you primarily like to use your Skills with People, or your Skills with Things, or your Skills with Information. As someone has said, the point of all career planning is to simplify the things you know about yourself, and pick out those few elements that give you your power in life.

What are you sensitive to, that you don't think everybody necessarily is? This could be things your eyes pick up (e.g., colors, facial expressions, bodies showing injury); *or* things your ears pick up (e.g., birdsongs); *or* things your nose picks up (e.g., faint odors in the air); *or* things your mouth picks up (e.g., peculiar tastes); *or* things your body picks up (e.g., air currents, temperature changes); *or* things your brain picks up (e.g., connections, disharmony, remembering details), etc., etc. What kinds of jobs would use this sensitivity?

What turns you on? If a thing turns you on, you'll be good at it; if it doesn't, you won't. *(This hint courtesy of David Maister.)*

8

☆ What exhausts you? What energizes you? Go for the work, and tasks, that energize you. What are your hobbies? Astronomy? Aerospace? Airplanes? Bicycling? Birding? Boating or kayaking? Books? Cars? Caves? Collecting coins, or stamps, or dolls, or anything else? Cooking? Crafts? Dance? Electronics? Fishing? Flowers or gardening? Genealogy? Horses? Hunting? Juggling? Magic? Martial arts or other physical stuff? Minerals or rocks? Models? Motorcycles? The outdoors? Pets? Photography? Puppetry? Trains? Travel? Woodworking? Or what? See what kinds of jobs any of these might point to, for you.

9

☆ What is, or what do you want to be, your gift to the world?

10

☆ What is it about the world that you hate the most, and would most love to help eradicate, correct or fix? How could your gifts plug into the doing of that? What is the product or service that you think your community really needs?

11

☆ What do you want out of life?

12

☆ What are your best (and favorite) skills? If you haven't a clue, following is a sampler of skill-verbs. The way in which this list is typically used by job-hunters or career-changers is to put a *separate* check mark in front of each skill that: a) you believe you possess. And a separate check mark in front of each skill that: b) you enjoy doing. And a separate check mark in front of each skill that: c) you believe you do well.

Thus a skill could end up with three check marks -- and

A List of 246 Skills as Verbs

- achieving
- acting
- adapting
- addressing
- administering
- advising
- analyzing
- anticipating
- arbitrating
- arranging
- ascertaining
- assembling
- assessing
- attaining
- auditing
- budgeting
- building
- calculating
- charting
- checking
- classifying
- coaching
- collecting
- communicating
- compiling
- completing
- composing
- computing
- conceptualizing
- conducting
- conserving
- consolidating
- constructing
- controlling
- coordinating
- coping
- counseling
- creating
- deciding
- defining
- delivering
- designing
- detailing
- detecting
- determining
- developing
- devising
- diagnosing
- digging
- directing
- discovering
- dispensing
- displaying
- disproving
- dissecting
- distributing
- diverting
- dramatizing
- drawing
- driving
- editing
- eliminating
- empathizing
- enforcing
- establishing
- estimating
- evaluating
- examining
- expanding
- experimenting
- explaining
- expressing
- extracting
- filing
- financing
- fixing
- following
- formulating
- founding
- gathering
- generating
- getting
- giving
- guiding
- handling
- having responsibility
- heading
- helping
- hypothesizing
- identifying
- illustrating
- imagining
- implementing
- improving
- improvising
- increasing
- influencing
- informing
- initiating
- innovating
- inspecting
- inspiring
- installing
- instituting
- instructing
- integrating
- interpreting
- interviewing
- intuiting
- inventing
- inventorying
- investigating
- judging
- keeping
- leading
- learning
- lecturing
- lifting
- listening
- logging
- maintaining
- making
- managing
- manipulating
- mediating
- meeting
- memorizing
- mentoring
- modeling
- monitoring
- motivating
- navigating
- negotiating
- observing
- obtaining
- offering
- operating
- ordering
- organizing
- originating
- overseeing
- painting
- perceiving
- performing
- persuading
- photographing
- piloting
- planning
- playing
- predicting
- preparing
- prescribing
- presenting
- printing
- problem solving
- processing
- producing
- programming
- projecting
- promoting
- proof-reading
- protecting
- providing
- publicizing
- purchasing
- questioning
- raising
- reading
- realizing
- reasoning
- receiving
- recommending
- reconciling
- recording
- recruiting
- reducing
- referring
- rehabilitating
- relating
- remembering
- rendering
- repairing
- reporting
- representing
- researching
- resolving
- responding
- restoring
- retrieving
- reviewing
- risking
- scheduling
- selecting
- selling
- sensing
- separating
- serving
- setting
- setting-up
- sewing
- shaping
- sharing
- showing
- singing
- sketching
- solving
- sorting
- speaking
- studying
- summarizing
- supervising
- supplying
- symbolizing
- synergizing
- synthesizing
- systematizing
- taking
- taking instructions
- talking
- teaching
- team-building
- telling
- tending
- testing and proving
- training
- transcribing
- translating
- traveling
- treating
- trouble-shooting
- tutoring
- typing
- umpiring
- understanding
- understudying
- undertaking
- unifying
- uniting
- upgrading
- using
- utilizing
- verbalizing
- washing
- weighing
- winning
- working
- writing

these, in fact, are the ones you want to look the hardest at, to see what kind of job they suggest.

If none of this works for you, and you just can't think of anything you'd really like to do, off the top of your head (or the tip of your tongue), then turn to the *Parachute Workbook,* in *The Parachute Resource Guide,* p. ***10***, and do the exercises there.

☆ Actually, the major issue you will face with employers, vis-à-vis your skills, is not which ones you have, but how you use them: whether you just try to *keep busy,* or try to actually solve problems, thus increasing your effectiveness and the organization's effectiveness, too.

☆ What problems could your skills help solve for an employer? For example, would your skills help an employer with: making customers want to return, the quality of service, the quality of the merchandise, the timeliness of deliveries, bringing costs down, inventing new products, *or what?*

15

☆ Spend some time considering what makes you stand out from nineteen other people who could do the same job you can do. It will usually be a matter of *style.* Do you do it more thoroughly, faster, or what? The more you can answer this question, in a job interview, the better your chances of being the one who gets hired, instead of the other nineteen. Don't expect an employer to figure that out, for you. Be prepared to say, however modestly, *This is what makes me stand out.*

Tips
About Deciding WHERE You Would Like to Do It

The next part of *every* job-hunt must be the question of *Where. Where* would you like to do it?

It makes a big difference *where* you do your favorite tasks. Everyone knows that the difference between working in an outdoor nursery, or at a law firm, is night and day.

Where you do your favorite tasks is partly a matter of what "field" you choose to work in. Hence, the questions you should be asking yourself (and jotting down the answers to) are:

16

☆ What are your favorite interests? *(Computers? Gardening? Spanish? Law? Physics? Department stores? Hospitals? etc., etc.)*

17

☆ If you just can't think of any favorite interest, ask yourself if you could talk about *something* with someone all day long, day after day, what would that subject or field of interest be?

If you were stuck on a desert island with a person who only had the capacity to speak on a few subjects, what would you pray those subjects were?

If you turn out to have more than one favorite subject, take two of them at a time, and ask yourself: if you were in a conversation with someone covering two of your favorite subjects at once, which way would you steer the conversation? Toward what subject?

18

☆ Once you know what fields interest you, look back at your answers to *What,* and see if you can put the two of them together, in terms of a particular job. For example, if you love to work with figures, and your favorite field is hospitals, you would want to think about working in the accounting department at a hospital.

19

☆ Once you have some idea of what jobs interest you, go visit places where those jobs are, and talk to people doing those jobs, to see if this *really* interests you, or not. This is called "informal research" or (sometimes) "informational interviewing."

20

☆ If you have decided to try to stay with your old career *(which you lost through downsizing or whatever)* there are ways of developing 'leads.' Ask yourself the question: *"Who might be interested in the skills and problem-solving that I learned at my last job?"*

Ask yourself who you served in your last job, or came in contact with, who might be in a position to hire someone with your talents.

Ask yourself who supplied training or staff development in your last company or field; would any of them be interested in hiring you?

Ask yourself what machines or technology you learned, mastered, improved on, at your last job; who is interested in those machines or technology?

Ask yourself what raw materials *(e.g., Kodak paper in a darkroom),* equipment, or support services you used at your last job; would any of those suppliers know of other places where their equipment or support services are used?

Ask yourself who were the subcontractors, outsourcing agencies, or temp agencies that were used at your last job; would any of them be interested in hiring you?

Ask yourself what community or service organizations were interested in your projects at your last job; would any of them be interested in hiring you? *(These suggestions courtesy of Chuck Young, Administrator for the Oregon Commission on the Blind; and Martin Kimeldorf, career counselor and author.)*

21

☆ If you have decided to try a new career (see the next chapter) or go into a new field (for you), and you are dismayed at how much preparation it looks as though it would take, go talk to people doing that work. And don't look for the rules or generalizations. Look for the exceptions to the rules. For example, everyone may tell you the rule is: *"In order to do this work you have to have a master's degree and ten years' experience at it."* But you want to find out about the exceptions. *"Yes, but do you know of anyone in the field who hasn't got all those credentials? And where might I find him or her?"*

22

☆ Once you know what kind of work you are looking for, tell everyone what it is; have as many other eyes and ears out there looking on your behalf, as possible.

23

☆ If you happen to own a telephone answering machine, you might even consider putting the kind of work you are looking for, on that machine, in your opening message: *"Hi, this is Sandra. I'm busy right now, looking for a job in the accounting department at a hospital. Leave me a message after the beep, and if you happen to have any leads or contacts for me, be sure to mention that too, along with your phone number. Thanks a lot."*

Tips

About HOW To Find The Work You're Looking For

How.

This is the final part of *any* job-hunt.

This is the most difficult part of *any* job-hunt.

After making sure you have the right *attitude* about your job-hunt in general.

After deciding *what* you are looking for,

And *where* you would like to do it,

You come to this question, which is after all the point of it all: *how* do you find such a job?

As we have seen in the previous chapter, the jobs are always out there, and some methods are much better than others for finding those jobs.

You, of course -- the Impatient Job-Hunter -- want to know how to do all of this *faster.* Okay, here are some tips.

24

☆ To speed up your search for one of the jobs that *are* out there, *you must think of yourself as having already found a job.* Your job, in this case, is that of hunting for work. Put in a larger context, think of yourself as one who always has a job. It's just that its nature varies, at different times in your life. If you were working for someone else, that was your job. If you were working for yourself, that was your job. If you are job-hunting, that is now your job. You are never without a job. Even when the world would call you 'unemployed,' you have a full-time job (without pay) from 9 to 5 every weekday, since job-hunting *is* a full-time job, just like any other in your life.

25

☆ When your job is this one -- hunting for work -- you should 'punch in' at 9, and 'punch out' at 5, just as a worker does. *You must determine to spend full-time on this phase of your hunt, if you want to speed up your job-search. Because, the swiftness with which you bring this part of your job-hunt to a successful conclusion, will be* directly *proportional to the time you spend on it.*

I emphasize this nine-to-five business, because studies have revealed the depressing fact that two-thirds of all job-hunters spend 5 hours or less hunting for a job, each week.[3] And believe me, this is true!

You must spend 35 hours a week, at least, on your search for one of the jobs that are *out there.* That should cut down, dramatically, the number of weeks it takes you to find work -- more so, than any other factor.

To illustrate, let us imagine a woman job-hunter who devotes only 5 hours a week to her search; and it turns out, in the end, to take 30 weeks, before she finds a job. That means it took a total of 150 hours.

Now let us suppose that same job-hunter were to be hurled back in time, but this time she knew it was going to take 150 hours. Therefore she decides to give 35 hours *a week* to the task, in order to 'eat up' the 150 hours faster. As you can figure out for yourself, her 150-hour job-hunt should then take only 4 weeks, or so, before she found work, other things being equal.[4]

3. According to the U.S. Census Bureau, discussed in "Job Search Assistance Programs: Implications for the School," authored by the late Robert G. Wegmann, and first appearing in *Phi Delta Kappan,* December 1979, pp. 271ff.

4. Of course, there are some factors beyond a job-hunter's control, that may prolong the job-hunt, such as how long it takes an interviewing-committee to schedule the next round of interviews at the place that interests you (you will often be invited back two or three times before they make up their mind about you), etc. Nonetheless, the main point of our illustration still remains.

26

☆ You must be mentally prepared (and financially prepared) for your job-hunt to last a lot longer than you think it will. *Even the shortest job-hunt still lasts between two and eighteen weeks, depending on a variety of factors, even if you work full-time at it.* It depends, of course, on what kind of job you are looking for, where you are living, how old you are, how high you are aiming, and what the state is of the local economy.

But don't count on the "two weeks" minimum. Be prepared for the eighteen weeks or longer. Experienced outplacement people have long claimed that *your search for one of the jobs that* are *out there* will probably take one month for every $10,000 of salary that you are seeking. This may be pure drivel, but you get the picture, don't you?

27

☆ Don't give up. Be gently, lovingly persistent about your job-hunt. One job-hunter out of every three gives up too soon. That is to say, one out of every three becomes an unsuccessful job-hunter *simply because* they abandon their search prematurely. And if you ask them why they abandoned it, they say, "I didn't think it was going to be this hard; I didn't think it was going to take this long." In other words, what 'does in' so many job-hunters is some *unspoken* mental quota in our head, which goes something like this: *I expect I'll be able to find a job after about 30 phone calls, 15 calls in person, and three interviews.* We go about our job-hunt, fill or exceed those quotas, and then give up. Without a job. At least one out of every three of us does. So, don't let this happen to you.

Keep going until you find a job. **Persistence** is the name of the game. *Persistent* means being willing to go back to places that interested you, at least a couple of times in the following months, to see if by any chance their 'no vacancy' situation has changed.

The one thing an individual needs above everything else is hope, and hope is born of persistence.

28

☆ To speed up your search for one of the jobs that *are* out there, find some kind of a support group, so that you don't have to face the job-hunt all by yourself. Ever. You'd be amazed how much the support of others can keep you going, when you might otherwise be discouraged, and thus help speed up your job-hunt. Here are the candidates you can choose from:

a. Job-hunting groups that already exist in your city or town, such as "Forty Plus" clubs, "Experience Unlimited" groups, job-hunt classes at your local Federal/state employment offices, or at the local Chamber of Commerce, or at your local college or community college, or at your local Adult Education center, or at your local church, synagogue, or place of worship.[5] The likelihood that such help is available in your community increases dramatically for you if you are from certain groups held to be disadvantaged, such as low income, or welfare recipients, or youth, or displaced workers, etc. Ask around.

b. A job-hunting group that doesn't currently exist, but that you could help form, with the aid of your priest, minister, rabbi or religious leader, at your local church, synagogue or religious center, or elsewhere -- even on the Internet. Some enterprising job-hunters, unable to locate any group, have formed their own by running an ad in the local newspaper, near the "help wanted" listings. *"Am currently job-hunting, would like to meet weekly with other job-hunters for mutual support and encouragement. Am using 'What Color Is Your Parachute?' as my guide."*

c. Your mate or partner, grandparent, brother or sister, or best friend. A loving 'taskmaster' is what you need. Someone who will make a regular weekly appointment to meet with you, check you out on what you've done that week, and be very stern with you if you've done little or nothing since you last

5. A U.S. listing of *some* of these kinds of places is to be found in the *National Business Employment Weekly*, on its pages called "Calendar of Career Events." It's available on many newsstands, $3.95 an issue, or you can order an issue directly from: National Business Employment Weekly, P.O. Box 300, Princeton, NJ 08543. Their phone is: 800-JOB-HUNT.

met. You want understanding, sympathy, and discipline. If your mate, brother or sister, or best friend, can offer you all of these, run -- do not walk -- to enlist them immediately.

d. A local career counselor. I grant you that career counselors aren't usually thought of as 'a support group.' But many of them do have group sessions; and even by themselves they can be of inestimable support. If you can afford their services, and none of the above suggestions have worked, this is a good fall-back strategy. Before choosing such a counselor, however, *please* read pp. *243ff* in the *Parachute Workbook and Resource Guide,* thoroughly. That will also tell you how to locate such counselors.

29

☆ To speed up your search for one of the jobs that *are* out there, *go after many different organizations, instead of just one or two.* Restricting your search to just one or two favorite places is *death.* No matter how much you love that place, no matter how much you would *die* to work for that person, no matter how promising the situation there looks, for you (*"We'll call you next week. Promise!"*) keep on searching every day.

Don't let your job-hunt go on 'hold' just because you *hope* this place will pan out. Continue searching, at other organizations, until the day you actually begin working!!! Otherwise you will lose valuable, valuable time, when something that looked like *a sure thing* falls through, at the last moment.

Many of you will have good cause to remember these words, later, if you ignore them now!

30

☆ To speed up your search for one of the jobs that *are* out there, *determine to go after* any *place that interests you. Pay no attention to whether or not there is a known vacancy at that place.*

Underline this rule, copy it, paste it on your bathroom mirror, memorize it, repeat it to yourself every morning. I'll say it again: Pay no attention to whether or not there is a known vacancy!

If you base your job-hunt just on places where there is a known vacancy, you will prolong your search *forever!* Vacancies often develop at places *long before* any notice is put out that this vacancy exists. Moreover, when bosses or managers are thinking of creating a new position, this *intention* often lies in their mind for quite some time before they get around to doing anything about it. If you contact them during this opportune, quiescent period, you come as the answer to their prayers.

31

☆ To speed up your search for one of the jobs that *are* out there, *concentrate on organizations with twenty or less employees.* There is a natural tendency for job-hunters to make large organizations *'the measure of all things'* going on in the job-market. If the newspapers are filled with the news of companies like AT&T, General Motors, and others laying off thousands of workers, most job-hunters *assume* things are bad everywhere. This is confirmed when job-hunters focus their job-hunt only on large, well-known organizations. When they can't find a job at any of these places, they assume that *no one* is hiring. This is a very common, and very costly, mistake.

The fact is, there are always companies that are hiring -- but they are usually small companies -- with 100 or less employees. It is these which have been creating two out of every three new positions since 1970. In the U.S., for example, during the 1980s, while the Fortune 500 companies were *cutting* 3.7 million jobs from their payrolls, smaller companies *created* 19 million new jobs.[6]

So, if you would speed up your job-hunt, you need to concentrate on every *small* firm in your field that is within commuting distance, and has one hundred or less employees. Personally, I would begin with firms that have twenty or less employees.

It is true that small firms tend to have fewer benefits, such as health care, but on the other hand, they are easier to approach, the boss there is easier to get in to see, there are no forbidding personnel or human resource departments to screen you out, *and* they have the jobs.

---

6. *The San Francisco Chronicle,* 2/1/93.

You may visit any small business that interests you, but if that doesn't pay off, then go looking in particular for small businesses that are *prospering, growing, and expanding.* "The lion's share of job creation over time," says Bennett Harrison, author of *Lean and Mean: The Changing Landscape of Corporate Power in the Age of Flexibility,* "is contributed by a tiny fraction of new firms." For example, of the 245,000 businesses begun in 1985, 735 of them accounted for 75% of the employment gains between 1985 and 1988. So you are looking for businesses which may be *relatively* small now, but are on their way to *bigger.* One thinks of companies like Apple Computer which started out in a garage, or ASK Group, of Mountain View, California, which started out in a spare bedroom. Anyway, read the business section of your newspaper, daily, talk to everyone you can, talk to your Chamber of Commerce, to find out which small businesses are growing and expanding.

32

☆ To speed up your search for one of the jobs that *are* out there, *contact* at least *four employers a day, if in person; or if contacting them by telephone, forty a day, minimum; or if you're contacting them only with your resume, hundreds each week.* I emphasize this, because studies have shown that the average U.S. job-hunter only visits six employers a month. That adds up to little more than one employer *per week.*[7] That's: *visits.* Of course you can contact hundreds a week by paper (resumes); but we're talking *face-to-face.*

Logic alone will tell you that this is one of the reasons the average job-hunt takes so long. Say you were an average job-hunter, you visited only *six employers a month,* and let us say it took you *twelve months* to find a job. That means, mathematically, you had to contact 72 employers, face-to-face, in order to find that job.

But were you to be flung back in time to start all over again, except that this time you knew it will take you 72 employers, face-to-face, before you got hired, you might determine to contact, say, *four* employers *per day,* each weekday, in which case you would cover the 72 employers, and then get a job, in just a little over *three weeks,* instead of twelve months!

All of this, which you may figure out for yourself by logic, was confirmed by an actual study, which found that if a job-hunter contacted two employers a week, the job-search typically lasted up to a year; if ten employers a week, the search typically ended with a job within six months; *and,* at twenty employers a week, the search time typically dropped to 90 days or less.[8]

Therefore, common sense will tell you that you should determine to see *at least* four employers per weekday, two in the morning and two in the afternoon, at a minimum. And you should determine to do this for as many weeks (or months) as your job-hunt may last. For thus you should greatly shorten your job-hunt.

---

7. A survey cited by the late Robert G. Wegmann in "Job Search Assistance: A Review," in the *Journal of Employment Counseling,* December 1979, p. 212.

8. Goodrich & Sherwood Co., reported in "How to Succeed in Rotten Times," Oct. 1992.

When you thus approach employers, be prepared always to tell them what makes you different from nineteen other people who can do the same thing that you do. And don't be put off by rejection, if they have nothing to offer you. Be polite, ask them if they know of anyone else who might be hiring. Keep going until you find someone who is hiring.

33

☆ To speed up your search for one of the jobs that *are* out there, *use the telephone.* Some experts, of course, advise against this strategy: never, never use the telephone, they say, under *any* circumstances: it only makes it easier for the employer to screen you out over the phone.

Nonetheless, all the successful group job-search programs that I have studied over the years, from Nathan Azrin's *Job Club* to Dean Curtis's *Welfare Reform* programs *(based on the Dave Perschau/Chuck Hoffman model)* have based their programs on the *heavy* use of the telephone.

The better a group job-hunting program has worked and the faster it has succeeded in its people finding jobs, the more phone calls it has their job-hunters make. Nathan has had job-hunters make at least 10 phone calls a day; Chuck has had them make 100 phone calls in the morning, and 100 in the afternoon.

So if you've tried *everything* and all else fails, telephoning is your fall-back strategy. It is almost guaranteed to turn up something, just by its sheer weight of numbers.

Of course, I know this isn't easy -- for most of us. Some are born to it, like a duck to water. But most of us *hate* telephone solicitation, when it is directed at us; and we hate the thought of doing it ourselves, even though it is directed toward others (namely, employers).

Anyway, if you decide to do it (because you're desperate, or *really* impatient) you can go to your local library or bookstore and find books telling you exactly how to go about this.

In essence, the eleven things the experts will emphasize are these:

1. Take the Yellow Pages of the Phone Book, and call up

every single company or organization in the Yellow Pages that looks interesting to you, to ask them if they might be hiring, for the kind of work you do.

2. Write out what you plan to say. This is akin to some experts' advice that before you make your call, you should set down the objective of that call in writing before you, and the key points you want to make during the conversation. But most experts say, *Write out every word.* This is your *script*; don't try to *wing it.* Unabashedly read it, but try not to sound like you're reading it. Rehearse it first, several times.

3. If you can, start the call with a specific benefit to the caller. "I just read that you . . . and I . . ." If you can't find a connection, don't try to invent one.

4. Stand up when you make your phone calls; your voice is more forceful that way.

5. Have a mirror in front of you, on the wall, at eye level, so you can watch yourself in it, to see if you are smiling as you talk.

6. Call before 8 a.m., shortly before noon, or after 5 p.m. If it's managers you're seeking, and if they're hardworking, they're likely to be there at those times -- without a screener.

7. When you are connected, ask to speak with the manager. When she or he comes on the line, address them by name, introduce yourself by name, and then *briefly* (in one sentence) describe your greatest personal strength or top skill, a *brief* description of your experience, and then ask if there is a job opening for someone with your skills and background. For example, *"I am an experienced writer, with three published books, and I wonder if you have any job openings for someone with my experience?"* If *"yes,"* set up an interview time, repeat it, and repeat your name; if *"no,"* ask if they know of anyone else who might be hiring a person with your background. *(Courtesy of Dean Curtis.)*

8. If someone suggested you call this person, use their name as a reference when you call. "Your name was given to me by . . . "

9. If you've done something in the community, written articles for the local paper, or served on a volunteer committee, work that into the conversation if it goes on for more than one minute.

10. If you run into an interviewer's sharp objections, try responding with:

I understand . . .

I can appreciate your position . . .

I see your point . . .

Of course! However . . .

11. Some experts advise you to make fewer calls, to places that *really* interest you, and research each of them before you call. Other experts advise you not to call about a job, but to call only for information. All advise you to thank the employer before signing off, whether they have a job lead, or not.

34

☆ To speed up your search for one of the jobs that *are* out there, *knock on doors* -- particularly if you *hate* to use the telephone.

Choose places where you would like to work. Either from the phone book, or by walking down those streets in your village, city, or town, where you would like to work. Then, physically go in there, at any place that looks interesting, and looks as though it might be hiring someone with your skills.

This tip, to state it in another way, is that if you want to speed up your job-hunt, you need to go *face-to-face* with employers whenever possible, rather than sending paper, such as a resume. 47.7% of those job-hunters who use this approach, get a hiring-interview and then a job, thereby.

Yes, I know this isn't easy, for most of us. But *if* nothing else is working, it's a good fall-back strategy for you to rely on.

Said one job-hunter: *"The very first real job I got was by knocking door-to-door, asking if they needed a draftsman. I got a favorable response at the fifth, but not the last, place I knocked; interviewed a few days after; and was working within the week. I was incredibly lucky, as were they: their current draftsman had given notice that day I knocked. I worked there two years and then went on to a much better position at the invitation of friends I had made at that first job."*

Generally speaking, and particularly at small organizations, it is the boss, or hiring manager -- the one who makes the actual decision to hire -- that you want to talk to, to ask if they're hiring.

When you knock on the doors of larger organizations, you will generally be well-advised to try to avoid the personnel or human resources department, since their primary function is often to *screen out* job-hunters, so as not to bother the people 'upstairs' -- though there are exceptions to this rule, where the department is helpful, kind, and capable of hiring. It's a judgment call, on your part. *(You are only likely to run into such departments if you are knocking on the door of larger organizations, inasmuch as only 15% of all organizations, mostly large ones, even have such departments.)*

Coming in 'cold' this way, if the only person you can manage to see is the receptionist or human resources department, they will ask you to fill out a job application.

Job applications are question-and-answer forms which have such simple questions as: Your Name, Address, Age, Places of Previous Employment. etc. Such applications vary greatly in their complexity, from ones used by fast-food chains, to those used by, say, engineering firms. *If* you decide to fill one out, use a black pen, *print* neatly, fill in every question or space, even questions that don't apply to you (write *n.a.* "not applicable" in that space), write *"Open"* for salary, and sign your name. If they ask your reasons for leaving a previous job, you can choose between: *the job ended, my family needed me at the time (no longer a problem), it was a seasonal job, it was a temporary job, I wanted to make a career change, I want more responsibility than they gave me.* (Courtesy of Dean Curtis.)

If you've never seen a job application in your life, and you plan to be approaching organizations *cold,* you should familiarize yourself with an application form ahead of time. One way to do this without jeopardizing your job chances at places you care about, is to go to visit some fast-food place or any large organization that has a personnel department where you *don't* care to work, and simply *ask* for a job application, then immediately go back out the door. Take the application form home with you, where you can study it, and take a stab at filling it out, just for practice. Then throw it in the waste basket, after you've learned what you need to know. Do *not* return it to the place you got it from, unless you are seriously interested in working there. The purpose of this exercise is simply to find out what an application form looks like, not to use it -- at least at this point. Anyway, now you know what an application form looks like, and how to fill it out. I hope you never need to.

This direct 'walk-in' approach may pay off for you, or it may not. The effectiveness of the approach to employers is probably in inverse proportion to the level sought: more effective for blue-collar jobs than for managerial ones. In their pioneering study of the job-hunt some years ago, *The Job Hunt: Job-Seeking Behavior of Unemployed Workers in a Local Economy,* Harvey Belitsky and Harold A. Sheppard discovered that going face-to-face at a workplace, without introduction or *leads,* was *the* most effective job-hunting method *if you were a blue-collar worker.* Blue-collar workers take note.

35

☆ To speed up your search for one of the jobs that *are* out there, be willing to look at different *kinds* of jobs: full-time jobs, part-time jobs, unlimited contract jobs *(formerly called 'permanent jobs')*, short-term contract jobs, temporary jobs, working for others, working for yourself, etc.

36

☆ To speed up your search for one of the jobs that *are* out there, always remember that no matter what handicaps you bring with you to the job-hunt, there are **two** kinds of employers out there: *those who will be put off by your handicap, and therefore won't hire you;*

AND

those who will not be put off by your handicap, and therefore will hire you, if you are qualified for the job.

You are not interested in the former kind of employer, no matter how many of them there are -- except as a source of referrals.

You are only looking for those employers who are not put off by your handicap, and therefore will hire you *if you can do the job.*

Once you get an invitation to come in for a hiring-interview with the-person-who-has-the-power-to-hire, you will of course want some tips about how to conduct the interview. Even at the interview stage, things can drag on and on. You want to do more than simply get interviews; you want them to result in your getting hired. Hence, the need for tips about how to conduct the interview successfully. Here they are:

37

☆ To increase your chances of getting hired early on, if it is you who is asking for the interview with the boss, only ask for twenty minutes; and keep to this, religiously. Don't stay *one minute longer!* This will always impress an employer!

38

☆ To increase your chances of getting hired early on, research the organization ahead of time, before going in for an interview. This will put you ahead (in the employer's mind) of the other people they talk to.

Toward this end, when the appointment is first set up, ask them right then and there if they have anything *in writing* about their organization; if so, request they mail it to you, so you'll have time to read it before the interview. Or, if the interview is the next day, offer to come down today and pick it up, yourself.

Also, go to your local library, and ask the librarian for help in locating any newspaper articles or other information about that organization.

Finally, ask all your friends if they know anyone who is working there, or used to work there; if they do, ask them to put you in touch with him or her, *please.*

You want to become familiar with the organization's history, their purposes and their goals. All organizations, be they large or small, profit or nonprofit, love to be loved. If you have gone to all this trouble, to learn so much about them -- before you ever walk in their doors, they will be impressed, believe me, because most job-hunters never go to this trouble. *They* walk in knowing little or nothing about the organization. This drives employers *nuts.* Want some examples?

One time, the first question an IBM college recruiter asked a graduating senior was, "What do the initials IBM stand for?" The senior didn't know, and the interview was over.

Another time, an employer said to me, "I'm so tired of job-hunters who come in, and say, *"Uh, what do you do here?"* that the next time someone walks in who already knows something about us, I'm going to hire him or her, on the spot." And he did, within the week.

Thus, if *you* come in, and have done your homework on the organization, this immediately makes you stand out from other job-hunters, and dramatically speeds up your chances of being offered a job there.

39

☆ To increase your chances of getting hired early on, do not hog the whole interview. Studies have revealed that generally speaking the people who get hired are those who mix speaking and listening fifty-fifty in the interview. That is, half the time they spend letting the employer do the talking, half the time in the interview the job-hunter does the talking. People who didn't follow that mix, were the ones who didn't get hired, according to the study.[9] My hunch as to the *reason* why this is so, is that if you talk too much about yourself, you come across as one who would ignore the needs of the organization; while if you talk too little, you come across as trying to hide something about your background.

40

☆ To increase your chances of getting hired early on, studies[10] have revealed that when it is your turn to speak, you should not speak any longer than two minutes at a time, if you want to make the best impression. In fact, a good answer to an employer's question sometimes only takes twenty seconds to give. This is useful information for you to know, in conducting a successful interview -- as you certainly want to do.

9. This one done by a researcher at Massachusetts Institute of Technology.

10. This one conducted by my colleague, Daniel Porot, in Geneva, Switzerland.

41

☆ To increase your chances of getting hired early on, stay focussed on what you can do for the employer, rather than on what the employer can do for you. You want the employer to see you as a potential *Resource Person* for that organization, rather than as simply *A Job Beggar* (to quote Daniel Porot). You want to come across as *a problem solver*, rather than as *one who simply keeps busy.*

42

☆ To increase your chances of getting hired early on, think of what a *bad* employee would do, in the position you are asking for -- come in late, take too much time off, follow his or her own agenda instead of the employer's, etc. Then emphasize to the employer how much you are the very opposite: your sole goal is to increase the organization's effectiveness and service and bottom line.

Every organization has two main preoccupations for its day-by-day work: the problems they are facing, and what solutions people are coming up with, there. Therefore, the main thing the employer is trying to figure out during the hiring-interview, is -- if they hire you -- will you be part of the *solution* there, or just another part of the *problem.*

During the course of the interview, you need to make it clear that you are there in order to make an oral proposal, followed hopefully by a written proposal, of what *you can do for them,* to help them with *their* problems. You will see immediately what a switch this is from the way most job-hunters approach an employer! *("How much do you pay, and how much time off will I have?")* Will he or she be glad to see you, with this different emphasis? In most cases, you bet they will. They *want* a resource person, and a problem-solver.

They are also looking for employees: *who are punctual, arriving at work on time or early; who stay until quitting time, or even leave late; who are dependable; who have a good attitude; who have drive, energy, and enthusiasm; who want more than a paycheck; who are self-disciplined, well-organized, highly motivated, and good at managing their time; who can handle people well; who can use language effectively; who can work on a computer; who are committed to team work; who are flexible, and can respond to novel situations, or adapt when circumstances at work change; who are trainable, and love to learn; who are project-oriented, and goal-oriented; who have creativity and are good at problem solving; who have integrity; who are loyal to the organization; who are able to identify opportunities, markets, coming trends. They also want to hire people who can bring in more money than they are paid.* Claim any of these that you *legitimately* can, during the hiring interview.

☆ To increase your chances of getting hired early on, be sure that you illustrate in the interview whatever it is you claim will be true of you, once hired. For example, if you claim you are very *thorough* in all your work, be sure to be thorough in the way you have researched the organization ahead of time. Overall, remember that the manner in which you do your job-hunt and the manner in which you would do the job you are seeking, are not assumed by most employers to be two unrelated subjects, but one and the same. They can tell when you are doing a slipshod, half-hearted job-hunt (*"Uh, what do you guys do here?"*) and this is taken as a clear warning that you might do a slipshod, half-hearted job, were they foolish enough to ever hire you. Employers know this simple truth: most people job-hunt the way they live their lives.

☆ To increase your chances of getting hired early on, try to think of some way to bring evidence of your skills. For example, if you are an artist, craftsperson or anyone who produces a product, try to bring a sample of what you have made or produced -- either in person, or through photos, or even videotapes.

As you will see from the diagram on the next page, employers have their own *hierarchy* of the ways in which they prefer to hire. Their most preferred method is at the bottom of the pyramid. Their least preferred method is at the apex.

The words within the triangle illustrate the typical employer's thoughts.

As you can see, the employer most prefers to hire from within, or to hire someone whose work he or she has seen. By bringing this evidence, this sort of *portfolio,* you are following the employer's preferred strategy: "I want to hire someone whose work I have seen."

Incidentally, while you are looking at this diagram, notice that the typical job-hunter hunts for a job *in exactly the opposite order* from the order that most employers prefer. This is why I call the job-hunting system in this country and most others, Neanderthal.

The way a typical job-hunter likes to hunt for a job (starts here)

6 "I will place an ad to find someone."

Newspaper Ads

Resumes

5 "I will look at some resumes which come in, unsolicited."

Employment Agency for Lower Level Jobs

4 "I want to hire someone for a lower level job, from a stack of potential candidates that some agency has screened for me."

This is called 'a private employment agency,' or - - if it is within the company - - 'the human resources department,' formerly the 'personnel department.' Incidentally, only 15% of all organizations have such an internal department.

Search Firm for Higher Level Jobs

3 "I want to hire someone for a higher level job, from among outstanding people who are presently working for another organization; and I will pay a recruiter to find this outstanding candidate for me."

The agency, thus hired by an employer, is called 'a search firm' or 'headhunter'; only employers can hire such agencies.

A Job-Hunter Who Offers Proof

2 "I want to hire someone who walks in the door and can show me samples of their previous work."

"I want to hire someone whose work a trusted friend of mine has seen and recommends."

That friend may be: mate, best friend, colleague in the same field, or colleague in a different field.

From Within

Employer's Thoughts:

1 "I want to hire someone whose work I have seen." (Promotion from within of a full-time employee, or promotion from within of a part-time employee; hiring a former consultant for a regular position (formerly on a limited contract); hiring a temp for a regular position; hiring a volunteer for a regular position.)

The way a typical employer prefers to fill vacancies (starts here)

Our Neanderthal Job-Hunting System

45

☆ To increase your chances of getting hired early on, never speak badly of your previous employer(s). Employers often feel as though they are a fraternity or sorority. During the interview you want to come across as one who displays courtesy toward all members of that fraternity or sorority. Bad-mouthing a previous employer only makes this employer worry that were they to hire you, you would end up bad-mouthing *them.*

I once spoke graciously about a previous employer, to my present employer. Unbeknownst to me, my present employer *knew* my previous employer had badly mistreated me. He therefore thought very highly of me because I didn't drag it up. In fact, he never forgot this incident; talked about it for years, afterward. It always makes a *big* impression when you don't bad-mouth a previous employer.

Say something nice about your previous employer, or if you know the previous employer is going to give you a very bad recommendation, just say something simple like, "I usually get along with everybody; but for some reason, my past employer and I just didn't get along. Don't know why. It's never happened to me before. Hope it never happens again."

46

☆ To increase your chances of getting hired early on, don't be wearied by rejection. Tom Jackson's model (from *Guerrilla Tactics in the Job Market*) of the typical job-hunt is:
NO NO NO NO NO NO NO NO NO NO NO NO NO NO
NO NO NO NO NO NO NO NO NO NO NO NO NO NO
NO NO NO NO NO NO NO NO NO NO NO NO NO NO
NO NO NO NO NO NO NO NO NO NO NO NO NO NO
NO NO NO NO NO NO NO NO NO NO NO NO NO NO
NO NO NO NO NO NO NO NO NO NO NO NO NO YES.[11]

11. This is my friend Tom Jackson's description of the typical job-hunt, in his famous book, *Guerrilla Tactics in the Job Market.*

Even in consecutive interviews at many places, the more NOs you get out of the way, the closer you are to YES. Ideally, of course, you want to end up with two YESes. Two, so that you'll have at least two things to choose between.

☆ To increase your chances of getting hired early on, every evening after an interview sit down and write (with pen, typewriter, keyboard/printer), or e-mail, a thank-you note to each person you saw that day. This means not only employers, but also their secretaries, receptionists, or anyone else who gave you a friendly helping hand, in any way. Don't make this *perfunctory*. Make it personal. Mention something individual about the way they treated you, or what you liked about them. Use the thank-you note to underline anything that was discussed during the interview, or to add anything you left out, that was important.

The thank-you note is *crucial*. A job-hunter presented herself for a hiring-interview as public relations officer for a major-league baseball team. That evening, she wrote and mailed a thank-you note. She was eventually hired for the job, and when she asked why, they told her that they had decided to hire her because, out of thirty-five applicants, she was the only one who had written a thank-you note after the interview.

If you want to stand out from the others applying for the same job, if you want to speed up your getting hired, send thank-you notes -- to *everyone* you met there, that day.

Treat every employer with courtesy, even if it seems certain they can offer you no job there; they may be able to refer you to someone else next week, if you made a good impression.

WHAT IF NOTHING WORKS?

Following the strategies in this chapter, learned from *successful* job-hunters, you should dramatically improve your chance of finding a job.[12] Good luck, and if you find one, congratulations. You do not need to read the rest of this book -- *until the next time.*

But if you faithfully try everything listed in this chapter, and *none of it works* for you, what then? Well, there is a life-preserver still available to you: flee to Chapters 5, 6, and 7. read them, and painstakingly do the exercises in *The Parachute Workbook* (it will take you no more than a good weekend, if you keep at it).

Above all, never abandon hope, my friend.

I close this chapter, with the story of a successful job-hunter, who wrote me as follows:

"I was a woman who majored in Humanities and then floated around after college in several jobs, which were just jobs. To be honest, I was in my early twenties (which I have nicknamed the decade of terror), and had no idea what I wanted to do. Only, I longed for self-expression and passion in my work. I purchased your book, did some informational interviews, even saw a career counselor, all to no avail.

"Five years later, now, I have come back to your book (the new edition, of course), and identified my values, skills and talents. With my values and skills in mind, I went to the library to research government and non-profit careers, and found myself much interested in the latter. I copied a list of them and began contacting the organizations whose values were closely related to mine: helping people in the community.

12. If you want more job-hunting strategies, I refer you to *The Complete Job and Career Handbook: 101 Ways to Get From Here to There,* by S. Norman Feingold and Marilyn N. Feingold. Garrett Park Press, PO Box 190B, Garrett Park, MD 20896. 1993. This $15 book lists many other strategies for you to explore, should your job-hunt reach a dead end. Chapter titles include: "Infrequently Used/Non-traditional Job and Career Search Techniques," "Check List of 177 Ways to Help Get A Job and Advance Your Career," etc. Very helpful, and detailed. Dr. Feingold is a pioneer in the career counseling field, and he and Marilyn really know their stuff.

"One organization in particular called me back the next day, and asked if I could interview for a professional position with them. I did, explored further to be sure I understood what the job entailed, interviewed a second time, and in less than one month was offered the position of my dreams!

"Thanks to you and your advice on the most successful ways to find employment -- previously, over a period of four months, I had applied for at least fifty jobs from the want ads, with no hits -- I am now happily employed doing the kind of work I like best, and I did so in record time."

To grow is to change, and to become perfect is to change often.

Cardinal Newman

CHAPTER FOUR

FOR THE IMPATIENT JOB-HUNTER

HOW TO QUICKLY CHOOSE A NEW CAREER

WHEN YOU HAVEN'T THE FOGGIEST IDEA WHAT YOU WANT TO DO

Chapter 4

Table of Contents

HOW DO PEOPLE CHOOSE CAREERS?

Once, I overheard two college students talking, in Central Park in New York City. We'll call them Jim and Fred. In half a minute of conversation they perfectly illustrated the way most people choose careers:

Jim: Hey, what are you majoring in?
Fred: Physics.
Jim: Physics? Man, you shouldn't major in physics. Computer science is the thing these days.
Fred: Naw, I like physics.
Jim: Man, physics doesn't pay much.

Fred: Really? What does?

Jim: Computer science. You should switch to computer science.

Fred: Okay, I'll look into it tomorrow.

In this way are many career choices (and career-changes) made in our culture -- on impulse and whim, in a moment, in the twinkling of an eye. A casual conversation with someone. A decision to just follow in our parents' footsteps. An article on a news broadcast. An invitation from a girlfriend or boyfriend to come work where they do.

> When you choose a career,[1] you have got to know what it is you *want* to do, or else someone is going to sell you a bill of goods somewhere along the line that can do irreparable damage to your self-esteem, your sense of worth, and your stewardship of the talents that God gave you.

Most of us spend more time planning next summer's vacation, which will consume about 80 hours of our life, than we spend planning our life in the world of work, which will consume 80,000 hours of our life.

You'd think we'd spend some time trying to figure out what we want to do with our lives. Instead, we take shortcuts in deciding on a career. And most of those shortcuts begin not by

---

1. The word career remains a very fuzzy word in the English language, because there are three senses in which it is used. It is used, first of all, to mean *work* in contrast to *learning* or *leisure*. Thus when clothing ads speak of "a career outfit," they are referring to clothes which are worn primarily at work, rather than during learning-activities or leisure-activities. It is used, secondly, to sum up *a person's whole life in the world of work*. Thus when people say of someone at the end of their life, "He or she had a brilliant career," they are not referring to a particular occupation, but to *all* the occupations this person ever held, and all the work this person ever did. Thirdly, in its most common sense, as I indicated earlier, it is used as a synonym for the word *occupation* or *job* -- particularly where that occupation or job offers opportunity for promotion and advancement, toward the top. (This *movement toward a goal* is its most primitive meaning, as it dates from the origin of the word. *Career* comes from the Latin *carrus*, referring to a racetrack where horses wildly *careen* while competing in a race.) The wild way in which people *careen* into careers thus preserves the original meaning of the word. *Adapted from the article on "Careers" in* Collier's Encyclopedia, *written by the author. Copyright © 1991 by Macmillan Educational Company.*

inquiring what *we* want to do, but by trying to figure out what *the job-market* supposedly is looking for.

U.S. Statistics

A survey found that 45% of all U.S. workers said they would change their careers if they could.[2]

In point of fact, each year about 10% of all U.S. workers actually do. In the most recent year surveyed, that equated to 10 million workers who changed careers that year. Of these:

5.3 million of them changed careers *voluntarily,* and in 7 out of 10 cases their income went up;

1.3 million of them changed careers *involuntarily,* because of what happened to them in the economy, and in 7 out of 10 cases, their income went down;

3.4 million of them changed careers for a *mixture* of voluntary and involuntary reasons (such as needing to go from part-time to full-time work, etc.), and there is no record of what happened to their income.

Despite the *myth* that career-change is primarily a mid-life phenomenon, in point of fact people can and do change careers at *all* ages. In this study, only one out of ten career-changers was actually in mid-life.[3] Many U.S. experts think, however, that the remainder of the '90s will see a lot more 'mid-life career-change,' inasmuch as 1996 was the year when the first of the U.S.'s 76 million 'baby boomers' turned fifty. The rest are only in their forties, at best.

---

2. The survey was done by the Roper Organization for Shearson Lehman Brothers, in 1992.

3. The year was 1986. The survey was published in the *Occupational Outlook Quarterly,* Summer 1989, and in the *Monthly Labor Review,* September 1989. Should you wish further resources dealing with career-change at mid-life, these include:

Betsy Jaffe, Ed.D., *Altered Ambitions: What's Next in Your Life? Winning Strategies To Reshape Your Career.* Donald I. Fine, Inc., 19 W. 21st St., New York, NY 10010. 1991.

Godfrey Golzen, and Philip Plumbley, *Changing Your Job After 35.* Kogan Page Ltd., 120 Pentonville Rd., London Nl 9JN. l988.

Tell me, we say, *what kinds of careers are doing a lot of hiring, these days?* Or, *Tell me,* we say, *what are the careers where I can make the most money?* Or, *Tell me,* we say, *what are the hot careers for the next ten years?* The answers we get, from so-called experts, are often far wide of the mark! *Beware of false prophets,* someone once said. Good advice, when trying to guess 'the best future careers.' We read about these supposedly great jobs, we go looking for one, and often we cannot find it no matter how hard we look. One year, two years, still can't find one.

But even when we do, it turns out there's often a chasm the size of the Grand Canyon between what we thought we were going to be doing vs. what we actually wind up doing. For example, we thought we were going to be working with people all day long, helping, caring, but we discover -- too late -- that most of the day we're only working with paper. Or we thought we were going to be working on the computer designing gorgeous images, and we discover -- too late -- that most of the day is spent in meetings. We start reading *Dilbert* avidly. *The vision vs. the reality.* What a letdown!

No wonder surveys of worker dissatisfaction find that up to 80%, or four out of every five workers, are dissatisfied with some important aspects of their jobs or careers. *It's not a pretty picture.*

Used by permission of Johnny Hart and Creators Syndicate, Inc.

WHAT PUSHES US TO CHANGE CAREERS?

It is no surprise that as time goes on, we decide to change careers. Not once, but several times in our life. In fact, people entering the job-market today should count on having anywhere between three and six careers during their lifetime.

We make this decision to change careers for one of several reasons:

• We got fired, and we can't find our old work any more; we *have* to 're-tool.'

• We are not earning enough, and we need a new career that pays us more money -- more of what we're worth.

• We made a bad choice when we first chose our career, and now we've decided to set it right.

• All we wanted from a job, in the past, was money; now we want *meaning*. Indeed, if truth be told, most of us are engaged in a life-long search for, and journey toward, *meaning* -- a process in which career-choice plays an important part.

• We're looking more and more for 'our mission in life,' and while we don't yet know what that is, we do know for sure that what we're presently doing *isn't it.*

• We've been asked to do the work of three, and we feel stressed out, angry, exhausted, burnt out, and grumpy; we want a job or career that is a little easier on us, so we'll have time to smell the flowers.

• We had hardly been stretched at all by our previous work, and we'd like something that offers a real challenge and 'stretches' us.

• We had a dream job, but our much-beloved boss moved on, we now find ourselves working for 'a jerk,' and the dream job has turned into 'the job from hell.' We not only want a new employer, we want a new career.

For any or all of these reasons, we change careers.

SELF-EMPLOYMENT

Sometimes the career we change to is that of self-employment. 12% of all the workers in the U.S. are self-employed. But of course, that means that 88% of all the workers in the U.S. are working for someone else.

In view of this disparity, I have put notes, about self-employment, in the *Workbook*, on page 177, for the 12% *(one would guess)* of my readers who are interested in that possibility; but am devoting the remainder of this chapter to the vast majority (88%) whose idea of career-change is that of moving to a new career, but still working for someone else.

I would, however, caution those leaning toward self-employment to read this chapter as well. For, self-employment is a career-change, for sure; and the better you understand what career-change is, the better your transition to self-employment may be.

WHAT CAREER-CHANGE IS

Okay, then, let's begin. Simply. Basically, a career is made up of two parts: an occupation-title, and a field. For example, let us suppose you decided you wanted to be a management consultant. That's an occupation-title. So far, so good. But, you have to go beyond that, and decide also on a field.

In what field do you want to be a management consultant? Do you want to do management consulting with . . . a law firm? . . . a gardening firm? . . . a camping firm? . . . a firm that manufactures cars? . . . a computer firm? . . . or what? Makes a big difference, doesn't it? Law, Gardening, Camping, Cars, Computers -- these are all *fields.*

Career-change = occupation-title + field. Memorize that, please. It will help you a lot, down the line. If you're trying hard to find a job as a management consultant, for example, and nothing is turning up, you know what your problem is. You only said, "I want to be a management consultant," and that by itself isn't enough. It's an occupation-title, to be sure. But, if you want your job-hunt to be successful you must also define a *field.* Until you've decided what field you want to do management consulting in, your job-hunt is going to be somewhere between *difficult* and *impossible.* Too broad a target, too dispersed, too scattered. You need to focus your job-hunt, or career-change. *Field* is the way you do that.

So, this is our first lesson: *Career-change = occupation-title + field.* And in the most complete career-change you move from one occupation-title to another, *and* from one field to another. Let me illustrate:

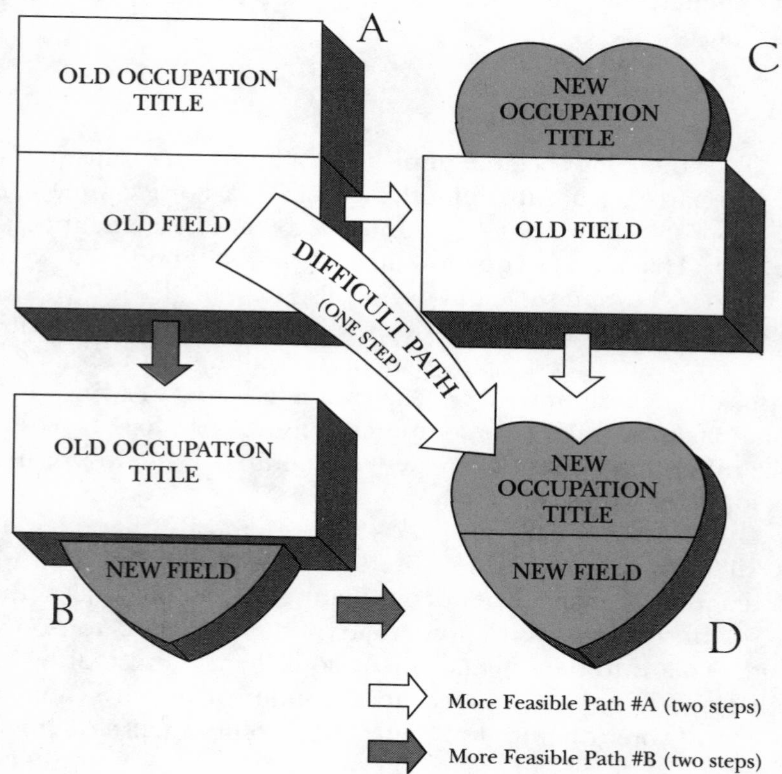

WHEN YOU KNOW WHAT CAREER YOU WANT: THE 'ONE STEP AT A TIME' METHOD OF CHANGING CAREERS

As the previous diagram makes clear, when you've decided it's time for you to make a career-change, there are three kinds of career change you can choose:

(1) You can just change your field but not your occupation-title. This is a move from A to B, in the diagram. *This is a career-change. You may be much happier just by getting into a new* field.

(2) You can just change your occupation-title, but not your field. This is a move from A to C, in the diagram. *This is a career-change. You may be much happier just by changing your* occupation, *in that same field.*

(3) You can decide you want to change both your occupation-title *and* your field. This is a move from A to D, in the diagram. *This is a career-change. You may decide you can only be happy if you change both* occupation *and* field.

Should you decide you want to make the latter kind of complete change, there are two ways you can go about it:

a) The move can be made all at once (The Difficult Path) -- going from A to D, in a single bound.

b) Or, the move can be made in two steps, as indicated by the two white arrows (that's one way), or by the two red arrows (that's another way). We call this the 'one-step-at-a-time' method of career change.

To illustrate all of this, let us suppose your present (or most recent) career is that of an accountant at a television station. Now, for whatever reason, you've decided that you would like to change careers, and be a reporter who covers the medical field.

If you decide to try to make this career-change in a single bound, you go and try to convince some newspaper, journal, or whatever that you have the expertise and background to be a good reporter, *and* that you also are familiar with the medical field. This is not easy -- unless you have some background

Types of Career Change Visualized

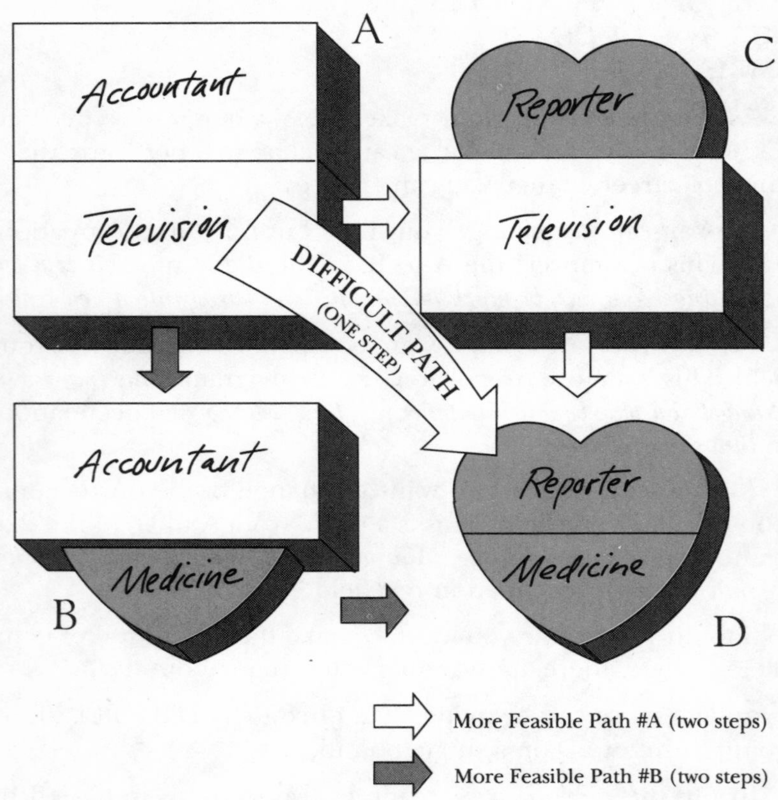

and experience in both -- and that's why we call this The Difficult Path. But there is another way -- two other ways, as a matter of fact.

In the diagram above, you can first move from A to B: stay an accountant, but get a new job at some medical journal or newspaper. You'd stay there one year, two, or three; then you move from B to D: try to get them to hire you as a reporter where you are, or try to get a different medical journal or newspaper to hire you as a reporter.

Alternatively, you can first move from A to C: ask the television station where you already work as an accountant to hire you as a reporter instead, or go to another television station and ask to be hired as a reporter. You'd stay there one year, two, or three; then you move from C to D: getting a job as a reporter at a medical journal or newspaper.

> In both cases, the tremendous advantage of this 'one-step-at-a-time' career-change method, is that *each time you make a move, you are already experienced in either the occupation or the field.* This carries much greater weight with would-be employers, than when you are inexperienced in both occupation *and* field at the same time.

SELLING YOURSELF TO AN EMPLOYER WHEN YOU ARE INEXPERIENCED

But suppose you've found the career of your dreams. You want to get there in a single bound. You don't want to take it in steps. How do you sell yourself to a would-be employer, when you are inexperienced in both occupation *and* field?

In such a case, you must remember that every occupation is composed of a series of tasks or assignments; and every task or assignment, in turn, requires that you have certain skills, to do it well.

You can quickly learn just exactly what skills are required for this new career of yours, by going and chatting with people who are already in that career. *What tasks or assignments do you have to do in this career?* you ask them. And, *What skills does it take to do such tasks or assignments?* Armed with such a list, after interviewing two or three, you can then compare it with the skills that *you* have, and put a check beside each skill that matches. After which, you can approach a would-be employer, for this new career you have chosen, as someone who is *experienced.* Of course you are brand new to both occupation and field, but you *are* experienced where it really counts. And that is, in your skills. Indeed, precisely those skills needed to do the tasks and assignments of this new job and career.

You can not only enumerate what those skills are, but you can give the employer convincing evidence and proof, from the past, that you have those skills.

True, you used them in a different occupation and field at the time. But all skills are *transferable.* That is, if you were good -- say -- at *analyzing things,* in the past, you will be good at *analyzing things* in this new occupation, and field. '*Analyzing things*' is not just a skill; it is a '*transferable* skill.'

If you did enough chatting with people in this new career of yours before you approach an employer, you will also have gained a considerable overview of the field and occupation -- even though you've never been in it -- and to that degree you will be *familiar* with both, in at least some small degree, as would not be the case if you had never done all that chatting.

It is obvious of course that before approaching an employer, you *will* have to do some homework on yourself. Specifically, you will need to take an inventory of just exactly what your transferable skills are.

That takes time. That takes patience. And it requires a systematic method.

Such a method is described in the next chapters, "For the Determined Job-Hunter," and in The Workbook that you will find in *The Parachute Workbook and Resource Guide,* attached to this book.

We can thus supply you with the method.

You have to supply the time. And the patience.

WHEN YOU DON'T KNOW WHAT CAREER YOU WANT

When you have no idea what you'd like to do next, there is only one route that makes any sense, as we have already seen:

> Don't decide on your future, until you have first inventoried your past.

The purpose of choosing or changing a career is to find career satisfaction, or -- in a word -- happiness. More than that, it is to find a career you will *love.* Work that you can't wait to get up in the morning and go do. Work that you love so much, you can't believe you are being paid to do it -- since you'd be willing to do it for nothing.

Finding a career you can love depends on there being a match between what you love most to do, and what is available *out there.* For example, if some *hot* new career is available, but involves working with paper, while you love working with people, then that career is going to make you miserable, no matter how easy it may be to find a job there.

Hence, it doesn't matter that a career is *hot* or *easy* to get into. What matters is that you and the career should be happy with each other, nay, be in love with each other. There are few greater joys in life, than to find such a career.

As we can see from the diagram on the next page, finding such a career depends upon it matching the skills you love to use, plus your favorite subjects, the people you love to help or work with, the kind of place where you love to work, your goals and that place's goals, and a salary that satisfies your needs.

Chief among these are the skills you love to use, and your favorite subjects. While you may think you know what these are, in most cases your self-knowledge could use a little more work. A weekend would do. In a weekend, you can inventory your past sufficiently so that you have a good picture of the *kind* of work you would love to be doing. You can, of course, stretch the inventory over a number of weeks, maybe doing an

THE ANATOMY OF MY IDEAL JOB

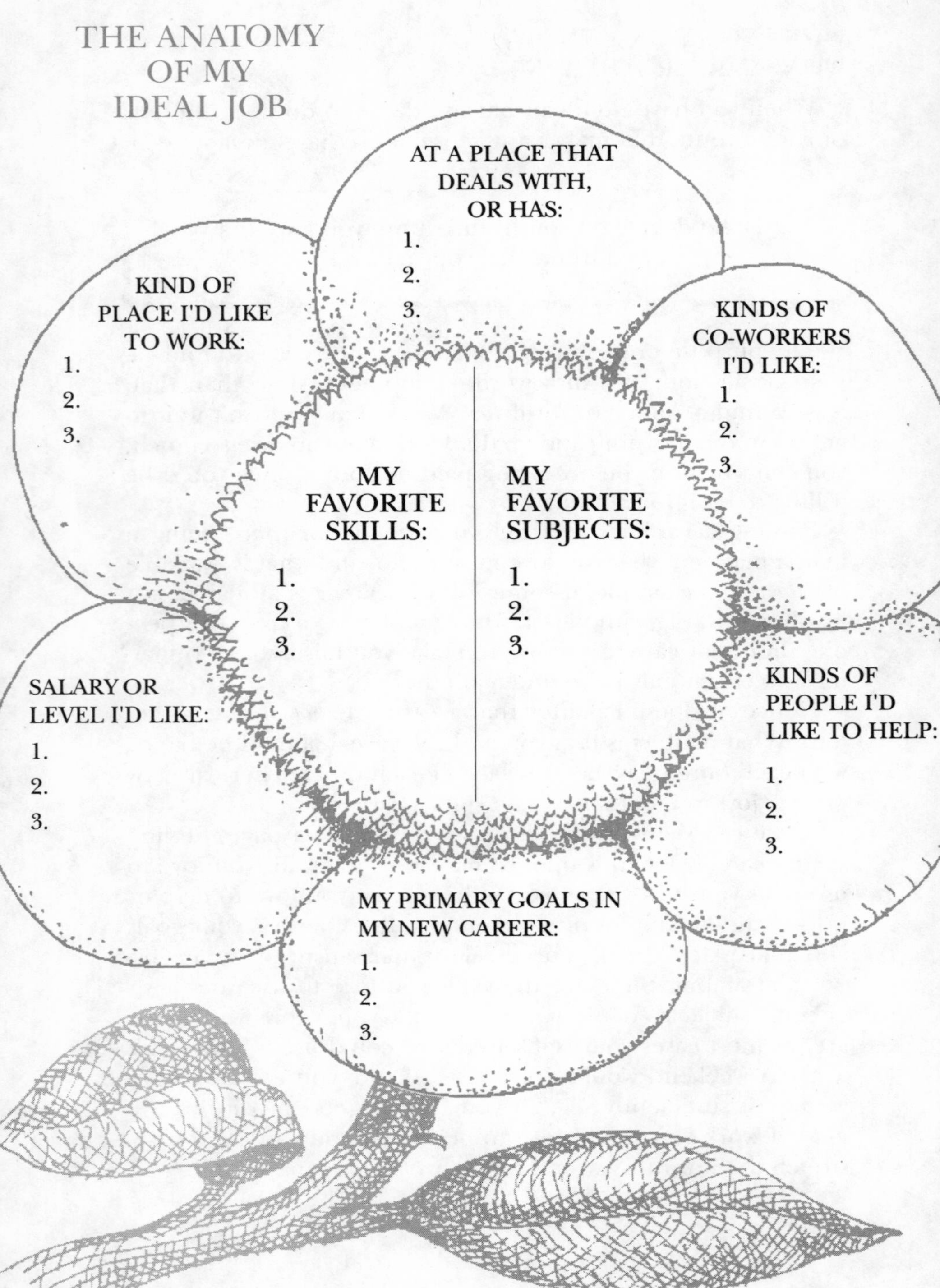

hour or two one night a week, if you prefer. It's up to you as to just how you do it.

But it is the best way. Indeed, it is the only sensible path to career satisfaction. *Don't decide on your future before you have first inventoried your past.*

The Best Way to Choose A New Career

You do a systematic inventory of the *transferable skills* which you already possess, and the *bodies of knowledge* which you already know, together with *the interests* that most fascinate you, and from all this you fashion a description -- a picture, if you will -- of what your new career *looks like*; then you interview people, with this picture, to find out *what its name is* (or names). The inventory takes a weekend. The finding out of the names takes several hours of research during the weeks following.

A detailed description of this process of career-change is in *The Parachute Workbook and Resource Guide* attached to this book at the back. The workbook is called "The Quick Job-Hunting Map," subtitled, *How to Create A Picture of Your Ideal Job or Next Career.*

SHORTCUTS

Now, this careful, reasoned way of going about choosing or changing a career is by far the best way. But you may feel that you just don't have the time or the patience to do all this work of inventorying your past.

That, of course, is how you feel *now.* It may be, that in a few weeks or months, you will feel quite differently, in which case we'll see you back here. Keep it in mind as *Plan B,* if the other things you try just don't work out.

In the meantime, for the Patience-Impaired, we'll devote the remainder of this chapter to looking at some shortcuts.

Ah, shortcuts, you say. *What a lovely word.*

Yes, shortcuts. But do remember that though they save time, you purchase that savings at a cost. You gain something, you lose something: accuracy. There's always the danger of *out of the frying pan, into the fire,* when you choose your new career in haste.

MIRROR, MIRROR, ON THE WALL, WHO'S THE FAIREST ONE OF ALL?

Well anyway, you want to know the simplest, fastest, easiest way to pick a career, I'm sure. Here is the fastest:

The Mirror Method of Choosing A New Career

In this method you use other people as though they were mirrors to yourself. You look at everyone you know, everyone you've ever seen on TV, or read about, and you think to yourself, "Well, whose job would I most like to have, in all the world?" Make a second and third choice. Write what each of these three people does, on three sheets of paper. Underneath each, then, break down their job into its parts: what is it about the job that attracts you? List as many things as possible. Then look at all three sheets of paper, choose which job is actually of greatest interest to you, and figure out how you could get such a job.

One woman who changed careers this way decided that the job she most admired was that of a woman she saw on national TV, who hosted a children's program. So, she prepared a careful outline of what she thought a good children's TV program should look like, then went to her local TV station (which had no such program) and told them her ideas. They liked her proposal, hired her to host just such a program, and she became a big success. Later, she triumphantly wrote me, "I am in my ideal career. . . . without ever having done any of the exercises in your book!" *Bravo,* say I.

This assumes, of course, that you can move from one career into another without spending much time 're-tooling.'

NEXT: A VOCATIONAL RESTAURANT

Now to our second shortcut: *Lists.*

When it's time to choose or change careers, many of us would like to be able to sit down in some kind of Vocational Restaurant, and just choose from a menu of options.

Big problem: there is no such Restaurant, *and* the number of options is bewildering. For example, experts can name at least 12,860 different occupations or careers that you might choose from, and these have 8,000 alternative job-titles, for a total of over 20,000.[4]

Twenty thousand! There's the problem, right there. Most of us find it is impossible to choose between 20,000 of anything. In fact, we have trouble choosing between twenty items on a restaurant menu!

That's why our experts have hacked this list down, essentially, to just 300 options. Yes, you can find 90% of the 125 million workers in the U.S. in a mere 300 of those 20,000 job-titles. The other 19,700 job titles are filled by just 10% of the workforce.

Some experts have hacked the list down further still, to just 50 options. You can find 50% of the 125 million workers in the U.S. in just 50 job-titles.

---

4. A description of all 20,000 of these occupations or careers can be found in any U.S. library, in a volume known as the U.S. *Dictionary of Occupational Titles.* It is known more familiarly as the *D.O.T.*, and is published by the Bureau of Labor Statistics. Other countries sometimes have similar volumes.

The *D.O.T.* is updated periodically -- most recently in 1991, with the previous revision having occurred in 1977, and supplemented (only) in 1982, 1986, and 1987. While vocational experts always recommend using this directory, our readers have found it a *terribly unhelpful* book for the end of the twentieth century. As one reader, a chemist, wrote: "While it claims to be updated to 1991, I found that *every* description I looked up was last updated in 1977! [That's twenty years ago!] . . . I read the description of my present occupation and it sounds quite good. I only wish I was doing what it described. That may have been what a chemist did 20 years ago but with most companies de-emphasizing research it is hardly what they do today." If you want to dabble in the D.O.T. despite these warnings, be prepared for its description of a particular job or career to be *widely* divergent from what that job is, currently. Be sure to go talk to people actually doing what you'd like to do. They'll tell you what the job or career is really like, *now.*

Fifty would seem to be a manageable number of careers to choose between, but in our culture we're always looking for someone who will hack the list down, further still -- say, to just ten options. That's why so many magazines, books, and newspapers, publish such lists as *The Ten Hottest Fields of the '90s.*

Anything so that we don't have to work our way through twenty thousand choices!

LISTS OF 'GUESSES'

> The 'Look Over This List' Method
> of Choosing A New Career
>
> In this method you look over a list of careers, or occupations, and see if any of them appeals to you. This approach assumes, of course, that you have at least a vague idea of what work these people do. If you don't know what 'a carpenter' does, then obviously you're not going to pick 'carpenter.' But, anyway, let's try it and see how it goes, for you.

We'll start with the shortest lists. They always have just ten items on them, and are usually titled "The Top Ten" something or other. They are *interesting,* sometimes helpful, sometimes useless. The most useless are lists of 'the ten *hottest* occupations.' (Whatever *that* means.)

• List #1. A Typical List of Someone's Idea of 'The Ten Best Careers':

Computer animator, Online content producer, *Mutual fund manager*, Industrial environmentalist, *Family doctor*, Management consultant, *Intellectual property lawyer*, Priest, rabbi, minister, *Interactive ad executive*, and Physical therapist.[5]

5. Or so *P.O.V.* Magazine says (quoted in *USA Today*, April 11, 1996).

How useful is such a list as this? Well, all such lists are highly subjective, they will differ from one magazine or book to another, there is no agreement between them all on which are really the 'ten hottest' careers, nor will they tell you what criteria they used when compiling that list.

That's for starters. More importantly, one person's *best career* is another person's *poison.* As you will recall, the best career *for You* has to: use *Your* favorite skills, *Your* favorite subjects, *Your* primary goals, and offer *Your* preferred people and things to work with, *Your* preferred workplace, that deals with *Your* preferred objectives, and all of this at *Your* preferred level and salary.

Thus it is, that each individual must form his or her *own* list of 'ten best careers.' (*See* The Workbook in *The Parachute Workbook and Resource Guide* attached to this book at the back.)

No one else can do this for you; therefore no one else's list should be taken seriously by you for even one minute -- unless you see something on that list that causes you to go, *Aha!*, triumphantly. It's given you an idea!

As a *primer of the pump*, such a list may be useful. As *a recipe* for where you should go next, it can be a disaster.

Next list?

Well actually, we have three -- all attempting to *predict* the labor market for the next decade:

• List #2. The top ten *occupations* that experts predict will grow the fastest between now and the year 2005:

Personal and home care aides, Home health aides, *Systems analysts,* Computer engineers, *Physical and corrective therapy assistants and aides,* Electronic pagination systems workers, *Occupational therapy assistants and aides,* Physical therapists, *Residential counselors,* and Human services workers.[6]

• List #3. The top ten *occupations* ranked by the number of additional workers that experts predict will be needed by the year 2005 are:

Cashiers, Janitors and cleaners, including maids and housekeeping cleaners, *Salespersons in retail,* Waiters and waitresses, *Registered nurses,* General managers and top executives, *Systems analysts,* Home health aides, *Guards,* and Nursing aides, orderlies and attendants.[7]

• List #4. The top ten *fields* that experts predict will grow the fastest between now and the year 2005:

Health services (they think this will grow 120% between 1995 and 2005), Residential care (83%), *Business services (79%),* Automobile services (except repair) (75%), *Computer and data processing services (70%),* Individual and other social services (69%), *Health practitioners not described elsewhere (65%),* Child daycare services (59%), *Personnel supply services (58%),* Services to buildings (58%), *Equipment rental and leasing (51%),* and Securities sales and services (50%).[8]

Please note: none of these three lists are lists of *facts.* They are all lists of *guesses.* This is what labor market experts *guess* will happen between now and the year 2005. And you know how reliable *guesses* or *predictions* are. Read any weather reports lately?

---

6. The *Bureau of Labor Statistics,* December 1, 1995.

7. Ditto.

8. Ditto.

LISTS OF FACTS

If you want facts instead of guesses, here are five such lists. They all describe what is actually the case, right now, rather than what someone *guesses* will be the case by the year 2005.

• List#5 . The fifty occupations that over half of the U.S. workforce are *actually* in, right now:

Automobile mechanics, carpenters, *electricians,* light- or heavy-truck drivers, *construction laborers*, welders & cutters, *groundskeepers & gardeners*, electrical and electronic engineers, *freight, stock, and material movers or handlers*, guards and police, *production occupations*, supervisors, *farmers*, commodities sales representatives, *laborers*, lawyers, *farm workers*, stockhandlers & baggers, *insurance sales*, janitors & cleaners, *managers & administrators*, supervisors & proprietors, *machine operators*, teachers -- university, college, secondary and elementary school, *stock & inventory clerks*, accountants & auditors, *underwriters and other financial officers*, secretaries, *receptionists,* childcare workers, *registered nurses*, typists, *bookkeepers*, textile sewing machine operators, *nursing aides,* orderlies & attendants, *hairdressers & cosmetologists*, waiters & waitresses, *maids and housemen*, cashiers, *general office clerks*, administrative support occupations, *sales workers,* computer operators, *miscellaneous food preparation occupations*, production inspectors, *checkers & examiners*, cooks, *real estate salespeople*, and assemblers.

• List #6 . The ten U.S. occupations that are considered the most prestigious (in case you're hunting for respect):

Physician (Prestige Score: 82), *College professor (78),* Judge (76), *Attorney (76),* Astronomer (74), *Dentist (74),* Bank officer (72), *Engineer (71),* Architect (71), and *Clergy (70).*[9]

• List #7 . The ten U.S. *occupations* that actually pay the most, right now (just *in case* this is of any interest to you):

Physicians (Median salary: $148,000), *Dentists ($93,000),* Lobbyists ($91,000), *Veterinarians ($63,069),* Management

9. Source: The National Opinion Research Center.

consultants ($61,900), *Lawyers ($60,500),* Electrical engineers ($59,100), *School principals ($57,300),* Aeronautical engineers ($56,700), *Airline pilots ($56,500),* and Civil engineers ($55,800).[10]

• List #8. The ten U.S. *fields* that actually pay the most, right now (we're talking 'median earnings' again):

Engineering, *mathematics*, computer and information sciences, *pharmacy*, architecture/environmental design, *physics*, accounting, *economics*, health/medical technologies, *and physical therapy*.[11]

• List #9. And finally, one extra list at no extra charge: the ten U.S. States with the lowest unemployment rate currently (just *in case* you are thinking about moving to where they're desperate for workers):

Nebraska (the lowest unemployment rate in the nation: only 2.39%), South Dakota (2.82%), *North Dakota (3.14%),* Iowa (3.28%), *Utah (3.36%),* Minnesota (3.45%), *Wisconsin (3.67%),* Colorado (3.84 %), *New Hampshire (3.89%),* and Delaware (4.11%).[12]

TRY ON THAT DRESS OR SUIT, FIRST, BEFORE YOU BUY

Now, let us suppose there is some career on the previous lists that sounds really intriguing to you. What should you do? Go get trained, get a degree (if that's necessary), and then go looking for jobs in the career you have chosen? No, no, no.

Before you take one single step toward pursuing that career, you *must* go talk to people in that career and see what it's *really* like -- lest you make a huge mistake.

Beyond chatting with them, you should, if the job lends itself to it,[13] ask if you can follow one of them around all day, to

10. Source: *Money* Magazine, and *The Bureau of Labor Statistics.*

11. Source: "Earnings of college graduates, 1993: Fields of study is a major determinant of the wide variations in earnings." *Monthly Labor Review,* December 1995.

12. *The Bureau of Labor Statistics.*

13. Well, I can think of some careers that don't: following a pilot around on his plane is one that comes to mind, and sitting in on a psychiatrist's sessions is another.

"Let's put it this way – if you can find a village without an idiot, you've got yourself a job."

see what the job actually involves on an hour-by-hour basis. *Don't* overlook this step. It is crucial, if you are to avoid being miserable in your new career.

Let's say you're thinking about a new career where you would be working in a beauty salon. You take the Yellow Pages, look up the ones in your city or neighborhood, go down there and ask to talk with someone who does the work you are thinking about doing. If you're still interested in the work, you then talk to them (and their manager), tell them you're thinking about going into this kind of work, and would it be possible for you to volunteer to help out there for a day, and follow someone around to see what the job actually involves? If they say No, for any reason, go visit another salon, and make the same request, until someone says, "Sure!"

You *need* to do this 'all-day visit,' because many jobs that look interesting and glamorous at a distance, don't look so glamorous up close. Standing on your feet all day, doing boring idle chit-chat, smelling awful odors, handling endless complaints -- well, you get the picture. If all of this strikes you, instead, as: painless exercise, good conversation, *interesting* odors, and challenges to be met and overcome, well then, you were probably born to do this work.

But that's exactly what you're trying to find out, one way or another. And you want to find it out, regardless of what career looks interesting on the list above. Before you go get trained to do it, you want to *try it on* first, even as you would a dress or suit before you buy. You want to understand the job fully and see what it feels like, from the inside, before you decide to commit.

Don't choose a career just because some expert says, *This is it!* Choose it because you love it, and you have taken the time to test that by 'on-the-job *shadowing*,' as I just described.

Otherwise, 'worker dissatisfaction' will soon be your favorite subject, and you're gonna be going through all this again, *real soon.*

GETTING A JOB BY DEGREES

But if you've explored this new career, and it still sounds interesting to you, then you can feel more confident you've made a good choice.

There is, however, another series of questions you *must* ask of those who are doing the work you are thinking about going into:

How do I get into this career, and how much of a demand is there for people who can do this work?

And, is it easy to find a job in this career, or is it hard?

You *want* to know this! Believe me, you *want* to know this! Especially if, in order to prepare for this career that interests you, it's going to take some time for you to go get some schooling, or perhaps a degree.

If you fail to ask such questions *ahead of time* you may be bitterly disappointed after you get all that training, or that degree.

You want to know this, before you start. So, *puh-leeze,* talk to people in the career you find so appealing, and ask them these questions I have just suggested. *Please!*

Ask at least three people in that career field those questions.

Make up your own mind whether this is one of 'the *hottest* careers of the '90s.' Don't believe what lists, experts, or well-meaning friends try to claim is a good career *for you.* Test it, make up your own mind. And don't go get a degree because you think that will guarantee you a job! No, mon ami, it will not.

I wish you could see my mail, filled with bitter letters from people who believed such lists as you have just seen, went and got a degree in that field, thought it would be a snap to find a job, but are still unemployed after two years. You would weep! They are bitter (often), angry (always), and disappointed in a society which they feel lied to them.

They found there was no job that went with that degree. They feel lied to, by our society and by the experts, about the value of going back to school, and getting a degree in this or that 'hot' field.

Now that they have that costly worthless degree, and still can't find a job, they find a certain irony in the phrase, "*Our country believes in getting a job by degrees.*"

If you already made this costly mistake, you know what I mean.

A FINAL WORD ABOUT CHANGING CAREERS

Well, you've ploughed your way through this chapter, and maybe you're thinking: "*Well, I want to change careers. But perhaps this just isn't the right time.*"

Friend, there will never be *a right time.* Conditions will always be *difficult.* Obstacles will always be *in your way,* which you must overcome. It will always be a challenge, should you decide to launch out into the deep and mysterious destiny to which you feel called, by the long-lost dreams of your soul.

By the way, if you're sharing your life with someone, please be sure to take them into your confidence. Sit down with that partner or spouse and ask what the implications are *for them* if you try this new thing. How do they feel about what you're about to do? What will it cost the two of you? Will it require all your joint savings? Will they have to give up things, along with you? If so, what? Are they willing to make those sacrifices? And so on.

If you aren't out of work, you will wrestle with the question of whether you should quit your present job, before you start up this new career.

The experts say that if you have a job, *don't* quit it. Better by far to move *gradually* into your new career, if that is at all possible -- doing it as a moonlighting activity at first, while you are still holding down that regular job somewhere else. That way, you can test out your new adventure, as you would test a floorboard in an old run-down house, stepping on it cautiously without yet putting your full weight on it, to see whether or not it will support you.[14]

Be sure to do your research first, weigh the risks, count the cost, get counsel from those intimately involved with you, and then if you decide you want to do it (whatever *it* is), go ahead and try -- no matter what your well-meaning but pessimistic acquaintances may say.

Just keep these three rules in mind:

1. There is always some risk, in trying something new. Your job is not to avoid risk -- there is no way to do that -- but to make sure ahead of time that the risks are *manageable.*

2. You find this out before you start, by first talking to others who have already done what you are thinking of doing; then you evaluate whether or not you still want to go ahead and try it.

3. Have a Plan B, already laid out, *before you start,* as to what you will do if it doesn't work out; i.e., know where you are going to go, next. Don't wait, p*uh-leaze!* Write it out, now. *This is what I'm going to do, if this doesn't work out:* ______________________________

14. See Philip Holland, *How To Start A Business Without Quitting Your Job: The Moonlight Entrepreneur's Guide.* Ten Speed Press, Post Office Box 7123, Berkeley, CA 94707. 1992.

These rules always apply, no matter where you are in your life: just starting out, already employed, unemployed, in mid-life, recovering after a crisis or accident, facing retirement, or whatever. Do take them very seriously.

And, *good luck!* In some ways this is a journey in which you cannot fail. Even if you are not able to *pull it off,* in any way that the world calls 'successful,' you will at the very least be a better man or woman for having tried. There is something about *adversity* and *challenge* that tests and refines *character,* even as fire tempers steel. A challenge toward growth and change -- willingly accepted -- can often bring out the very best in us.

You have something unique to contribute to this Earth, while you are here. Any journey you take, toward finding out what that is, will be well worth the adventure.

It's not what we have, but what we are,
that makes the poverty or richness of our life.

Phillips Brooks

CHAPTER FIVE

FOR THE DETERMINED JOB-HUNTER OR CAREER-CHANGER

The Systematic Approach To
Career-Change
And Job-Hunting

WHAT

SKILLS DO YOU MOST ENJOY USING?

You Must Figure Out What Kinds of Tasks
You Most Enjoy Doing
and Which of Your Skills
You Most Delight to Use

Chapter 5

Table of Contents

The major difference between successful and unsuccessful job-hunters is not some factor out there (such as a tight job-market), but the way they go about their job-hunt.

Yes, and that has always been true! When a job-hunter tells me: *"I can't find a job"* that tells me nothing, until he tells me *how* he has been looking for it. The method one uses, is everything!

The best method, by far, has over the years turned out to be the so-called **creative job-hunting approach**. This method leads to a job for 86 out of every 100 job-hunters who faithfully follow it. Such an effectiveness-rate -- 86% -- is *astronomically higher* than all other job-hunting methods.[1] That's why when nothing else is working for you, this is the method that you will thank your lucky stars for.

This is also the method you must turn to, if you've decided you would like to find a new career -- and you'd prefer not to have to take years out of your life to go back to school and get retrained with a new degree, etc., etc.

But it is only for the *determined* job-hunter. Making a pass at it, only taking a swipe at it, trying to do it in just a day and a night, will not do. If, to paraphrase an old hymn, *you want to be carried to your job on flowery beds of ease,* this is not the method for you. It requires dedication, determination, time, and hard work -- as most good things in life do. But if you are a *determined* job-hunter or career-changer, you certainly can do it, as millions have before you.

The creative approach to career-change has three parts to it. These parts are in the form of our old familiar questions: *What, Where,* and *How,* here more fully defined:

• WHAT?

The full question here is *what are the skills you most enjoy using?*

To answer this question, you need to identify or inventory what **skills/gifts/talents** you have; and then you need to prioritize them, in their order of importance and enjoyment for you. Experts call these 'transferable skills,' because they are transferable to any field/career that you choose, regardless of where you first picked them up, or how long you've had them.

1. I speak of individual job-hunting strategies. Group strategies, such as Nathan Azrin's 'job-club' concept, Chuck Hoffman's Self-Directed Job-Search, Dean Curtis' Group Job Search program, etc., have achieved success-rates in the 85–90% range, using telephone approaches to employers.

• **WHERE?**

The full question here is *where do you most want to use those skills?*

This has to do *primarily* with the **fields of knowledge** *you have already acquired,* which you most enjoy using. But *where* also has to do with your preferred working conditions, what kinds of data or people or things you enjoy working with, etc.

• **HOW?**

The full question here is *how do you find such jobs, that use your favorite skills and your favorite fields of knowledge?*

To answer this question, you need to do some **interviewing of various people in order to find the information you are looking for**. You begin this interviewing with the awareness that *skills* point toward job-titles; and *knowledges* point toward a career *field,* where you would use those skills. You want also to find out the names of *organizations* in your preferred geographical area which have such jobs to offer. *And,* the names of the people or person there who actually has the *power* to hire you, as well as the challenges they face. You then secure an interview with them, by using your contacts, and show them how your skills can help them with their challenges.

With this overview in mind, we must now go through each of these three steps in greater detail. This chapter deals with WHAT? Chapter 6 deals with WHERE? And Chapter 7 deals with HOW?

THE CRUCIAL IMPORTANCE OF "WHAT?"

When you first approach the job-hunt, if you are normal you will instinctively want to leap over *What* and *Where*, and go directly to *How*. You know: *how* do we find vacancies, *how* do we do our resume, *how* do we conduct an interview? There is, in fact, a vast industry in this country and many others, dedicated to conducting workshops that teach people only the *How* part of the job-hunt: resumes, interviews, salary negotiation.

This is a *huge* mistake.

I will explain *why*. Suppose I ask you to look around your house to see if you can find some minor object that is of interest to your cousin Ned, twice-removed, whom you don't much like. Since this assignment is of close to zero interest to you, you can imagine the listless way in which you might go hunting for that object. You'd do the search because you're a good-hearted person, but you'd give it *just a lick and a promise.*

Now, suppose there is some other object in your house, and this one is a beloved object, the only thing left to you by your dear departed grandmother, and you have been hunting for it, in vain, for years. It is *tremendously* important to you. And now I tell you that I saw it, somewhere in the house, just the other day, but can't remember exactly where. Armed with this fresh evidence that it still exists, you can imagine that you'd practically tear that house apart, to find this thing you care about so much, and have been looking for, for years.

The moral of our tale, you've already guessed: *the fervor of your hunt will be directly proportional to how much you care about* WHAT *you are hunting for.* That's true in life. It's true also in job-hunting.

THE POWER OF THE VISION

You can now understand why I say: I can teach you all the techniques, job-hunting tricks, and shortcuts in the world, but if your definition of *what you're looking for* leaves you cold, the techniques will be purely academic. You'll likely figure out some way unconsciously to botch them up, to do them incorrectly, to do them half-heartedly, all the while unaware that this is what you're doing. And if you botch them up, it will be for a very healthy reason: your soul does not want *to settle for* anything less than its destiny.

> *The Secret of Job-Hunting Success*
>
> It's an old rule, which you must never forget: Search for a job you only half-care about, and you'll search for it with only half your being; but search for a job you are desperately anxious to find, and you'll hunt for it with all of your being. The more you die to find a particular thing that you most love to do, the more you will alter not only your job-hunt, but your life. Determination is born from Vision, Vision, burning bright.

No matter what other people tell you, you don't increase your job-hunting success by memorizing a few more techniques, a few better answers to an employer's interview questions. You increase your success by working on your vision for your life. By asking yourself: Why am I not happier? What is it that I most want to be doing with my life? What vision, what hunches, what yearnings, do I have about why I was put here, on earth? What are my unfulfilled dreams?

Let's face it, dear reader, you aren't getting any younger. If you don't go after your dreams *now*, when will you?

Now is the time to fulfill your dreams and your vision that you once had of what your life could be. Even if it means hard work. Even if it means changing careers. Even if means going out into the unknown, and taking risks. Manageable risks.

You may think this is a selfish activity -- but it is not. It is related to what *the world most needs* from you. That world currently is *filled* with workers whose weeklong motto is, *When is the weekend going to be here?* And, then, **T**hank **G**od **I**t's **F**riday! They are bored out of their skulls. Some of them are bored because even though they know what they'd rather be doing, they can't get out of their deadend jobs, for one reason or another.

But too many others, unfortunately, are bored simply because they have *never* taken the time to *think* -- to think out what they uniquely can do, and what they uniquely have to offer to the world. They've flopped from one job to another, letting accident, circumstance, coincidence, and whim carry them where it will.

What the world most needs from you is not to add to their number, but to figure out, and then contribute to the world, what you came into this world to do.

It's time for you to fulfill your destiny.

Dust off those dreams.

Let the vision burn brightly! And let it beckon you on.

Then you'll have a job-hunt that truly sets your heart on fire!

HOW DO YOU BEGIN?

You begin this systematic approach -- whether you're just doing a normal job-hunt or you want this to be a full-fledged career-change -- in exactly the same way: by first of all identifying your skills.

Now, many people just "freeze" when they hear the word "skills." It begins with high school job-hunters: "I haven't really got any skills," they say. It continues with college students: "I've spent four years in college. I haven't had time to pick up any

skills." And it lasts through the middle years, especially when a person is thinking of changing his or her career: "I'll have to go back to college, and get retrained, because otherwise I won't have any skills in my new field." Or: "Well, if I claim any skills, I'll start at a very entry kind of level." All of this fright about the word "skills" is very common, and stems from a total misunderstanding of what the word means. A misunderstanding that is shared, we might add, by altogether too many employers, personnel or human resources departments, and other so-called "vocational experts."

By understanding the word, you will automatically put yourself way ahead of most job-hunters. And, especially if you are weighing a change of career, you can save yourself much waste of time on the folly called "I can only change careers by going back to school for extensive retraining." I've said it before, and I'll say it again: *maybe* you need some retraining, but very often it is possible to make a dramatic career-change without any retraining. It all depends. And you won't really *know* if you need further schooling, until you have finished all the exercises in this and the next chapter.

THE MOST MISUNDERSTOOD WORD IN THE WORLD OF WORK: SKILLS

You begin career-change (or a thorough job-hunt) by first identifying your transferable, functional, skills. Here you are looking for what you may think of as the basic building-blocks of your work.

'. . . *and give me good abstract-reasoning ability, interpersonal skills, cultural perspective, linguistic comprehension, and a high sociodynamic potential.*'

The skills you need to inventory, for yourself, are called functional or transferable skills. Here is a famous diagram of them:

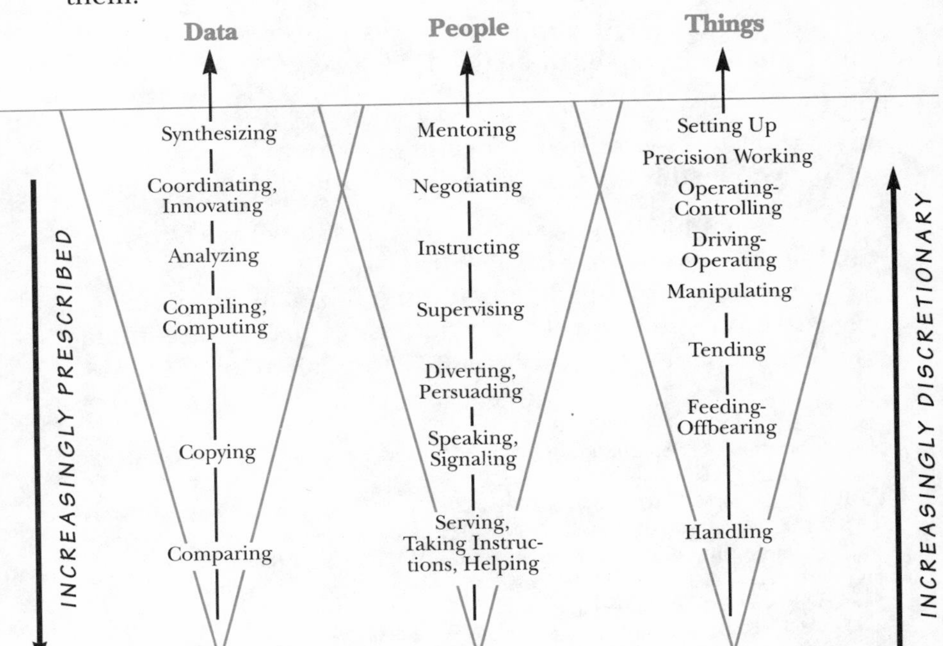

That's what skills are. Most people, however, think skills are such things as: *has lots of energy, gives attention to details, gets along well with people, shows determination, works well under pressure, is*

sympathetic, intuitive, persistent, dynamic, dependable, etc. Despite popular misconceptions, these are not functional/transferable skills, but the *style* with which you do your transferable skills. For example, let's take *"gives attention to details."* If one of your *transferable skills* is *"conducting research"* then *"gives attention to details"* describes the manner or style with which you do that transferable skill called *conducting research.* These phrases which identify *your style* of doing things are commonly called your **traits, temperaments**, or **type.** Popular tests, such as the *Myers-Briggs,* measure this sort of thing.[2]

A CRASH COURSE ON *TRANSFERABLE SKILLS*

All right, then, if transferable skills are the heart of your vision and your destiny, let's see just exactly what transferable skills *are.*

Here are the most important truths you need to keep in mind about transferable, functional, skills:

1. Your transferable *(functional)* skills are the most basic unit -- the atoms -- of whatever career you may choose.
You can see this from the diagram on page 111.

2. You should always claim the *highest* skills you legitimately can, on the basis of your past performance.

As we saw in the functional/transferable skills diagram on page 109, your skills break down into three *families,* according to whether you use them with **Data (Information)**, or **People** or

---

2. The Myers-Briggs Type Indicator, or 'MBTI,' measures what is called *psychological type.* For further reading about this, see:

Paul D. Tieger & Barbara Barron-Tieger, *Do What You Are: Discover the Perfect Career for You Through the Secrets of Personality Type.* 1992. Little, Brown & Company, Inc., division of Time Warner Inc., 34 Beacon St., Boston MA 02108. For those who cannot obtain the MBTI, this book includes a method for readers to identify their personality types. This is a very popular book.

David Keirsey and Marilyn Bates, *Please Understand Me: Character & Temperament Types.* 1978. Includes the Keirsey Temperament Sorter -- again, for those who cannot obtain the MBTI® (Myers-Briggs Type Indicator) -- registered trademarks of Consulting Psychologists Press.

A publication list of other readings about psychological type can be obtained from the Center for Application of Psychological Type, 2720 N.W. 6th St., Gainesville, FL 32609. 904-375-0160.

Skills as The Basic Unit of Work

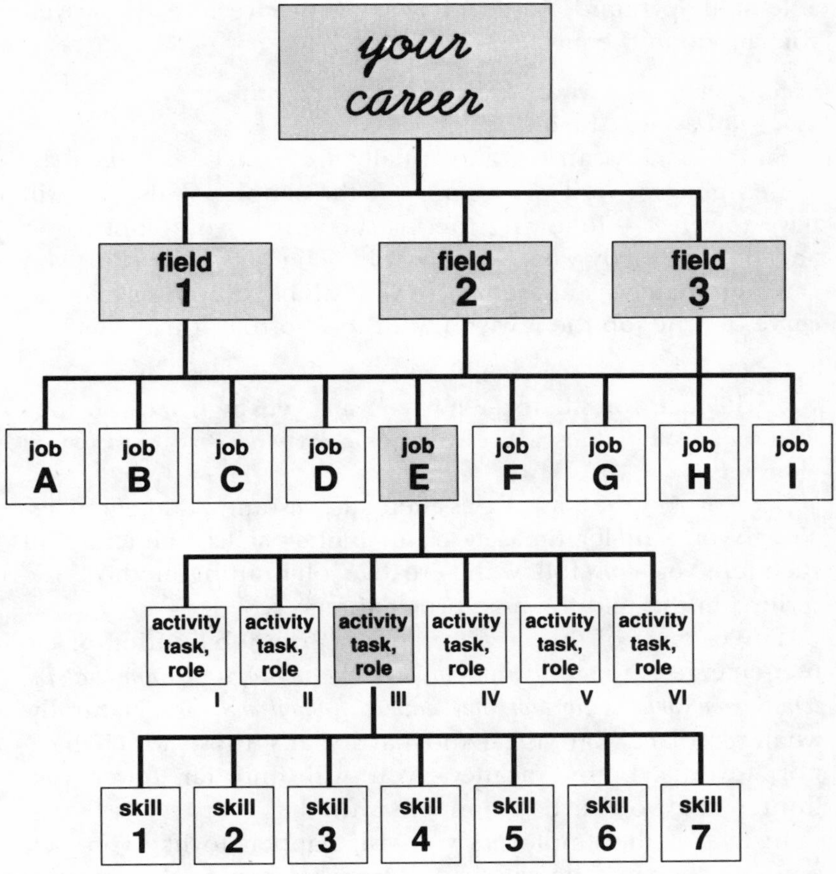

Things. And again, as that diagram makes clear, within each family there are *simple* skills, and there are higher, or *more complex* skills, so that these can be listed as vertical pyramids, with the simpler skills at the bottom, and the more complex ones in order above it, as in the diagram.

Incidentally, as a general rule -- to which there are exceptions -- each *higher* skill requires you to be able also to do all those skills listed below it, on the diagram. So of course you can usually claim *those,* as well. But you want to particularly claim the highest skill you legitimately can, on each transferable skills pyramid, based on what you have already proven you can do in the past.[3]

3. The higher your transferable skills, the more freedom you will have on the job.

Simpler skills can be, and usually are, heavily *prescribed* (by the employer), so if you claim *only* the simpler skills, you will have to *'fit in'*-- following the instructions of your supervisor, and doing exactly what you are told. The *higher* the skills you can legitimately claim, the more you will be given discretion to carve out the job the way you want to -- so that it truly fits *you.*

4. The higher your transferable skills, the less competition you will face for whatever job you are seeking, because jobs which use such skills will rarely be advertised through normal channels.

Not for you the way of classified ads, resumes, and agencies. No, if you can legitimately claim higher skills, then to find such jobs you *must* follow the creative job-hunting methods described in this and the next two chapters.

The essence of this creative approach to job-hunting or career-change is that you may approach *any organization that interests you, whether or not they have a known vacancy.* Naturally, whatever place you visit -- and particularly those which have not advertised any vacancy -- you will find far fewer job-hunters that you have to compete with.

In fact, if the employers you visit happen to like you well enough, they may be willing to create for you a job that does not presently exist. *In which case, you will be competing with no one, since you will be the sole applicant for that newly created job.* While this doesn't happen all the time, it is astounding to me how many times it *does* happen. *The reason* it does is that the employers often have been *thinking* about creating a new job within their organization, for quite some time -- but with this

3. If you desire more explanation of what these skills are, I refer you in the U.S. to *The Dictionary of Occupational Titles,* the 1991 revised fourth edition, pp. 1005–1006 in vol. II. It should be available in any public library in the U.S. Other countries (such as Canada) have similar dictionaries.

and that, they just have never gotten around to *doing* it. Until they saw you.

Then they decided they didn't want to let you get away, since *good employees are as hard to find as are good employers.* And they suddenly remember that job they have been thinking about creating for many weeks or months, now. So they dust off their *intention,* create the job on the spot, and offer it to you! And if that new job is not only what *they* need, but is exactly what *you* were looking for, then you have: Match-match. Win-win.

From our country's perspective, it is also interesting to note this: by this job-hunting initiative of yours, you have helped *accelerate* the creation of more jobs in your country, which is so much on everybody's mind here in the '90s. How nice to help your country, as well as yourself!

> And so, the paradoxical moral of all this: The less you try to 'stay loose' and open to *anything,* the more you define your skills with *Data/Information* and/or *People* and/or *Things* in detail, and at the highest level you legitimately can, **the more likely you are to find a job**. *Just the opposite of what the typical career-changer starts out believing.*

"I WOULDN'T RECOGNIZE MY SKILLS IF THEY CAME UP AND SHOOK HANDS WITH ME"

Well, now that you know what skills technically *are,* the problem is figuring out your own. If you are one of the few lucky people who already know what your transferable skills are, blessed are you. Write them down, and put them in the order of preference, for you.

If, however, you don't know what your skills are (and 95% of all workers *don't*), then you will need some help. That help is to be found in *The Parachute Workbook* on page 7.

It involves writing seven stories from your life.

Here is a specific example of such a story, so you can see how it is done:

"I wanted to be able to take a summer trip with my wife and four children. I had a very limited budget, and could not afford to put my family up, in motels. I decided to rig our station wagon as a camper.

"First I went to the library to get some books on campers. I read those books. Next I designed a plan of what I had to build, so that I could outfit the inside of the station wagon, as well as topside. Then I went and purchased the necessary wood. On weekends, over a period of six weeks, I first constructed, in my driveway, the shell for the 'second story' on my station wagon. Then I cut doors, windows, and placed a six-drawer bureau within that shell. I mounted it on top of the wagon, and pinioned it in place by driving two-by-fours under the station wagon's rack on top. I then outfitted the inside of the station wagon, back in the wheelwell, with a table and a bench on either side, that I made.

"The result was a complete homemade camper, which I put together when we were about to start our trip, and then disassembled after we got back home. When we went on our summer trip, we were able to be on the road for four weeks, yet stayed within our budget, since we didn't have to stay at motels.

"I estimate I saved $1900 on motel bills, during that summer's vacation."

Ideally, each story you write should have the following parts, as illustrated above:

I.) **Your goal: what you wanted to accomplish**: *"I wanted to be able to take a summer trip with my wife and four children."*

II.) **Some kind of hurdle, obstacle, or constraint that you faced** (self-imposed or otherwise): *"I had a very limited budget, and could not afford to put my family up, in motels."*

III.) **A description of what you did, step by step** (how you set about to ultimately achieve your goal, above, in spite of this hurdle or constraint): *"I decided to rig our station wagon as a camper. First I went to the library to get some books on campers. I read those books. Next I designed a plan of what I had to build, so that I could outfit the inside of the station wagon, as well as topside. Then I went and purchased the necessary wood. On weekends, over a period of six weeks, I . . ." etc., etc.*

IV.) **A description of the outcome or result**: *"When we went on our summer trip, we were able to be on the road for four weeks, yet stayed within our budget, since we didn't have to stay at motels."*

V.) **Any measurable/quantifiable statement of that outcome, that you can think of**: *"I estimate I saved $1900 on motel bills, during that summer's vacation."*

The Parachute Workbook will take you through the whole process of analyzing seven such stories, identifying your transferable skills therein, and prioritizing them.

Once you have identified your eight top favorite transferable skills *(or however many you wish)*, you need to *flesh out* your skill-description for each of those eight, so that you are able to describe each of your talents or skills with more than just a one-word verb or gerund, like: *organizing.*

Let's take *organizing* as our example. You tell us proudly: "I'm good at *organizing.*" That's a fine start at defining your skills, but unfortunately it doesn't yet tell us much. Organizing WHAT? *People,* as at a party? *Nuts and bolts,* as on a workbench? Or *lots of information,* as on a computer? These are three entirely different skills. The one word *organizing* doesn't tell us which one is *yours.*

An Overview of This Process

a
PUT THEM IN CATEGORIES
△ PEOPLE
□ THINGS
○ DATA
△ PEOPLE
□ THINGS
○ DATA
PRIORITIZE THEM ACCORDING TO ENJOYMENT

So, please *flesh out* each of your favorite transferable skills with an object -- some kind of *Data/Information*, or some kind of *People*, or some kind of *Thing*, and then add an adverb or adjective, too.

Why adjectives? Well, "I'm good at organizing information *painstakingly and logically*" and "I'm good at organizing information *in a flash, by intuition,*" are two *entirely different* skills. The difference between them is spelled out not in the verb, nor in the object, but in the adjectival or adverbial phrase there at the end. So, expand each definition of your eight favorite skills, in the fashion I have just described.

> When you are face-to-face with a person-who-has-the-power-to-hire-you, you want to be able to explain what makes you different from nineteen other people who can basically do the same thing that you can do. It is often the adjective or adverb that will save your life, during that explanation.

A PICTURE IS WORTH A THOUSAND WORDS

When you have your eight top favorite skills, in order, and *fleshed out*, it is time to put them on the central petal of the diagram, which we call *The Flower Diagram*, that you will find on page 75.

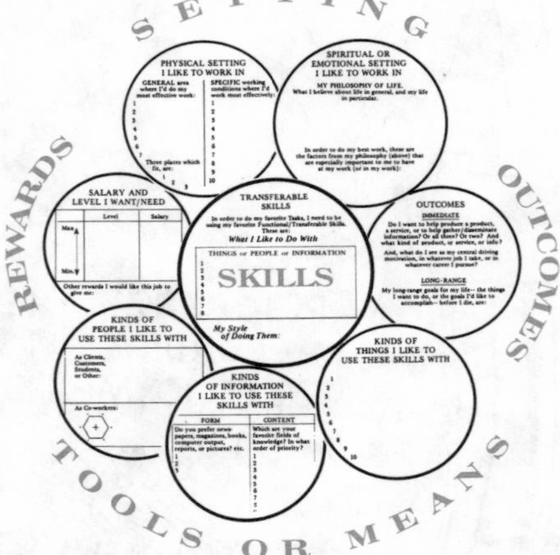

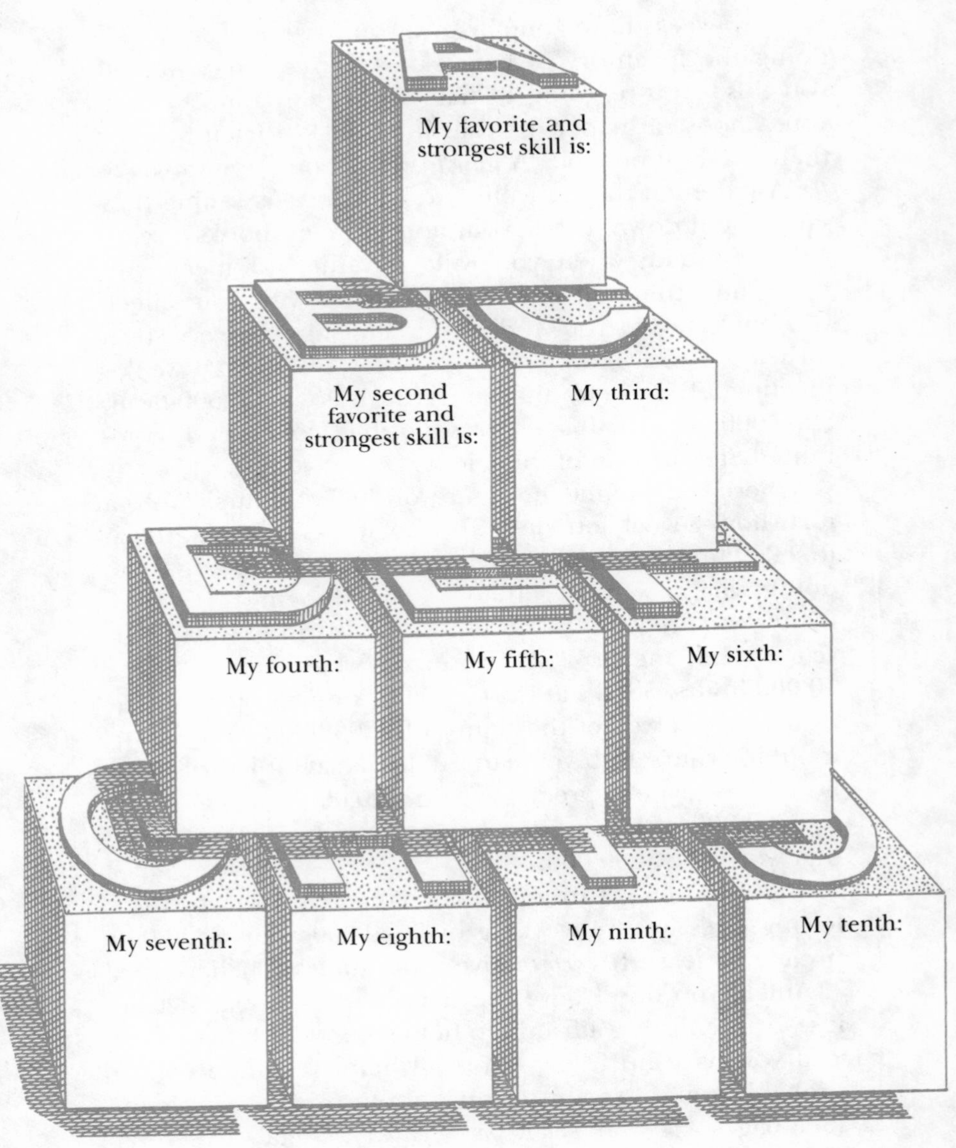

You may also, or alternatively, want to enroll them on the building-block diagram here -- in which case, you can list your top ten. And that's it, for this chapter.

Voila! You now have finished with **WHAT**.

A Friendly Word to Procrastinators

If two weeks have gone by, and you haven't even *started* doing the inventory of your skills, then -- I hate to tell you this -- you're going to have to get someone to help you. Choose a helper for your job-hunt -- a friend rather than family, if possible. A *tough* friend. You know, *taskmaster.* Ask them if they're willing to help you. Assuming they say yes, put down in *both* your appointment books a regular *weekly* date when you will guarantee to meet with them, and they will guarantee to meet with you, check you out on what you've done already, and be very stern with you if you've done little or nothing since last week's meeting. Tell them that it is at least a 20,000-hour, $200,000 project. It's also responsible, concerned, committed Stewardship of the talents God gave you.

Where did we get the figure of 20,000 hours? Well, a forty-hour-a-week job, done for fifty weeks a year, adds up to 2,000 hours annually. So, how long are you going to be doing this new career that you are looking for? How many years do you plan to stay in the world of work? Ten years? That means 20,000 hours. Twenty years? That's 40,000 hours. So, it's at least a 20,000-hour project.

Where did we get the figure of $200,000? Well, figure it out for yourself. If you earned, let us say, at least $10 an hour in your new career, that *times* 20,000 hours adds up to $200,000. If by chance you were to earn $20 an hour, that would be $400,000.

So, in working through this chapter and the two following ones, you're working on a 20,000-hour, $200,000 project, at least. It's *worth* giving the time to, believe me.

And if you don't have the self-discipline to stick at it, it's worth enlisting a friend to help you.

If you have no friend who will help you, then you're probably going to want to think about professional help. (See pages 243 *ff*, in *The Resource Guide*). Go talk to several career-counselors. Choose the one you like best, and *get on with it.*

You've only one life to live, my friend. And every day is precious.

"Same career, change of career, same career . . . change of . . ."

Chapter Five Postscript
SOME PROBLEMS YOU MAY RUN INTO, WHILE DOING YOUR SKILL-IDENTIFICATION

In doing the aforementioned skill-identification, it will not be surprising if you run into some problems. Let us look at the five more common ones that have arisen for job-hunters, in the past:

1. "I don't know exactly what is an achievement."

When you're looking for a story/achievement to illustrate one of your skills, you're *not* looking for something that only you have done, in the history of the world. What you're looking for is a lot simpler than that. You're looking for *any* time in your life when you did something that was, at that time of your life, a source of pride and accomplishment *for you.* It might have been learning to ride a bike. It might be achieving your first quota, at work. It might be a particularly significant project that you designed, in mid-life. It doesn't matter whether or not it pleased anybody else; it only matters that it pleased you.

I like Bernard Haldane's definition of an achievement. He says it is: something you yourself feel you have done well, that you also enjoyed doing and felt proud of. In other words you are looking for an accomplishment which gave you two pleasures: enjoyment while doing it, and satisfaction from the outcome. That doesn't mean you may not have sweated as you did it, or hated *some parts* of the process, but it does mean that basically you enjoyed *most of* the process. The pleasure was not simply in getting it done. Generally speaking, an achievement will have all the parts outlined on page 115.

2. *"I don't see why I should look for skills I enjoy; it seems to me that employers will only want to know what skills I do well. They will not care whether I enjoy using the skill or not."*

Well, sure, it is important for you to find the skills you do well, above all else. But, generally speaking, that is hard for you to evaluate about yourself. *Do I do this well, or not? Compared to whom?* Even aptitude tests can't resolve this dilemma for you. So it's better to take the following circular equation, which experience has shown to be true:

If it is a skill you do well, you will generally enjoy it.

If it is a skill you enjoy, it is generally because you do it well.

With these equations in hand, you will see that -- since they are equal anyway -- it is much more useful to ask yourself, "Do I enjoy doing it?" instead of hunting for the elusive "Do I do it well?" I repeat: listing the skills you most *enjoy* is -- in most cases -- just another way of listing the skills you do *best.*

The reason why this idea -- of making *enjoyment* the key -- causes such feelings of uncomfortableness in so many of us is that we have an old historical tradition in this country which insinuates you shouldn't really enjoy yourself in life. To suffer is virtuous.

Sample: Two girls do babysitting. One hates it. One enjoys it thoroughly. Which is more virtuous in God's sight? According to that old tradition, the one who hates it is more virtuous. Some of us feel this instinctively, even if more logical thought says, Whoa!

We have this subconscious fear that if we are caught enjoying life, punishment looms. Thus, the story of two Scotsmen who met on the street one day: "Isn't this a beautiful day?" said one. "Aye," said the other, "but we'll pay for it."

We feel it is okay to talk about our failures, but not about our successes. To talk about our successes appears to be boasting, and that is manifestly a sin. Or so we think. We shouldn't be enjoying so much about ourselves.

But look at the birds of the air, or watch your pets at play. You will notice one distinctive fact about that part of God's creation: when a bird or a pet does what it is meant to do, by God and nature, it manifests true joy.

Joy is so clearly a part of God's plan for us. God wants us to eat; therefore He made eating enjoyable. God wants us to sleep; therefore He made sleeping enjoyable. God wants us to procreate, love, and make love; therefore He made sex enjoyable, and love even more so.

Likewise, God gives to each of us unique combinations of skills and talents which He wants us to contribute to His general plan -- to the symphony of the world, and the music of the spheres. Therefore, **when we use the talents He most wants each of us to use, He attends it with a feeling of great joy**. Everywhere in God's plan for His creation, joy rewards right action.

You need to identify the skills you enjoy using -- not only now, as you are in the process of choosing a new career, but also later when you are face-to-face with an employer. True, bad employers will not care whether you enjoy a particular task, or not. But good employers will care greatly. They know that unless a would-be employee has **enthusiasm** for his or her work, the quality of that work will always suffer.

3. "I have no difficulty finding stories to write up, from my life, that I consider to be enjoyable achievements; but once these are written, I have great difficulty in seeing what the skills are -- even if I stare at the skills keys diagram for hours. *I need somebody else's insight."*

You will want to consider getting two friends or two other members of your family to sit down with you, and do skill identification through the practice of 'Trioing' which I invented some twenty years ago to help with this very problem. This practice is fully described in my book, *Where Do I Go From Here With My Life?* But to save you the trouble of reading it, here is -- in general -- how it goes:

a. Each of the three of you quietly writes up some story of an accomplishment in their life that was enjoyable.

b. Each of the three of you quietly analyzes just your own story to see what skills you see there; you jot these down.

c. One of you then volunteers to go first. You read your story aloud. The other two jot down on a piece of paper whatever skills they hear you using. They ask you to pause if they're having trouble keeping up. You finish your story. You read aloud the skills *you* picked out in that story.

d. Then the second person tells you what's on their list: what skills *they* heard you use in your story. You copy them down, below your own list, even if you don't agree with every one of them.

e. Then the third person tells you what's on their list; what skills *they* heard you use in your story. You copy them down, below your own list, even if you don't agree with every one of them.

f. When they're both done, you ask them any questions for further elaboration that you may have. *"What did you mean by this skill? Where did you think you heard me using it?"*

g. Now it is the next person's turn, and you repeat steps 'c' through 'f' with them. Then it is the third person's turn, and you repeat steps 'c' through 'f' with them..

h. Now it is time to move on to a second story for each of you, so you begin with steps 'a' through 'g' all over again, except that each of you writes a new story. And so on, through seven stories.

4. "How do I know if I've done this all correctly? What if I just think I understood what I was supposed to do, but I really didn't? I want to be sure the stuff I've identified is really going to help me in my job-hunt."

It will, if you've followed *all* the directions in *The Parachute Workbook* plus this chapter *(no shortcuts)* and *if* you avoided stating your skills in the jargon or language of your past career, such as the military or the clergy. It is not useful to state your transferable skills in the jargon of your old profession, such as, *"I am good at preaching."* If you are going to choose a new career, out there in what you call the secular world, you must not use language that locks you into the past -- or suggests that you were good in one field and one field only. Therefore, it is important to take *preaching* and ask yourself what is its larger form? *"Teaching?"* Perhaps. *"Motivating people?"* Perhaps. *"Inspiring people to the depths of their being?"* Perhaps. *Only you can say what is true, for you.* But in one way or another be sure to get your skills out of *any jargon that locks you into your past career.*

5. Do you have any final advice, for me while I'm doing skill-identification?

Yes. Once you've finished your skill-identification, steer clear of prematurely putting a job-title on the skills you see. In actual fact, skills can point to *many* different jobs, which have a multitude of titles, as you will see in the next chapter. Therefore, don't lock yourself in, prematurely. *"I'm looking for a job where I can* ***use*** *the following skills,"* is fine. But, *"I'm looking for a job where I can* ***be*** *a (job-title)"* is a no-no, at this point in your job-hunt. *Narrowing down* will come later; but at this point, keep *all* your options open.

In case you feel, after all of this, you just can't do the stories, you will be interested in this account from a woman job-hunter in England, who wrote me as follows:

"I have a Ph.D. in Chemistry, but the last thing I wanted to do on graduating was to work in a laboratory or a research group. I read your book, and tried -- but failed -- to write the stories; it required too much soul-searching! Consequently, it took me nine months before I decided on a new career path. It was Daniel Porot's PIE method that got me there -- Practice Interviewing, Informational Interviewing, Employment Interviewing. It helped build my confidence enormously, and I felt I had the power -- rather than being the victim of the employment market. I followed your ideas and advice, and have just been offered my first permanent position. I am overjoyed, because I chose this new career looking at my interests and skills, rather than my qualifications. Now I am a Clinical Research Scientist in a hospital. I feel now at long last, at 27 years of age, I am finally on the right track to finding my mission in life."

A realist is more correct about things in life than an optimist. But the optimist seems to have more friends and much more fun.[1]

Megan, Age 14

The latest self-help book for pessimists

1. From H. Jackson Brown, Jr.'s *When You Lick a Slug, Your Tongue Goes Numb: Kids share their wit and wisdom.* Rutledge Hill Press, Nashville, Tennessee. 1994. Used with permission.

CHAPTER SIX

FOR THE DETERMINED JOB-HUNTER OR CAREER-CHANGER

The Systematic Approach To
Career-Change
And Job-Hunting

WHERE

DO YOU MOST WANT TO USE THOSE SKILLS?

You Must Figure Out
Just Exactly What Field
and What Kinds of Places
You Would Most Delight to Work In

Chapter 6

Table of Contents

THE LANGUAGE OF YOUR CAREER

I once worked as a secretary/typist. That is WHAT I did.

But, of course, I had a lot of choices about WHERE I did it.

I could have worked as a legal secretary, or as a secretary at a gardening store, or as a secretary at an airline, or as a secretary at a church, or as a secretary at a photographic laboratory, or as a secretary at a bank, or as a secretary at a chemical plant, or as a secretary in the Federal government.

The point I am making is: it is not sufficient to simply say WHAT you want to do: *I want to be a secretary.* You must define for yourself WHERE you want to do that kind of work. These various places where you *might* work as a secretary -- law, gardening, airlines, church, photography, banking, chemistry, or government, etc., etc. -- are commonly called ***Majors***, or ***Subjects***, or ***Fields***, or ***Fields of interest***, or ***Fields of knowledge***.

There is, however, another way of thinking about them, and that is as if they were *languages.* If you're puzzled as to what field you would like to be in, for your next career or job, begin by asking yourself what *language* or *languages* you love to listen to, speak, and work in, all day long.

If you work as a legal secretary, you'll have to endure a lot of talk there, all day long, about legal procedures. Therefore, Law is the *language* you have to live with, every day, at that workplace. Do you like that *language?* If so, choose law as your field -- for your next career or job.

Again, if you work as a secretary at a gardening store, there's a lot of talk there, all day long, about gardens and such. Therefore, Gardening is the *language* you have to live with, all day, at that workplace. Do you like that *language?* If so, choose horticulture as your field -- for your next career or job.

If you work as a secretary at an airline, there's a lot of talk there, all day long, about airlines procedures. Therefore, Airlines is the *language* you have to live with, all day, at that workplace. Do you like that *language?* If so, choose air transportation as your field -- for your next career or job.

If you work as a secretary at a church, there's a lot of talk there, all day long, about church procedures and matters of faith. Therefore, Religion is the *language* you have to live with, all day, at that workplace. Do you like that *language?* If so, choose religion as your field -- for your next career or job.

If you work as a secretary in a photographic laboratory, there's a lot of talk there, all day long, about photographic procedures. Therefore, Photography is the *language* you have to live with, all day, at that workplace. Do you like that *language?* If so, choose photography as your field -- for your next career or job.

If you work as a secretary at a bank, there's a lot of talk there, all day long, about banking procedures. Therefore, Banking is the *language* you have to live with, all day, at that workplace. Do you like that *language?* If so, choose banking as your field -- for your next career or job.

If you work as a secretary at a chemical plant, there's a lot of talk there, all day long, about chemicals manufacturing. Therefore, Chemistry is the *language* you have to live with, all day, at that workplace. Do you like that *language?* If so, choose chemistry as your field -- for your next career or job.

If you work as a secretary for the Federal government, there's a lot of talk there, all day long, about government procedures. Therefore, Government is the *language* you have to live with, all day, at that workplace. Do you like that *language?* If so, choose government as your field -- for your next career or job.

As a general rule, if you enjoy the *language* you deal with all day, then you will be happy in that field or career.

However, if you don't enjoy the *language* spoken at work -- if, say, *gardening* is your favorite subject, but you work at a place where *law* -- a language you hate -- is what you have to listen to, and work with, all day long, then you are not going to be happy in that career.

WHAT DO YOU LOVE TO TALK ABOUT OR BE IMMERSED IN?

It is important for you to begin your consideration of "WHERE do I want to use my (favorite) skills?" by making a list of your ***Favorite Subjects*** (*i.e., languages*). In the case of each *field* or *language* you list, it is only necessary that you love talking about this subject, and know *something* about it -- it is not necessary that you have a *mastery* of it.

Also, it doesn't have to be a subject you studied in school. As I mentioned in Chapter 4, most people think that if they're going to change careers, they have to go back and master some new field at a college, or university. Well, sometimes that's the case; but not always, by any means. Your next career can be in a field that you just picked up along the way in life -- say, *antiques,* or *cars,* or *interior decorating,* or *music* or *movies* or *psychology,* or *the kind of subjects that come up on television 'game shows.'*

The only important thing is that you *like* the subject a lot, and that you picked up a working knowledge of it -- who cares where or how? As the late John Crystal used to say, it doesn't matter whether you learned it in college, or sitting at the end of a log.

Let's take *antiques* as an example. Suppose it's one of your favorite subjects, yet you never studied it in school. You picked up your knowledge of antiques by going around to antique stores, and asking lots of questions. And you supplemented this by reading a few books on the subject, and you subscribe to an antiques magazine. You've also bought a few antiques, yourself. That's enough, for you to put *antiques,* on your list of fields/interests/languages. Your degree of *mastery* of this whole field of antiques is irrelevant -- *unless you want to work at a level in the field that demands and requires* mastery.

THE FLOWER DIAGRAM

How, exactly, do you go about figuring out what your favorite *languages,* i.e., fields, are?

Well, you need a series of checklists, and we have provided these for you, in that part of *The Parachute Workbook* that begins on page 55.

It will guide you not only through *languages,* but through the whole process of identifying WHERE -- after which, you can enroll what you discover on the *petals* on the Flower Diagram there.

All of this will take you a bit of time, but not more than a few hours, normally.

When you've got all eight *petals* of the *Flower Diagram* filled in (page 75), you might then want to cut out all eight *petals* -- and paste them together on one large sheet.

Put that sheet on a wall, or on the door of your refrigerator. And there you have it: Your Flower Diagram.

But, what exactly is it that you have there? Well, it's a picture of *you* (sort of) and it's also a picture of *the job or career* you're looking for. It's both these things at once, because you've constructed a picture of a job or career *that matches you.*

A LIGHT BULB GOES ON

And when you're looking at that diagram, what should happen? Well, for some of you *(about three in every hundred of those reading this book)* there will be a big *Aha!* as you look at your Flower Diagram. A light bulb will go off, over your head, and you will say, "My goodness, I see *exactly* what sort of career this points me to."

If you are one of these extremely intuitive people, I say, "Good for you!" Just two gentle warnings, if I may: don't prematurely close out *other* possibilities. And *don't* say to yourself: "Well, I see what it is that I would die to be able to do, but I *know* there is no job in the world like that, that *I* would be able to get." Dear friend, you don't know any such thing. You haven't done your research yet.

To be sure, it is possible that when you've completed all that research, and conducted your search, you still may not be able to find *all* that you want -- down to the last detail.

But you'd be surprised at how much of your dream you may be able to find.

Sometimes it will be found in *stages.* One retired man I know, who had been a senior executive with a publishing company, found himself bored to death in retirement, after he turned 65. He contacted a business acquaintance, who said apologetically, "We just don't have anything open that matches or requires your abilities; right now all we need is someone in our mail room." The 65-year-old executive said, "I'll take that job!" He did, and over the ensuing years steadily advanced once again, to just the job he wanted: as a senior executive in that organization, where he utilized all his prized skills, for some time. He retired as senior executive for the second time, at the age of 85.

Other times, you may be able to find your dream, directly, without having to go through stages.

It is amazing how often people do get their dreams, whether in stages or directly. The more you don't *cut* the dream down, because of what you *think* you know about *the real world,* the more likely you are to find what you are looking for.

Most people don't find their heart's desire, because they decide to pursue just half their dream -- and consequently they hunt for it with only *half a heart.*

If you decide to pursue your whole dream, your best dream, the one you die to do, I guarantee you that you will hunt for it *with all your heart.* It is this *passion* which often is the difference between successful career-changers, and unsuccessful ones.

YOU LOOK AT YOUR FLOWER DIAGRAM AND. . . NOTHING!

Most of you will look at your Flower Diagram, and you won't have *a clue* as to what job or career it points to. Soooo, you're going to have to do some additional research, *of course.*

Here's how you begin. Take a pad of paper, with pen or pencil, or go to your computer, keyboard in hand, and make some notes.

First, look at your Flower Diagram, and write down your three to five most *favorite* skills.

Then, look at your Flower Diagram and write down your three to five most *favorite* vocational *languages,* alias *fields of knowledge,* or *fields of interest.*

Take your notes, and show them to at least five friends, family, or professionals whom you know.

As you will recall from Chapter 4, skills usually point toward a **job-title** or job-level, while fields of interest or knowledge usually point toward a **career field**. So, you want to ask them, in the case of your skills, *What job or jobs do these suggest to you?*

Then ask them, in the case of your favorite vocational *languages, What career fields do these suggest to you?*

Jot down *everything* these five people tell you.

After you have finished talking to them, you want to go home and look at what the five have told you. Incidentally, if none of it looks valuable, go talk to five more of your friends or acquaintances, plus any people you know in the business world and non-profit sector.

When you've got some worthwhile ideas, sit down, look over their combined suggestions, and ask yourself some questions.

• First, you want to look at what they suggested about your skills: *what job or jobs came to their mind?* It will help you to know that most jobs can be classified under 19 headings or families, as listed on the next page.

Which of these nineteen do your friends' suggestions predominantly point to? Which of these nineteen grabs you?

• Next, you want to look at what they suggested about your *favorite languages*: *what fields or careers came to their mind?* It will help you to know that most career fields can be classified, first of all, under four broad headings: *Agriculture, Manufacturing, Information industries,* and *Service industries.*

Which of these four do your friends' suggestions predominantly *point to?* Which of these four grabs you?

• The next question you want to ask yourself is: both job-titles and career-fields can be broken down further, according to whether you like to work primarily with *people* **or** primarily with *information/data* **or** primarily with *things.*

Let's take agriculture as an example. Within agriculture, you could be driving tractors and other farm machinery -- and thus working primarily with *things;* or you could be gathering

JOB FAMILIES

1. Executive, Administrative, and Managerial Occupations
2. Engineers, Surveyors, and Architects
3. Natural Scientists and Mathematicians
4. Social Scientists, Social Workers, Religious Workers, and Lawyers
5. Teachers, Counselors, Librarians, and Archivists
6. Health Diagnosing and Treating Practitioners
7. Registered Nurses, Pharmacists, Dieticians, Therapists, and Physician Assistants
8. Health Technologists and Technicians
9. Writers, Artists, and Entertainers
10. Technologists and Technicians, Except Health
11. Marketing and Sales Occupations
12. Administrative Support Occupations, Including Clerical
13. Service Occupations
14. Agricultural, Forestry, and Fishing Occupations
15. Mechanics and Repairers
16. Construction and Extractive Occupations
17. Production Occupations
18. Transportation and Material Moving Occupations
19. Handlers, Equipment Cleaners, Helpers, and Laborers

statistics about crop growth for some state agency -- and thus working primarily with *information/data;* or you could be teaching agriculture in a college classroom, and thus working primarily with *people* and *ideas.* Almost all fields as well as career families offer you these three kinds of choices, though *of course* many jobs combine two or more of the three.

Still, you do want to tell yourself what your *preference* is, and what you *primarily* want to be working with. Otherwise your job-hunt or career-change is going to leave you very frustrated, at the end. In this matter, it is often your favorite skill that will give you the clue. If it *doesn't*, then go back and look at your total skills *petal*, on pages 47. What do you think? Are your favorite skills weighted more toward working with *people*, or toward working with *information/data*, or toward working with *things?*

And, no matter what that *petal* suggests, which do you think you prefer?

THE TRANSCENDENT IMPORTANCE OF PEOPLE

Once you have these *clues* from your friends, you need to go gather some further information. Specifically, you want to find answers to these four WHERE questions, in the sequence indicated:

• QUESTION #1

What are the **names of jobs or careers** that would give me a chance to use my most enjoyable skills, in a field that is based on my favorite subjects?

• QUESTION #2

What **kinds of organizations** would and/or do employ people in these careers?

• QUESTION #3

Among the kinds of organizations uncovered in the previous question, what are the names of **particular places** that I especially like?

• QUESTION #4

Among the places that I particularly like, **what needs do they have** or what outcomes are they trying to produce, that my skills and knowledge could help with?

And how do you find the answers to these four questions? Well, let's begin with the first one; because in seeing how you explore that question, you will understand how to explore the other three, in turn.

The first question is: What are the **names of jobs or careers** that would give me a chance to use my most enjoyable skills, in a field that is based on my favorite subjects?

Where do you begin? The Internet is one place, if you're on the Internet. Libraries are another, if you like to do research in libraries.

The bad news, unfortunately -- for the shy -- is that the most dependable and up-to-date information on jobs and careers is *not* found in either of these two ways. It's found by going and talking to *people.* The reason for this is that last week's absolutely true, certifiably guaranteed, 100% accurate information about jobs and careers is, today, completely outdated. *Things are just moving too fast.* Books can't keep up. They're outdated before they're in print. So, if you want to identify a new career or job that *fits* you, you must go see people -- with *some*

reading on the side, to *supplement* what they tell you. It's no time to be shy!

If shyness is a problem for you, I have a word to say about how to deal with that, at the end of this chapter.

But let us return to our train of thought, here. To gather the information you need, you must go talk to people. Ah, but how do you decide *which people?* Well, it's relatively easy. Let me give you an actual example of how it's done. (We'll take an actual career-changer I've known.)

After doing his Flower Diagram, it turned out that his top/favorite skill was: diagnosing, treating, or healing.

His three top/favorite *languages* or fields of knowledge were: psychiatry, plants, and carpentry.

After showing five friends this information, and mulling over what they said, he concluded:

Among the 19 *Job families,* he was most attracted to (6) Health diagnosing and treating practitioners.

Among the four *broad divisions of career-fields,* he was most attracted to Service industries.

Among the *three kinds of skills,* he most wanted to use his skills with people.

So far, so good. Now, where does he go from here?

He's going to have to go talk to people. But, how does he choose who to talk to? Easy. He takes his favorite *languages* or fields of knowledge, above -- psychiatry, plants, and carpentry -- and mentally translates them into *people* with particular occupations: namely, a psychiatrist, a gardener, and a carpenter.

Then he has to go find at least one of each. That's relatively easy: the Yellow Pages of the telephone directory will do, or he may know some of these among the friends or acquaintances he already has. What he wants to do, now, is go visit them and ask them: *how do you combine these three fields into one occupation?* He knows it may be a career that already exists, *or* it may be he will have to create this career for himself.

And, how does he decide which of these three to go interview *first?* He asks himself which of these persons is most likely to have the *largest overview. (This is often, but not always, the same as asking: who took the longest to get their training?)* The particular answer here: the psychiatrist.

He would then go see two or three psychiatrists -- say, the heads of the psychiatry departments at the nearest colleges or universities,[2] and ask them: *Do you have any idea how to put these three subjects -- carpentry, plants, and psychiatry -- together into one job or career? And if you don't know, who do you think might?* He would keep going until he found someone who had a bright idea about how you put this all together.

In this particular case *(as I said, this is from an actual career-changer's experience)*, he was eventually told: "Yes, it can all be put together. There is a branch of psychiatry that uses plants to help heal people. That takes care of your interest in plants and psychiatry. As for your carpentry interests, I suppose you could use that to build the planters for your plants."

INFORMATIONAL INTERVIEWING

There is a name for this process I have just described. It is called *Informational Interviewing* -- a term I invented many many years ago. But it is sometimes, incorrectly, called *by other names.* Some even call this gathering of information *Networking,* which it is not.

To avoid this confusion, I have summarized in the chart on the next pages just exactly what *Informational Interviewing* is, and how it differs from the other ways in which *people* can help and support you, during your job-hunt or career-change -- namely, *Networking, Support Groups,* and *Contacts.* I have also thrown in, at no extra charge, a *first* column in that chart, dealing with an aspect of the job-hunt that *never* gets talked about: namely, the importance before your job-hunt ever begins, of *nurturing the friendships you have let slip* -- by calling them or visiting them early on in your job-hunt -- just re-establishing relationships *before* you ever need anything from them, as you most certainly may, later on in your job-hunt. The first column in the chart explains this further.

---

2. If there were no psychiatrists at any academic institution near him, then he would do all his research with psychiatrists in private practice -- getting their names from the phone book -- and asking them for, and paying for, *a half session.* This, if there is no other way.

The Job-Hunter's or Career-Changer's

The Process	1. Valuing Your *Community* Before the Job-Hunt	2. Networking
What Is Its Purpose?	To make sure that people whom you may someday need to do you a favor, or lend you a hand, know long beforehand that you value and prize them *for themselves.*	To gather a list of contacts *now* who might be able to help you with your career, or with your job-hunting, at some future date. And to go out of your way to *regularly* add to that list. *Networking is a term often reserved only for the business of adding to your list; but, obviously, this presupposes you first listed everyone you* already *know.*
Who Is It Done With?	Those who live with you, plus your family, relatives, friends, and acquaintances, however near (geographically) or far.	People in your present field, or in a field of future interest that you yourself meet; also, people whose names are given to you by others.
When You're Doing This Right How Do You Go About It? (Typical Activities)	You make time for them in your busy schedule, long before you find yourself job-hunting. You do this by: (1) Spending 'quality time' with those you live with, letting them know you really appreciate who they are, and what kind of person they are, (2) Maintaining contact (phone, lunch, a thank-you note) with those who live nearby, (3) Writing friendly notes, regularly, to those who live at a distance -- *thus letting them all know that you appreciate them* for themselves.	You deliberately attend, for this purpose, meetings or conventions in your present field, or the field/ career you are thinking of switching to, someday. You talk to people at meetings and at 'socials,' exchanging calling cards after a brief conversation. Occasionally, someone may suggest a name to you as you are about to set off for some distant city or place, recommending that while you are there, you contact them. A phone call may be your best bet, with follow-up letter after you return home, unless *they* invite *you* to lunch during the phone call. Asking *them* to lunch sometimes 'bombs.' (See below.)
When You've Really Botched This Up, What Are The Signs?	You're out of work, and you find yourself having to contact people that you haven't written or phoned in ages, suddenly asking them out of the blue for their help with your job-hunt. *The message inevitably read from this is that you don't really care about them at all, except when you can* use *them. Further, you get perceived as one who sees others only in terms of what they can do for you, rather than in a relationship that is 'a two-way street.'*	It's usually when you have approached a very busy individual and asked them to have lunch with you. If it is an aimless lunch, with no particular agenda -- they ask during lunch what you need to talk about, and you lamely say, "Well, uh, I don't know, So-and-So just thought we should get to know each other" -- you will not be practicing *Networking.* You will be practicing *antagonizing.* Try to restrict your *Networking* to the telephone.

Guide To Relationships With Others

3. Developing A Support Group	4. Informational Interviewing	5. Using Contacts
To enlist some of your family or close friends specifically to help you with your emotional, social, and spiritual needs, when you are going through a difficult transition period, such as a job-hunt or career-change -- so that you do not have to face this time all by yourself.	To screen careers *before* you change to them. To screen jobs *before* you take them, rather than afterward. To screen places *before* you decide you want to seek employment there. To find answers to *very specific questions* that occur to you during your job-hunt.	It takes, let us say, 77 pairs of eyes and ears to find a new job or career. Here you recruit those 76 other people (don't take me literally -- it can be any number you choose) to be your eyes and ears -- once you know what kind of work, what kind of place, what kind of job you are looking for, *and not before.*
You try to enlist people with one or more of the following qualifications: you feel comfortable talking to them; they will take initiative in calling you, on a regular basis; they are wiser than you are; and they can be a hard taskmaster, when you need one.	Workers, workers, workers. You *only* do informational interviewing with people actually doing the work that interests you as a potential new job or career for yourself.	Anyone and everyone who is on your 'networking list.' (See column 2.) It includes family, friends, relatives, high school alumni, college alumni, former co-workers, church/ synagogue members, places where you shop, etc.
There should be three of them, at least. They may meet with you regularly, once a week, as a group, for an hour or two, to check on how you are doing. One or more of them should also be available to you on an "as needed" basis: the Listener, when you are feeling 'down,' and need to talk; the Initiator, when you are tempted to hide; the Wise One, when you are puzzled as to what to do next; and the Taskmaster, when your discipline is falling apart, and you need someone to encourage you to 'get at it.' It helps if there is also a Cheerleader among them, that you can tell your victories to.	You get names of workers from your co-workers, from departments at local community colleges, or career offices. Once you have names, you call them and ask for a chance to talk to them *for twenty minutes.* You make a list, ahead of time, of all the questions you want answers to. If nothing occurs to you, try these: (1) How did you get into this line of work? Into this particular job? (2) What kinds of things do you like the most about this job? (3) What kinds of things do you like the least about this job? (4) Who else, doing this same kind of work, would you recommend I go talk to?	Anytime you're stuck, you ask your contacts for help *with specific information.* For example: When you can't find workers who are doing the work that interests you. When you can't find the names of places which do that kind of work. When you have a place in mind, but can't figure out the name of 'the person-who-has-the-power-to-hire-you.' When you know that name, but can't get in to see that person. At such times, you call every contact you have on your Networking list, if necessary, until someone can tell you the specific answer you need.
You've 'botched it' when you have no support group, no one to turn to, no one to talk to, and you feel that you are in this, all alone. You've 'botched it' when you are waiting for your friends and family to notice how miserable you are, and to prove they love you by taking the initiative in coming after you; rather than, as is necessary with a support group, *your* choosing and recruiting them -- asking them for their help and aid.	You're trying to use this with people-who-have-the-power-to-hire-you, rather than with *workers.* You're claiming you want information when really you have some other hidden agenda, with this person. *(P.S. They usually can smell the hidden agenda, a mile away.)* You've botched it, whenever you're telling a lie to someone. The whole point of informational interviewing is that it is a search for Truth.	Approaching your 'contacts' too early in your job-hunt, and asking them for help only in the most general and vague terms: "John, I'm out of work. If you hear of anything, please let me know." *Any what thing?* You must do all your own homework *before* you approach your contacts. They will not do your homework for you.

TALKING TO WORKERS, 'TRYING ON' JOBS

Now, when you go talk to people, you are hoping they will give you ideas, as we saw, about *what careers* will use your skills and languages or fields of knowledge and interest.

That's the first step.

The second step is that you want also to get some idea of *what that work feels like, from the inside.*

In the example above, you don't just want the job-title: *psychiatrist working with plants.* You want some feel for the substance that is underneath the title. In other words, you want to find out what the day-to-day work is like.

For this purpose you must leave your *overview people* and go talk to actual living examples of people doing the work you think you'd love: in the particular example we have been discussing, you must go talk to actual *psychiatrists who use plants, in their healing work.*

Why do you want to ask them what the work feels like, from the inside? Well, in effect, you are mentally *trying on jobs* to see if they fit you.

It is exactly analogous to your going to a clothing store and trying on different suits (or dresses) that you see in their window or on their racks. Why do you try them on? Well, the suits or dresses that look *terrific* in the window don't always look so hotsy-totsy when you see them on *you.* Lots of pins were used, on the backside of the figurine in the window. On you, without the pins, the clothes don't hang quite right, etc., etc.

Likewise, the careers that *sound* terrific in books or in your imagination don't always look so great when you see them up close and personal, in all their living glory.

You need to know that. What you're ultimately trying to find is a career that looks terrific in the window, *and* on you. Toward that end, you are asking what *this* job feels like. There are some questions that will help *(you are talking, of course, with workers who are actually doing the career you think you might like to do):*

- How did you get into this work?
- What do you like the most about it?
- What do you like the least about it?

• And, where else could I find people who do this kind of work? *(You should always ask them for more than one name, so that if you run into a dead end at any point, you can easily go back and visit the other people they suggested.)*

If it becomes apparent to you, during the course of any of these Informational Interviews, that this career, occupation, or job you are exploring definitely *doesn't* fit you, then the last question (above) gets turned into a different kind of inquiry:

• Do you have any ideas as to who else I could go talk to, about my skills and fields of knowledge/interest -- so I can find out how they all might fit together, in one job or career?

Then go visit the people they suggest.

If they can't think of anyone, ask them if they know who *might* know. And so on. And so forth.

"THEY SAY I HAVE TO GO BACK TO SCHOOL, BUT I HAVEN'T THE TIME OR THE MONEY"

Next step: having found the names of jobs or careers that interest you, having mentally *tried them on* to see if they fit, you next want to find out *how much training, etc., it takes, to get into that field or career.* You ask the same people you have been talking to, thus far.

More times than not, you will hear *bad news.* They will tell you something like: "In order to be hired for this job, you have to have a master's degree and ten years' experience at it."

If you're willing to do that, if you have the time, and the money, fine! But what if you don't? Then this is what you do: you search for *the exception:*

"Yes, but do you know of anyone in this field who got into it without that master's degree, and ten years' experience?

And where might I find him or her?

And if you don't know of any such person, who might know some names?"

Throughout your Informational Interviewing, don't assume anything ("But I just assumed that . . ."). Question *all* assumptions, no matter how many people tell you that 'this is the way things are.'

Keep clearly in mind that there are people *out there* who will tell you something that absolutely *isn't* so, with every conviction in their being -- because they *think* it's true. Sincerity they have, one hundred percent. Accuracy is something else again. You will need to check and cross-check any information that people tell you or that you read in books (even this one).

Therefore, no matter how many people tell you that such-and-so are the rules about getting into a particular occupation, and there are no exceptions -- believe me, there *are* exceptions, to almost *every* rule, except where a profession has rigid entrance examinations, as in, say, medicine or law.

Of course rules are rules. But what you are counting on is that somewhere in this vast country, somewhere in this vast world, *somebody* found a way to get into this career you dream of, without going through all the hoops that everyone else is telling you are *absolutely essential.*

You want to find out who these people are, and go talk to them, to find out *how they did it.*

WHEN *SOME* TRAINING IS UNAVOIDABLE

Okay, but suppose you are determined to go into a career that takes *years* to prepare for; and you can't find *anyone* who took a shortcut? What then?

Even here, you can get *close* to the profession *without* such long preparation. Every professional speciality has one or more *shadow* professions, which require much less training. For example, instead of becoming a doctor, you can go into paramedical work; instead of becoming a lawyer, you can go into paralegal work, etc., etc.

CHOOSE TWO CAREERS

Anyway, sooner or later, as you interview one person after another, you'll begin to get some definite ideas about a career that is of interest to you. It uses your favorite skills. It employs your favorite fields of knowledge or fields of interest. You've interviewed people *actually doing that work*, and it all sounds fine. This part of your Informational Interviewing is over.

Just be sure that you get the names of at least *two* careers, or jobs, that you think you could be happy doing. Never, ever, put all your eggs in one basket. The secret of surviving out there in the jungle is *having alternatives.*

Be careful. Be thorough. Be persistent. This is your life you're working on, and your future. Make it glorious. Whatever it takes, find out the name of your ideal career, your ideal occupation, your ideal job -- *or jobs.*

Then you are ready to turn to the next two questions:

• QUESTION #2

What **kinds of organizations** would and/or do employ people in these careers?

Before you think of individual places where you might like to work, it is necessary to step back a little, as it were, and think of all the *kinds* of places where one might get hired.

Let's take an example. Suppose in your new career you want to be a teacher. You must then ask yourself: *what kinds of places hire teachers?* You might answer, *"just schools"* -- and finding that schools in your geographical area have no openings, you might say, *"Well, there are no jobs for people in this career."*

But that is not true. There are countless other *kinds* of organizations and agencies out there, besides schools, which employ *teachers.* For example, corporate training and educational departments, workshop sponsors, foundations, private research firms, educational consultants, teachers' associations, professional and trade societies, military bases, state and local councils on higher education, fire and police training academies, and so on, and so forth.

'*Kinds* of places' also means places with different *hiring modes,* besides full-time hiring, such as:

• places that would employ you part-time (maybe you'll end up deciding to hold down two or even three part-time jobs, which altogether would add up to one full-time job, in order to give yourself more variety);

• places that take temporary workers, on assignment for one project at a time;

• places that take consultants, one project at a time;

• places that operate with volunteers, etc.

• places that are nonprofit;

• places that are for profit;

• and, don't forget, places which you yourself would start up, should you decide to be your own boss.

Don't forget that as you talk to workers about their jobs or careers (in the previous section), they will accidentally volunteer information about the *kinds* of organizations. Listen keenly, and keep notes.

> **• QUESTION #3**
>
> Among the kinds of organizations uncovered in the previous question, what are the names of **particular places** that I especially like?

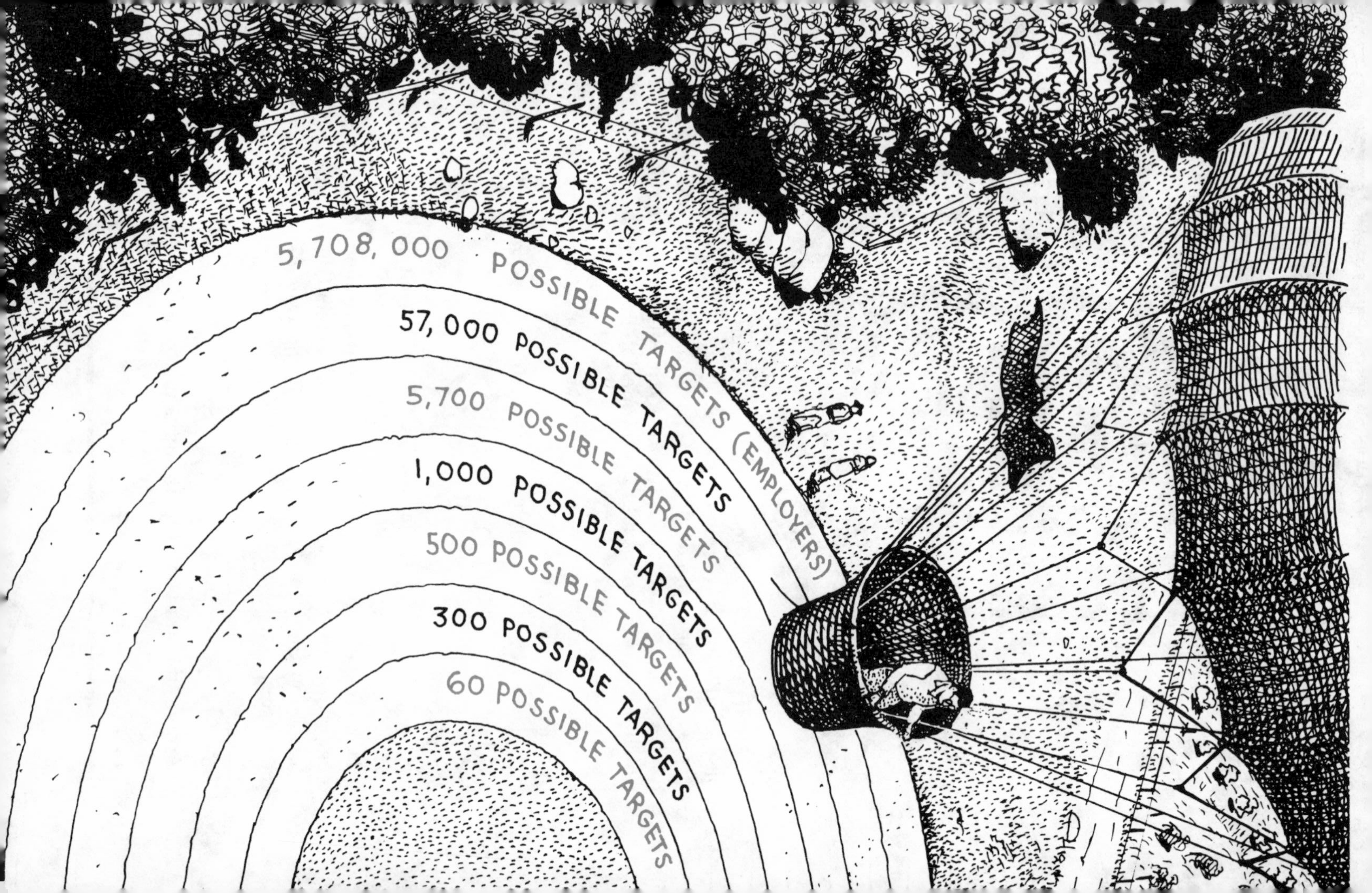

5,708,000 POSSIBLE TARGETS (EMPLOYERS)
57,000 POSSIBLE TARGETS
5,700 POSSIBLE TARGETS
1,000 POSSIBLE TARGETS
500 POSSIBLE TARGETS
300 POSSIBLE TARGETS
60 POSSIBLE TARGETS

10 POSSIBLE TARGETS
YOUR SPIRITUAL VALUES
YOUR PREFERRED LEVEL AND SALARY
YOUR PREFERRED WORKING CONDITIONS
THINGS, KINDS OF PEOPLE, AND INFORMATION YOU PREFER
YOUR PREFERRED TASKS OR SKILLS
YOUR PREFERRED FIELD (OF KNOWLEDGE) OR CAREER FIELD
YOUR PREFERRED GEOGRAPHICAL LOCATION

CUTTING DOWN THE TERRITORY

As you interview workers about their jobs or careers, they will incidentally volunteer actual names of organizations that have such jobs -- including what's good or bad about the place where *they* work. This is important information for you. Jot it all down. Keep notes as though it were part of your religion.

You're going to run into two scenarios: you'll be left with too few names of places to work, or you'll end up with too much information -- too many names of places which hire people in the career that interests you.

We'll take this last scenario, first. If you end up with too many places, you will want to **cut the territory down,** so that you are left with *a manageable number* of 'targets' for your job-hunt.[3]

Let's take an example. Suppose you discovered that the career which interests you the most is *welding*. You want to be a welder. Well, that's a beginning. You've cut the 16 million U.S. job-markets down to:

I want to work in a place that hires welders.

But the territory is still too large. There might be thousands of places in the country, that use welders. You can't go visit them all. So, you've got to cut the territory down, further. Suppose that on your Geography *petal* you said that you really want to live and work in the San Jose area of California. That's helpful: that cuts the territory down further. Now your goal is:

I want to work in a place that hires welders,
within the San Jose area.

But, the territory is still too large. There could be 100, 200, 300 organizations which fit that description. So you look at your Flower Diagram for further help, and you notice that under *preferred working conditions* you said you wanted

3. If you resist this idea of *cutting the territory down* -- if you feel you could be happy *anywhere* just as long as you were using your favorite skills - - then almost no organization in the country can be ruled out. In the U.S. alone there are currently over 16 million

to work for an organization with fifty or less employees. Good, now your goal is:

I want to work in a place that hires welders, within the San Jose area, and has fifty or less employees.

This territory may still be too large. So you look again at your Flower Diagram for further guidance, and you see that on the Things *petal* you said you wanted to work for an organization which works with, or produces, *wheels*. So now your statement of what you're looking for, becomes:

I want to work in a place that hires welders, within the San Jose area, has fifty or less employees, and makes wheels.

Using your Flower Diagram, you can thus keep cutting the territory down, until the *'targets'* of your job-hunt are no more than 10 places. That's a manageable number of places for you to *start with*. You can always expand the list later, if none of these 10 turn out to be very promising or interesting.

EXPANDING THE TERRITORY

Sometimes your problem will be just the opposite. We come here to the second scenario: if your Informational Interviewing doesn't turn up enough names of places where you could get hired in your new career, then you're going to have to consult some directories.

If it's the name of large organizations that you're looking for, see the list on pages *84ff* , in the *Resource Guide*. There are *many* directories of such large organizations.

If it's the name of smaller organizations that you're looking for, your salvation is going to be The Yellow Pages of your local phone book. Look under every related heading that you can think of. Also, see if the Chamber of Commerce publishes a business directory; often it will list not only small companies

---

employers, hence 16 million job-markets, out there. (And a *proportional* number in other countries.) So if you aren't willing to cut the territory down, then you'll have to go visit them all. Good luck! We'll see you in about 43 years.

but also local divisions of larger companies, with names of department heads; and sometimes will even include the (SIC) industry codes. You won't likely lack for names, believe me -- unless it's a very small town you live in, in which case you'll need to cast your net a little wider, to include other towns or villages that are within commuting distance.

Once you have about 10 names of organizations or businesses that might hire you for the kind of work you are dying to do, you proceed to the fourth question:

> • **QUESTION #4**
>
> Among the places that I particularly like, **what needs do they have** or what outcomes are they trying to produce, that my skills and knowledge could help with?

RESEARCHING PLACES BEFORE YOU APPROACH THEM

Why should you research places, before you approach them for a hiring-interview? Well, first of all, you want to know something about the organization from the inside: what kind of work they do there. And what their needs or problems or challenges are. And what kind of goals are they trying to achieve, what obstacles are they running into, and how can your skills and knowledges help them? *(When you do at last go in for a hiring-interview, you want above all else to be able to show them that you have something to offer, which they need.)*

Secondly, you want to find out if you would enjoy working there. You want to take the measure of that organization or organizations. Everybody takes the measure of an organization, sooner or later. The problem with most job-hunters or career-changers is they take the measure of an organization *after* they are hired there.

In the U.S., for example, a survey of the Federal/State employment service found that 57% of those who found jobs through that service were not working at that job just 30 days later.

They were not working at that job just thirty days later, *because* they used the first ten or twenty days *on the job* to screen out the job (and some were temorary workers, as well).

By doing this research of a place ahead of time, you are choosing a better way, by far. Essentially, you are *screening out* careers, jobs, places *before* you commit to them. How sensible! How smart!

So, what you do is try to think of every way in the world that you could find out more about those organizations *(plural, not singular)* that interest you, *before you go to see if you can get hired there.* There are several ways you can do this research ahead of time:

- **Friends and Neighbors**. Ask *everybody* you know if they know anyone who works at the place that interests you. And, if they do, ask them if they could arrange for you and that person to get together, for lunch, coffee, or tea. At that time, tell them why the place interests you, and indicate you'd like to know more about it. *(It helps if your mutual friend is sitting there with the two of you, so the purpose of this little chat won't be misconstrued.)* This is the vastly preferred way to find out about a place. However, obviously you need a couple of additional alternatives up your sleeve, in case you run into a dead end here:

- **What's In Print**. The organization itself may have stuff in print, about its business, purpose, etc. The CEO or head of the organization may have given talks. The organization may have copies of those talks. In addition, there may be brochures, annual reports, etc. that the organization has put out, about itself. How do you get ahold of these? The person that answers the phone is the person to check with, in small organizations. In larger organizations, the publicity office, or human relations office, are the places to check. Also, if it's a decent-sized organization that you are interested in, one of the numerous directories mentioned beginning on page *84ff*, in the *Resource Guide,* may furnish additional information. As well, public libraries may have files on the organization -- newspaper clippings, articles, etc. You never know; and it never hurts to ask your friendly neighborhood research librarian.

• **People at the Organizations in Question, or at Similar Organizations.** You can also go directly to organizations and ask questions about the place, but here I must caution you about several *dangers.*

First, you must make sure you're not asking them questions that are in print somewhere, which you could easily have read for yourself instead of bothering *them.*

Secondly, you must make sure that you approach the people at that organization *whose business it is to give out information* -- receptionists, public relations people, 'the personnel office,' etc., *before* you ever approach other people higher up.

Thirdly, you must make sure that you approach *subordinates* rather than the top person in the place, if the subordinates would know the answer to your questions. Bothering the boss there with some simple questions that someone else could have answered is committing *job-hunting suicide.*

Fourth, you must make sure you're not using this approach simply as a sneaky way to get in to see the boss, and make a pitch for them hiring you. This is information gathering. Keep it at that. Keep it honest.

Job-Hunters Who Are Tricksters

I regret to report that there is no honest, open-hearted job-hunting *technique* that cannot be twisted by those with clever, devious spirits, into some kind of *trick.* This has happened with Informational Interviewing. *Some* job-hunters have thought, "Wouldn't this be a great *trick* to use so as to get in to see employers (not workers) -- asking them for some of their time, claiming you need *information,* and then hitting them up for a job?"

In case *you,* even for a moment, are tempted to follow in their footsteps, let me gently inform you that employers universally detest this particular deception, and have usually thrown the liar/trickster out of their offices.

One New York employer told me what he said to such a trickster: "You came to see me to ask for some information. And I gladly gave you my time. But now, it is apparent you really want a job here, and you think you found a clever 'trick' that would get you in my door. You've essentially lied. Let me tell you something: on the basis of what I have just seen of your style of doing things, I wouldn't hire you if you were the last person on earth."

In this Age of Rudeness, Lies, Manipulation, and Getting Ahead At Any Cost, *you* will want, above all else, to be a beacon of integrity, truth, and kindness throughout your job-hunt or career-change -- including the time you are doing Informational Interviewing. *That's* the kind of employee employers are *dying* to find.

• **Temporary Agencies** . Many job-hunters and career-changers have found that a useful way to explore organizations is to go and work at a temporary agency. Employers turn to these agencies in order to find: a) job-hunters who can work part-time for a limited number of days; and b) job-hunters who can work full-time for a limited number of days. This is an increasing trend. Some companies whose temporary workers comprised only 10% of their total workforce as recently as 1989 are now hiring temps at such a rate that their temporary workers represent from 25 to 60% of their total workforce.[4]

The advantage to you of temporary work is that if there is an agency which loans out people with your particular skills and expertise, you get a chance to visit a number of different employers over a period of several weeks, and see each one from the inside. Maybe temps won't send you to exactly the place you hoped for; but sometimes you can develop contacts over there, even while you're temporarily working somewhere else -- if both organizations are in the same field.

Some of you, of course, may balk at the idea of enrolling with a temporary agency, because you remember the old days when such agencies were solely for clerical workers and secretarial help. But the field has seen an explosion of services in recent years -- according to the Bureau of Labor Statistics, temporary or part-time workers in the U.S. now number over 35 million, and represent 29% of the total civilian labor force.

There are temporary agencies these days *(at least in the larger cities)* for many different occupations. In your city you may find temporary agencies for: accountants, industrial workers, assemblers, drivers, mechanics, construction people, engineering people, software engineers, programmers, computer technicians, production workers, management/executives, nannies (for young and old), health care/dental/medical people, legal specialists, insurance specialists, sales/marketing people, underwriting professionals, financial services, and the like, as well as for the more obvious specialties: data processing, secretarial, and office services. See your local phone book, under 'Temporary Agencies.'

• **Volunteer Work**. Another useful way to research a place before you ever ask them to hire you there, is to volunteer your services at that place that interests you. Of course, some places will turn your offer down, cold. But others will be interested. If they are, it will be relatively easy for you to talk them into letting you work there for a while, because you offer your services *without pay,* and for a brief, limited period of time. In

4. *San Francisco Chronicle,* 6/30/94.

other words, from their point of view, if you turn out to be a *pain*, they won't have to endure you for long.

In this fashion, you get a chance to learn about organizations from the inside. Not so coincidentally, if you do decide you would really like to work there, and permanently, they've had a chance to see you in action, and when you are about to end your volunteer time there, *may* want to hire you permanently. I say *may*. Don't be mad if they simply say, "Thanks very much for helping us out." (That's what *usually* happens.) Even so, you've learned a lot, and this will stand you in good stead, in the future -- as you approach other organizations.

SEND A THANK-YOU NOTE

After *anyone* has done you a favor, during this Informational Interviewing phase of your job-hunt, you must *be sure* to send them a thank-you note by the very next day, at the latest. Such a note goes to *everyone* who helps you, or who talks with you. That means friends, people at the organization in question, temporary agency people, secretaries, receptionists, librarians, workers, or whoever.

Ask them, at the time you are face-to-face with them, for their calling card (if they have one), or ask them to write out their name and work-address, on a piece of paper, for you. You *don't* want to misspell their name. It is difficult to figure out how to spell people's names, these days, simply from the sound of it. What sounds like "Laura" may actually be "Lara." What sounds like "Smith" may actually be "Smythe," and so on. Get that name and address, *but get it right,* please. And let me reiterate: write them the thank-you note that same night, or the very next day at the latest. A thank-you note that arrives a week later, completely misses the point.

Ideally it should be handwritten, but if your handwriting is the least bit difficult to read (ranging on up to *indecipherable*), by all means type it. It can be just two or three sentences. Something like: "*I wanted to thank you for talking with me yesterday. It was very helpful to me. I much appreciated your taking the time out of your busy schedule, to do this. Best wishes to you,*" and then your signature. *Do* sign it, particularly if the thank-you note is typed. Typed letters without any signature seem to be multiplying like rabbits in the world of work, these days; the absence of a signature is usually perceived as making your letter *real* impersonal. You don't want to leave that impression.

WHAT IF I GET OFFERED A JOB ALONG THE WAY, WHILE I'M STILL GATHERING ALL THIS INFORMATION?

You probably won't. Let me remind you that during this information gathering, you are *not* talking primarily to employers. You're talking to workers.

Nonetheless, an occasional employer *may* stray across your path during all this Informational Interviewing. And that employer *may* be so impressed with the carefulness you're showing, in going about your career-change and job-search, that they want to hire you, on the spot. So, it's *possible* that you might get offered a job while you're still doing your information gathering. Not *likely,* but *possible.* And if that happens, what should you say?

Well, if you're desperate, you will of course say *yes.* I remember one wintertime when I had just gone through the knee of my last pair of pants, we were burning old pieces of furniture in our fireplace to stay warm, the legs on our bed had just broken, and we were eating spaghetti until it was coming out our ears. In such a situation, *of course* you say yes.

But if you're not *desperate,* if you have a little time to be more careful, then you respond to the job-offer in a way that will buy you some time. You tell them what you're doing: that the average job-hunter tries to screen a job *after* they take it. But you are doing what you are *sure* this employer would do if they were in your shoes: you are examining careers, fields, industries, jobs, organizations *before* you decide where you can do your best and most effective work.

And you tell them that since your Informational Interviewing isn't finished yet, it would be premature for you to accept their job offer, until you're *sure* that this is the place where you could be most effective, and do your best work.

But, you add: "Of course, I'm tickled pink that you would want me to be working here. And when I've finished my personal survey, I'll be glad to get back to you about this, as my preliminary impression is that this is the kind of place I'd like to work in, and the kind of people I'd like to work for, and the kind of people I'd like to work with."

In other words, *if you're not desperate yet,* you don't walk immediately through any opened doors; but neither do you allow them to shut.

A Closing Word to Those Who Are Shy

The late John Crystal[5] had to often counsel the shy. They were often *frightened* at the whole idea of going to talk to people for information, never mind for hiring. So John developed a system to help the shy. He suggested that before you even begin doing any Informational Interviewing, you first go out and talk to people about *anything* just to get good at *talking to people.* Thousands of job-hunters and career-changers have followed his advice, over the past twenty-five years, and found it really helps. Indeed, people who have followed John's advice in this regard have had a success rate of 86% in finding a job --and not just any job, but *the* job or new career that they were looking for.

Daniel Porot, the job-hunting expert in Europe, has taken John's system, and brought some organization to it. He observed that John was really recommending three types of interviews: this interview we are talking about, just for practice. Then Informational Interviewing. And finally, of course, the hiring-interview. Daniel decided to call these three the *'The PIE Method,'* which has helped thousands of job-hunters and career-changers in both the U.S. and in Europe. Porot's "PIE Chart" follows on the next page:

---

5. John also was the inventor of WHAT, WHERE, and HOW -- which I have used as the basic framework for Chapters 5, 6, and 7, here.

Initial:	Pleasure P	Information I	Employment E
Kind of Interview	Practice Field Survey	Informational Interviewing or Researching	Employment Interview or Hiring Interview
Purpose	To Get Used to Talking with People to Enjoy It; To "Penetrate" Networks	To Find Out If You'd Like a Job, Before You Go Trying to Get It	To Get Hired for the Work You Have Decided You Would Most Like to Do
How You Go to the Interview	You Can Take Somebody with You	By Yourself or You Can Take Somebody with You	By Yourself
Who You Talk To	Anyone Who Shares Your Enthusiasm About a (for You) Non-Job-Related Subject	A Worker Who Is Doing the Actual Work You Are Thinking About Doing	An Employer Who Has the Power to Hire You for the Job You Have Decided You Would Most Like to Do
How Long a Time You Ask For	10 Minutes (and DON'T run over -- asking to see them at 11:50 may help keep you honest, since most employers have lunch appointments at noon)	Ditto	
What You Ask Them	Any Curiosity You Have About Your Shared Interest or Enthusiasm	Any Questions You Have About This Job or This Kind of Work	You Tell Them What It Is You Like About Their Organization and What Kind of Work You Are Looking For.

Initial:	Pleasure P	Information I	Employment E
What You Ask Them *(continued)*	If Nothing Occurs to You, Ask: 1. How did you start, with this hobby, interest, etc.? 2. What excites or interests you the most about it? 3. What do you find is the thing you like the least about it? 4. Who else do you know of who shares this interest, hobby or enthusiasm, or could tell me more about my curiosity? a. Can I go and see them? b. May I mention that it was you who suggested I see them? c. May I say that you recommended them? ***Get their name and address***	If Nothing Occurs to You, Ask: 1. How did you get interested in this work and how did you get hired? 2. What excites or interests you the most about it? 3. What do you find is the thing you like the least about it? 4. Who else do you know of who does this kind of work, or similar work but with this difference: ______________? 5. What kinds of challenges or problems do you have to deal with in this job? 6. What skills do you need in order to meet those challenges or problems? ***Get their name and address***	 You tell them the kinds of challenges you like to deal with. What skills you have to deal with those challenges. What experience you have had in dealing with those challenges in the past.
AFTERWARD: That Same Night	SEND A THANK YOU NOTE	SEND A THANK YOU NOTE	SEND A THANK YOU NOTE

Why is it called *'PIE'*?[6]

P is for the *warmup* phase. John Crystal named this warmup 'The Practice Field Survey.'[7] Daniel Porot calls it **P** for *pleasure.*

I is for 'Informational Interviewing.'

E is for the employment interview with the-person-who-has-the-power-to-hire-you.

How do you use this **P** for *practice* to get comfortable about going out and talking to people *one-on-one?*

This is achieved by choosing a topic -- *any* topic, however silly or trivial -- that is a pleasure for you to talk about with your friends, or family. To avoid anxiety, it should not be a topic that is connected to any present or future career that you are considering. Rather, the kinds of topics that work best, for this exercise, are:

- **a hobby** you *love,* such as skiing, bridge playing, exercise, computers, etc.
- **any leisure-time enthusiasm** of yours, such as a movie you just saw, that you liked a lot
- **a long-time curiosity**, such as how do they predict the weather, or what do policemen do
- **an aspect of the town or city you live in**, such as a new shopping mall that just opened
- **an issue** you feel strongly about, such as the homeless, AIDS sufferers, ecology, peace, health, etc.

There is only one condition about choosing a topic: it should be something you *love* to talk about with other people: a subject you know nothing about, but you feel a great deal of enthusiasm for it, is far preferable to something you know an awful lot about, but it puts you to sleep.

6. Daniel has summarized his system in a new book published here in the U.S.: it is called *The PIE Method for Career Success: A Unique Way to Find Your Ideal Job,* 1996, and is available from its publisher, JIST Works, Inc., 720 North Park Avenue, Indianapolis IN 46202-3431. Phone 317-264-3720. Fax 317-264-3709. It is a fantastic book, and I give it my highest recommendation.

7. If you want further instructions about this whole process, I refer you to "The Practice Field Survey," pp. 187–196 in *Where Do I Go From Here With My Life?* by John Crystal and friend. Ten Speed Press, Box 7123, Berkeley, CA 94707.

Enthusiasm

Throughout the job-hunt and career-change, the key to 'interviewing' is not found in memorizing a dozen rules about what you're supposed to say.

No, the key is just this one thing: now and always, be *sure* you are talking about something you feel *passionate about.*[8]

Enthusiasm is the key -- to *enjoying* 'interviewing,' and conducting *effective* interviews, at any level. What this **P** exercise teaches us is that shyness always loses its power and its painful self-consciousness -- *if* and *when* you are talking about something *you love.*

For example, if you love gardens you will forget all about your shyness when you're talking to someone else about gardens and flowers. *"You ever been to Butchart Gardens?"*

If you love movies, you'll forget all about your shyness when you're talking to someone else about movies. *"I just hated that scene where they . . ."*

If you love computers, then you will forget all about your shyness when you're talking to someone else about computers. *"Do you work on a Mac or an MS-DOS machine?*

That's why it is important that it be your enthusiasms -- here, your hobbies -- later, in Informational Interviewing, your *favorite* skills and your *favorite* subjects -- that you are exploring and pursuing in these conversations with others.

Having identified your enthusiasm, you then need to go talk to someone who is as enthusiastic about this thing, as you are. *For best results with your later job-hunt, this should be someone you don't already know.* Use the Yellow Pages, ask around among your friends and family, *who do you know that* loves *to talk about this?* It's relatively easy to find the kind of person you're looking for.

You love to talk about skiing? *Try a ski-clothes store, or a skiing instructor.* You love to talk about writing? *Try a professor on a nearby college campus, who teaches English.* You love to talk about physical exercise? *Try a trainer, or someone who teaches physical therapy.*

Once you've identified someone you think shares your enthusiasm, you then go talk with them. When you are face-to-face with your *fellow enthusiast,* the first thing you must do is relieve their understandable anxiety. *Everyone* has had someone visit them who has stayed too long, who has worn out their welcome. If your *fellow enthusiast* is worried about you staying too long, they'll be so preoccupied with this that they won't hear a word you are saying.

So, when you first meet them, ask for *ten minutes of their time, only.* Period. Stop. Exclamation point. And watch your wristwatch *like a hawk,* to be sure

8. This is what the late Joseph Campbell used to call 'your bliss.'

you stay no longer. *Never* stay longer, unless they *beg* you to. And I mean, *beg, beg, beg.*[9]

Once they've agreed to give you ten minutes, you tell them why you're there -- that you're trying to get comfortable about talking with people, for information -- and you understand that you two share a mutual interest, which is . . .

Then what? Well, a topic may have its own unique set of questions. For example, I love movies, so if I met someone who shared this interest, my first question would be, "What movies have you seen lately?" And so on. If it's a topic you love, and often talk about, you'll *know* what kinds of questions you begin with. But, if no such questions come to mind, no matter how hard you try, the following ones have proved to be good conversation starters for thousands of job-hunters and career-changers before you, no matter what their topic or interest.

So, look these over, memorize them *(or copy them on a little card that fits in the palm of your hand),* and give them a try:

Questions Shy People Can Practice With

Addressed to the person you're doing the Practice Interviewing with:

- How did you get involved with/become interested in this? ("*This*" is the hobby, curiosity, aspect, issue, or enthusiasm, that you are so interested in.)
- What do you like the most about it?
- What do you like the least about it?
- Who else would you suggest I go talk to that shares this interest?
- Can I use your name?
- May I tell them it was you who recommended that I talk with them?
- *Then, choosing one person off the list of several names they may have given you, you say,* Well, I think I will begin by going to talk to this person. Would you be willing to call ahead for me, so they will know who I am, when I go over there?

9. A polite, "Oh do you have to go?" should be understood for what it is: politeness. Your response should be, "Yes, I promised to only take ten minutes of your time, and I want to keep to my word." This will almost always leave a *very* favorable impression behind you.

Incidentally, during *this* Practice Interviewing, it's perfectly okay for you to take someone with you -- preferably someone who is more outgoing than you feel you are. And on the first few interviews, let them take the lead in the conversation, while you watch to see how they do it.

Once it is *your turn* to conduct the interview, it will by that time usually be easy for you to figure out what to talk about.

Alone or with someone, keep at this Practice Interviewing until you feel very much at ease in talking with people and asking them questions about things you are curious about.

In all of this, *fun* is the key. If you're having fun, you're doing it right. If you're not having fun, you need to keep at it, until you are. It may take your seeing four people. It may take ten. Or twenty. You'll know.

Summary of This Chapter

There is no limit to what you can find out about WHERE you'd like to work -- careers, and places which hire for those careers -- if you go out and talk to people. When you find places that interest you, it is irrelevant whether they happen to have a vacancy, or not. In this dance of life, called the job-hunt, you get to decide first of all whether or not *you* want *them*, through your research. Only after you have decided that, is it appropriate to ask, as in the next chapter, if they also want you.

You're a bunch of jackasses. You work your rear ends off in a trivial course that no one will ever care about again. You're not willing to spend time researching a company that you're interested in working for. Why don't you decide who you want to work for and go after them?

Professor Albert Shapiro,
The late William H. Davis Professor of The American Free Enterprise System at Ohio State University

CHAPTER SEVEN

FOR THE DETERMINED JOB-HUNTER OR CAREER-CHANGER

The Systematic Approach To
Career-Change
And Job-Hunting

HOW

DO YOU OBTAIN SUCH A JOB?

You Must Identify The Person Who Has The Power to Hire You, and Show Them How Your Skills Can Help Them With Their Problems

Chapter 7

Table of Contents

HOW
To Get A Hiring Interview

Okay, so you've identified a job you love, you've found a place -- better yet, *places* -- where you'd *love* to work. But . . .

But, the person you'd have to see, in order to get hired there, is in an office with a ring of fire around it, three knights in full armor guarding it, in a castle with fifty-foot walls, surrounded by a wide moat whose deep waters are filled with hungry alligators.

And you want to know how to get a hiring-interview with this person. Right? Well, it isn't as difficult as it might at first seem . . . if you are *determined.* And if you know a few simple principles.

THE FIRST CRUCIAL QUESTION: HOW LARGE IS THE ORGANIZATION?

To begin with, most discussions of job-interviewing proceed from a false assumption. That is, they *assume* you are going to be approaching a large organization -- you know, the ones where you need a floor-plan of the building, and an alphabetical directory of the staff.

There are admittedly *huge* problems in approaching such giants for a hiring-interview, not the least of which is that many are doing more downsizing than hiring, during these cost-cutting times.[1]

But many job-hunters don't want to work for large corporations, anyway. They want to go after the so-called 'small organizations' -- those with 50 or less employees -- which, in the U.S., for example, total 80% of all private businesses, and represent one-fourth of all workers in the private sector.

These small organizations create -- experts say -- two-thirds, or more, of all new jobs.[2] Which is a good thing, because small organizations are *much* easier to get into than large ones, believe me.

With a small organization, you don't need to wait until there's a *known* vacancy, because they rarely advertise vacancies

---

1. Like all generalizations, this one of course has a number of exceptions. In the U.S., Wal-Mart, Pepsico, U.P.S., Chrysler, Sara Lee, General Mills, Motorola, and Home Depot all added jobs -- in Wal-Mart's case, 182,000 -- between 1992 and 1994. Wal-Mart thus became the second largest employer in the U.S. *(New York Times,* 3/25/94*)*.

2. This statistic, first popularized by David Birch of M.I.T., and 'bandied about' for years, has been widely debated, during the '90s, by economists such as Nobel laureate Milton Friedman and Harvard economist James Medoff. The debate has been fueled by a study conducted jointly by Steven J. Davis, a labor economist at the University of Chicago, John Haltiwanger at the University of Maryland, and Scott Schuh at the Federal Reserve. Their study, however, was of U.S. *manufacturing,* not of the economy as a whole. Anyway, picky-smicky, what these researchers discovered is that small *manufacturing* companies with 50 or fewer employees created only *one-fifth* of all new manufacturing jobs. *(New York Times,* 3/25/94*)*. Other researchers, such as Birch, had attributed a much larger percentage to small companies. Here and elsewhere, critics often concede that small companies do create a lot of the new jobs in the *overall economy,* but then *sniff,* "Small businesses are not the places you see *the best* jobs," as one economist put it. (The emphasis is mine.) 'Best jobs' mean -- to these critics -- jobs with high pay, high benefits, government-mandated health and safety regulations, and union representation. *(San Francisco Chronicle,* 3/29/93*)*.

even when there is one. You just go there and ask if they need someone.

With a small organization, there is no Personnel or Human Resources Department to screen you out.

With a small organization, there's no problem in identifying the person-who-has-the-power-to-hire-you. It's *the boss.* Everyone there knows who it is. They can point to his or her office door, easily.

With a small organization, you do not need to approach them through the mail; you can go in to see the boss. And if, by chance, he or she is well-protected from intruders, it is relatively easy to figure out how to get around *that.* Contacts are the answer, as we shall see.

With a small organization, if it is growing, there is a greater likelihood that they will be willing to create a new position for you, *if you quietly convince them that you are too good to let slip out of their grasp.*

For all of these reasons and more, small organizations must be kept in mind, as much as large organizations, when we begin talking about techniques or strategies for securing a hiring-interview. And, we therefore need to talk about two different techniques:

How you approach a large organization.

And, how you approach a small organization.

Two different approaches, altogether.

APPROACHING LARGE ORGANIZATIONS FOR AN INTERVIEW

In securing hiring-interviews, it's the large organizations that are the problem -- the ones, as I mentioned before, where you need a floor-plan of the building, and an alphabetical directory of the staff.

But we can simplify our task, if we keep certain things in mind. To begin with, you don't want to just get into the building. You want to see *a particular person* in that building, and only that person: namely, the person-who-has-the-power-to-hire-you for the job you are interested in.

Most job-hunters *don't* even *try* to find out *who* that person is, before approaching a large organization. Rather, they approach each large organization in what can only be described as a haphazard, scatter-shot fashion -- sending them their resume or c.v.[3] -- with or without some covering letter -- hoping

3. C.v. stands for *curriculum vitae,* a term for *resume* that is favored in academic circles in the U.S. and in other countries.

that resume or covering letter will function as a kind of extended calling-card, arousing employers' interest, so they will ask the job-hunter to come in and see them.

This is many job-hunters' favorite way of approaching an organization, particularly a large organization, for a hiring-interview. It's their favorite because you don't have to *go* somewhere needlessly, you don't have to look into the employers' eyes when they reject you, and -- let's admit it, sometimes it actually works: you do get invited in for a possible hiring-interview.

On the other hand, *some* employers also love this 'mail approach,' but for very different reasons. They love it, because it enables them to screen you out *in about eight seconds,* without ever 'wasting their time' on your coming in for an interview.

It is therefore *very common* for job-hunters to approach eight hundred organizations or more in this fashion and not get *one* single invitation to come in for a hiring-interview. You, of course, falsely thinking this is a method that works well for *most* job-hunters, will wonder what is wrong with you; you not only don't find a job this way, but you end up with much-lowered self-esteem. If you try this approach and it doesn't work, don't feel there is something wrong with you. There's something wrong with this method!!

It goes without saying that there are certain situations where you may *want* to have a resume -- for example, if you're talking to some employer who is halfway across the country, or if you're having a *series* of interviews with some particular place locally, and you want to *leave* a resume behind you, *after* the first interview, for the interviewing officer to share with those there who haven't met you yet.

The most important rule about preparing your resume or c.v. is that there is no such thing as a *right* format or form for a resume or c.v. I used to have a hobby of collecting 'winning' resumes -- that is, resumes that had actually gotten someone a hiring-interview and, ultimately, a job. Being playful by nature, I delighted in showing these, without comment, to employers whom I knew. Many of them didn't like the winning resumes at all. "That resume will never get anyone a job," they would say.

Then, I would tell them, "Sorry, you're wrong. It already has. What you are saying is that it wouldn't get them a job *with you.*"

The resume reproduced on the next page is a good example of what I mean. (*You did want an example of what I mean, didn't you?*) Jim Dyer, who had been in the Marines for twenty years, wanted a job as a salesman for heavy construction and mining equipment thousands of miles from where he was then living. He devised the resume you see, and had fifteen copies made. "I used," he said, "a grand total of seven before I got the job in the place I wanted!"

Like the employer who hired him, I loved this resume. Yet, other employers have criticized it for using a picture, for being too long (or too short), etc., etc. In other words, had Jim sent his resume to *them,* they wouldn't have been impressed enough to invite him in for an interview. So, don't believe anyone who tells you there's one right format for a resume, or one style that's guaranteed to win. After four thousand years, we've still gotten no further than the *ink-blot* stage in hiring, where one thing means something to one employer, but something quite different to another. So, when you mail it out, basically what you're doing is hoping and praying that this resume of yours will appeal to *those employers who appeal to you.*

There are always going to be millions of employers who don't like resumes in general, or don't like *your* resume in particular. Some employers are so highly allergic to resumes -- period -- that they break out into a rash, if they see even one in their mail. Hence, oftentimes a brief individual letter, summarizing the same stuff, is preferable to sending someone your resume.

There is a far far more effective way to approach employers -- and that is to identify *who* at that organization has the power to hire you for the position you have in mind, and then to discover what mutual friend the two of you might have in common, who could help you get an appointment. **The person-who-has-the-power-to-hire-you** will see you because of that mutual friend having gotten the appointment for you.

It is astonishing how often this approach works -- it has, in fact, an 86% effectiveness rate for getting a hiring-interview and, subsequently, a job.

E.J. DYER Street, City, Zip Telephone No.

I SPEAK
THE LANGUAGE
OF
MEN
MACHINERY
AND
MANAGEMENT
...

OBJECTIVE: Sales of Heavy Equipment

QUALIFICATIONS
* Knowledge of heavy equipment, its use and maintenance.
* Ability to communicate with management and with men in the field.
* Ability to favorably introduce change in the form of new equipment or new ideas... the ability to sell.

EXPERIENCE

Men and Machinery
* Maintained, shipped, budgeted and set allocation priorities for 85 pieces of heavy equipment as head of a 500-man organization (1975-1977).
* Constructed twelve field operation support complexes, employing a 100-man crew and 19 pieces of heavy equipment (1965-1967).
* Jack-hammer operator, heavy construction (summers 1956-1957-1958).

Management
* Planned, negotiated and executed large scale equipment purchases on a nation to nation level (1972-1974).

Sales
* Achieved field customer acceptance of two major new computer-based systems:
  - Equipment inventory control and repair parts expedite system (1968-1971)
  - Decision makers' training system (1977-1979).
* Proven leader ... repeatedly elected or appointed to senior posts.

EDUCATION
* B.A. Benedictine College, 1959. (Class President; Editor Yearbook; "Who's Who in American Colleges").
* Naval War College, 1975. (Class President; Graduated "With Highest Distinction").
* University of Maryland, 1973-1974. (Chinese Language).
* Middle Level Management Training Course, 1967-1968 (Class Standing: 1 of 97).

PERSONAL
* Family: Sharon and our sons Jim (11), Andy (8) and Matt (5) desire to locate in a Mountain State by 1982, however, in the interim will consider a position elsewhere in or outside the United States ... Health: Excellent ... Birthdate: December 9, 1937 ... Completing Military Service with the rank of Lieutenant Colonel, U.S. Marine Corps.

SUMMARY
A seeker of challenge ... experienced, proven and confident of closing the sales for profit.

Of course, there is that 14% of the time when it *doesn't* work. There are places where it is absolutely *impossible* to get in to see 'the boss,' i.e., the one who has the power to hire you, in spite of *contacts*, mutual friends, or whatever. As mentioned earlier, he or she may be isolated in a castle surrounded by a moat, with eight large, oversized, hungry alligators in that moat. You of course will hurl yourself against the ramparts of that castle a half-dozen times, anyway, furious that you can't get in to see that person, despite all the techniques recommended in this book.

But, could I ask you a question: "*Why* do you want to work for *a place like that?*" I mean, never mind that you're understandably taking this very personally. *Rejection, rejection, rejection,* is flashing on and off in your brain. But, haven't they *(by these actions)* told you something about *the way they work* that is important information for you to have? And having gained that information, isn't it time for you to reassess *whether you really want to work at a place so guarded, so impenetrable, so 'un-user-friendly'*?

How
To Use Your Contacts To Get That Interview

HOW DO I FIND OUT EXACTLY WHO HAS THE POWER TO HIRE ME?

In a small organization with 50 or less employees, this is a relatively easy problem. Calling the place and asking for the name of the boss, should do it. It's what we call *The One-Minute Research Project.*

But if the place where you are dying to work is a much larger organization, then the answer is: "Through the *research* you already learned how to do in Chapter 6; *and* by asking every *contact* you have."

Let's say the one of the places you are interested in is an organization which we will call *Mythical Corporation.*

You know the kind of job you'd like to get there, but first you know you need to find out the name of **the person-who-has-the-power-to-hire-you** there. What do you do?

If it's a large organization, you go on the Internet or you go to your local public library, and search the directories there. I have listed these on pages 84 and 141. Hopefully that search will yield the name of the person you want.

But if it doesn't, which will particularly be the case with smaller organizations, *then you turn to your contacts.*

Who or What Is "A Contact"?

Since this subject of *contacts* is widely misunderstood by job-hunters and career-changers, let's be very specific, here.

Every person you know, is a contact.

Every member of your family.

Every friend of yours.

Every person in your address book.

Every person on your Christmas-card list.

Every merchant or salesperson you ever deal with.

Every person who comes to your apartment or house to do any kind of repairs or maintenance work.

Every check-out clerk you know.

Every gas station attendant you know.

Every leisure partner you have, as for walking, exercising, swimming, or whatever.

Every doctor, or medical professional you know.

Every professor, teacher, etc., you once knew or maybe still know how to get ahold of.

Every clergyperson, rabbi, or religious leader you know.

Every person in your church, synagogue, mosque, or religious assembly.

Everyone you know in Rotary, Kiwanis, Lions, or other service organizations.

Every person you are newly introduced to.

Every person you meet, stumble across, or blunder into, during your job-hunt, whose name, address, and phone number you have the grace to ask for. (*Always* have the grace to ask for it.)

Got the picture?

So now, to our task. You approach as many people as necessary, among all those you know, and you ask each of them, "Do you know anyone who works, or used to work, at *Mythical Corporation*?"

You ask that question again and again of *everyone* you know, or meet, until you find someone who says, "*Yes, I do.*"

Then you ask them:

- "What is the name of the person you know who works, or used to work, at *Mythical Corporation*? Do you have their phone number and/or address?"
- "Would you be willing to call ahead, to tell them who I am?"
- You then either phone them yourself or make an appointment to go see them ("*I won't need more than 10 minutes of your time.*") Once you are talking to them, after the usual polite chit-chat, you ask them the question you are dying to know. Because they are *inside* the organization that interests you, they are usually able to give you the exact answer to the question that has been puzzling you: "Who would have the power to hire me at *Mythical Corporation*, for this kind of position *(which you then describe)*?" If they answer that they do not know, ask if they know *who* might know. If it turns out that they do know, then you ask them not only for that hiring person's name, address, phone, and e-mail address, but also what they can tell you about that person's job, that person's interests, and their style of interviewing.
- Then, you ask them if they could help you get an appointment with that person. You repeat once again the familiar refrain:
- "Given my background, would you recommend I go see them?"
- "Do you know them, personally? If not, could you give me the name of someone who does?"
- "If you know them personally, may I tell them it was you who recommended that I talk with them?"
- "If you know them personally, would you be willing to call ahead, to tell them who I am, and to help set up an appointment?"

Also, before leaving, you can also ask them about the organization, in general.

Then you thank them, and leave; and you *never never* let the day end, without sitting down to write them a thank-you note. *Always* do it. *Never* forget to.

RESCUING THE EMPLOYER

As you can see, getting in to see someone, even for a hiring-interview, is not all that difficult. Everyone has friends, including this **person-who-has-the-power-to-hire-you**. You are simply approaching them through *their* friends. And you are doing this, not *wimpishly*, as one who is coming to ask a favor. You are doing it *helpfully*, as one who is asking to help rescue them.

Rescue? Yes, rescue! I cannot tell you the number of employers I have known over the years, who can't figure out how to find the right employee. It is absolutely mind-boggling, particularly in those hard times when job-hunters would seem to be gathered on every street corner.

You're having trouble finding the employer. The employer is having trouble finding you. *What a great country!*

So, if you now present yourself directly to **the person-who-has-the-power-to-hire-you**, you are not only answering your own prayers. You are hopefully answering the employer's, as well. You will be *just* what the employer is looking for, but didn't know how to find, if . . .

if you took the trouble to do Chapters 5 and 6, and

if you took the trouble to figure out what are your favorite and best skills, and

if you took the trouble to figure out what are your favorite and best subjects or *languages,* and

if you took the trouble to figure out what places *might* need such skills and such *languages,* and

if you researched this place with the intent of finding out what their tasks, challenges, and problems are, and

if you took the trouble to figure out who there has the power to hire you.

Of course, you don't for sure *know* they need you; that remains for the hiring-interview to uncover. But at least by this thorough preparation you have *increased* the chances that you are at the right place -- whether they have an announced vacancy or not. And, if you are, you are not imposing on this employer. You are coming not as 'job-beggar,' but as 'resource person.' You may well be rescuing him or her, believe me.

MAY-DAY, MAY-DAY!

Whenever a job-hunter writes me and tells me they've run into a brick wall, and just can't find out the name of **the person-who-has-the-power-to-hire-them**, the problem *always* turns out to be: they aren't making *sufficient* use of their contacts. They're making a *pass* at using their contacts, but they aren't putting their whole heart and soul into it.

My favorite (true) story in this regard, concerns a job-hunter I know, in Virginia. He decided he wanted to work for a particular health-care organization in that State, and not knowing any better, he approached them by visiting their Human Resources Department. After dutifully filling out a job application, and talking to someone there in that department, he was told there were no jobs available. Stop. Period. End of story.

Approximately three months later he learned about this technique of approaching your favorite organization by using contacts. He explored his contacts *diligently,* and succeeded in getting an interview with the person-who-had-the-power-to-hire-him for the position he was interested in. The two of them hit it off, immediately. The appointment went swimmingly. "You're hired," said the person-who-had-the-power-to-hire-him. "I'll call Human Resources and tell them you're hired, and that you'll be down to fill out the necessary stuff."

Our job-hunter never once mentioned that he had previously approached that same organization through that same Human Resources Department, and been turned down cold.

Just remember: contacts are the key. It takes about eighty pairs of eyes, and ears, to help find the career, the workplace, the job that you are looking for.

Your contacts *are* those eyes and ears.

They are what will help you get the ideal job you are looking for, and they are key to finding out the name of the person-who-has-the-power-to-hire-you.

The more people you know, the more people you meet, the more people you talk to, the more people you enlist as part of your own personal job-hunting network, the better your job-finding success is likely to be.

Some job-hunters cultivate new contacts wherever they go, during their time of unemployment. For example, if they go to hear a speaker on some subject that interests them, they make it a point to join the crowd that gathers 'round the speaker at the end of the talk, and -- with notepad poised -- ask such questions as: "Is there anything special that people with my expertise can do?" And here they mention their *generalized* job-title: computer scientist, health professional, chemist, writer, or whatever. Very useful information has thus been turned up. You can also go up to the speaker afterwards, and ask if you can contact him or her for further information -- "and at what address?"

Conventions, likewise, afford rich opportunities to make contacts. Says one college graduate: "I snuck into the Cable Advertisers Convention at the Waldorf in N.Y.C. That's how I got my job."

Another way people have cultivated contacts, is to leave a message on their telephone answering machine which tells

everyone who calls, what information they are looking for. One job-hunter used the following message: "This is the recently laid off John Smith. I'm not home right now because I'm out looking for a good job as a computer trouble-shooter in the telecommunications field; if you have any leads or just want to leave a message, please leave it after the tone."

You may also cultivate contacts by studying the *things* that you like to work with, and then writing to the manufacturer of that *thing* to ask them for a list of organizations in your geographical area which use that *thing*. For example, if you like to work on a particular machine, you would write to the manufacturer of that machine, and ask for names of organizations in your geographical area which use that machine. Or if you like to work in a particular environment, think of the supplies used in that environment. For example, let's say you love darkrooms. You think of what brand equipment or supplies is usually used in darkrooms, and then you contact the sales manager of the company that makes those supplies, to ask where his (or her) customers are. Some sales managers will not be at all responsive to such an inquiry; but others graciously will, and thus you may gain some very helpful leads.

Because your memory is going to be overloaded during your job-hunt or career-change, it is useful to set up a filing system, where you put the name of each contact of yours on a 3×5 card, with addresses, phone numbers, and anything about where they work or who they know that may be of use at a later date. Go back over those cards frequently.

That does add up to *a lot* of file cards, just because you've got *a lot* of contacts. But that's the whole point.

You may need *every one* of them, *when push comes to shove.*

GETTING IN

If the contact you talked to, doesn't know **the person-who-has-the-power-to-hire-you** well enough to get you an interview, then you go back to your other contacts -- now armed with the name of the person you are trying to get in to see -- and pose a new question. Approaching as many of your contacts as necessary, you ask each of them, "Do you know Ms. or Mr. See, at *Mythical Corporation* or do you know someone who does?"

You ask that question again and again of *everyone* who is on your file cards, until you find someone who says, "*Yes, I do.*"

Then of course, over the phone or -- better -- in person, you ask them the same familiar questions, carefully, and in this exact order:

- "What can you tell me about him -- or her?"
- "Given the kind of job I am looking for *(which you here describe)*, do you think it would be worth my while to go see them?"
- "Do you have their phone number and/or address?"
- "May I tell them it was you who recommended that I talk with them?"
- "Would you be willing to call ahead, to set up an appointment for me, and tell them who I am?"

When you've gotten an appointment, in this fashion, *that* is the time of course that you will begin to sweat. *"The hiring-interview! I'm actually there."*

THE TEN GREATEST MISTAKES MADE IN JOB INTERVIEWS

Whereby Your Chances of Finding a Job Are Greatly Decreased

I. Going after large organizations only (such as the Fortune 500).

II. Hunting all by yourself for places to visit, using ads and resumes.

III. Doing no homework on an organization before going there.

IV. Allowing the Personnel Department (or Human Resources) to interview you--*their primary function is to screen you OUT.*

V. Setting no time limit when you make the appointment with an organization.

VI. Letting your resume be used as the agenda for the job interview.

VII. Talking primarily about yourself, and what benefit the job will be for you.

VIII. When answering a question of theirs, talking anywhere from 2 to 15 minutes, at a time.

IX. Basically approaching them as if you were a job-beggar, hoping they will offer you a job, however humble.

X. Not sending a thank-you note right after the interview.

THE TEN COMMANDMENTS FOR JOB INTERVIEWS

Whereby Your Chances of Finding a Job Are Vastly Increased

I. Go after small organizations, with twenty or less employees, since they create 2/3 of all new jobs.

II. Hunt for interviews using the aid of friends and acquaintances, because a job-hunt requires fifty eyes and ears.

III. Do thorough homework on an organization before going there, using Informational Interviews plus the library.

IV. At any organization, identify who has the power to hire you there, for the position you want, and use your friends and acquaintances' contacts, to get in to see that person.

V. Ask for just 20 minutes of their time, when asking for the appointment; and keep to your word.

VI. Go to the interview with your own agenda, your own questions and curiosities about whether or not this job fits you.

VII. Talk about yourself only if what you say offers some benefit to that organization, and their 'problems.'

VIII. When answering a question of theirs, talk only between 20 seconds and 2 minutes, at any one time.

IX. Basically approach them as if you were a resource person, able to produce better work for that organization than any predecessor.

X. Always write a thank-you note the same evening of the interview, and mail it at the latest by the next morning.

How
To Conduct An Interview

Yes, you're there. But do not be afraid as you go to meet the person-who-has-the-power-to-hire-you. There are several comforting thoughts you may cling to.

FIRST COMFORTING THOUGHT: IN A HIRING-INTERVIEW, YOU'RE STILL DOING RESEARCH

Your natural question, as you approach any job-interview, tends to be, "How do I convince this employer to hire me?" Wrong question. It implies that you have already made up your mind that this would be a grand place to work at, and a grand person to work for, so that all that remains is for you to sell yourself. This is rarely the case. In most cases, despite your best attempts to research the place thoroughly, you don't know enough about it yet, to say that. You have *got* to use the hiring-interview as a chance to gather further information about this organization, and this boss.

If you understand *this* about an interview, you will be ahead of 98% of all other job-hunters -- who all too often go to the hiring-interview as a lamb goes to the slaughter, or as a criminal goes on trial before a judge.

You *are* on trial, of course, in the employer's eyes.

But, so is that employer and that organization, in *your* eyes.

This is what makes the job interview tolerable or even enjoyable: you are studying everything about this employer, at the same time that they are studying everything about you.

Two people, both sizing each other up. You know what that reminds you of. Dating, of course. Well, the job interview is every bit like 'the dating game.' Both of you have to like each other, before you can even discuss the question of *'going steady,'* i.e., a job. So, you're sitting there, sizing each other up. *Great!*

The importance of your doing your own weighing of this person, this organization, and this job, *during* the hiring-interview, cannot be overstated. The tradition in the U.S., and throughout the world for that matter, is to find a job, take it, and *then* try to figure out in the next three months, after you're in it, whether it is a good job or not -- quitting if you decide it isn't.

You are going against that stupid tradition, as any sensible job-hunter or career-changer should, by using the hiring-interview to screen the organization *before you go to work there* -- saving yourself grief, guilt, and lost time.

For thus, in effect, *quitting before you're offered the job,* rather than *quitting after you've taken the job,* the employer will thank you, your Mother will thank you, your spouse or partner will thank you, and of course you yourself will thank you.

"I'm hoping to find something in a meaningful, humanist, outreach kind of bag, with flexible hours, non-sexist bosses, and fabulous fringes."

SECOND COMFORTING THOUGHT: HIRING-INTERVIEWS ARE NOT A SCIENCE

As you go to the interview, do remember that the person-who-has-the-power-to-hire-you is sweating too. Why? Because, the hiring-interview is not a very reliable way to choose an employee. In a survey conducted among a dozen top United Kingdom employers,[4] it was discovered that the chances of an employer finding a good employee through the hiring interview was only ***3% better*** than if they had picked a name out of a hat. In a further ironic finding, it was discovered that if the interview were conducted by someone who would be working directly with the candidate, the success rate dropped to ***2% below*** that of picking a name out of a hat. And if the interview were conducted by a so-called personnel expert, the success rate dropped to ***10% below*** that of picking a name out of a hat.

No, I don't know how they came up with these figures. But they are totally consistent with what I know of the world of hiring. I have watched so-called personnel or human resources experts make *wretchedly* bad choices about hiring in their own office, and when they would morosely confess this to me some months later, over lunch, I would tease them with, "If you don't even know how to hire well, yourselves, how do you keep a straight face when you're called in as consultant by another organization?" And they would ruefully reply, "We treat it *as though it were* a science."

Well, let me tell you, dear reader, the hiring-interview is *not* a science. It is a very very hazy art, and done badly by most of its employer-practitioners, in spite of their good heart, their very best intentions, and their carloads of goodwill.

---

4. Reported in the *Financial Times Career Guide 1989* in the United Kingdom.

THIRD COMFORTING THOUGHT: OFTENTIMES THE EMPLOYER IS AS SCARED AS YOU ARE

So, you are sitting there with sweaty palms, but you have been probably assuming that the person-who-has-the-power-to-hire-you will be sitting there *enjoying* this whole masochistic process. That is sometimes, but rarely, true.

No, no, you do not have one individual *(you)* sitting there, scared to death, in the hiring-interview.

You have two individuals *(you* and *the employer)* sitting there, scared to death. It's just that the employer has learned to *hide* his or her fears better than you have, because they've had more practice.

But he or she is, after all, a human being just like you are. He or she may *never* have been hired to do *this. This* just got thrown in with all their other duties. And they may *know* they're not very good at it.

It will help give you confidence if you mentally catalog ahead of time *not your fears, but the employer's.* They include:

A. That you won't be able to do the job: that you lack the necessary skills or experience, and the hiring-interview didn't uncover this.

B. That if hired, you won't put in a full working day, regularly.

C. That if hired, you'll be frequently "out sick," or otherwise absent whole days.

D. That if hired, you'll only stay around for a few weeks or at most a few months, and then quit without advance warning.

E. That it will take you too long to master the job, and thus it will be too long before you're profitable to that organization.

F. That you won't get along with the other workers there, or that you will develop a personality conflict with the boss himself (or herself).

G. That you will do only the minimum that you can get away with, rather than the maximum that they hired you for.

H. That you will always have to be told what to do next, rather than displaying initiative -- always in a responding mode, rather than an initiating mode (and mood).

I. That you will have a work-disrupting character flaw, and turn out to be: dishonest, or totally irresponsible, a spreader of dissension at work, lazy, an embezzler, a gossip, a sexual harasser, a drug-user or substance abuser, a drunk, a liar, incompetent, or -- in a word -- bad news.

J. *(If this is a large organization, and your would-be boss is not the top person)*: that you will bring discredit upon them, and upon their department/section/division, etc., for ever hiring you in the first place -- making them lose face, possibly also costing your would-be boss a raise or promotion.

K. That you will cost a lot of money, if they make a mistake by hiring you. Currently, in the U.S. the cost to an employer of a bad hire can run $50,000 or more, including relocation costs, lost pay for the period for work not done or aborted, and severance pay -- if *they* let you go.

No wonder the employer is sweating.

In the old days, an employer might have gotten useful information to guide them in the hiring decision, from *outside* the hiring-interview, by obtaining references from your previous employers. No more. In the past decade, as job-hunters have started filing lawsuits left and right, alleging 'unlawful discharge,' or 'being deprived of an ability to make a living,' more than half of all *Previous Employers* have adopted the policy of refusing to volunteer *any* information about Past Employees, except name, rank, and serial number -- i.e., the person's job-title and dates of employment.

The interviewer is therefore completely on his own -- or her own -- in trying to figure out, *during this interview, or during a series of interviews* -- whether or not to hire you. The hiring interview these days has become *everything.*

FOURTH COMFORTING THOUGHT: YOU DON'T HAVE TO MEMORIZE A LOT OF ANSWERS

To help them figure out whether or not to hire you, they will be asking you some questions. Books on interviewing, of which there are many, often publish lists of these questions -- or at least some *typical* ones that employers ask, such as:

- Tell me about yourself.
- Why are you applying for this job?
- What do you know about this job or company?
- How would you describe yourself?
- What are your major strengths?
- What is your greatest weakness?
- What type of work do you like to do best?
- What are your interests outside of work?
- What accomplishment gave you the greatest satisfaction?
- What was your worst mistake in previous jobs?
- Why did you leave your last job?
- Why were you fired (if you were)?
- How does your education or experience relate to this job?
- Where do you see yourself five years from now?
- What are your goals in life?
- How much did you make at your last job?

Well, the list goes on and on. It sometimes totals eighty-nine questions, or more.

You are then told that you should prepare for a hiring-interview by writing out, practicing, and memorizing some clever answers to *all* these questions -- answers which some books furnish for you. Well, not the best advice.

Dear friend, your preparation for the hiring-interview does not need to be that complicated.

Beneath the dozens and dozens of possible questions like those above that employers could ask you, there are really only *five basic questions,* that you need to remember.

Five. Just five. And they are:

The person-who-has-the-power-to-hire-you wants to know:

1. **"Why are you here?"** *They mean by this, "Why are you knocking on my door, rather than someone else's door?"*

Then, the person-who-has-the-power-to-hire-you wants to know:

2. **"What can you do for us?"** *They mean by this, "If I were to hire you would you be part of the problems I already have, or would you be a part of the solution to those problems? What are your skills, and how much do you know about some subject or field that is of interest to us?"*

Then, the person-who-has-the-power-to-hire-you wants to know:

3. "What kind of person are you?" *They mean by this, "Do you have the kind of personality that makes it easy for people to work with you, and do you share the values which we have at this place?"*

Then, the person-who-has-the-power-to-hire-you wants to know:

4. "What distinguishes you from nineteen other people who can do the same tasks that you can?" *They mean by this, "Do you have better work habits than the nineteen others, do you show up earlier, stay later, work more thoroughly, work faster, maintain higher standards, go the extra mile, or . . . what?"*

Lastly, the person-who-has-the-power-to-hire-you wants to know:

5. "Can I afford you?" *They mean by this, "If we decide we want you here, how much will it take to get you, and are we willing and able to pay that amount -- governed, as we are, by our budget, and by our inability to pay you as much as the person who would be above you, on the organizational chart?"*

These are the five *main* questions that *bug* employers most. *This is the case, even if the interview begins and ends with these five questions never once being uttered aloud.* They're still floating in the room there, beneath the surface of the conversation, beneath the eighty-nine questions they may ask.

The good news is that since there are really only five basic questions on the employer's mind, and not eighty-nine, there are really only five answers you need to know.

But, you had *better* know those five answers. If you did your homework in Chapters 5 and 6 plus the Workbook on page 7, you will. If you didn't, you won't. Period. End of story.

You, of course, have the right -- nay, the duty -- to be asking yourself the same five questions, in only a slightly different form:

1. What does this job involve?
2. Do my skills truly match this job?
3. Are these the kind of people I would like to work with, or

not? *Do not ignore your intuition if it tells you that you would not be comfortable working with these people!!*

4. If we like each other, and both want to work together, can I persuade them there is something unique about me, that makes me different from nineteen other people who can do the same tasks?

5. Can I persuade them to hire me at the salary I need or want?

You don't, of course, ask these questions in the interview. Rather, you might begin your part of the hiring-interview by reporting to them just exactly how you've been conducting your job-hunt, and what impressed you so much about *their* organization during your research, that you decided to come in and talk to them about a job. Then you can devote your attention, during the remainder of the interview, to exploring the five questions above, in your own way.[5]

If you're not there about a job that already exists, but rather, you want them to *create* a job for you, then your five questions get changed into five *statements,* that you make to this person-who-has-the-power-to-hire-you:

1. What you **like** about this organization.
2. What sorts of **needs** you find intriguing in this field and in this organization (don't ever use the word "*problems,*" as most employers prefer synonyms, such as '*needs*' -- unless you first hear the word '*problems*' coming out of their mouth).
3. What **skills** seem to you to be needed in order to meet such needs.
4. **Evidence** from your past experience that demonstrates you have the very skills in question, and that you perform them in the manner or style you claim.
5. What is **unique** about the way *you* perform those skills. As I have mentioned before, this is something you *must* devote

---

5. Additional questions you may want to ask, to elaborate upon these five:
What significant changes has this company gone through in the last five years?
What values are sacred to this company?
What characterizes the most successful employees this company has?
What future changes do you see in the work here?
Who do you see as your allies, colleagues, or competitors in this business?

some thought to, ahead of time. For example, if you analyze problems, how do you do that? *Painstakingly? Intuitively, in a flash? By consulting with greater authorities in the field?* You see the point. You are trying to put your finger on the 'style' or 'manner' in which you do your work, that is distinctive and hopefully appealing, to this employer.

I have said this before, but I will say it again: every prospective employer wants to know *what makes you different* from nineteen other people who can do the same kind of work as you do. You *have* to know what that is. And then not only talk about it, but actually demonstrate it, by the way you conduct your part of the hiring-interview. *E.g., "I am very thorough in the way I would do the job for you"* = be thorough in the way you have researched the place before you go in for the hiring-interview.

FIFTH COMFORTING THOUGHT: THE EMPLOYER DOESN'T REALLY CARE ABOUT YOUR PAST

In most cases, as I have been emphasizing, the person-who-has-the-power-to-hire-you is *scared.* If you think that is too strong a word, let's settle for *anxious,* or *afraid,* or *worried.* And this worry lies beneath all the questions they may ask.

Their fear, by definition, is about the future. No employer cares about your past. In fact, in the U.S., employers must only ask you questions related to the requirements and expectations of the job. They cannot ask about such things in your past (or present) as your creed, religion, race, age, sexual orientation, or marital status.

Rules aside, you must realize that the only thing any employer should possibly care about is your future . . . with *them.* But the future is difficult to uncover, so they usually try to gauge your future behavior by asking about your past behavior.

Do not be fooled by this absorption with your past. Your whole focus during the time the employer is questioning you should be to sense what fear about the *future* lies beneath each question that the employer asks you concerning your past -- and then answer that fear.

Here are some *examples:*

Employer's Question	The Fear Behind The Question	The Point You Try To Get Across	Phrases You Might Use To Get This Across
"Tell me about yourself"	The employer is afraid he/she isn't going to conduct a very good interview, by failing to ask the right questions. Or is afraid there is something wrong with you, and is hoping you will blurt it out.	You are a good employee, as you have proved in the past at your other jobs. (Give the briefest history of who you are, where born, raised, interests, hobbies, and kind of work you have enjoyed the most to date.) *Keep it to two minutes, max.*	In describing your past work history, use any *honest* phrases you can about your work history, that are self-complimentary: "Hard worker." "Came in early, left late." "Always did more than was expected of me." Etc.
"What kind of work are you looking for?"	The employer is afraid that you are looking for a different job than that which the employer is trying to fill. E.g., he/she wants a secretary, but you want to be an office manager, etc.	You are looking for precisely the kind of work the employer is offering (but don't say that, if it isn't true). Repeat back to the employer, in your own words, what he/she has said about the job, and emphasize the skills you have to do *that.*	If the employer hasn't described the job at all, say, 'I'd be happy to answer that, but first I need to understand exactly what kind of work this job involves." *Then* answer, as at left.
"Have you ever done this kind of work before?"	The employer is afraid you don't possess the necessary skills and experience to do this job.	You have skills that are transferable, from whatever you used to do; and you did it well.	"I pick up stuff very quickly." "I have quickly mastered any job I have ever done."

Employer's Question	The Fear Behind The Question	The Point You Try To Get Across	Phrases You Might Use To Get This Across
"When did you leave your last job?" -- *or* "How did you get along with your former boss and co-workers?"	The employer is afraid you don't get along well with people, especially bosses, and is just waiting for you to 'bad-mouth' your previous boss- or co-workers, as proof of that.	Say whatever positive things you possibly can about your former boss and co-workers (*without telling lies*). Emphasize you usually get along very well with people -- and then let your gracious attitude toward your previous boss(es) and co-workers prove it, right before this employer's very eyes (and ears).	If you left voluntarily: "*My boss and I* both felt I would be happier and more effective in a job where [here describe your strong points, such as] I would have more room to use my initiative and creativity." If you were fired: "Usually, I get along well with everyone, but in this particular case the boss and I just didn't get along with each other. Difficult to say why." *You don't need to say any more than that.* If you were laid off and your job wasn't filled after you left: "My *job* was terminated."
"How is your health?" -- *or* "How much were you absent from work during your last job?"	The employer is afraid you will be absent from work a lot, if they hire you.	You will not be absent. If you have a health problem, you want to emphasize that it is one which will not keep you from being at work, daily. Your productivity, compared to other workers', is excellent.	If you were *not* absent a lot at your last job: "I believe it's an employee's job to show up every work day. Period." If you *were* absent a lot, say why, and stress that it was due to a difficulty that is now *past*.

Employer's Question	The Fear Behind The Question	The Point You Try To Get Across	Phrases You Might Use To Get This Across
"Can you explain why you've been out of work so long?" *-- or* **"Can you tell me why there are these gaps in your work history?"** ***(Usually said after studying your resume.)***	The employer is afraid that you are the kind of person who quits a job the minute he/she doesn't like something at it; in other words, that you have no 'stick-to-it-iveness.'	You love to work, and you regard times when things aren't going well as challenges, which you enjoy learning how to conquer.	"During the gaps in my work record, I was studying/doing volunteer work/doing some hard thinking about my mission in life/finding redirection." (Choose one.)
"Wouldn't this job represent a step down for you?" *-- or* **"I think this job would be way beneath your talents and experience."** *-- or* **"Don't you think you would be underemployed if you took this job?"**	The employer is afraid you could command a bigger salary, somewhere else, and will therefore leave him/her as soon as something better turns up.	You will stick with this job as long as you and the employer agree this is where you should be.	"This job isn't a step down for me. It's a step up -- from welfare." "We have mutual fears: every employer is afraid a good employee will leave too soon, and every employee is afraid the employer might fire him/her, for no good reason." "I like to work, and I give my best to every job I've ever had."
And, lastly: **"Tell me, what is your greatest weakness?"**	The employer is afraid you have some character flaw, and hopes you will now rashly blurt it out, or confess it.	You have limitations just like anyone else but you work constantly to improve yourself and be a more and more effective worker.	Mention a weakness and then stress its positive aspect, e.g., "I don't like to be oversupervised, because I have a great deal of initiative, and I like to anticipate problems before they even arise."

As the interview proceeds, you want to quietly notice (*but not comment on*) the *time-sequence* of the questions the employer is asking. When the interview is turning out favorably for you, the time-sequence of the employer's questions will often move -- *however slowly* -- through the following stages.

1. Distant past: *e.g., "Where did you attend high school?"*

2. Immediate past: *e.g., "Tell me about your most recent job."*

3. Present: *e.g., "What kind of a job are you looking for?"*

4. Immediate future: *e.g., "Would you be able to come back for another interview next week?"*

5. [*Optional:* Distant future: *e.g., "Where would you like to be five years from now?"*]

The more the interviewer's questions move from the past to the future, the more favorably the interview is going for you. On the other hand, if the interviewer's questions stay firmly in the past, the outlook is not so good. *Ah well, y' can't win them all!*

If the time-frame of the interviewer's questions moves firmly into the future, *then* is the time for you to get more specific about the job. Experts suggest you ask these kinds of questions:

What is the job, specifically, that I am being considered for?
If I were hired, what duties would I be performing?
What responsibilities would I have?
What would you be hiring me to accomplish?
Would I be working with a team, or group? To whom would I report?
Whose responsibility is it to see that I get the training I need, here, to get up to speed?
How would I be evaluated, how often, and by whom?
What were the strengths and weaknesses of previous people in this position?
Why did *you* yourself decide to work here?
What do you wish you had known about this company before you started here? What particular characteristics do you think have made you successful in your job here?
May I meet the person I would be working for (if it isn't you)?

Remember, throughout this *weighing of each other*, we're not talking scientific measurement here. As Nathan Azrin has said for many years, *The hiring process is more like choosing a mate, than*

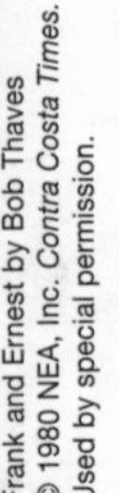

it is like deciding whether or not to buy a new house. This of course is not to be taken literally. To say that hiring is like choosing a mate does not mean that if you get hired, you will literally be marrying the organization or someone in the organization. No, no, no.

'Choosing a mate' here is a metaphor. To elaborate upon the metaphor a little bit, it means that *the mechanisms* by which human nature decides to hire someone, are *similar to* the mechanisms by which human nature decides whether or not to marry someone. Those mechanisms, of course, are impulsive, intuitional, non-rational, and often made on the spur of the moment -- often revolving around some small idiotic *oops,* that only their sister Ann would understand.

SIXTH COMFORTING THOUGHT: INTERVIEWS ARE OFTEN LOST IN THE FIRST TWO MINUTES

To continue our discussion of the metaphor of *choosing a mate and hiring,* think about this: you can have all the skills in the world, have researched this organization to death, have practiced *interviewing* until you are a master at giving 'right answers,' be absolutely the perfect person for this job, and yet lose the hiring-interview because . . . *your breath smells terrible.* Or some other small personal reason. It's akin to your being ready to fight dragons, and then being killed by a mosquito.

"I'll tell you why I want this job. I thrive on challenges. I like being stretched to my full capacity. I like solving problems. Also, my car is about to be repossessed."

It's the reason why interviews are most often lost, when they are lost, *during the first two minutes.*

Let me hold in abeyance, for a moment or two, my strange claim, above, that this is *a comforting thought.* And let us first look at *what* interview-mosquitoes (*as it were*) can fly in, during the first 30 seconds to two minutes of your interview with *the person-who-has-the-power-to-hire-you,* so that they start muttering to themselves, *"I sure hope we have some other candidates besides this person"*:

1. Your appearance and personal habits: interview after interview has revealed that if you are a male, *you are much more likely to get the job if--*

• you have obviously freshly bathed, have your face freshly shaved or your hair and beard freshly trimmed, have clean fingernails; and are using a deodorant;

• you have on freshly laundered clothes, and a suit rather than a sports outfit, pants with a sharp crease, and shoes freshly polished;

• you do not have bad breath, do not dispense gallons of garlic, onion, stale tobacco, or the odor of strong drink, into the enclosed office air; but have brushed and flossed your teeth, plus used a mouthwash if necessary;

• you are not wafting tons of after-shave cologne fifteen feet ahead of you, as you enter the room.

Remember, since the hiring process is more like choosing a mate, than deciding whether or not to buy a new house, the employer is simply trying to determine if they like you. If you 'bomb' in one of these areas just listed, the person-who-has-the-power-to-hire-you may decide they really don't like you, in which case you're not going to get hired there, no matter how qualified you otherwise may be.

If you are a female, interview after interview has revealed that *you are much more likely to get the job if--*

• you have obviously freshly bathed, have not got tons of makeup on your face; have had your hair newly 'permed' or 'coiffed'; have clean or nicely manicured fingernails, that don't stick out ten inches from your fingers; and are using a deodorant;

• you wear a bra, have on freshly cleaned clothes, a suit or sophisticated-looking dress, shoes not sandals, and ones which don't call *a lot* of attention to themselves;

• you do not have bad breath, do not dispense gallons of garlic, onion, stale tobacco, or the odor of strong drink, into the enclosed office air; but have brushed and flossed your teeth, plus used a mouthwash if necessary;

• you are not wafting tons of perfume fifteen feet ahead of you, as you enter the room.

Remember, since the hiring process is more like choosing a mate, than deciding whether or not to buy a new house, the employer is simply trying to determine if they like you. If you 'bomb' in one of these areas just listed, the person-who-has-the-power-to-hire-you may decide they really don't like you, in which case you're not going to get hired there, no matter how qualified you otherwise may be.

2. Nervous mannerisms: *it is a turn-off for employers if--*

• you give a limp handshake, *or*

• you slouch in your chair, or endlessly fidget in your seat, during the interview, *or*

• you continually avoid eye contact with the employer, *or*

• you crack your knuckles, *or* are constantly playing with your hands, or your hair.

Remember, since the hiring process is more like choosing a mate, than deciding whether or not to buy a new house, the employer is simply trying to determine if they like you. If you 'bomb' in one of these areas just listed, the person-who-has-the-power-to-hire-you may decide they really don't like you, in which case you're not going to get hired there, no matter how qualified you otherwise may be.

3. Lack of self-confidence: *it is a turn-off for employers if--*

• you are continuously being extremely self-critical,

• you are downplaying your achievements or abilities,

• you are speaking so softly you cannot be heard, or so loudly you can be heard two rooms away,

• you are giving one-word answers to all the employer's questions,

• you are constantly interrupting the employer,

• or you are giving answers in an extremely hesitant fashion.

Remember, since the hiring process is more like choosing a mate, than deciding whether or not to buy a new house, the employer is simply trying to determine if they like you. If you 'bomb' in one of these areas just listed, the person-who-has-the-power-to-hire-you may decide they really don't like you, in which case you're not going to get hired there, no matter how qualified you otherwise may be.

4. Your considerateness toward other people: *it is a turn-off for employers if--*

• you show a lack of courtesy to the receptionist, secretary, and (at lunch) to the waiter or waitress,

• you display extreme criticalness toward your previous employers and places of work,

• you drink strong stuff (ordering a drink if and when the employer takes you to lunch is always a bad idea, as it raises the question in the employer's mind, *Do they normally stop with one, or do they normally keep on going*? Don't . . . do . . . it!)

• you forget to thank the interviewer as you're leaving, or forget to send a thank-you note afterward. Says one human resources manager: "A prompt, brief, faxed business letter thanking me for my time along with a (brief!) synopsis of his/

her unique qualities communicates to me that this person is an assertive, motivated, customer service-oriented salesperson who utilizes technology and knows the rules of the 'game.' These are qualities I am looking for. At the moment I receive approximately one letter for every fifteen candidates interviewed."

Remember, since the hiring process is more like choosing a mate, than deciding whether or not to buy a new house, the employer is simply trying to determine if they like you. If you 'bomb' in one of these areas just listed, the person-who-has-the-power-to-hire-you may decide they really don't like you, in which case you're not going to get hired there, no matter how qualified you otherwise may be.

- Incidentally, *many* an employer watches to see if you smoke, either in the office or at lunch. *(In a race between two equally qualified people, the nonsmoker will win out over the smoker 94% of the time, according to a study done by a professor of business at Seattle University.) Some experts give the following advice to smokers who are therefore determined to hide the fact that they smoke from the interviewer: "If you are a smoker, do not think it will be easy to hide it. It will take a lot of work, on your part. The more that smoke has been hovering around you and your clothes, the more your clothes, hair, and breath will reek of smoke when you go in for the interview. You are so inured to it, that you will not be able to detect this; but the employer will know it,* instantly, *as you move forward to greet them. Breath mints and perfume/cologne will NOT cover it up; it will take much*

more formidable measures than that. Like what? Like this: don't smoke for at least four hours prior to the interview, bathe completely, including your hair, immediately before leaving for the interview, keep a set of smoke-free interview clothes, underwear, and shoes (at home) in a tight plastic bag in a room far-removed from any place you smoke in the house, and wear those smoke-free clothes to the interview." That's the advice of the You-Can-Hide-It school of thinking. Personally, I think all such deceptions practiced upon the employer are, in the end, self-defeating. So what if you do pull it off? It will *come out that you smoke, after you are hired, and the employer who hates smoking can always manage to get you out of there after you are hired, on one pretext or another, without ever mentioning the word 'smoke.' So, don't try to hide it. Nonetheless,* wait *to reveal it.* Never *smoke during the time you are with the person-who-has-the-power-to-hire-you, unless* they *are smoking like a chimney themselves; -- and so as to prevent yourself from having to run out and take 'a smoke break,' I'd suggest you take chewing gum (or nicotine patches) with you to the interview, as you may be stuck there a long time).* Once a job-offer has been made, *then* I think it is important for you to tell the employer you smoke, and to offer an easy way out: "If this is a truly offensive habit to you, and one you don't want in any of your employees, I'd rather bow out gracefully now, than have it become an issue between us down the road." Such consideration, thoughtfulness, and graciousness on your part may go a long way to soften the employer's resistance to the fact that you are a smoker. Many places, in fact, allow their employees to go outside for a 'smoke break' at stated intervals.

5. Your values: *it is a complete turn-off for most employers, if they see in you --*

- any signs of dishonesty or lying, on your resume or in the interview;
- any signs of irresponsibility or tendency to goof off;
- any sign of arrogance or excessive aggressiveness; any sign of tardiness or failure to keep appointments and commitments on time, including the hiring-interview;
- any sign of not following instructions or obeying rules;
- any sign of constant complaining or blaming things on others;

• any sign of laziness or lack of motivation;

• any sign of a lack of enthusiasm for this organization and what it is trying to do;

• any sign of instability, inappropriate response, and the like.

• the other ways in which you evidence your *values,* such as: what things impress you or don't impress you in the office; what you are willing to sacrifice in order to get this job *and* what you are *not* willing to sacrifice in order to get this job; your enthusiasm for work;

• the carefulness with which you did or didn't research this company before you came in;

and blah, blah, blah.

Remember, since the hiring process is more like choosing a mate, than deciding whether or not to buy a new house, the employer is simply trying to determine if they like you. If you 'bomb' in one of these areas just listed, the person-who-has-the-power-to-hire-you may decide they really don't like you, in which case you're not going to get hired there, no matter how qualified you otherwise may be.

Anyway, these are the *mosquitoes* that can kill you, when you're out to fight dragons, in the hiring-interview.

Now please, dear friend, do not write me, telling me how picayune some of this is. Believe me, I already *know* that. I'm not reporting the world as it *should* be. I'm only reporting what study after study has revealed about the world as it *is.*

You may take this all to heart, or just ignore it. However, if you decide to ignore these points, and then -- despite interview after interview -- you never get hired, you might want to rethink your position on all of this. It may be the mosquitoes, not the dragons, that are killing you.

And you can *fix* these mosquitoes. That's why I said, back at the beginning of *this* section: that the fact the interview can thus be lost in the first two minutes over such picayune things as *these,* is a *comforting* thought. It's comforting, because *all* of these picayune things *are in your control.* Yes, you control *every one* of these factors.

Read them all over again. There isn't a one of them that you don't have the power to determine, or the power to change. You can decide to bathe before going to the interview, you can decide to shine your shoes, you can decide not to smoke, etc., etc. All the little things which could torpedo your interview are within your control, and *you can fix* them, if they are keeping you from getting hired.

I'd say that was a comforting thought, wouldn't you?

HOW
To End The Inteview

Before you let the interview end, there are six questions you should *always* ask:

#1. *"Given my skills and experience, is there work here that you would consider me for?"* This is if you haven't come after a specific job, from the beginning.

#2. *"Can you offer me this job?"* I know this seems stupid, but it is astonishing how many job-hunters have secured a job simply by being bold enough to ask for it, at the end of the interview, either with the words *May I have this job,* or something similar to it, in language they feel comfortable with. I don't know *why* this is so. I only know *that* it is so. Maybe it has something to do with employers not liking to say "No," to someone who directly asks them for something. Anyway, if after hearing all about this job at this place, you decide you'd really like to have it, *ask for it.* The worst thing the employer can say is "No," or "We need some time to think about all the interviews we're conducting."

#3. *"Do you want me to come back for another interview, perhaps with some of your colleagues here?"* If you are a serious candidate, in this employer's mind, for this job, there usually *is* a second round of interviews. And, often, a third, and fourth. You, of course, want to be in that second round. Indeed, many experts say the *only* purpose you should have in the first interview, at a particular place, is to be invited back for a second interview. If you've secured *that,* say they, it has been a successful first interview.

#4. *"When may I expect to hear from you?"* You *never* want to leave control of the ensuing steps in this process in the hands of the employer. You want it in your own hands. If the employer says, *"We need time to think about this,"* or *"We will be calling you for a second interview,"* you don't want to leave this as an undated good intention on the employer's part. You want to nail it down.

#5. *"What would be the latest I can expect to hear from you?"* The employer has probably given you their *best* guess, in answer to your previous question. Now you want to know *what is the worst-case* scenario? One employer, when I asked him the *worst-case* scenario replied, *"Never!"* I thought he had a great sense of humor. Turned out he was dead serious.

#6. *"May I contact you after that date, if for any reason you haven't gotten back to me by that time?"* Some employers resent this question. You'll know that is the case if they snap at you, *"Don't you trust me?"* But most employers appreciate your offering them what is in essence a safety-net. They know they can get busy, become overwhelmed with other things, forget their promise to you. It's reassuring, in such a case, for you to offer to rescue them.

[Optional: #7. *"Can you think of anyone else who* might *be interested in hiring me?"* This question is invoked *only* if they replied *"No,"* to your first question, above.]

Jot down any answers they give you to the questions above, then stand up, thank them sincerely for their time, give a firm handshake, and leave. Write a thank-you note *that night,* to them, and mail it without fail the next morning.

In the following days, rigorously keep to this covenant, and don't contact them except with that mandatory thank-you note, until after the *latest* deadline you two agreed upon, in answer to question #4, above. If you do have to contact them after that date, and if they tell you things are still up in the air, you ask questions #3, #4, and #5, all over again. And so on, and so forth.

Incidentally, it is entirely appropriate for you to insert a thank-you note into the running stream, after *each* interview or telephone contact. That will help them remember you.

How
(And When) To Negotiate Your Salary

Assuming things went favorably in the first interview, and assuming they weren't ready at that time to point-blank offer you the job, you *will* be invited back for another interview, *or interviews* at that place -- either with the person you saw before, and/or with a committee. Eventually, after the second, third, or fourth interview, if *you* like them and *they* increasingly like you, a job offer *will* be made.

Then, and only then, it is time to deal with the question that is inevitably on any employer's mind -- as we saw on page 192 -- *how much is this person going to cost me?* And the question that is on *your* mind: *how much does this job pay?*

It's time for salary negotiation. While whole books can be (and have been) written on this subject, there are basically just five keys for you to keep in mind:

FIRST KEY TO SUCCESSFUL SALARY NEGOTIATION:

THE EMPLOYER WILL RARELY TELL YOU THE MOST THEY ARE WILLING TO PAY

Salary negotiation would never happen if *every* employer in *every* hiring-interview were to mention, right from the start, the top figure they are willing to pay for that position. *Some* employers do. And that's the end of any salary negotiation. But, of course, most of them don't. Hoping they'll be able to get you for less, they start *lower* than they're ultimately willing to go. This creates *a range.* And that range is what salary negotiation is all about.

For example, if the employer wants to hire somebody for no more than $12 an hour, they may start *the bidding* at $8 an hour. In which case, their *range* runs from $8 to $12 an hour. Or if they want to pay no more than $20 an hour, they may start the bidding at $16 an hour. In which case their range runs from $16 to $20 an hour.

So, why do you have to negotiate? Because, if a range *is* thus involved, you have every right to try to negotiate the highest salary possible *within that range.*

The employer's goal, is to save money, if possible. Your goal is to bring home to your family, your partner, or your own household, the best salary that you can, for the work you will be doing. Nothing's wrong with the goals of either of you. But it does mean that, where the employer starts lower, salary negotiation is proper, and expected.

SECOND KEY TO SUCCESSFUL SALARY NEGOTIATION:

NEVER DISCUSS SALARY UNTIL THE END OF THE INTERVIEWING PROCESS, WHEN THEY HAVE DEFINITELY SAID THEY WANT YOU

If the employer raises the salary question earlier, but seems like a kindly man or woman, your best reply might be: "Until you've decided you definitely want me, and I've decided I definitely could help you with your tasks here, I feel any discussion of salary is premature." That will work, in most cases.

But suppose you are face-to-face with an employer, and they *demand* to know what salary you are looking for, within the first two minutes that you're in the room. You try the excellent response you rehearsed, for this very eventuality: "I'll gladly come to that, but could you first help me to understand what this job involves?"

Good response, *in most cases.* But this time it doesn't work. The employer with rising voice says, "Come, come, don't play games with me. I want to know what salary you're looking for." You have a response prepared for *this* eventuality, too. You answer in terms of a *range,* but this employer insists on a single figure. "How much per hour?" they bark.

In today's market, many interviews begin here, and this is increasingly where many interviews end. The employer has no range in mind. The beginning figure is the ending figure. No negotiation is possible.[6]

This happens, when it happens, because many employers are making salary their major criterion for deciding who to hire, and who not to hire, out of -- say -- nineteen possible candidates.

If you run into this situation, and you want that job badly enough, you have no choice but to capitulate. Ask what they are offering, and make your decision. (Of course you may always say, *"I need a little time, to think about this."*)

However, this is the *worst-case scenario.* Things don't always go this way. Not by a long shot. In lots and lots of interviews, these days, salary is still negotiable -- *if you save the discussion to the very end of the interviewing process.*

6. One job-hunter said his interviews *always* began with the salary question, and no matter what he answered, that ended the interview. Turned out, this job-hunter was doing all the interviewing *over the phone.* That was the problem. Once he went *face-to-face,* salary was no longer the first thing discussed in the interview.

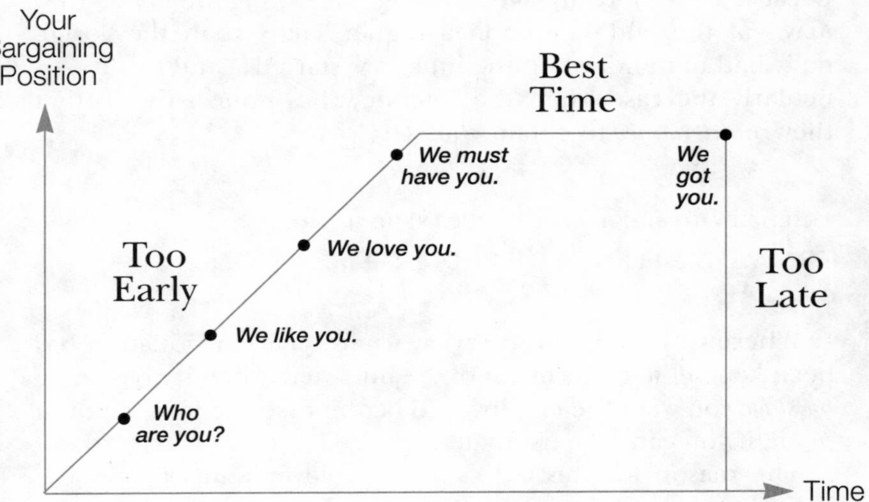

Don't Discuss Salary

Until all of the following conditions have been fulfilled --

- Not until they've gotten to know you, at your best, so they can see how you stand out above the other applicants.
- Not until you've gotten to know them, as completely as you can, so you can tell when they're being firm, or when they're flexible.
- Not until you've found out exactly what the job entails.
- Not until they've had a chance to find out how well you match the job-requirements.
- Not until you're in the final interview at that place, for that job.
- Not until you've decided, "I'd really like to work here."
- Not until they've said, "We want you."
- Not until they've said, "We've got to have you."

-- should you get into salary discussion with this employer.

---

7. Reprinted, by permission of the publisher, from *Ready, Aim, You're Hired,* by Paul Hellman, © 1986 Paul Hellman. Published by AMACOM, a division of American Management Association, New York. All rights reserved.

Why is it to your advantage to delay salary discussion? Because, if you really *shine* during the hiring-interview, they may -- at the end -- mention a higher salary than they originally had in mind, when the interview started -- and this is particularly the case when the interview has gone so well, that they're *determined* to obtain your services.

THIRD KEY TO SUCCESSFUL SALARY NEGOTIATION:

TRY *NEVER* TO BE THE FIRST TO MENTION A SALARY FIGURE

Where you are in an interview where salary negotiation has been kept *off stage* for much of the interview, when it does come *on stage* you want the employer to be the first one to mention *a figure*, if you can manage that.

The reason for this is that the employer wants to pay the least they can, while on the other hand you want them to pay the most they can, *within their range.* So, it's going to be a kind of verbal arm-wrestling. And, never mind the reason why, what has been observed over the years is that in this contest *whoever mentions a salary figure first, generally loses salary negotiation, at the last.*

Inexperienced employer/interviewers don't know this. Experienced ones do; that's why they will *always* toss the ball to you, with some innocent-sounding question, such as: "What kind of salary are you looking for?" *Well, how kind of them to ask me what I want* -- you may be thinking. No, no, no. Kindness has nothing to do with it. They are hoping *you* will be the first to mention a figure, because they know this obscure rule well, that *whoever mentions a salary figure first, generally loses salary negotiation, at the last.*

So of course, you will *always* want to respond, if you can: "Well, you created this position, so you must have some figure in mind, and I'd be interested in knowing what that is."

FOURTH KEY TO SUCCESSFUL SALARY NEGOTIATION:

BEFORE YOU GO TO THE INTERVIEW, DO HOMEWORK ON HOW MUCH YOU NEED.

When you are in an interview process where salary discussion is indeed saved *(as it should be)* to the end, salary negotiation *within their range* is wide open -- *except* for this one horrible scenario: *What if* their *highest figure is so far below* your *lowest figure, that you will starve, if you accept it?* You need $14 an hour, to barely survive, and the highest they are willing to pay is $8 an hour.

You see the problem. You've *got* to know, beforehand, just how much it is you need to make, at a minimum.

You can determine this in one of two ways: a) take a wild guess -- and risk finding out after you take the job that it's simply impossible for you to live on that salary *(the favorite strategy in this country, and most others)*; or, b) make out a detailed outline of your estimated expenses *now*, listing what you need *monthly* in the following categories:[8]

---

8. If this kind of financial figuring is not your cup of tea, find a buddy, friend, relative, family member, or *anyone*, who can help you do this. If you don't know anyone who could do this, go to your local church, synagogue, religious center, social club, gym, or wherever you hang out, and ask the leader or manager there, to help you find someone. If there's a bulletin board, put up a notice on the bulletin board.

Housing
- Rent or mortgage payments . . . . $ __________
- Electricity/gas . . . . $ __________
- Water . . . . $ __________
- Telephone . . . . $ __________
- Garbage removal . . . . $ __________
- Cleaning, maintenance, repairs[9] . . . . $ __________

Food
- What you spend at the supermarket and/or meat market, etc. . . . . $ __________
- Eating out . . . . $ __________

Clothing
- Purchase of new or used clothing . . . . $ __________
- Cleaning, dry cleaning, laundry . . . . $ __________

Automobile/transportation[10]
- Car payments . . . . $ __________
- Gas . . . . $ __________
- Repairs . . . . $ __________
- Public transportation *(bus, train, plane)* . . . . . $ __________

Insurance
- Car . . . . $ __________
- Medical or health-care . . . . $ __________
- House and personal possessions . . . . $ __________
- Life . . . . $ __________

Medical expenses
- Doctors' visits . . . . $ __________
- Prescriptions . . . . $ __________
- Fitness costs . . . . $ __________

---

9. If you have extra household expenses, such as a security system for example, be sure and include the quarterly (or whatever) expenses here, divided by three.

10. Your checkbook stubs will tell you a lot of this stuff. But you may be vague about your cash or credit card expenditures. For example, you may not know how much you spend at the supermarket, or how much you spend on gas, etc. But there is a simple way to find out. Just carry a little notepad and pen around with you for two weeks or more, and jot down *everything* you pay cash *(or use credit cards)* for -- *on the spot, right after you pay it.* At the end of those two weeks, you'll be able to take that notepad and make a realistic guess of what should be put down in these categories that now puzzle you. *(Multiply the two-weeks figure by two, and you'll have the monthly figure.)*

Support for Other Family Members
 Child-care costs *(if you have children)*. . . . . $ ________
 Child-support *(if you're paying that)* . . . . $ ________
 Support for your parents *(if you're helping out)*. $ ________
Charity giving/tithe *(to help others)* . . . . $ ________
School/learning
 Children's costs *(if you have children in school)*. . $ ________
 Your learning costs *(adult education, job-hunting classes, etc.)* . . . . $ ________
Pet care *(if you have pets)* . . . . $ ________
Bills and debts *(usual monthly payments)*
 Credit cards . . . . $ ________
 Local stores . . . . $ ________
 Other obligations you pay off monthly . . . . . . $ ________
Taxes
 Federal[11] *(next April's due, divided by months remaining until then)*. . . . . $ ________
 State *(likewise)* . . . . $ ________
 Local/property *(next amount due, divided by months remaining until then)*. . . . . $ ________
 Tax-help *(if you ever use an accountant, pay a friend to help you with taxes, etc.)*. . . . . . . $ ________
Savings . . . . $ ________
Retirement (Keogh, IRA, SEP, etc.) . . . . $ ________
Amusement/discretionary spending
 Movies, video rentals, etc.. . . . . $ ________
 Other kinds of entertainment . . . . $ ________
 Reading, newspapers, magazines, books . . . . . $ ________
 Gifts *(birthday, Christmas, etc.)* . . . . $ ________

Total Amount You Need Each Month . . . . $ ________

11. Incidentally, looking ahead to next April 15th, be sure and check with your local IRS office or a reputable accountant to find out if you can deduct the expenses of your job-hunt on your Federal (and State) income tax returns. At this writing, some job-hunters can, if -- big IF -- this is not your first job that you're looking for, if you haven't been unemployed too long, and if you aren't making a career-change. Do go find out what the latest "if"s are. If IRS tells you you are eligible, keep careful receipts of everything related to your job-hunt, as you go along: telephone calls, stationery, printing, postage, travel, etc.

Multiply the total amount you need each month by 12, to get the yearly figure. Divide the yearly figure by 2000, and you will be reasonably near the *minimum* hourly wage that you need. Thus, if you need $3333. per month, multiplied by 12 that's $40,000 a year, and then divided by 2,000, that's $20 an hour.

Parenthetically, you may want to prepare two different versions of the above budget: one with the expenses you'd ideally *like* to make, and the other a minimum budget, which will give you what you are looking for, here: the floor, below which you simply cannot afford to go.

FIFTH KEY TO SUCCESSFUL SALARY NEGOTIATION:

BEFORE YOU GO IN, DO RESEARCH ON SALARIES FOR YOUR FIELD AND FOR THAT ORGANIZATION

As I said earlier, salary negotiation is possible *anytime* the employer does not open their discussion of salary by naming the top figure they have in mind, but starts instead with a lower figure.

Okay, so here is our $64,000 question: how do you tell whether the figure the employer first offers you is only their *starting bid*, or is their *final final offer?* The answer is: by doing some research on the field *and* that organization, first.

Oh, come on! I can hear you say. *Isn't this all more trouble than it's worth?* Well, yes, if we were in the chapters on the Impatient Job-Hunter. But this chapter, you recall, is for The Determined Career-Changer or Job-Hunter.

And if you're determined, this is one step you don't want to overlook. Trust me, salary research pays off *handsomely.*

Let's say it takes you from one to three days to run down this sort of information on the three or four organizations that interest you the most. And let us say that because you've done this research, when you finally go in for the hiring-interview you are able to ask for and obtain a salary that is $4,000 a year higher in range, than you would otherwise have gotten. In just the next three years, you will be earning $12,000 extra, because of your salary research. *Not bad pay, for one to three days' work!* And it can be even more. I know *many* job-hunters and career-changers to whom this has happened. Thus you can see that there is a financial penalty exacted from those who are too lazy, or in too much of a hurry, to go gather this information. In plainer language: you don't do this research, it'll cost ya!

Well then, how do you do this research? There's a simple rule: **abandon books, and go talk to people**. Preferably to people who are in the same job *at another company or organization.* Or, go talk to people at the nearby university or college who *train* such people: whatever the department is, where people get trained for this kind of job. These teachers will usually know what their graduates are getting.

Use books, libraries, and the Internet only as a *second,* or *last,* resort. I have listed on page *140* the kind of places on the Internet where you can find salary research. The Internet is particularly helpful in this regard. But talking to people is still your best bet.

Now, exactly how do you go about talking to people, in order to get this information? Let's look at some examples:

First Example: Working at your first entry-level job, say at a fast-food place.

You may not need to do any salary research. They pay what they pay. You can walk in, ask for a job application, and interview with the manager. He or she will usually tell you the pay, outright. It's usually *inflexible.* But at least you'll find it easy to discover what the pay is. (Incidentally, filling out an application, or having an interview there, doesn't commit you to take the job -- but you probably already know that. You can always decline an offer from *any place.* That's what makes this approach harmless.)

> *Second Example:* Working at a place where you can't discover what the pay is, say *at a construction company.*

If that construction company where you would *hope* to get a job is difficult to research, go visit a *different* construction company in the same town -- one that isn't of much interest to you -- and ask what they make *there.* Or, if you don't know who to talk to there, fill out one of their applications, and talk to the hiring person about what kinds of jobs they have (or might have in the future), at which time prospective wages is a legitimate subject of discussion. Then, having done this research on a place you don't care about, go back to the place that *really* interests you, and apply. You still don't know *exactly* what they pay, but you do know what their competitor pays -- which will usually be *close.*

> *Third Example:* Working in a one-person office, say *as a secretary.*

Here you can often find useful salary information by perusing the *Help Wanted* ads in the local paper for a week or two. Most of the ads probably won't mention a salary figure, but a few *may.* Among those that do, note what the lowest salary offering is, and what the highest is, and see if the ad reveals some reasons for the difference. It's interesting how much you can learn about salaries, with this approach. I know, because I was a secretary myself, once upon a time.

Another way to do salary research is to find a *Temporary Work Agency* that places secretaries, and let yourself be farmed out to various offices: the more, the merrier. It's relatively easy to do salary research when you're *inside* the place. (Study what that place pays *the agency,* not what the agency pays you.) If it's an office where the other workers *like* you, you'll be able to ask questions about a lot of things, including salary. It's like *summertime,* where the research is easy.

Before you finish your research, before you go in to that organization for your final interview, you want more than just one figure. You want *a range.* In any organization which has more than five employees, that range is relatively easy to figure out. It will be less than what the person *who would be above you* makes, and more than what the person *who would be below you* makes.

If The Person Who Would Be Below You Makes	*And The Person Who Would Be Above You Makes*	*The Range For Your Job Would Be*
$22,000	$27,000	$23,000 – $26,000
$10,000	$13,500	$10,500 – $12,500
$ 6,240	$ 7,800	$ 6,400 – $7,600

One teensy-tiny little problem: *how* do you find out the salary of those who would be above and below you? Well, first you have to find out their *names* or the names of their *positions.* If it is a small organization you are going after -- one with twenty or less employees -- finding this information out should be *duck soup.* Any employee who works there is likely to know the answer, and you can usually get in touch with one of those employees, or even an ex-employee, through your contacts. Since two-thirds of all new jobs are created by companies of that size, that's the size organization you are likely to be researching, anyway.

If you are going after a larger organization, then you have our familiar life-preserver to fall back on, namely, every contact you have (family, friend, relative, business, or church acquaintance) who might know the company, and therefore, the information you seek. You are looking for Someone Who Knows Someone who either is working, or has worked, at the particular place or places that interest you, who therefore has or can get this information for you.

If you absolutely run into a blank wall on a particular organization (everyone who works there is pledged to secrecy, and they have shipped all their ex-employees to Siberia), then seek out information on their nearest *competitor* in the same geographic area. *For example,* let us say you were researching Bank X, and they were proving to be inscrutable about what they pay their managers. You would then try Bank Y as your research base, to see if the information were easier to come by, there. And if it were, you would then assume the two were similar in their pay scales, and that what you learned about Bank Y was applicable also to Bank X.

Also experts say that in researching salaries, you should take note of the fact that most governmental agencies have civil service positions matching those in private industry, and their job descriptions and pay ranges are available to the public. Go to the nearest City, County, Regional, State, or Federal Civil Service office, find the job description nearest what you are seeking in private industry, and then ask for the starting salary.

When all this research is done, when you are in the actual hiring-interview, and the employer mentions the figure *they* have in mind, you are then ready to respond: "I understand of course the constraints under which all organizations are operating in the '90s, but I believe my productivity is such that it would *justify* a salary in the range of . . . " -- *and here you mention a figure near the top of* their *range.*

It will help a lot if during this discussion, you are prepared to show in what ways you will *make money* or in what ways you will *save money* for that organization, such as will justify the higher salary you are seeking. Hopefully, this will succeed in getting you the salary you want.[12]

During your salary negotiation, do not forget to pay attention to so-called fringe benefits. 'Fringes' such as life insurance, health benefits or health plans, vacation or holiday plans, and retirement programs typically add another 28% to many workers' salaries. That is to say, if an employee receives $800 salary per month, the fringe benefits are worth another $200 per month.

If your job is at a higher level, benefits may include but not be limited to: health, life, dental, disability, malpractice insurance; insurance for dependents; sick leave; vacation; personal leave/personal days; educational leave; educational cost reimbursement for coursework related to the job; maternity and or parental leave; health leave to care for dependents; bonus system or profit sharing; stock options; expense accounts for entertaining clients; dues to professional associations; travel reimbursement; fee sharing arrangements for clients that the employee generates; organizational memberships; parking; automobile allowance; relocation costs; sabbaticals; professional conference costs; time for community service; flextime work schedules; fitness center memberships.

You should therefore remember to ask what benefits are offered, and negotiate if necessary for the raises you want. Thinking this out ahead of time, of course, makes your negotiating easier, by far. You can prepare the ground during your salary negotiation, by saying: *"If I accomplish this job to your satisfaction, as I fully expect to -- and more -- when could I expect to be in line for a raise?"*

---

12. Daniel Porot, in Europe, suggests that if you and an employer really hit it off, and you're *dying* to work there, but they cannot afford the salary you need, consider offering them part of your time. If you need, and believe you deserve, say $25,000, but they can only afford $15,000, you might consider offering them three days a week of your time for that $15,000 (15/25 = 3/5). This leaves you free to take other work those other two days.

Once all salary negotiation is concluded to your satisfaction, do remember to ask to have it summed up in a letter of agreement -- or employment contract -- that they give to you. It may be you cannot get it in writing, but do try! The Road to Hell is paved with oral promises that went unwritten, and -- later -- unfulfilled.

Many executives unfortunately 'forget' what they told you during the hiring-interview, or even deny they ever said such a thing.

Also, many executives leave the company for another position and place, and their successor or the top boss may disown any *unwritten* promises: *"I don't know what caused them to say that to you, but they clearly exceeded their authority, and of course we can't be held to that."*

Plan to keep track of your accomplishments at this new job, on a weekly basis -- jotting them down, every weekend, in your own private diary. Career experts, such as Bernard Haldane, recommend you do this without fail. You can then summarize these accomplishments annually on a one-page sheet, for your boss's eyes, when raise or promotion is a legitimate subject for you to bring up.[13]

13. In any good-sized organization, you will often be amazed at how little attention your superiors pay to your noteworthy accomplishments, and how little they are aware at the end of the year that you really are *entitled* to a raise. Noteworthy your accomplishments may be, but no one is taking notes . . . unless *you* do.

What
To Do, When Employers Never Invite You Back

WHEN IT'S NOT YOUR FAULT

I hear regularly from job-hunters who report that they pay attention to all the matters I have mentioned in this chapter, and are quite successful at getting interviews -- but they still don't get hired. And they want to know what they're doing wrong. Well, unfortunately, the answer *sometimes* is: "Maybe nothing."

I don't know *how often* this happens, but I know it does happen -- because more than one employer has confessed it to me, and in fact at one point in my life it actually happened to *moi*: namely, *some* employers play games, whereby they invite you in for an interview despite the fact that they have already hired someone for the position in question!

You are cheered, of course, by the ease with which you get these interviews. But unbeknownst to you, the manager who is interviewing you (we'll say it's a *he*) has a personal friend he already agreed to give the job to. Of course, one small problem remains: the State or the Federal government gives funds to this organization, and has mandated that this position be opened to all. So this manager must comply. He therefore pretends to choose ten candidates, including his favorite, and pretends to interview them all as though the job opening were wide open and available. But, he intended, from the beginning, to reject the first nine and choose his favorite, and since you were selected for the honor of being among those nine, you automatically get rejected -- even if you are a much better candidate. This tenth person is, after all, his *friend.* The manager then claims that he followed the mandated hiring procedures to the letter.

If you are one of the nine, you will of course be baffled as to *why* you got turned down. Trouble is, you won't know if it was because you met an employer who was playing this game, or not. You're just depressed.

WHEN IT IS YOUR FAULT

There is always the chance that no games are being played, by the employer: but you are getting rejected, at place after place, because there is something really wrong with the way you are coming across, during these hiring-interviews.

Employers will rarely ever tell you this. You will never hear them say something like, "You're too cocky and arrogant during the interview." You will almost always be left completely in the dark as to what it is you're doing wrong.

One way around this deadly silence, is to ask for *generalized* feedback, from whoever was the *friendliest* employer that you saw a while back. If your interviews, time and again, are leading nowhere, you can always try phoning them, reminding them of who you are, and then asking the following question -- deliberately kept generalized, vague, unrelated just to *that* place, and above all, *future-directed: "You know, I've been on several interviews at several different places now, where I've gotten turned down. From what you've seen, is there something about me in an interview, that is causing me not to get hired at those places? If so, I'd really appreciate your giving me some pointers so I can do better in my future hiring-interviews."*

Most of the time they'll *still* duck saying anything hurtful or helpful. First of all, they're afraid of lawsuits. Secondly, they don't know how you will use what they might have to say. (Said an old veteran to me once, "I used to think it was my duty to hit everyone with the truth. Now I only give it to those who can use it.")

But *occasionally* you will run into an employer who is willing to risk giving you the truth, because they think you know how to use it. In the absence of any such help from employers who interviewed you, you might want to get a good business friend of yours to role-play a mock hiring-interview with you, in case they see something glaringly wrong with how you're 'coming across.'

If, from either friend or employer-on-the-phone, you do get feedback, thank them from the bottom of your heart -- no matter how painful their feedback is. Such advice, seriously heeded, can bring about just the changes in your interviewing strategy that you most need, in order to win the interview.

When all else fails, I would recommend you go to a career counselor that charges by the hour, and put yourself in their tender knowledgeable hands.

Never
Put All Your Eggs In One Basket

In conclusion, I would like to say this: I have studied successful and unsuccessful job-hunters for over a quarter of a century, now, and the single greatest thing I have ever learned is that the secret of *successful* job-hunters is *that they always have alternatives.* Alternative ways of describing what they want to do. Alternative ways of going about the job-hunt (not just resumes, agencies, and ads). Alternative *job prospects.* Alternative 'target' organizations that they go after. Alternative ways of approaching employers. And so on, and so forth.

Be sure you have more than just one employer that you are pursuing. That organization, that office, that group, that church, that factory, that government agency, that volunteer organization may be *the ideal place* where you would like to work. But no matter how appetizing this *first choice* looks to you, no matter how much it makes your mouth water at the thought of working there, *you are committing job-hunting suicide* if you don't have some alternative places in mind. Sure, maybe you'll get that dream-come-true. But -- *big question* -- what are your plans if you don't? You've *got* to have other plans **now** -- not when that first target runs out of gas, three months from now. You must go after more than one organization. I recommend five, at least.

Target Small Organizations

Were I myself looking for a job tomorrow, this is what I would do. After I had figured out, as in the previous chapters, what my ideal job looked like, and after I had collected a list of those workplaces that have such jobs, in my chosen geographical area, I would then circle the names and addresses of those which are *small* organizations (personally I would restrict my *first draft* to those with 25 or less employees) -- and then go after them, in the manner I have described in this chapter. However, since small organizations can sometimes be static or dying, I would look particularly for small organizations that are ***established*** or ***growing***. And if '*organizations with 25 or less employees*' eventually didn't turn up enough *leads* for me, only then would I broaden my search to '*organizations with 50 or less employees*,' and finally -- if that turned up nothing -- to '*organizations with 100 or less employees*.' But I would *start* small. Very small.

Remember, job-hunting always involves luck, to some degree. But with a little bit of luck, and a lot of hard work, plus determination, these instructions about how to get hired, should work for you, even as they have worked for so many hundreds of thousands before you.

Take heart from those who have gone before you, such as this determined job-hunter, who just wrote me this heartfelt letter, with which I close:

"Before I read this book, I was depressed and lost in the futile job-hunt using Want Ads Only. I did not receive even one phone call from any ad I answered, over a total of 4 months. I felt that I was the most useless person on earth. I am female, with a 2½ year old daughter, former professor in China, with no working experience at all in the U.S. We came here seven months ago because my husband had a job offer here.

"Then, on June 11th of this year (1996), I saw your book in a local bookstore. Subsequently, I spent 3 weeks, 10 hours a day except Sunday, reading every single word of your book and doing all of the flower

petals in the Quick Job-Hunting Map. After getting to know myself much better, I felt I was ready to try the job-hunt again. I used Parachute throughout as my guide, from the very beginning to the very end, namely, salary negotiation.

"In just two weeks I secured (you guessed it) two job offers, one of which I am taking, as it is an excellent job, with very good pay. It is (you guessed it again) a small company, with 20 or so employees. It is also a career-change: I was a professor of English; now I am to be a controller!

"I am so glad I believed your advice: there are jobs out there, and there are two types of employers out there, and truly there are!

"I hope you will be happy to hear my story."

Other Resources

Additional materials by Richard N. Bolles to help you with your job-hunt:

JOB-HUNTING ON THE INTERNET
The inaugural book in our new Parachute Library, this stand-alone extract from *Parachute* is frequently updated with the latest and hottest Internet addresses and Websites for job-hunters of all types.

HOW TO CREATE A PICTURE OF YOUR IDEAL JOB OR NEXT CAREER
This 8½ by 11 inches workbook is designed to lead the reader through a series of detailed exercises, almost identical to The Workbook here in *Parachute.*

THE ANATOMY OF A JOB
This full size (24 by 36 inches) poster serves as a worksheet to supplement *How to Create a Picture of Your Ideal Job or Next Career* (described above). The "Skills Keys" are on one side, the "Flower" on the other.

HOW TO FIND YOUR MISSION IN LIFE
This is a gift-book version of the current Epilogue from *Parachute.* Judging by the mail the author receives, this is a favorite of readers who want their work to fulfill a purpose and bring more than simply money to their lives.

THE MISSION POSTER
This colorful 24-by-36-inch-poster summarizes the main ideas in *How to Find Your Mission in Life.*

JOB-HUNTING TIPS FOR THE SO-CALLED "HANDICAPPED" OR PEOPLE WHO HAVE DISABILITIES
Originally published as an appendix in *Parachute,* this popular resource is now available only as a separate booklet. In this work, Bolles uses his unique perspective on job-hunting and career-changes to address the special experiences of the disabled.

WHAT COLOR IS YOUR PARACHUTE? Audiotapes
Read by the author, this series of audiotapes supplements the book with additional material, including an introduction and overview of the job-hunting process, and a helpful question-and-answer session.

For more information, or to order, call the publisher at the number below. We accept VISA, Mastercard, and American Express. You may also wish to write for our free catalog of over 500 books, posters, and audiotapes.

Update for 1999

TO: PARACHUTE
P.O. Box 379
Walnut Creek, CA 94597

I think that the information in the '98 edition needs to be changed, in your next revision, regarding (or, the following resource should be added):

____

____

____

____

____

____

I cannot find the following resource, listed on page _______:

____

____

____

____

____

____

Name ____

Address ____

Please make a copy.

Submit this so as to reach us by February 1, 1998. Thank you.

What Color Is Your Parachute?

Helping People Find Jobs & New Careers, Shaping People's Lives

> "We always wish we could give this book more than a 'Magna Cum Laude' award but, fortunately, it just received what must be the ultimate compliment, The Library of Congress recently placed it on the list of '25 Books That Have Shaped Readers' Lives' along with *The Bible, Treasure Island*, and *Gone With the Wind*."
>
> —*Career Opportunity News*, Jan-Feb, 1997

Letters from various readers:

"Eighteen years ago, when I was between 'real' jobs and waiting tables to pay the bills, I picked up a copy of What Color Is Your Parachute? *I never imagined it would become a friend for life. The book is really about life planning. I highly recommend it to everyone, even if they like their job and plan to stay in it for the rest of their career. We should never stop learning."*

"I am an American, living in Japan, and I find the *Parachute* book *so* uplifting and inspiring. My husband is Japanese—and to him your book is a true gift, inspired by God. I hope to see a Japanese version sometime . . . this country needs it."

"Although incarcerated (or maybe because *I am incarcerated), I have greatly enjoyed* What Color Is Your Parachute? *This is a superb motivational book, not just for job searches and career changes, but for life in general. It has made quite a difference in how I see my present situation and my future potential. Thank you for authoring such a great book!"*

"My father applied the key points of *What Color Is Your Parachute?* to his career in the early '70s, and he is currently CEO and chairman of a successful business. What worked for him, he was positive would work for me. I warded off my father's urgings to delve into the book . . . However, at the age of 27, turns of events led me to quit my job and travel around the world. Finding myself in the depth of despair in my career, I begrudgingly picked up the book . . . ironically in, of all places, Peru. What completely bowled me over was your exercise with the stories. I was able to concentrate on what I most enjoyed, not what I achieved, an important difference . . . I returned home, and within 2 and a half months, I found myself in San Francisco, a new city, with a job as production manager and assistant editor of a television documentary. I'm forever fortunate . . ."

Richard Bolles, known the world over as the author of *What Color Is Your Parachute?*, is acknowledged as "America's top career expert" (*Modern Maturity* magazine), "the one responsible for the renaissance of the career counseling profession in the U.S. over the past decade" (*Money* magazine), and "the most widely read and influential leader in the whole career-planning field" (*U.S. Law Placement Assn.*) He is listed in *Who's Who in America*, and *Who's Who in the World*. He has been featured in countless magazines (including *Reader's Digest, Fortune, Money*, and *Business Week*), newspapers, radio, and TV (CNN, Ted Koppel, ABC's *Nightline*, Diane Sawyer, *CBS News*, and many others.)

Richard Bolles

1998 Parachute Workbook

and Resource Guide

Ten Speed Press

YOU'VE BEEN A DOG ALL YOUR LIFE, HAVEN'T YOU?
© 1989 United Feature Syndicate, Inc.

I'VE OFTEN WONDERED WHAT MADE YOU DECIDE TO BECOME A DOG..
8-16

I WAS FOOLED BY THE JOB DESCRIPTION
SCHULZ

1998
Edition

The Parachute Workbook & Resource Guide

by
Richard Nelson Bolles

Ten Speed Press

PUBLISHER'S NOTE

This publication is designed to provide accurate and authoritative information in regard to the subject matter covered. It is sold with the understanding that the publisher is not engaged in rendering professional career services. If expert assistance is required, the service of the appropriate professional should be sought.

Photograph of parachutist on book divider © Bernard Parker. Used with permission.

The drawings on pages 8 and 9 are by Steven M. Johnson, author of *What The World Needs Now.*

Library of Congress Catalog Card Information on file with the publisher.
ISBN 0-89815-931-8, paper
ISBN 0-89815-932-6, cloth

Published by Ten Speed Press, P.O. Box 7123, Berkeley, California 94707

Typesetting by Star Type, Berkeley
Printed in the United States of America

3 4 5 6 7 8 9

Parachute Workbook and Resource Guide

Contents

I. The Parachute Workbook

The Quick Job-Hunting Map

for

Determined

Job-Hunters & Career-Changers

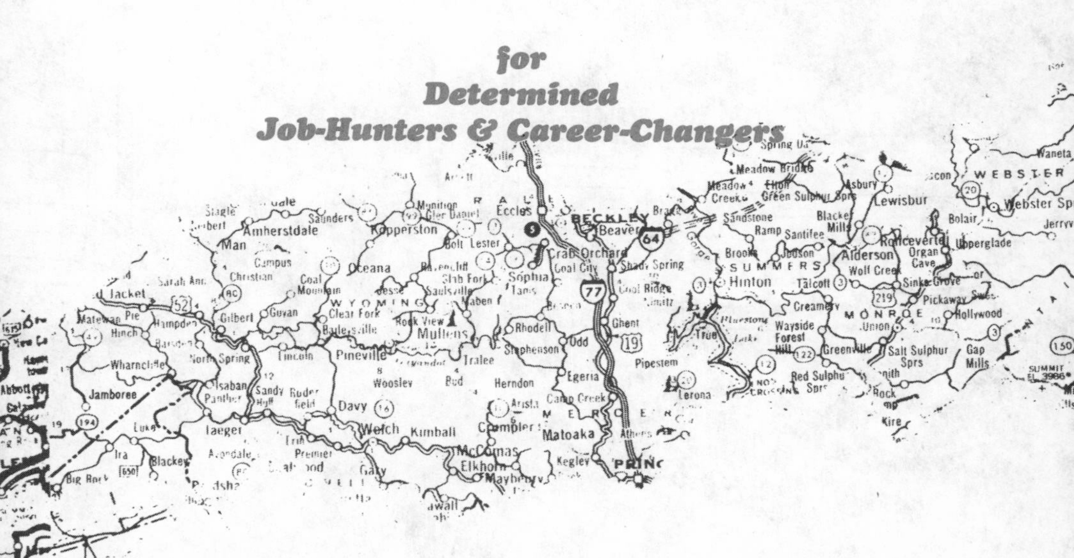

THE MANY PATHS YOU CAN TAKE
STAYING AT YOUR PRESENT ORGANIZATION
SAME CAREER BUT IN A NEW PLACE
DOING TEMP WORK
CONTINUING IN YOUR PRESENT CAREER
STARTING A NEW CAREER
YOUR NEXT STEP
STAYING WHERE YOU LIVE NOW
OR MOVING TO A NEW PLACE

PART-TIME WORK
FULL-TIME WORK
A COMPOSITE CAREER (2, 3 OR MORE PART-TIME CAREERS)
ONE CAREER
WORKING FOR SOMEONE ELSE
WORKING FOR YOURSELF
WORKING AT HOME
DOING VOLUNTARY WORK OR AN INTERNSHIP
GOING BACK TO SCHOOL FOR LEGITIMATE RETRAINING
STEVEN M. JOHNSON

The Quick Job-Hunting Map

INTRODUCTION

A job-hunt, done well, is a process. A process which has three steps. Those steps are: WHAT, WHERE, and HOW. When you need to change careers, this three-step process will often save you from having to go back to school. If you're out of work, this three-step process, done thoroughly, usually *works* when all other job-hunting efforts have failed. Do not be discouraged, therefore, if you have tried to find a job *without* doing the hard work that this three-step process requires, and failed. You can still succeed. WHAT, WHERE, and HOW is the key.

What

What are your favorite transferable skills, that you most enjoy using? And, in what fields would you most like to use these skills?

1. *Before* you go job-hunting, or changing careers, you must figure out what **you want to do**. Our natural tendency is to answer this in terms of a job title. Like: "I want to be an accountant." Try to avoid such an easy, premature answer. Instead, ask yourself what **are your favorite transferable skills, that you most enjoy using?**

   Skills are the key. Skills are your gifts, talents that you were born knowing how to do. Like: "persuading people." They are transferable, which means that you can use them in any field you choose, at any job you choose. You want to identify your *favorite* skills. The clue is often to be found in what skills you are using, when you most lose track of time.

What also includes the question: **where -- specifically, in which field -- would you most like to use your favorite skills?** The clue is often to be found in what fields you most love to read about, talk about, or master.

Where

Where would you most like to live and work?

2. *Before* you go job-hunting, or changing careers, you must also figure out where **you want to work.** It is obvious that *where* includes "city or place." But it also includes "the kind of organization, large or small," where you'd most like to work; and what that organization produces, etc., etc.

How

How do you find those jobs or careers that allow you to use your favorite transferable skills in your favorite field, in your favorite city or place?

3. *Before* you go job hunting, or changing careers, you must have a plan for figuring out **how to find the kind of job that you most want to do.** Newspaper ads, employment agencies, and resumes *may* work for you. But more often than not, they don't. So you *must* have a "Plan B." A careful, systematic, step-by-step "Plan B." The key to such a plan is to enlist people you know, to help you find the information you want: such as the names of fields, the names of organizations, and actual job-leads, plus introductions to the people who have the power to hire, there. There are **always** jobs out there, but whether you can find them or not depends on what methods of job-hunting you are using to locate them.

WHAT, WHERE, HOW. That is the process, whether you're job-hunting or changing careers. It's simple, and it needn't take very long to do -- at least, for the first part. (You can usually do the WHAT and the WHERE in one good weekend, if it's solely dedicated to this task -- *no radio, no TV, and your meals are slipped under your door.)*

A Picture is Worth A Thousand Words

It is useful to put all this information, as it unfolds, on a diagram. The diagram which has worked the best, for millions of job-hunters over the years, is a Flower Diagram. It is an interesting and accurate metaphor, because we are like a flower; that is to say, in the world of work there are certain environments in which we blossom, and other environments in which we wither away. Hence, throughout this workbook, you will be filling out your own Flower Diagram, on pages 74–75.

Optional Exercise: To help you become familiar with this diagram, many have found it useful to begin by quickly filling out a *copy* of this diagram, wherein you describe your present, or most recent, job. Just jot down those things which occur to you off the top of your head -- it is not even necessary to fill out all the lines on each petal. A completed analysis of your present job might look something like this:

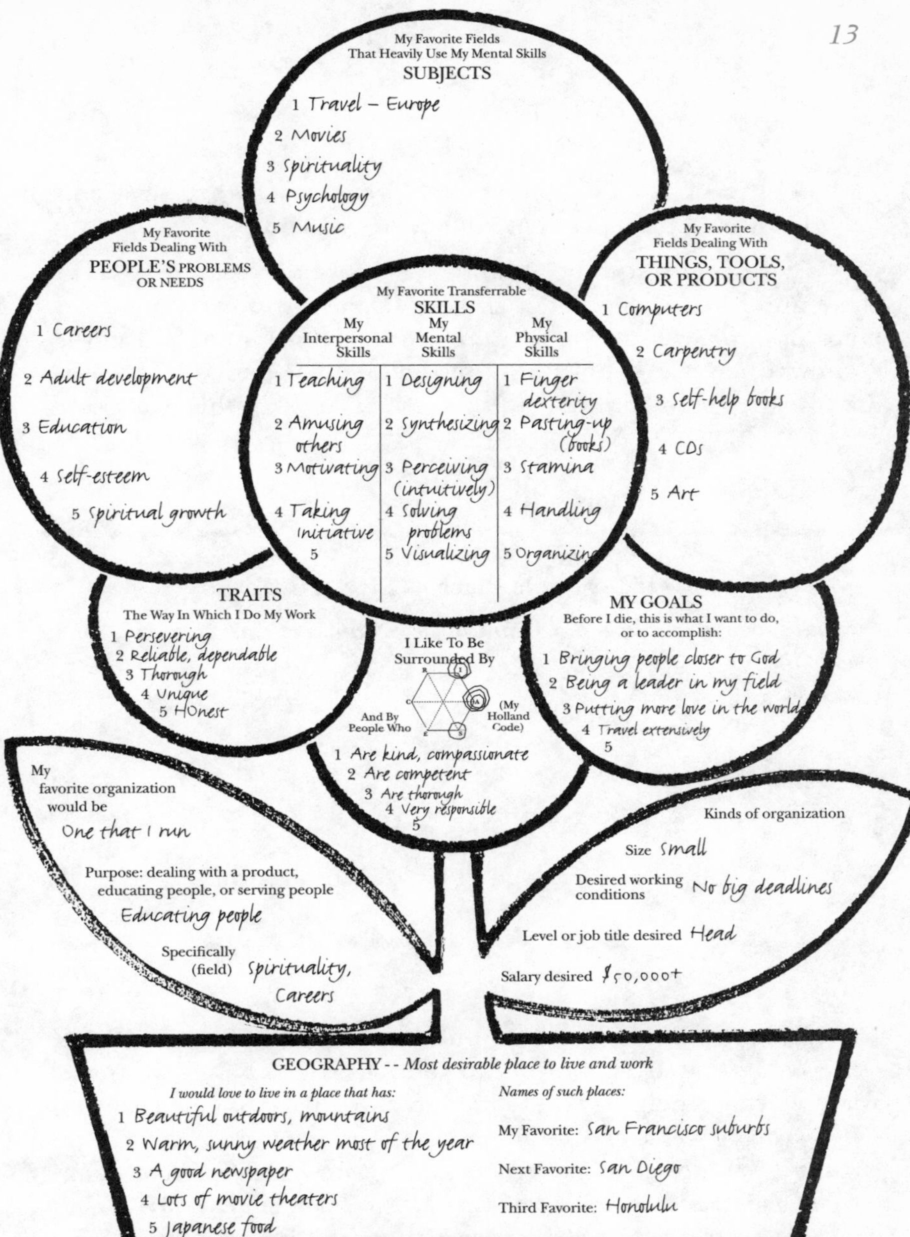

The remainder of The Quick Job-Hunting Map is devoted to filling out this Flower Diagram, step-by-step, through What, Where, and How. We begin, not with the What, but with the Where -- because this is often where we naturally start.

Where **Where would you most like to live and work? In what place, in what kind of organization?**

Where begins with geography. Where would you most like to live and work, if you had a choice? (Even if you *love* where you are now, or even if you're *stuck* where you are now, you never know when an opportunity may suddenly open up for you, down the road. You want to be ready. *Don't* skip this exercise!)

Geography

Most Desirable Place to Live and Work

I would love to live in a place that has:	*Names of such places:*
1.	My Favorite:
2.	
3.	Next Favorite:
4.	
5.	Third Favorite:

It is important to know not only the names of places, but also the *factors* that are important to you. On pages 16 and 17 there is a chart, for helping you to identify those factors. *(You may copy it onto a larger piece of paper if you wish, before you begin working on it. And, if you are doing this exercise with a partner, make a copy of the chart, for them also, before you start filling it out, so that each of you may have a 'clean' copy of your own.)* Then, this is how you use that chart. There are five easy steps:

1. List all the places you have ever lived. *These go in Column 1.*

2. Then, considering each place by itself, list the factors you *disliked* and still dislike about that place. *All of these negative factors go in Column 2.*

3. Then take each of those negative factors and translate the negatives into positives. This will not *necessarily* be the opposite. For example, "rains all the time" does not necessarily translate into "sunny all the time." It might be more like: "sunny at least 200 days a year." It's your call. *All these positive factors go in Column 3. Feel free to add at the bottom of the column here, any positive factors you remember straightaway about the places in Column 1.*

4. Now, rank your positive factors list (Column 3) in their order of importance, to you. They will be things like: "has cultural opportunities," "skiing in the winter," "good newspaper," etc. *List your top 10 positive factors, in exact order, in Column 4.* **If you are baffled as to how to prioritize these factors in exact order, use the Prioritizing Grid in Appendix B**, on page 71. The question to ask yourself, there, as you confront each 'pair' is: "If I could live in a place that had this first 'factor,' but not the second; or if I could live in another place that had the second 'factor,' but not the first, which place would I choose to live in?"

5. When you are done, show this list of ten prioritized, positive factors to *everyone* you know, and ask them what cities, towns, or places they know of that have all or most of these factors, *beginning with the top ones.* From all the names your friends suggest to you, choose the three that look most intriguing to you, in order of your personal preference, based on what you now know. *This goes in Column 5. These are the places you will want to find out more about, until you are sure which is your absolute first preference, second, and third.*

Voila! You are done with Geography. You now have the ground, out of which your Flower may grow.

N.B. If you are doing this with a partner, you will not use Column 5. Instead, copy *their* Column 4 into your Column 6. Then alternately combine *their* first five factors and *your* first five factors, so that you wind up with a list of ten altogether. (First you list their top one, then your top one, then their second preference, then your second preference, etc.) *This goes in Column 7.* It is *this* list of ten positive factors which you both then show to *everyone* you know, to ask them what cities, towns, or places they know of that have all or most of these factors, *beginning with the top ones.* From all the names those friends suggest to you, you then choose the three places that look the most intriguing to both of you, and rank them in order. *This goes in Column 8.*

Now, go back to the Geography diagram on page 75, and copy Column 4 (or 7) on to it, under *I Would Love to Live in a Place That Has;* and Column 5 (or 8) on to it, under *Names of Such Places.*

My Geographical Preferences

Decision Making for Just You

Column 1 Names of Places I Have Lived	*Column 2* From the Past: Negatives	*Column 3* Translating the Negatives into Positives	*Column 4* Ranking of My Positives
	Factors I Disliked and still Dislike about That Place		1.
			2.
			3.
			4.
			5.
			6.
			7.
			8.
			9.
			10.
			11.
		Factors I Liked and Still Like about That Place	12.
			13.
			14.
			15.

Column 5 Places Which Fit These Criteria

Our Geographical Preferences

Decision Making for You and A Partner

Column 6 Ranking of His/Her Preferences	*Column 7* Combining Our Two Lists (Column 4 & 6)	*Column 8* Places Which Fit These Criteria
a.	a.	
	1.	
b.	b.	
	2.	
c.	c.	
	3.	
d.	d.	
	4.	
e.	e.	
	5.	
f.	f.	
	6.	
g.	g.	
	7.	
h.	h.	
	8.	
i.	i.	
	9.	
j.	j.	
	10.	
k.	k.	
	11.	
l.	l.	
	12.	
m.	m.	
	13.	
n.	n.	
	14.	
o.	o.	
	15.	

The next part of the WHERE question is "The Organization Where You Would Most Like To Work." This begins with the right-hand leaf of your Flower Diagram, which contains five questions or issues:

Here are the questions or issues, in more detail:

Kind of Organization

What kind of organization do you think you would most like to work for? Here are the sort of choices you may choose between *(check one, in each of the three families of choices that follow)*:

Its Location:

- ❑ A place in the city
- ❑ A place in the suburbs
- ❑ A place in the country
- ❑ An organization that sends you outdoors to work

Its Office Politics and Problems:

- ❑ A new organization
- ❑ A place that is growing and expanding
- ❑ An old organization
- ❑ An organization with lots of problems
- ❑ A place that is downsizing and reducing its size
- ❑ I don't care

Its Nature:

- ❑ A profit-making firm
- ❑ A nonprofit organization
- ❑ A service organization
- ❑ My own business
- ❑ The government
- ❑ The military
- ❑ A religious organization

Enter your three answers on the Leaf of your Flower, where it says: KINDS OF ORGANIZATIONS. *(You may first wish to copy the Leaf on to a larger piece of paper so that there is more room to write.)*

Size

What size organization do you think you would most like to work for, in terms of "number of employees"? Here, again, are the sort of choices you face:

- ❑ A large corporation
- ❑ A place with 100 or less employees
- ❑ A place with 20 or less employees
- ❑ A place with 5 or less employees
- ❑ Two employees (yourself and the boss, or your own business with an assistant),

Or what? Maybe you don't know for sure, at this point, but make a guess anyway. *Don't say: "It doesn't matter." Believe me, it does.* Enter your answer on the Leaf of your Flower, where it says: SIZE.

Working Conditions

What are your favorite working conditions -- those conditions under which you do, or would do, your most effective work? The best way to approach this is by starting with the things you *disliked* about all your previous jobs, using the following chart to list these. The chart, as you can see, has three columns, and you fill them out in the same order, and manner, that you filled out the previous geography chart. You may copy this chart onto a larger piece of paper if you wish, before you begin filling it out. *Column A may begin with such factors as: "too noisy," "too much supervision," "no windows in my workplace," "having to be at work by 6 a.m.," etc.*

DISTASTEFUL WORKING CONDITIONS

	Column A — Distasteful Working Conditions	Column B — Distasteful Working Conditions Ranked	Column C + The Keys to My Effectiveness At Work
Places I Have Worked Thus Far In My Life	*I Have Learned From the Past that My Effectiveness at Work is Decreased When I Have To Work Under These Conditions:*	*Among the Factors or Qualities Listed in Column A, These Are The Ones I Dislike Absolutely The Most (in order of Decreasing Dislike):*	*The Opposite of These Qualities, in order* *"I Believe My Effectiveness Would Be At An Absolute Maximum, If I Could Work Under These Conditions:"*

Of course, when you get to Column B, you must rank these factors that are in Column A, in their exact order of importance, to you. **If you are baffled as to how to prioritize these factors in exact order, use the Prioritizing Grid in Appendix B**, on pages *71*. The question to ask yourself, there, as you confront each 'pair' is: "If I were offered two jobs, and in the first job I would be rid of this first distasteful working condition, but not the second; while in the second job, I would be rid of the second distasteful working condition, but not the first, which distasteful working condition would I choose to get rid of?"

Note that when you later come to Column C, the factors will be already prioritized. Your only job, there, is to think of the "positive" form of that factor that you hated so much (in Column B). (It is not always "the exact opposite." For example, *too much supervision* (listed in Column B) does not always mean *no supervision* (in Column C). It *might* mean: *a moderate amount of supervision, once or twice a day.*

Once you've finished Column C, enter the top five factors from there, on to the Leaf of your Flower, on page *19*, where it says DESIRED WORKING CONDITIONS.

Level

What level would you like to work at, in the organization? Level is a matter of how much responsibility you want, in an organization:

- ❑ Boss or CEO (this may mean you'll have to form your own business)
- ❑ Manager or someone under the boss who carries out orders, but also gives them
- ❑ The head of a team
- ❑ A member of a team of equals
- ❑ One who works in tandem with one other partner
- ❑ One who works alone, either as an employee or as a consultant to an organization, or as a one-person business.

Enter your answer on the Leaf of your Flower, on page *19*, where it says LEVEL OR JOB-TITLE DESIRED. *Keep in mind that this is something you may wish to alter or change, after you do more exercises in this workbook.*

Salary and Rewards

What salary would you like to be aiming at? Here you have to think in terms of minimum or maximum. ***Minimum*** is what you would need to make, if you were just barely 'getting by.' And you need to know this *before* you go in for a job interview with anyone *(or before you form your own business, and need to know how much profit you must make, just to survive).* To compute your basic survival budget, if you don't already have one, you can use the worksheets on pages 214 and 215 in the main volume of this book, to help.

Maximum could be any astronomical figure you can think of, but it is more useful here to put down the salary you realistically think you could make, with your present competency and experience, were you working for a real, *but generous,* boss. (If this maximum figure is still depressingly low, then put down the salary you would like to be making five years from now.)

Enter your two answers on the Leaf of your Flower, on page 19, where it says SALARY DESIRED.

Optional Exercise: You may wish to put down other rewards, besides money, that you would hope for, from your next job or career. These might be:

❑ Adventure ❑ Challenge ❑ Respect ❑ Influence
❑ Popularity ❑ Fame ❑ Power ❑ A chance to be creative
❑ Intellectual stimulation from the other workers there
❑ A chance to exercise leadership
❑ A chance to make decisions
❑ A chance to use my expertise
❑ A chance to help others
❑ A chance to bring others closer to God
❑ Other:

If you do check off things on this list, arrange your answers in order of importance to you, and then add them on the Leaf, just below *Salary.*

Well now, you are done with *this* Leaf. ***Just remember, as we go on to the other Leaf, that all the answers you wrote here should be regarded as preliminary and tentative. You are free to come back and modify, or completely change, them any time that you wish.***

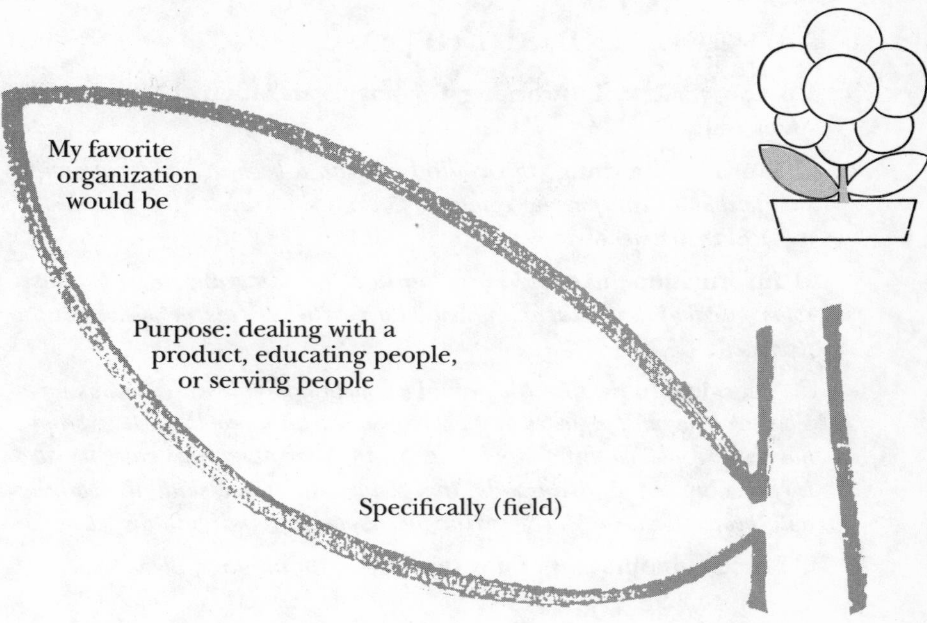

The next part of the WHERE question takes us to Part II of the questions about "The Organization Where You Would Most Like To Work." These are on the left-hand leaf of your Flower Diagram:

A word of warning: for many, it is difficult to fill out this petal at this stage of the game. You may not have a clue, as to how to answer these questions -- at this point. That's fine. We put these questions *here* so that -- even if you can't answer them -- you'll have a clearer understanding of what you need to get out of the rest of the Flower Diagram. This Leaf, put here now, is intended to pique your curiosity, perhaps even motivate you to finish the rest of the Flower. Then, come back here. At that point, filling out this petal will be 'a piece of cake.'

And so, to the questions:

Organizational Purpose

Do you want to be working for an organization that primarily turns out:

❑ **A product, a thing** *(this could be: a car, a book, a gadget, organizers, telephone equipment, computers, clothes, airline tickets, concerts, musical instrument, etc.)*

❑ **Information** *(this could be: statistics, text, diagrams, reports, classroom curricula, magazine or newspaper articles, Internet newsgroups, flyers, etc.)*

❑ **A service, to people** *(this could be: helping people with various problems, waiting on people, caring for people, teaching people, feeding people, housing people, clothing people, etc. Strangely enough, this category also includes flowers and animals; they require the same skills as working with people: viz., patience, nurturing, responding individually, etc.)*

❑ **Some combination of any two above** *(or all three, above).*

Okay, those are the options. Now, you have two choices here: answering this question now, or answering this question later.

Answering This Now: Upon reading these categories you may instantly know the answer. You *know* you want to work with your hands (hence, things), or with your mind (hence, information), or with people (hence, . . . well . . . people). Or, with more than one of these. If so, enter your *tentative* answer(s) on the petal, in the appropriate place. I recommend using a pencil here, for the time being.

Answering This Later: It may be you *don't* know the answer *at this point.* That's normal. You're not expected to, at this stage of the game. In which case, wait until you've finished all the flower petals, and then come back to this Leaf. You'll know the answer by then. Be patient with yourself in the meantime, and don't try to force an answer out of your undecided brain, prematurely.

General Field

In what field do you want to be working? You can only answer this if you know *which* product, or *what kinds* of information, or *which* service to people you want to be involved with. *For example, if you want to work with* cars, *that's the automobile field. If you want to do* newsgroups, *that's the computer field. If you want to* help feed people, *that's the human services field, or the agricultural field.*

You have the same two choices here, as before: answering this question now, or answering this question later.

Answering This Now: It may be there is some field you have always been *dying* to work in, and you know its name right this minute. Fine, jot it down -- *in pencil.* You may want to come back later and change it.

Answering This Later: Probably, most likely, you don't have enough information yet to know which field you want to work in; that's why you're going to be filling out the petals on the Flower. After you've done all the exercises, and filled in the petals, you'll be able to see what fields appeal the most to you. So, for now, leave this part of the Leaf blank. Come back to it later.

"The Petals"

Where are we now? Well, you have established *the ground* of your Flower, plus *the stem and leaves.* We move up now to the Flower itself, and more particularly to the petal that sits *just where the stem joins the Flower.* (It deals with Your Preferred People Environments at work.)

Its petal sits in that particular spot, because *People Environments* is a transitional question between WHERE and WHAT. That is, partly it describes the organization where you want to work; but partly it also describes your skills and what you enjoy doing. Thus, it helps *determine* both WHERE you work, as well as WHAT you do there.

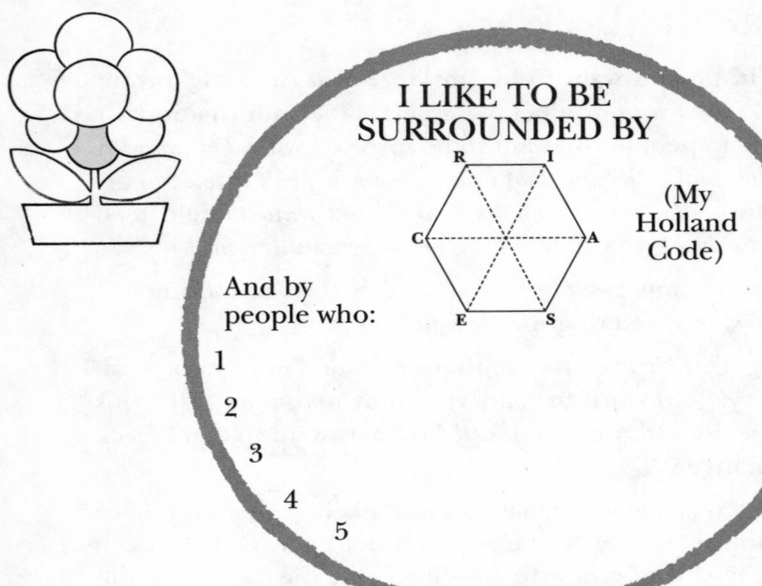

People Environment

In almost every job, including your *ideal* job, you are surrounded by people. Therefore, before you take *any* job, you need to think out an answer to the question: "*What kinds* of people do I most like to be surrounded by?"

I invented (many years ago) a quick and easy way for you to get at this. I call it "The Party Exercise." It is based on the research of John Holland, *Professor Emeritus at Johns Hopkins University*, who found that all people divide into basically six categories or *families*: Realistic, Investigative, Artistic, Social, Enterprising, or Conventional. Here is how the exercise goes (do it!):

On the next page is an aerial view of a room in which a two-day (!) party is taking place. At this party, people with the same or similar interests have (for some reason) all gathered in the same corner of the room.

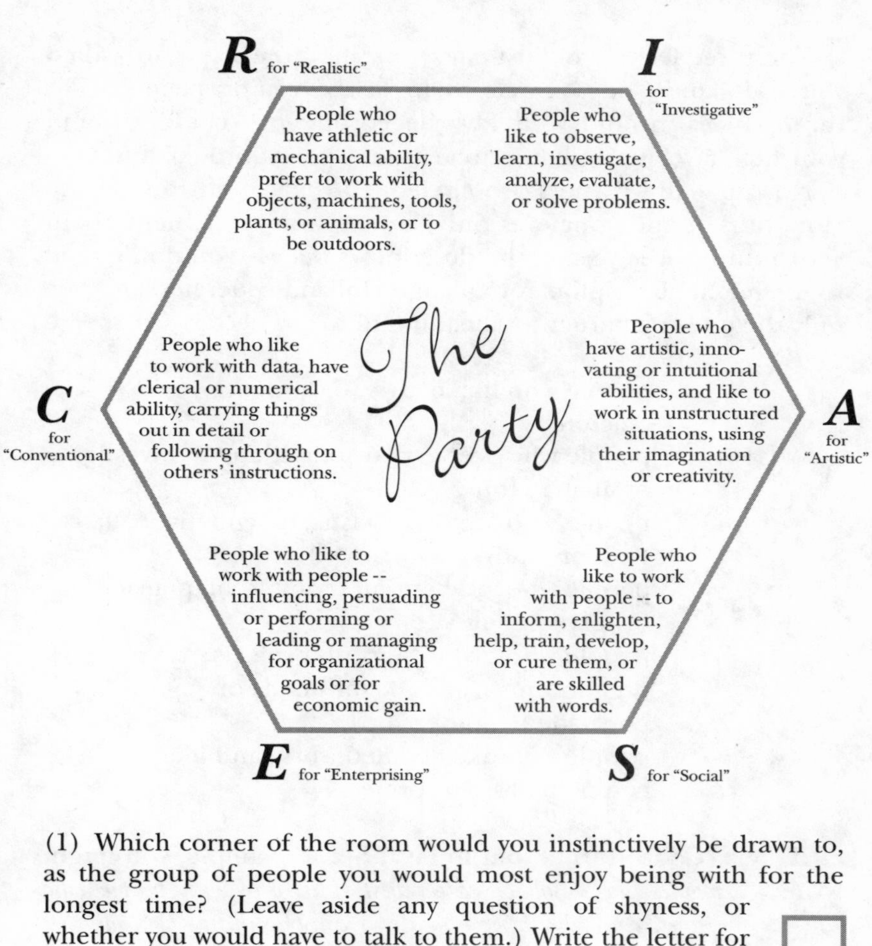

(1) Which corner of the room would you instinctively be drawn to, as the group of people you would most enjoy being with for the longest time? (Leave aside any question of shyness, or whether you would have to talk to them.) Write the letter for that corner here: ☐

(2) After fifteen minutes, everyone in the corner you have chosen leaves for another party crosstown, except you. Of the groups that still remain now, which corner or group would you be drawn to the most, as the people you would most enjoy being with for the longest time? Write the letter for that corner here: ☐

(3) After fifteen minutes, this group too leaves for another party, except you. Of the corners, and groups, which remain now, which one would you most enjoy being with for the longest time? Write the letter for that corner here: ☐

The three letters you just chose, in the three steps, are called your "Holland Code." Circle them *on the petal* on page 26. Put three circles around your favorite corner; two circles around your next favorite; and one circle around your third favorite.

Now that the corners are circled, you may wish to write up (for yourself and your eyes only) a temporary statement about your future career, using the descriptors below (you don't need to use *all* the descriptors for any one Holland code, here; choose only the ones that are most meaningful to you):[1]

R = people who like nature, or athletics, or tools & machinery

I = people who are very curious, liking to investigate or analyze things

A = people who are very artistic, imaginative and innovative

S = people who are bent on trying to help, teach, or serve people

E = people who like to start up projects or organizations, and/or influence or persuade people

C = people who like detailed work, and like to complete tasks or projects

If your "Code" turned out to be IAS, for example, you might write: *"I would like a job or career best if it were with people who are very curious, and like to investigate or analyze things (I); who are also very innovative (A); and who are bent on trying to help or serve people (S)."*

There is one further use you might put this information to. What I call "The Mirror Theory" holds that we often see *ourselves*

1. There is, incidentally, a relationship between the people you like to be surrounded by *and* your skills *and* your values. See John Holland's book, *Making Vocational Choices.* You can procure it by writing to Psychological Assessment Resources, Inc., Box 998, Odessa, FL 33556. Phone: 1-800-331-8478. *The book is $19.95 at this writing.* They also have John Holland's instrument, called *The Self-Directed Search* (or SDS, for short). It takes about an hour to take, and gives a more accurate reading of your "Code" than the Party Exercise can. Ask for a "Specimen Set" of the SDS. *Its price varies, but at this writing it costs $15.*

best by looking into the faces of others. Hence, once we have described the people we would most like to be surrounded by, and their skills, in many cases we have thereby described ourselves, and *our* favorite skills. So, look over the skills you have just described *in others,* and see how much of this is also true of *you.* Are these, perchance, *your* favorite skills, tasks, work, also? Or not?

Before leaving this petal on People Environments, there are a few other things you may wish to say about the people you would like to work for, and be surrounded by. Most of our data for such a list tends to come from memories of past working experiences. We all have such memories (they're not *complaints;* we call them "*learnings*"), *and* we tend to store such learnings in their negative form (*"I never again want to work for a person who . . ."*)

So, the key here is to dredge up those negative learnings, from the past, in all their glory; and then turn them into *positives* directed toward the future. The following exercise, which is a twin to the earlier exercise on "Distasteful Working Conditions," should help you do that.

PEOPLE I HAVE DISLIKED WORKING WITH (OR FOR)

	Column A −	Column B. −	Column C +
Places I Have Worked Thus Far In My Life	I Have Learned From the Past that My Effectiveness is Decreased When I Have To Work With (or For) People Who:	Among the Factors or Qualities Listed in Column A, These Are The Ones I Dislike The Most (in order of Dislike):	The Opposite of These Qualities, and therefore The Kinds of People I Would Like to Work With, (or For)

Using the Prioritizing Grid, prioritize the factors in Column C, and then copy the top 5 on to the petal on page *26*. Enter them right below the Holland hexagon, where it reads "And by people who:"

And now you are done, for the time being, with your first attempts to answer the WHERE questions. We move fully now into the WHAT

What What would you most like to do there? What are your favorite skills, that you most delight using?

The WHAT questions break down into two major subjects: **transferable skills**, and **fields**.

The precise questions are: What are your **favorite** transferable skills? And, what are the fields **you are most drawn to**? The answers to these two questions are found by filling out the next four petals of the Flower diagram -- three for fields, and one for transferable skills.

Both **transferable skills**, and **fields** divide (somewhat artificially) into three main categories.

Your favorite transferable **skills,** which may be thought of as your *energies* that go forth from you to act upon the world, divide into:

1. *Your Physical Skills:* the transferable skills you enjoy, **using primarily** *your hands or body* -- with things, or nature;
2. *Your Interpersonal Skills:* the transferable skills you enjoy, **involving primarily** *personal relationships* -- as you serve or help people or animals, and their needs or problems;[1]
3. *Your Mental Skills:* the transferable skills you enjoy, **using primarily** *your mind* -- with subjects, data/information, or ideas.

Fields may be thought of as the *stuff* that your skills (or energies) act upon; they also divide into three groups, *roughly* corresponding with the three kinds of skills:

1 (Physical) Those fields which deal primarily with **things**, or nature;

2. (Interpersonal) Those fields which deal primarily with **people** or animals, their needs or problems;
3. (Mental) Those fields which deal primarily with **subjects** not covered in 1 or 2 (above).

---

1. For the curious, "animals" are placed in this category with "people," because **the skills** required to deal with animals are more like those used with people, than like those used with "things."

Transferable Skills, and Fields; here's how it all fits together:[2]

The One "You," Artificially-Looked-At In Terms of Your "Three-ness"

Your Skills	What These Skills Act Upon	Examples	Typical "Holland Codes"
Physical Skills	Things	animals plant / trees machinery tools products	R, A, C
Mental Skills	Subjects	Spanish Music Computer-Science	I, A, C
Interpersonal Skills	Needs or Problems of People	people who are starving; people with: marriage problems, or loneliness, or certain handicaps, or AIDS.	S, E, A

We turn, now, to the appropriate petals. We begin with the three **Fields** petals, because we have discovered that if you begin instead with your **Transferable Skills**, you then tend to look *only* at those fields which correspond to your *favorite* transferable skills. Therefore, it is best to begin with Fields *before* you identify your favorite Transferable Skills. That way, you stay "wide" and get to weigh *all* the possibilities. Which you want to do. For, as the old *cardplayers' saying* has it, "Never choose a card, from less than a full deck."

2. Adapted from the work of Sidney Fine, author of *Benchmark Tasks for Job Analysis*, 1995. Used with permission.

Your Favorite Fields:

1. Fields That Use Your Mental Skills

Before you begin looking at Fields, you must fight against the natural tendency to think that a Field will automatically determine what job you will do. It does not.

Think of a Field of Knowledge as, literally, *a field* -- a meadow, a *large* meadow. Lots of people are standing in that meadow, or Field, no matter what Field it is. And they have many different skills, do many different things, have many different job titles.

Let us take the Field called "Movies" as our example. Suppose you love Movies, and want to choose this Field for your next job or career. Your first instinct will be to think that this automatically means you have to be either *an actor or actress, or a screen writer, or a director, or a movie critic.* Not so. There are many other people standing out in that Field, helping to produce Movies. Just look at the closing credits at the end of any movie, and you will see: *Researchers (especially for movies set in another time), Travel experts (to scout locations), Interior designers (to design sets), Carpenters (to build them), Painters (for backdrops, etc.), Artists, Computer graphics designers (for special effects), Costume designers, Make-up artists, Hair stylists, Photographers (camera operators), Lighting technicians, Sound mixers and sound editors, Composers (for soundtrack), Conductors, Musicians, Singers, Stunt people, Animal trainers, Caterers, Drivers, First aid people, Personal assistants, Secretaries, Publicists, Accountants, etc., etc.* My, there are a lot of people standing in that Field -- some of whom are *outstanding* in their Field!

And so it is with any Field. No matter what your skills are, they *can* be used in *any* meadow or Field that you may choose as your favorite.

For some people, incidentally, this particular Fields petal yields *the least* helpful information about future Fields. Reason? Subjects often *don't* point to jobs. Example? Liberal Arts. But, might as well inventory everything we've learned so far, *just in case* (using the exercise called **The Subjects Chart**). *Then* you can go on to the other Fields petals: using the exercise called **The People List**, and then the exercise called **The Things Phone Book**).

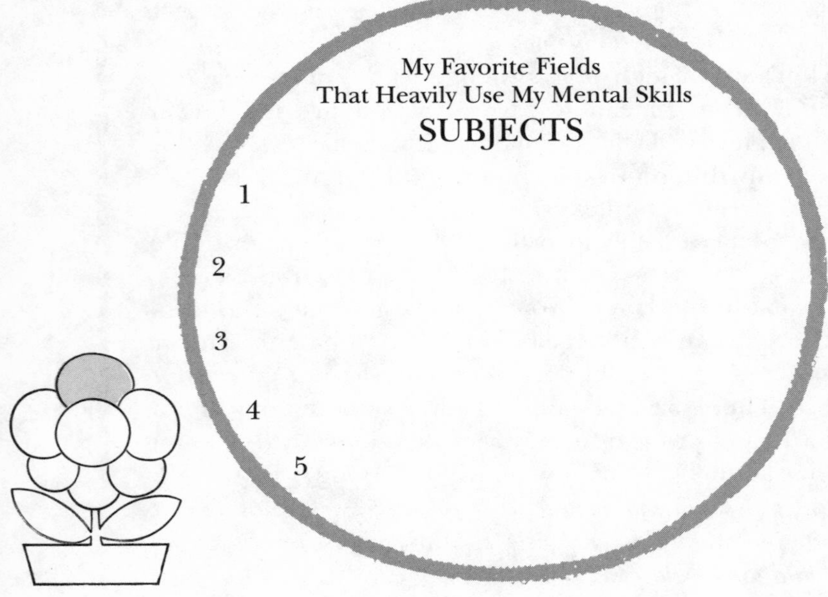

Your mental skills are such things as: *the ability to gather information, to analyze information, to organize information, to present information,* and the like. The question here is: **what kinds of information, subjects, bodies of knowledge, ideas, or languages, do you like to use your mental skills with?**

In order for you to answer this question, it is helpful to fill out the following chart; *you may first copy it on to a larger piece of paper, if you wish, in order to have more room to write.*

Please note that this chart is asking you what subjects you know *anything* about, whether you *like* the subject or not. (*Later*, you will ask yourself which of these you like or even *love.*) For now, the task facing you is merely *inventory*. That is a task similar

The Subjects Chart

Subjects I Know Something About

Which column you decide to put a subject in, below, doesn't matter at all. The columns are only a series of pegs, to hang your memories on. Which peg, is of no concern. Jot down a subject anywhere you like.

Column 1 Studied in High School or College or Graduate School	Column 2 Learned on the Job	Column 3 Learned from Conferences, Workshops, Training, Seminars	Column 4 Learned at Home: Reading, TV, Tape Programs, Study Courses	Column 5 Learned in My Leisure Time: Volunteer Work, Hobbies, etc.
Examples: Spanish, Typing, Accounting, Computer Literacy, Psychology, Geography	*Examples: Publishing, Computer graphics, How an organization works, How to operate various machines*	*Examples: Welfare rules, Job-hunting, Painting, How to Use the Internet*	*Examples: Art Appreciation, History, Speed Reading, A Language*	*Examples: Landscaping, How to sew, Antiques, Camping, Stamps,*

to inventorying what clothes you've got in your closet, before you decide which ones to give away. Only, here, *the closet is your head,* and you're inventorying all the stuff that's in *there.* Don't try to evaluate your degree of mastery of a particular subject. Put down something you've only read a few articles about *(if it interests you)* side by side with a subject you studied for three semesters in school.

Throwaway comes later *(though, obviously, if there's a subject you hate so much you can barely stand to write it down, then . . . don't . . . write . . . it . . . down.)*

When filling this chart out, do not forget to list those things you've learned -- no matter how -- about *Organizations (including volunteer organizations),* and what it takes to make them *work.*

It is not necessary that you should have ever taken a course in management or business. As John Crystal used to say, "Who cares *how* you learned it, whether in school or by sitting on the end of a log?" Examples of things you *may* know something about (and should list here) are: *Accounting or bookkeeping; Administration; Applications; Credit collection of overdue bills; Customer relations and service; Data analysis; Distribution; Fiscal analysis, controls, reductions; Government contracts; Group dynamics or work with groups in general; Hiring, Human resources; or manpower; International business; Management; Marketing, sales; Merchandising; Packaging; Performance specifications; Planning; Policy development; Problem solving or other types of troubleshooting with operations or management systems; Production; Public speaking/addressing people; R & D program management; Recruiting; Show or conference planning, organization and management; Systems analysis; Travel or travel planning, especially International travel; etc.*

Prioritizing "The Subjects Chart"

When you're done, you may want to let this Chart just sit on your refrigerator door for a few days, while you see if there's anything you want to add.

But when you're sure you've listed all you want to, on the chart, it is crucial then to sort and then prioritize all these subjects. The instruments for doing this are in Appendix A, and Appendix B.

When you're done with Appendix A and Appendix B, and you've got your ten prioritized Fields, then copy *the top Five* on to the "Fields Dealing with My Favorite Subjects" petal, on page 34 or on page 74 -- or both.

Your Favorite Fields:

2. Fields Dealing with People's Problems or Needs

Now, on to the second 'Fields petal,' the one on the top left-hand side of your Flower. It's entitled:

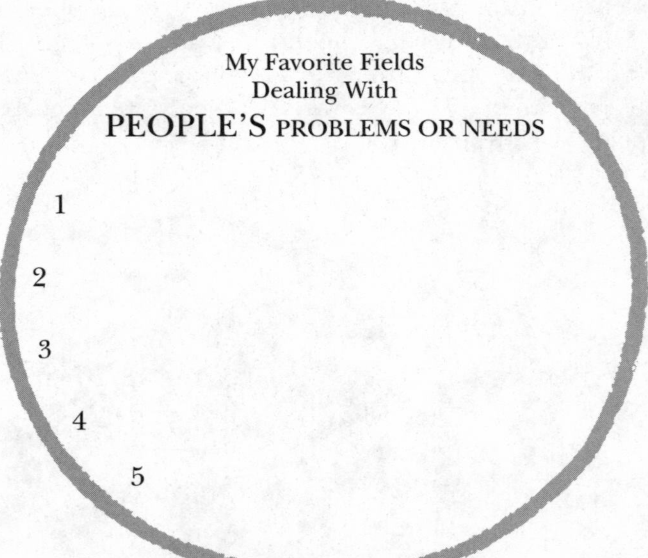

The question here is: **if you like to help people, what problems or needs do you like to help them with?** Each of these is a field.

In order to answer this question, it is helpful to fill out either of two kinds of exercises: *A Checklist,* or *"Fill in the blank."* Better yet, the two together, *like this:*

1. Check off any kind of need you think you *might* like to help people with, and then
2. Add *which part of it,* or *what aspect of it,* you find particularly interesting or *appealing.*

The People List

I'd like to help people with their need for:

- ❑ **Clothing** (people's need to find and choose appropriate and affordable clothing); *and in my case what interests me particularly is*____.
- ❑ **Food** (people's need to be fed, to be saved from starvation or poor nutrition) *and in my case what interests me particularly is*____.
- ❑ **Housing** and **Real estate** (people's need to find appropriate and affordable housing, apartment, office, or land); *and in my case what interests me particularly is*____.
- ❑ **Languages** (people's need for literacy, to be able to read, or to learn a new language); *and in my case what interests me particularly is*____.
- ❑ **Personal services** or **service occupations** (people's need to have someone do tasks they can't do, or haven't time to do, or don't want to do, for themselves -- ranging from childcare to helping run a farm); *and in my case what interests me particularly is*____.
- ❑ **Family and consumer economics** (people's need to have help with budgeting, taxes, financial planning, money management, etc.); *and in my case what interests me particularly is*____.
- ❑ **Retail sales** (people's need for help in buying something); *and in my case what interests me particularly is*____.
- ❑ **Automobile sales** (people's need for transportation); *and in my case what interests me particularly is*____.

- ❑ **Legal services** (people's need for expert counseling concerning the legal implications of things they are doing, or things that have been done to them); *and in my case what interests me particularly is*______________________________________.
- ❑ **Child development** (people's need for help with various problems as their children are moving from infancy through childhood, including behavioral disabilities); *and in my case what interests me particularly is*______________________________________.
- ❑ **Physical fitness** (people's need to get their body in tune through physical or occupational therapy, 'body-work,' exercise, or diet); *and in my case what interests me particularly is*______________________________________.
- ❑ **Health services** (people's need to have preventative medicine or help with ailments, allergies, and disease); *and in my case what interests me particularly is*______________________________________.
- ❑ **Healing** including **Alternative medicine** and **Holistic health** (people's need to have various injuries, ailments, maladies, or diseases healed); *and in my case what interests me particularly is*______________________________________.
- ❑ **Medicine** (people's need to have help with diagnosing, treating various diseases, or removing diseased or badly-injured parts of their body, etc.); *and in my case what interests me particularly is*______________________________________.
- ❑ **Mental health** (people's need for help with stress, depression, insomnia, or other forms of emotional or mental disturbance); *and in my case what interests me particularly is*______________________________________.
- ❑ **Psychology** or **psychiatry** (people's need for help with mental illness); *and in my case what interests me particularly is*______________________________________.
- ❑ **Personal counseling and guidance**, (people's need for help with family relations, with dysfunctions, or with various crises in their life, including a lack of balance in their use of time); *and in my case what interests me particularly is*______________________________________.

- ❑ **Career counseling, career-change, or life/work planning** (people's need for help in choosing a career or planning a holistic life); *and in my case what interests me particularly is*____________________________________.
- ❑ **Job-hunting, job-placement or vocational rehabilitation** (people's need to have help in finding the work they have chosen, particularly when handicapped, or unemployed, or enrolling for welfare under the new regulations); *and in my case what interests me particularly is*____________________________________.
- ❑ **Training or learning** (people's need to learn more about something, at work or outside of work); *and in my case what interests me particularly is*____________________________________.
- ❑ **Entertainment** (people's need to be entertained, by laughter, wit, intelligence, or beauty); *and in my case what interests me particularly is*____________________________________.
- ❑ **Spirituality** or **religion** (people's need to learn as much as they can about God, character, and their own soul, including their values and principles); *and in my case what interests me particularly is*____________________________________.
- ❑ **I'm interested in working with animals or plants** (their need for nurturing, growth, health and other life cycles which require the kinds of sensitivities often referred to as 'interpersonal skills'); *and in my case what interests me particularly is*____________________________________.
- ❑ **Other fields** (or people's needs) not listed above, or a new field I just invented (I think): ____________________________________.

In each question where it says "*. . . and in my case what interests me particularly is . . .*" think whether or not there are *particular age groups* you prefer to work with, *a particular sex* you prefer to work with (*or sexual orientation*), and whether you prefer to work with *individuals or groups, people of a particular background or set of beliefs, or people in a particular place (the Armed Forces, government, prison, mental institutions, etc.)*? If so, write it in.

Prioritizing "The People List"

When you're done, you may want to let this List just sit on your refrigerator door for a few days, while you see if there's anything you want to add.

But when you're sure you've listed all you want to, on the List, it is crucial then to sort and then prioritize all these Fields. The instruments for doing this are in Appendix A, and Appendix B.

When you're done with Appendix A and Appendix B, and you've got your ten prioritized Fields, then copy *the top Five* on to the "Fields Dealing with People's Problems or Needs" petal, on page *38* or on page *74* -- or both.

Your Favorite Fields:

3. Fields Dealing with Things, Tools, or Products

When you're done with the list above, go on to this third 'Fields petal,' the one on the right-hand side of your Flower. It's entitled:

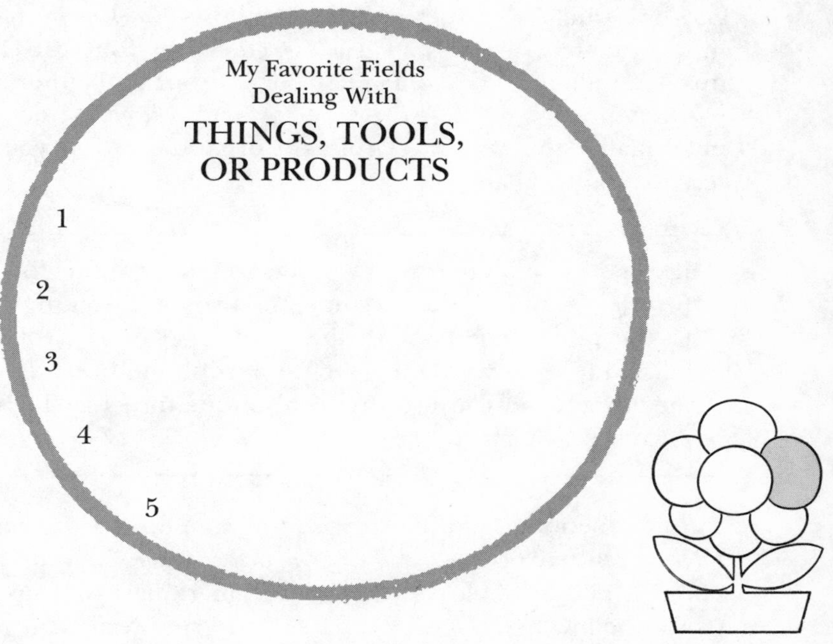

The question here is: **what things or products interest you the most?** (A product may be "a service," incidentally.)

Sampler: do you love to deal with, handle, or construct, or operate, or market, or repair: *airplanes, antiques, bicycles, blueprints, books, bridges, buildings, bushes, cameras, campers, cars, catalogs, chemicals, cooking utensils, clothing, computers, crops, diagrams, electricity, electronics, drugs, farms, farm machinery, fish, flowers, gardens, groceries, guidebooks, houses, kitchen appliances, lawns, machines, magazines, makeup, manuals, medicines, minerals, money, music, musical instruments, newspapers, office machines, paints, paper, plants, radios, rivers, rooms, sailboats, security systems, sewing machines, skiing equipment, soil, telephones, toiletries, tools, toys, trains, trees, valuable objects, videotapes, wine, wood -- or what?*

What things or products do you *love* to deal with? In order to answer this question, you need to compile *A List.* And it is important that it is complete -- that is, it's important that it list *all* the things or products that you love to deal with, in any way, shape, or form.

So, the brief *Sampler* above will not do. You need a longer list, and one which identifies what Fields those *things or products* are in. Fortunately, there is such a directory -- at your very fingertips. It's called: *The Yellow Pages,* from your local telephone company. It has it all: things, products, fields -- *and,* -- what you'll need later -- the *location* of relevant organizations in your chosen geographical area.

> If you don't plan to stay in your current community for this next job-hunt or career-change, then you will want to write to the phone company in the geographical area you are planning to move to, and secure *their* phone book. In the meantime, you can use the local phone directory for this exercise (just ignore locations).

The instructions for this exercise are simple. Go through the *table of contents* or *the index* of *The Yellow Pages* in your phone book (a phone book you don't mind marking up), and hi-lite (with a yellow hi-liter pen or marker) any and every category or field where you think you *might* like to deal with, or handle, or construct, or operate, or market, or repair *that thing, product, or service.* It is best to work your way backwards, from Z to A. Then, go back, and looking only at the items you hi-lited, circle *in red* the ones that you care the most about. Jot down their names on the next page.

> Incidentally, during the Phone Book exercise, you *will* run across fields that attract you, but which you might think *really* belong on the other 'Fields petals.' It really isn't important *which* petal the item falls on.

The Things Phone Book

Prioritizing "The Things Phone Book"

When you're done, you may want to let this Phone Book exercise just sit on your refrigerator door for a few days, while you see if there's anything you want to add.

But when you're sure you've listed all you want to, on the Phone Book exercise, it is crucial then to sort and then prioritize all these Fields. The instruments for doing this are in Appendix A, and Appendix B.

When you're done with Appendix A and Appendix B, and you've got your ten prioritized Fields, then copy *the top Five* on to the "Fields Dealing with Things, Tools, or Products" petal, on page 43 or on page 74 -- or both.

Putting All Your Favorite Fields Together

And now that you are done with all three Fields petals of the Flower diagram, it is time to put all three petals together, and make one unified list of Your Favorite Fields. Just prioritize all fifteen Fields that you have listed on the three Fields petals, using one 24-Item Prioritizing Grid (page 72), until you have them in the exact order of your personal preference.

And then, choose your top five Favorite Fields, and copy them in the space provided on page 66.

Your Favorite Transferable Skills

We are done with *Fields*; and so, we move on to the other WHAT question: **What are your favorite transferable *Skills*, that you most enjoy using?**

My Favorite Transferrable

SKILLS

My Interpersonal Skills	My Mental Skills	My Physical Skills
1	1	1
2	2	2
3	3	3
4	4	4
5	5	5

What exactly are your transferable skills? Well, they may be thought of as your *"directed energies,"* in which case Fields are *"the materials"* that *you* direct those energies to act upon.

To identify your favorite **transferable skills** (or *directed energies*) you will need to write **seven stories** about things you did just because they were fun, or gave you a sense of adventure, or gave you a sense of accomplishment. It does not matter whether anyone else ever knew about this accomplishment, or not.

Each story can be about something you did at work, or in school, or at play -- and can be from any time period of your life. It should not be more than two or three paragraphs, in length.

To the right is a form to help you write each of your Seven Stories, one story per form. *(You will obviously want to make seven copies of this form* before *you begin filling it out, for the first time. The copies work best if you make them on seven pieces of $8\frac{1}{2}'' \times 11''$ paper,* turned sideways.)

If you need an example of what to put in each of the five columns, turn to pages 114 and 115 in *Parachute.*

Once you have written your Story #1 (and before you write the other six), you should go to the list of skills found on pages *50–55*, which resemble a series of typewriter keys. There is one set of "Transferable Skills Keys" for Your Physical Skills, and another set for Your Mental Skills, and a third set for Your Interpersonal Skills. Arm yourself with a red pen or pencil.

Story # ________

My Seven Life Stories

Column 1	Column 2	Column 3	Column 4	Column 5
Your Goal: What You Want to Accomplish	Some Kind of Obstacle (or limit, hurdle or restraint you had to overcome before it could be accomplished)	What You Did Step-by-Step (It may help if you pretend you are telling this story to a whining 4-year-old child, who keeps asking, after each of your sentences, "An' then whadja do? An' then whadja do?")	Description of the Result (What you accomplished)	Any Measure or Quantities To Prove Your Achievement

My Interpersonal Skills

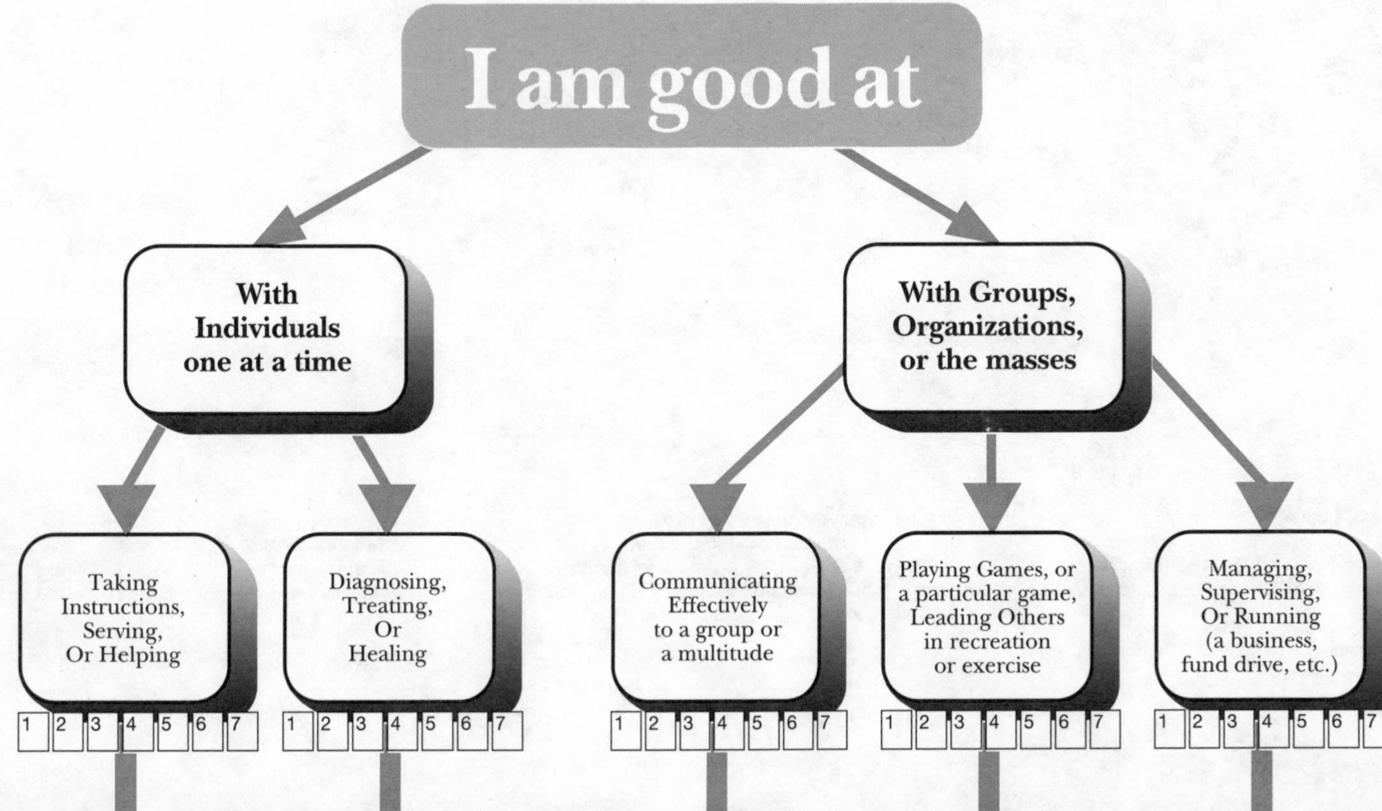

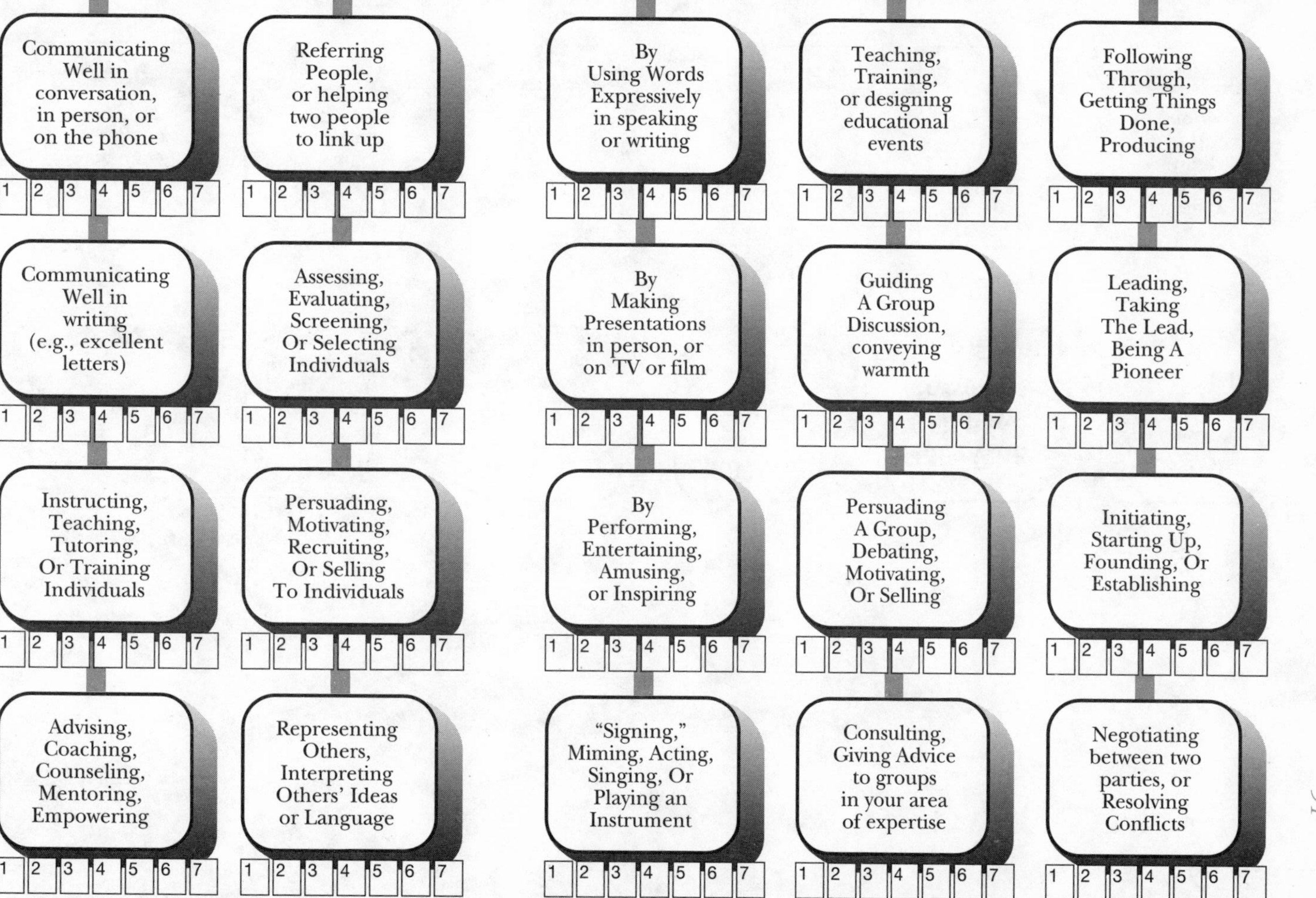
Communicating Well in conversation, in person, or on the phone
1 2 3 4 5 6 7
Communicating Well in writing (e.g., excellent letters)
1 2 3 4 5 6 7
Instructing, Teaching, Tutoring, Or Training Individuals
1 2 3 4 5 6 7
Advising, Coaching, Counseling, Mentoring, Empowering
1 2 3 4 5 6 7
Referring People, or helping two people to link up
1 2 3 4 5 6 7
Assessing, Evaluating, Screening, Or Selecting Individuals
1 2 3 4 5 6 7
Persuading, Motivating, Recruiting, Or Selling To Individuals
1 2 3 4 5 6 7
Representing Others, Interpreting Others' Ideas or Language
1 2 3 4 5 6 7
By Using Words Expressively in speaking or writing
1 2 3 4 5 6 7
By Making Presentations in person, or on TV or film
1 2 3 4 5 6 7
By Performing, Entertaining, Amusing, or Inspiring
1 2 3 4 5 6 7
"Signing," Miming, Acting, Singing, Or Playing an Instrument
1 2 3 4 5 6 7
Teaching, Training, or designing educational events
1 2 3 4 5 6 7
Guiding A Group Discussion, conveying warmth
1 2 3 4 5 6 7
Persuading A Group, Debating, Motivating, Or Selling
1 2 3 4 5 6 7
Consulting, Giving Advice to groups in your area of expertise
1 2 3 4 5 6 7
Following Through, Getting Things Done, Producing
1 2 3 4 5 6 7
Leading, Taking The Lead, Being A Pioneer
1 2 3 4 5 6 7
Initiating, Starting Up, Founding, Or Establishing
1 2 3 4 5 6 7
Negotiating between two parties, or Resolving Conflicts
1 2 3 4 5 6 7

My Physical Skills

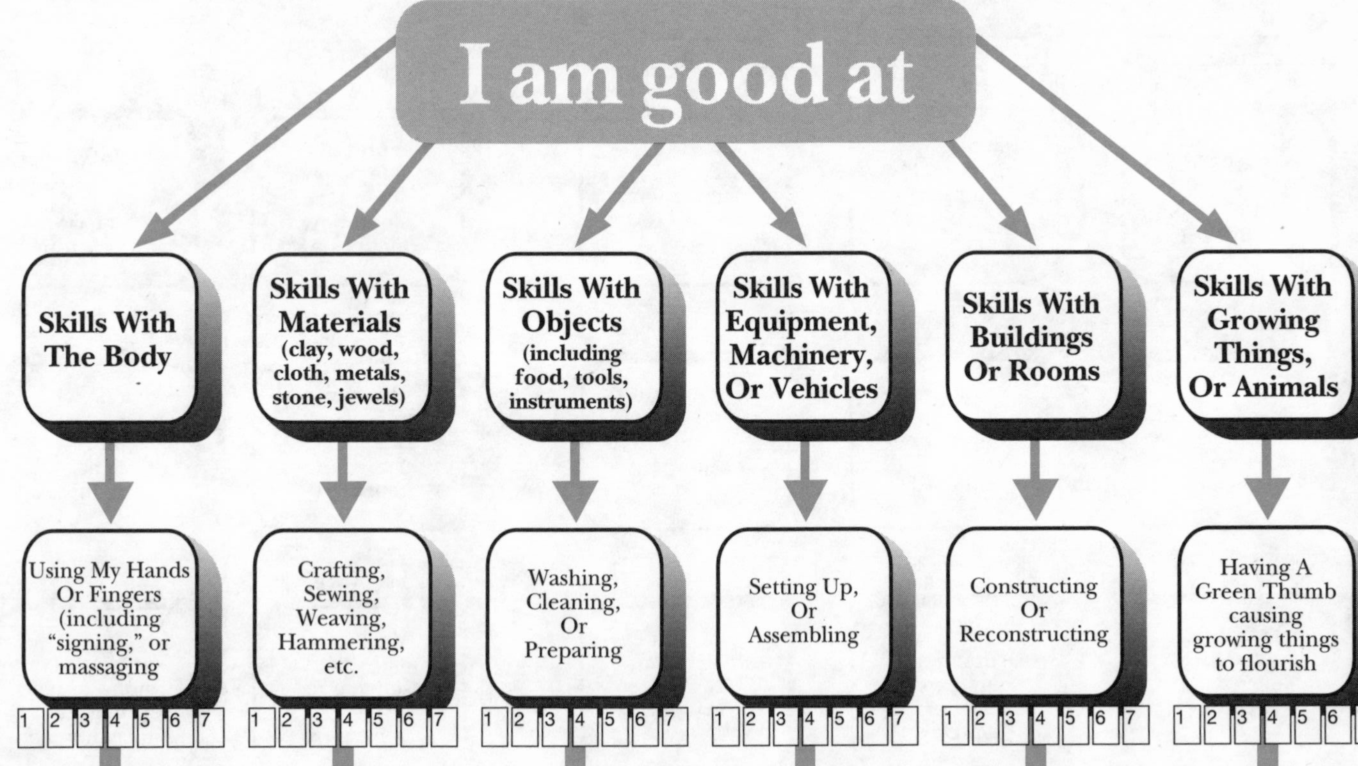

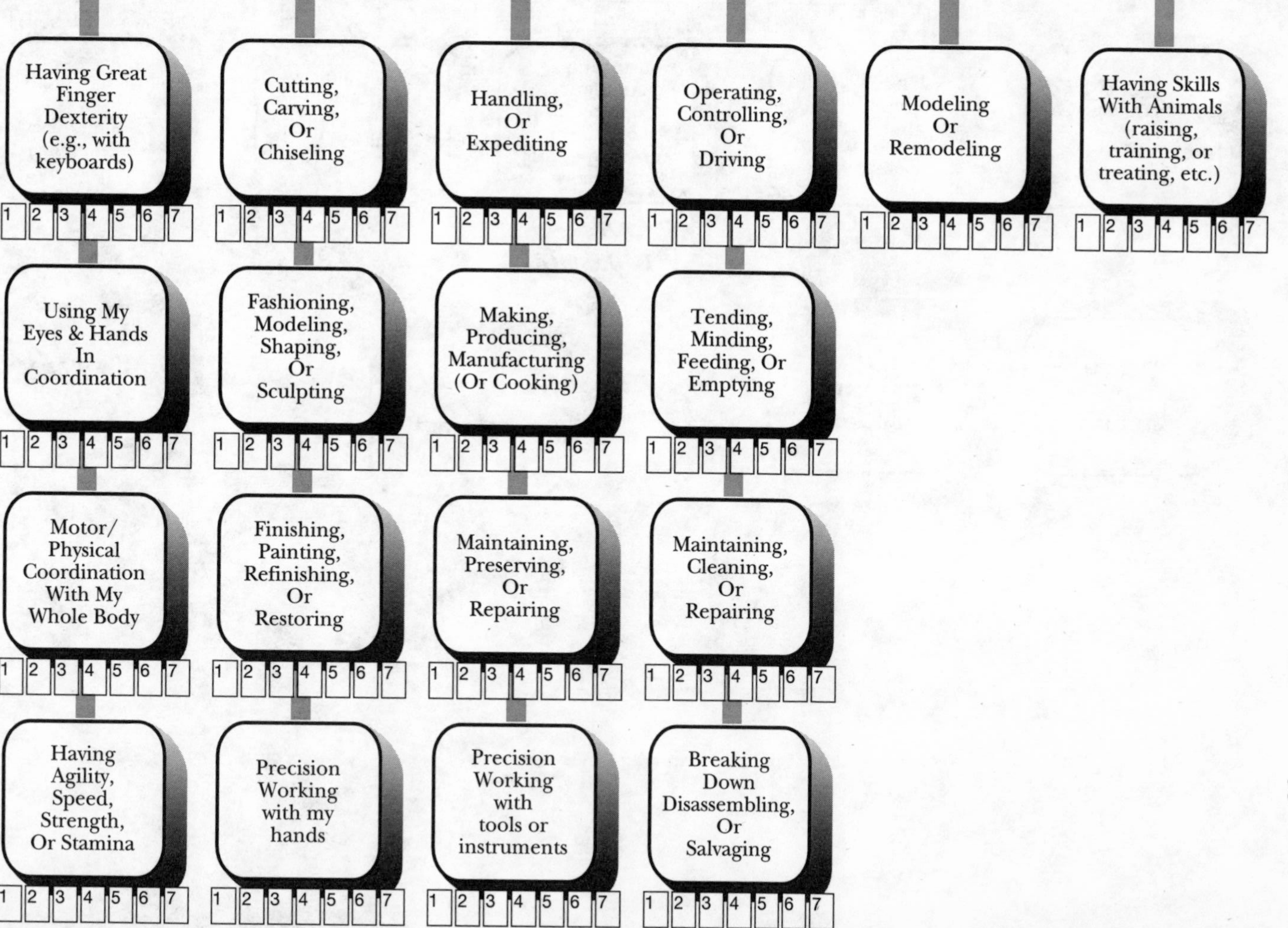

Having Great Finger Dexterity (e.g., with keyboards)
1 2 3 4 5 6 7
Using My Eyes & Hands In Coordination
1 2 3 4 5 6 7
Motor/ Physical Coordination With My Whole Body
1 2 3 4 5 6 7
Having Agility, Speed, Strength, Or Stamina
1 2 3 4 5 6 7
Cutting, Carving, Or Chiseling
1 2 3 4 5 6 7
Fashioning, Modeling, Shaping, Or Sculpting
1 2 3 4 5 6 7
Finishing, Painting, Refinishing, Or Restoring
1 2 3 4 5 6 7
Precision Working with my hands
1 2 3 4 5 6 7
Handling, Or Expediting
1 2 3 4 5 6 7
Making, Producing, Manufacturing (Or Cooking)
1 2 3 4 5 6 7
Maintaining, Preserving, Or Repairing
1 2 3 4 5 6 7
Precision Working with tools or instruments
1 2 3 4 5 6 7
Operating, Controlling, Or Driving
1 2 3 4 5 6 7
Tending, Minding, Feeding, Or Emptying
1 2 3 4 5 6 7
Maintaining, Cleaning, Or Repairing
1 2 3 4 5 6 7
Breaking Down Disassembling, Or Salvaging
1 2 3 4 5 6 7
Modeling Or Remodeling
1 2 3 4 5 6 7
Having Skills With Animals (raising, training, or treating, etc.)
1 2 3 4 5 6 7

My Mental Skills

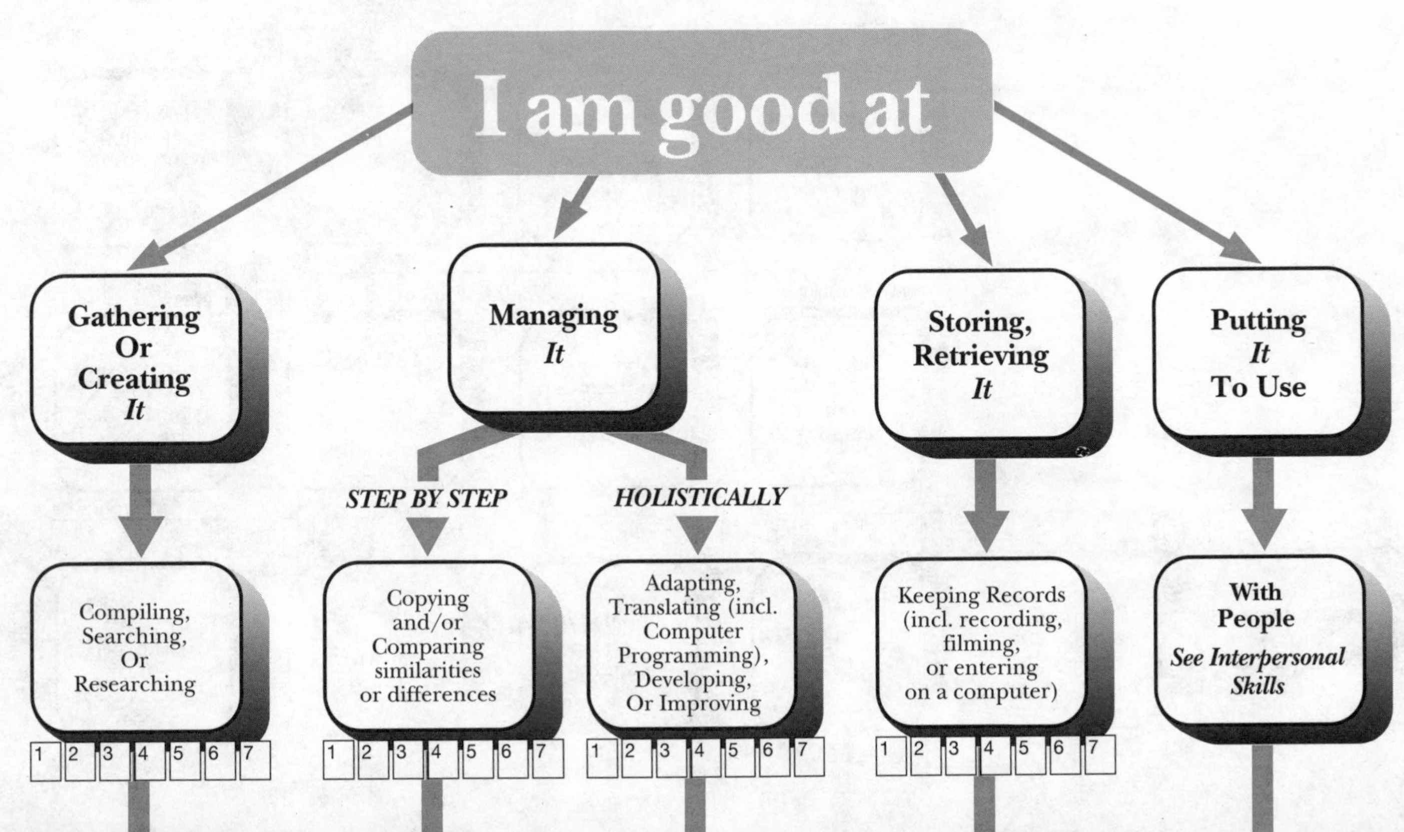

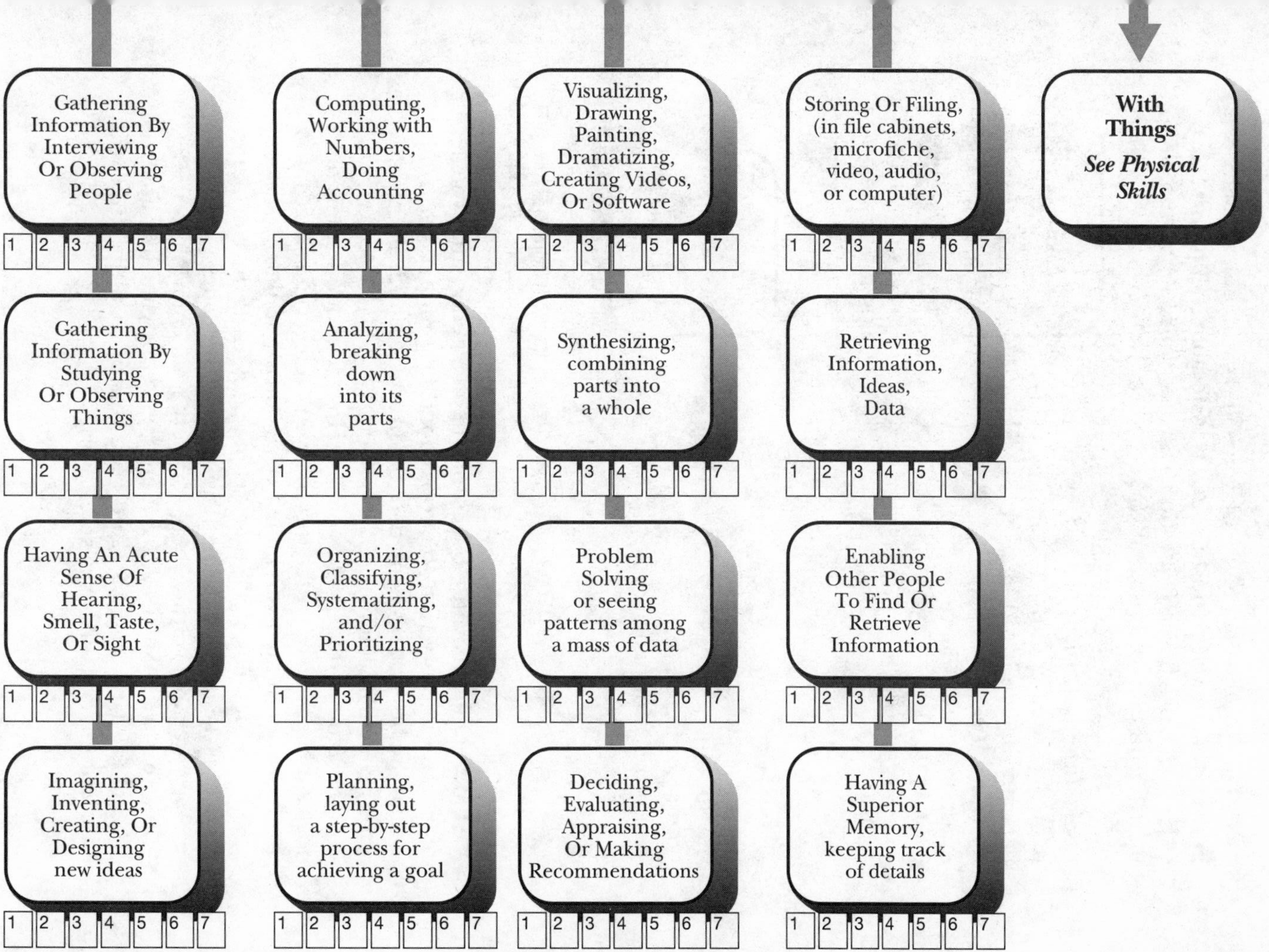

Gathering Information By Interviewing Or Observing People

1 2 3 4 5 6 7

Gathering Information By Studying Or Observing Things

1 2 3 4 5 6 7

Having An Acute Sense Of Hearing, Smell, Taste, Or Sight

1 2 3 4 5 6 7

Imagining, Inventing, Creating, Or Designing new ideas

1 2 3 4 5 6 7

Computing, Working with Numbers, Doing Accounting

1 2 3 4 5 6 7

Analyzing, breaking down into its parts

1 2 3 4 5 6 7

Organizing, Classifying, Systematizing, and/or Prioritizing

1 2 3 4 5 6 7

Planning, laying out a step-by-step process for achieving a goal

1 2 3 4 5 6 7

Visualizing, Drawing, Painting, Dramatizing, Creating Videos, Or Software

1 2 3 4 5 6 7

Synthesizing, combining parts into a whole

1 2 3 4 5 6 7

Problem Solving or seeing patterns among a mass of data

1 2 3 4 5 6 7

Deciding, Evaluating, Appraising, Or Making Recommendations

1 2 3 4 5 6 7

Storing Or Filing, (in file cabinets, microfiche, video, audio, or computer)

1 2 3 4 5 6 7

Retrieving Information, Ideas, Data

1 2 3 4 5 6 7

Enabling Other People To Find Or Retrieve Information

1 2 3 4 5 6 7

Having A Superior Memory, keeping track of details

1 2 3 4 5 6 7

With Things
See Physical Skills

The question you need to ask yourself, as you look at each key in the three sets, is: "Did I use *this* transferable skill in *this* Story (#1)?" That is the *only* question you ask yourself (at the moment). And then, this is what you do:

Look at the little box named #1, that lies just beneath the key. If you feel the answer to the question is, "No," leave the box blank.

If you feel the answer to the question is, "Yes," then color it in. Use your red pen or pencil, as here:

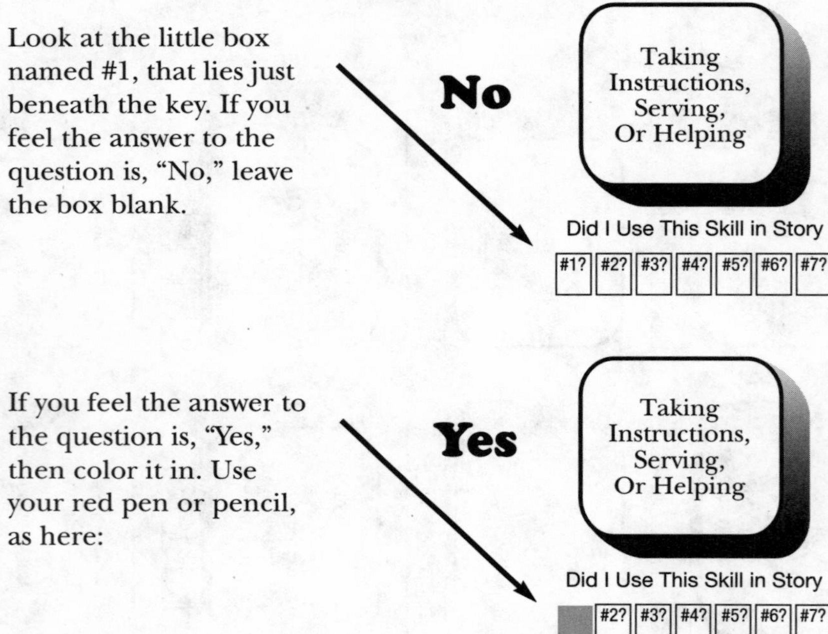

(Ignore the other little boxes for the time being, until you are analyzing the Story with the corresponding number; for example, all the little boxes named #2 belong to Story #2, all the little boxes named #3 belong to Story #3, etc.)

Voila! You are done with Story #1. However, 'one swallow doth not a summer make,' so the fact that you used certain skills in this first Story doesn't tell you much. What you are looking for is **patterns** -- transferable skills that keep reappearing in story after story. They keep reappearing because they are your favorites (assuming you chose stories where you were *really* enjoying yourself).

So, now, write Story #2, from any period in your life, analyze it using the keys, etc., etc. And keep this process up, until you have written, and analyzed, seven stories.

Prioritizing Your Favorite

. . . Interpersonal Skills

When you're done writing and analyzing all Seven Stories, you should now go back and look over the page of "Skills Keys" devoted to Interpersonal Skills. And now, in whatever way appeals to you, pick out your *five favorite* Interpersonal Skills. Most likely, these are the ones that got colored-in the most times. But not always. You get to make some judgment-calls here. And, of course, as always, **if you just can't make up your mind which are your five favorites, then use the Prioritizing Grid in Appendix B**, on page 72. The question to ask yourself, there, as you confront each 'pair' is: "If I were offered two jobs, and in one job I could use the first skill, but not the second; while in the other job, I could use the second skill, but not the first, which job would I choose?" When you've got your five favorite Interpersonal Skills, *and you have them in exact order of preference*, copy them on to the Transferable Skills petal, in the left-hand column there, on page 47.

. . . Mental Skills

Now look over the page of "Skills Keys" devoted to Mental Skills. And again, in whatever way appeals to you, pick out your *five favorite* Mental Skills. Most likely, these are the ones that got colored-in the most times. But not always. You get to make some judgment-calls here. And, of course, as always, **if you just can't make up your mind which are your five favorites, then use the Prioritizing Grid in Appendix B**, on page 72. The question to ask yourself, there, as you confront each 'pair' is: "If I were offered two jobs, and in one job I could use the first skill, but not the second; while in the other job, I could use the second skill, but not the first, which job would I choose?" When you've got your five favorite Mental Skills, *and you have them in exact order of preference*, copy them on to the Transferable Skills petal, in the center column there, on page 47.

. . . Physical Skills

Finally, here, look over the page of "Skills Keys" devoted to Physical Skills. And again, in whatever way appeals to you, pick out your *five favorite* Physical Skills. Most likely, these are the ones that got colored-in the most times. But not always. You get to make some judgment-calls here. And, of course, as always, **if you just can't make up your mind which are your five favorites, then use the Prioritizing Grid in Appendix B**, on page 72. The question to ask yourself, there, as you confront each 'pair' is: "If I were offered two jobs, and in one job I could use the first skill, but not the second; while in the other job, I could use the second skill, but not the first, which job would I choose?" When you've got your five favorite Physical Skills, *and you have them in exact order of preference*, copy them on to the Transferable Skills petal, in the right-hand column there, on page 47.

Putting All Your Transferable Skills Together

And now that you are done filling-in the three columns on your Transferable Skills petal, it is time to put all three columns together, and make one unified list of Your Favorite Transferable Skills. Just prioritize all fifteen in the three columns *together*, using one 24-Item Prioritizing Grid (page 72) -- until you have them in the exact order of your personal preference.

And then, write in your top five Favorite Transferable Skills, in the space provided on page 66.

Your work on **What** (and of course **Where**) is almost over. Only two petals now remain to be filled out, on your Flower diagram.

Your Strongest Traits

TRAITS
The Way In Which I Do My Work

1
2
3
4
5

You may think of Traits as "those characteristics which pervade *all* your behavior." Traits are qualities like: "thoroughness," "great attention to detail," "perseverance," and the like. Traits describe, in a sense, *the style* with which you do everything -- or almost everything.[3]

Traits divide into *at least* seven basic groups:

1. How you deal with time, and promptness.
2. How you deal with people and emotions.
3. How you deal with authority, and being told *what* to do at your job.
4. How you deal with supervision, and being told *how* to do your job.
5. How you deal with impulse vs. self-discipline, within yourself.
6. How you deal with initiative vs. response, within yourself.
7. How you deal with crises or problems.

---

3. They are the subject of such popular 'instruments' as the Myers-Briggs Type Indicator, or MBTI.

To expand upon these categories, and help you figure out *which* traits are your 'strong-suit,' a check-list is useful.

A Check-List of My Strongest Traits

- ❑ Accurate
- ❑ Achievement-oriented
- ❑ Adaptable
- ❑ Adept
- ❑ Adept at having fun
- ❑ Adventuresome
- ❑ Alert
- ❑ Appreciative
- ❑ Assertive
- ❑ Astute
- ❑ Authoritative
- ❑ Calm
- ❑ Cautious
- ❑ Charismatic
- ❑ Competent
- ❑ Consistent
- ❑ Contagious in my enthusiasm
- ❑ Cooperative
- ❑ Courageous
- ❑ Creative
- ❑ Decisive
- ❑ Deliberate
- ❑ Dependable/have dependability
- ❑ Diligent
- ❑ Diplomatic
- ❑ Discreet
- ❑ Driving
- ❑ Dynamic
- ❑ Extremely economical
- ❑ Effective
- ❑ Energetic
- ❑ Enthusiastic
- ❑ Exceptional
- ❑ Exhaustive
- ❑ Experienced
- ❑ Expert
- ❑ Firm
- ❑ Flexible
- ❑ Humanly oriented
- ❑ Impulsive
- ❑ Independent
- ❑ Innovative
- ❑ Knowledgeable
- ❑ Loyal
- ❑ Methodical
- ❑ Objective
- ❑ Open-minded
- ❑ Outgoing
- ❑ Outstanding
- ❑ Patient
- ❑ Penetrating
- ❑ Perceptive
- ❑ Persevering
- ❑ Persistent
- ❑ Pioneering
- ❑ Practical
- ❑ Professional
- ❑ Protective
- ❑ Punctual
- ❑ Quick/work quickly
- ❑ Rational
- ❑ Realistic
- ❑ Reliable
- ❑ Repeatedly
- ❑ Resourceful
- ❑ Responsible
- ❑ Responsive
- ❑ Safeguarding
- ❑ Self-motivated
- ❑ Self-reliant
- ❑ Sensitive
- ❑ Sophisticated, very sophisticated
- ❑ Strong
- ❑ Supportive
- ❑ Tactful
- ❑ Thorough
- ❑ Unique
- ❑ Unusual
- ❑ Versatile
- ❑ Vigorous

• I am a person who:

With respect to execution of a task, and achievement

- ❑ Takes initiative
- ❑ Is able to handle a great variety of tasks and responsibilities simultaneously and efficiently
- ❑ Takes risks
- ❑ Takes calculated risks
- ❑ Is expert at getting things done

• I am a person who:

With respect to time, and achievement

- ❑ Consistently tackles tasks ahead of time
- ❑ Is adept at finding ways to speed up a task
- ❑ Gets the most done in the shortest time
- ❑ Expedites the task at hand
- ❑ Meets deadlines
- ❑ Delivers on promises on time
- ❑ Brings projects in on time and within budget

With respect to working conditions

- ❑ Maintains order and neatness in my workspace
- ❑ Is attendant to details
- ❑ Has a high tolerance of repetition and/or monotonous routines
- ❑ Likes planning and directing an entire activity
- ❑ Demonstrates mastery
- ❑ Promotes change
- ❑ Works well under pressure and still improvises
- ❑ Enjoys a challenge
- ❑ Loves working outdoors
- ❑ Loves to travel
- ❑ Has an unusually good grasp of . . .
- ❑ Is good at responding to emergencies
- ❑ Has the courage of his or her convictions

When you're done checking off all the traits that you think describe the real You, go back, and pick out the ten Traits that you are proudest of -- the ones you would most like to emphasize to a prospective employer, because you feel these distinguish you from nineteen other job-hunters who basically 'do what you do' and 'know what you know.' As always, **if you just can't make up your mind which are your ten favorite traits, then use the Prioritizing Grid in Appendix B**, on page 71. The question to ask yourself, there, as you confront each 'pair' is: "If I were only given time in a job interview to emphasize *one* of these two traits of mine, which trait am I *proudest* of?"

When you've identified your ten Traits, that you are proudest of, *and you have them in exact order of emphasis,* copy the top five on to the Traits petal, on page 59 or on page 74 -- or both.

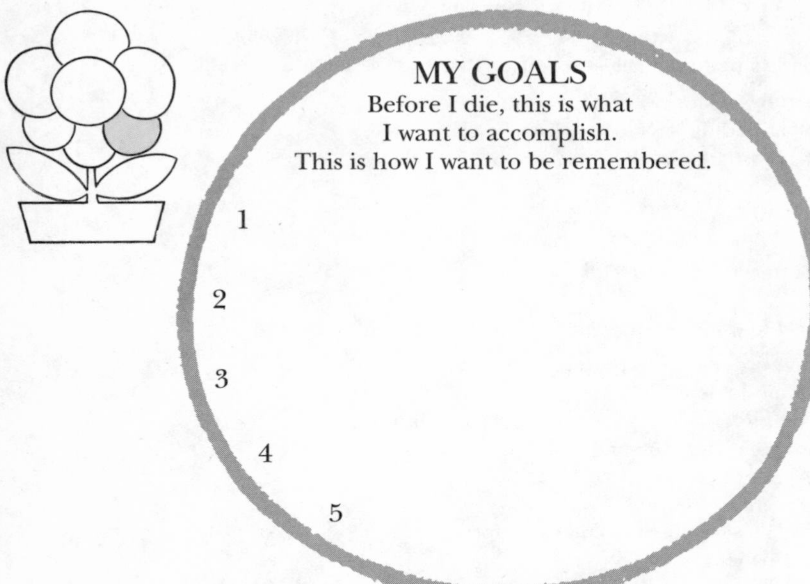

This petal deals with your **Goals**. Goals describe what it is you are ultimately trying to do, in life, with all your skills and all your fields of knowledge. It asks the question, *where is all this heading?*

To help you discover the answer, there is:

The Testimonial Dinner Exercise

Scene: It is one week before the end of your life, and everyone knows it. You are invited to dinner and to your great surprise this turns out to be a huge dinner, attended by everyone you value; they have secretly come in from all over the country and all over the world. It is to be a testimonial dinner, for You.

At the dinner, to your great embarrassment, there is one testimonial after another about the good things you did, or the good person that you were, in your lifetime. No mention of any parts of your life that you don't want to have remembered. Just the good stuff.

So, this brings us to some questions. What would you hope to hear, at that dinner? What about you would you like to have remembered, after you are gone from this earth? What traits? What physical qualities, if any? What spiritual qualities? What skills or talents? What achievements? Here is a checklist to help you:

I want people to remember me as one who, among other things:

- ❑ Served or helped those who were in need.
- ❑ Impressed people with my going the second mile, in meeting their needs.
- ❑ Was always a great listener.
- ❑ Was always good at carrying out orders, or bringing projects to a successful conclusion.
- ❑ Mastered some technique, or field.
- ❑ Did something that everyone said couldn't be done.
- ❑ Did something that no one had ever done before.
- ❑ Excelled and was the best at whatever it is I did.
- ❑ Pioneered or explored some new technology.
- ❑ Fixed something that was broken.
- ❑ Made something work, when everyone else had failed or given up.
- ❑ Improved something, made it better, or perfected it.
- ❑ Combatted some bad idea/philosophy/force/influence/pervasive trend -- and I persevered and/or prevailed.
- ❑ Influenced people and gained a tremendous response from them.
- ❑ Had an impact, and caused change.
- ❑ Did work which brought more information/truth into the world.
- ❑ Did work which brought more beauty into the world, through gardens, or painting, or decorating, or designing, or whatever.
- ❑ Did work which brought more justice, truth, and ethical behavior into the world.
- ❑ Brought people closer to God.
- ❑ Growing in wisdom and compassion was my great goal all my life.

- ❑ Had a vision of what something could be, and helped that vision to come true.
- ❑ Developed or built something, where there was nothing.
- ❑ Began a new business, or did some project from start to finish.
- ❑ Exploited, shaped and influenced some situation, market, before others saw the potential.
- ❑ Put together a great team, which made a huge difference in its field, industry, or community.
- ❑ Was a good decision-maker.
- ❑ Was acknowledged by everyone as a leader, and was in charge of whatever it was that I was doing.
- ❑ Had status in my field, industry, or community.
- ❑ Was in the spotlight, gained recognition, and was well-known.
- ❑ Made it into a higher echelon than I was, in terms of reputation, and/or prestige, and/or membership, and/or salary.
- ❑ Was able to acquire possessions, things or money.
- ❑ Other goals which occur to me:
- ❑ ____________________
- ❑ ____________________
- ❑ ____________________

Adapted from *The Truth About You: Discover What You Should Be Doing with Your Life,* by Arthur F. Miller and Ralph T. Mattson. Used by permission.

When you're done checking off all the goals that are important to you, go back, and pick out the ten that you care the most about, and then prioritize them in exact order of importance to you. As always, **if you just can't prioritize them by guess and by gosh, then use the Prioritizing Grid in Appendix B**, on page 71. The question to ask yourself, there, as you confront each 'pair' is: "If I could only have this true about me, at the end of my life, but not the other, which would I prefer?" *Try not to pay attention to what others might or might not think of you, if they knew this was your heart's desire. This is just between you and God.*

When you've got your top ten goals in exact order of importance to you, copy the top five on to the Goals petal, on page 62 or on page 74 -- or both.

Cleanup

Your flower should now be complete, with the possible exception of the two "leaves" dealing with organizations. If there were questions on either Leaf that were difficult for you to answer at the time, go back to them now and -- looking particularly at your answers on the "Fields" petals and the "Goals" petal -- see if you can now fill in the answers to those questions.

Voila! Your Flower Diagram should now be complete!

HOW

How do you find those jobs or careers that allow you to use your favorite transferable skills in your favorite field, in your favorite city or place?

Here is the heart of what you learned from your Flower:

My Top Five Favorite Transferable Skills, whether Interpersonal, Physical or Mental, Are:*

1. ______________________________

2. ______________________________

3. ______________________________

4. ______________________________

5. ______________________________

My Top Five Favorite Fields, whether with People, Things, or Ideas/Information, Are:**

1. ______________________________

2. ______________________________

3. ______________________________

4. ______________________________

5. ______________________________

*You get these by prioritizing your top 5 Interpersonal, your top 5 Physical and your top 5 Mental Skills *all together.*

** You get these by prioritizing your top 5 People Fields, your top 5 Things Fields and your top 5 Idea/Information Fields *all together.*

The question is: what kind of job or career does this point to? Chapter 6, in the main body of this book, describes exactly how you find that out -- *in detail* -- from page 131 on. Follow those steps faithfully.

The rest of the "HOW" is found in Chapter 7. Keep in mind, as mentioned earlier, this truth: there are **always** jobs out there. Whether you can find them or not depends on what methods of job-hunting you are using to locate them. *Before* you go job hunting, or changing careers, you must have a plan for figuring out how to find the kind of job that you most want to do. Newpaper ads, employment agencies, and resumes *may* work for you. But more often than not, they don't

So you *must* have a "Plan B." A careful, systematic, step-by-step "Plan B." The key to such a Plan, described in Chapter 6, is to enlist people you know, to help you find the information you want, after completing your Flower: such as the names of jobs or careers that your skills and fields (above) point to; the names of organizations offering such jobs or careers; actual job-leads, plus (most importantly) introductions to the people who have the power to hire, there.

Now that you've done all this homework on your Flower, Chapters 6 and 7 (faithfully followed) should produce good results for you in locating that new job or career you are looking for.

I wish you perseverance, and the very best of luck.

Appendix A

The Enthusiasm/Expertise Grid

You use this whenever you are working with any of the "Fields exercises" preparatory to filling out "The Fields" petals: either "**The Subjects Chart**," or "**The People List**," or "**The Things Phone Book**." Once you have a completed list from any one of the three exercises, you then proceed to the following three steps.

(1) Look back at the fields you listed in the exercise. Distribute all the Fields into one of the two columns below, according to only one principle: the enthusiasm you feel for them. (Expertise, at this point, has nothing to do with it.)

Low Enthusiasm Fields That I Have Low Enthusiasm For *(Regardless of My Expertise in This Field)*	High Enthusiasm Fields That I Have High Enthusiasm For *(Regardless of My Expertise in This Field)*

If you're puzzled as to whether or not a particular subject is an enthusiasm for you, imagine you are at a party -- meeting a lot of people you don't know very well, if at all -- and you get involved in a whole bunch of conversations during the evening. If all the subjects on your Chart got discussed at some point during the evening, which conversations would you hope would go on the longest? Another way to find out which ones you have enthusiasm for: If you were forced to kill a lot of time in a bookstore, which of the above subjects would you gravitate toward, to see what new books had come out?

(2) When you are done with this part of the exercise, proceed to the next: take only the items you put in the "High Enthusiasm" column previously, and distribute them now between these three new columns, in the diagram below:

High Enthusiasm

Fields
That I Have High Enthusiasm For
(Regardless of My Expertise in This Field)

 High Enthusiasm, High Expertise	 High Enthusiasm, Medium Expertise	 High Enthusiasm, Low Expertise

(3) When you are done distributing the items thus, choose *your ten favorites* from *the first two* columns: "High Enthusiasm, High Expertise," "High Enthusiasm, Medium Expertise," and prioritize them in the exact order of your personal preference.

Q: *"Can I throw in an item from the third column? Granted I have low expertise in it, but I like it a lot; and I could easily learn more about this field I've listed there."* A: *Of course.*

If you are baffled as to how to prioritize these Fields in exact order, use the Prioritizing Grid, following. The question to ask yourself, there, as you confront each 'pair' is: "If I were offered two jobs, both of them as the boss's assistant: but one job was in the first field, while the other job was in the second field -- which job would I choose?"

Appendix B

The Prioritizing Grid

How to Prioritize Your Lists of Anything

Here is a method for taking (say) ten items, and figuring out which one is most important to you, which is next most important, etc.

• Insert the items to be prioritized, in any order, in Section A. Then compare two items at a time, circling the one you prefer -- between the two -- in Section B. Which one is more important to you? State the question any way you want to: In the case of geographical factors, you might ask. "If I were being offered two jobs, one in an area that had factor #1, but not factor #2; the other in an area that had factor #2, but not factor #1, all other things being equal, which job would I take? Circle it. Then go on to the next pair, etc.

(directions continued on page 73)

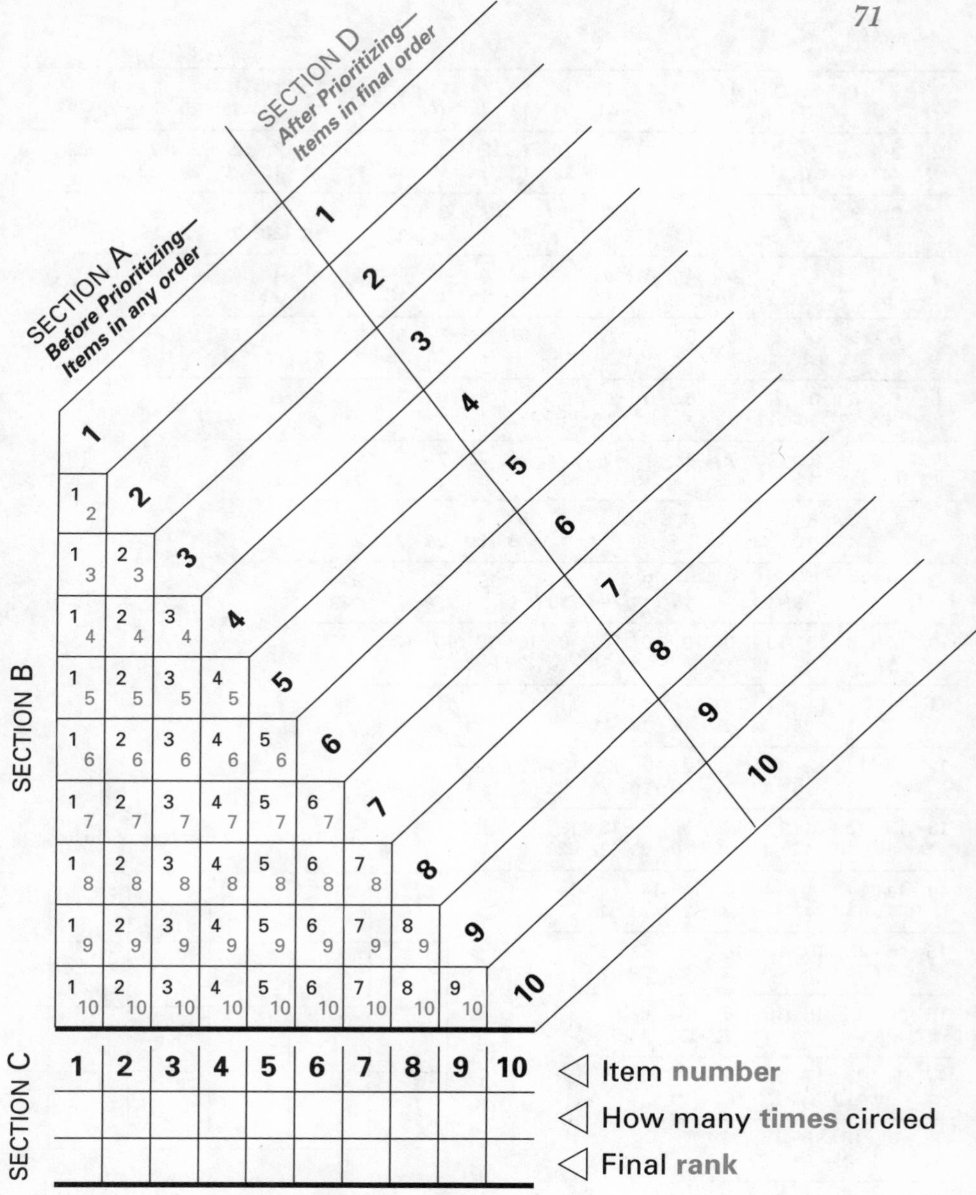

Prioritzing Grid
for 10 Items

1 1 1 1 1 1 1 1 1 1 1 1 1 1 1 1 1 1 1 1 1 1 1
2 3 4 5 6 7 8 9 10 11 12 13 14 15 16 17 18 19 20 21 22 23 24

2 2 2 2 2 2 2 2 2 2 2 2 2 2 2 2 2 2 2 2 2 2
3 4 5 6 7 8 9 10 11 12 13 14 15 16 17 18 19 20 21 22 23 24

3 3 3 3 3 3 3 3 3 3 3 3 3 3 3 3 3 3 3 3 3
4 5 6 7 8 9 10 11 12 13 14 15 16 17 18 19 20 21 22 23 24

4 4 4 4 4 4 4 4 4 4 4 4 4 4 4 4 4 4 4 4
5 6 7 8 9 10 11 12 13 14 15 16 17 18 19 20 21 22 23 24

5 5 5 5 5 5 5 5 5 5 5 5 5 5 5 5 5 5 5
6 7 8 9 10 11 12 13 14 15 16 17 18 19 20 21 22 23 24

6 6 6 6 6 6 6 6 6 6 6 6 6 6 6 6 6 6
7 8 9 10 11 12 13 14 15 16 17 18 19 20 21 22 23 24

7 7 7 7 7 7 7 7 7 7 7 7 7 7 7 7 7
8 9 10 11 12 13 14 15 16 17 18 19 20 21 22 23 24

8 8 8 8 8 8 8 8 8 8 8 8 8 8 8 8
9 10 11 12 13 14 15 16 17 18 19 20 21 22 23 24

9 9 9 9 9 9 9 9 9 9 9 9 9 9 9
10 11 12 13 14 15 16 17 18 19 20 21 22 23 24

10 10 10 10 10 10 10 10 10 10 10 10 10 10
11 12 13 14 15 16 17 18 19 20 21 22 23 24

11 11 11 11 11 11 11 11 11 11 11 11 11
12 13 14 15 16 17 18 19 20 21 22 23 24

12 12 12 12 12 12 12 12 12 12 12 12
13 14 15 16 17 18 19 20 21 22 23 24

13 13 13 13 13 13 13 13 13 13 13
14 15 16 17 18 19 20 21 22 23 24

14 14 14 14 14 14 14 14 14 14
15 16 17 18 19 20 21 22 23 24

15 15 15 15 15 15 15 15 15
16 17 18 19 20 21 22 23 24

16 16 16 16 16 16 16 16
17 18 19 20 21 22 23 24

17 17 17 17 17 17 17
18 19 20 21 22 23 24

18 18 18 18 18 18
19 20 21 22 23 24

19 19 19 19 19
20 21 22 23 24

20 20 20 20
21 22 23 24

21 21 21
22 23 24

22 22
23 24

23
24

Total times each number got circled

1	2	3	4	5	6
7	8	9	10	11	12
13	14	15	16	17	18
19	20	21	22	23	24

Prioritizing Grid for 24 Items

• When you are all done, count up the number of times each number got circled, all told. Enter these totals on the TIMES line in Section C. Then notice the number of times each item was circled ("Times" = "Times Circled"). This determines the item's ranking. Most circled = #1, next most circled = 2, etc. Enter this ranking on the RANK line in Section C. If two items are circled the same number of times, look back in Section B to see -- when those two were compared there -- which one you preferred. Give that one an extra half point. List the items, now in their proper rank, in Section D.

Each time you use this grid, make a photocopy of it, and fill in the photocopy rather than the original. You will need to photocopy this grid many times as you go through this map.

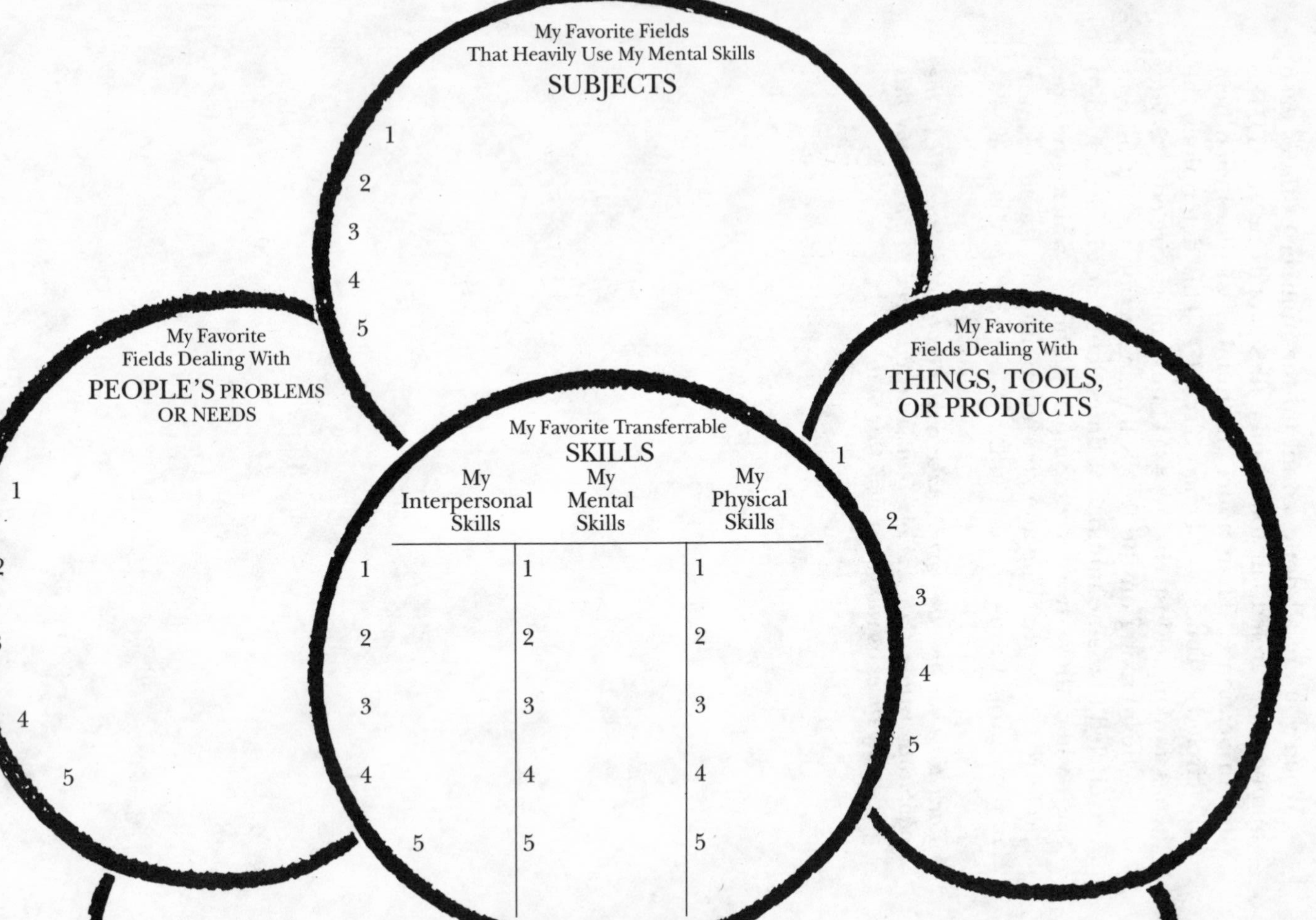
My Favorite Fields
That Heavily Use My Mental Skills
SUBJECTS
1
2
3
4
5
My Favorite
Fields Dealing With
PEOPLE'S PROBLEMS
OR NEEDS
1
2
3
4
5
My Favorite
Fields Dealing With
THINGS, TOOLS,
OR PRODUCTS
1
2
3
4
5
My Favorite Transferrable
SKILLS
My
Interpersonal
Skills
1
2
3
4
5
My
Mental
Skills
1
2
3
4
5
My
Physical
Skills
1
2
3
4
5

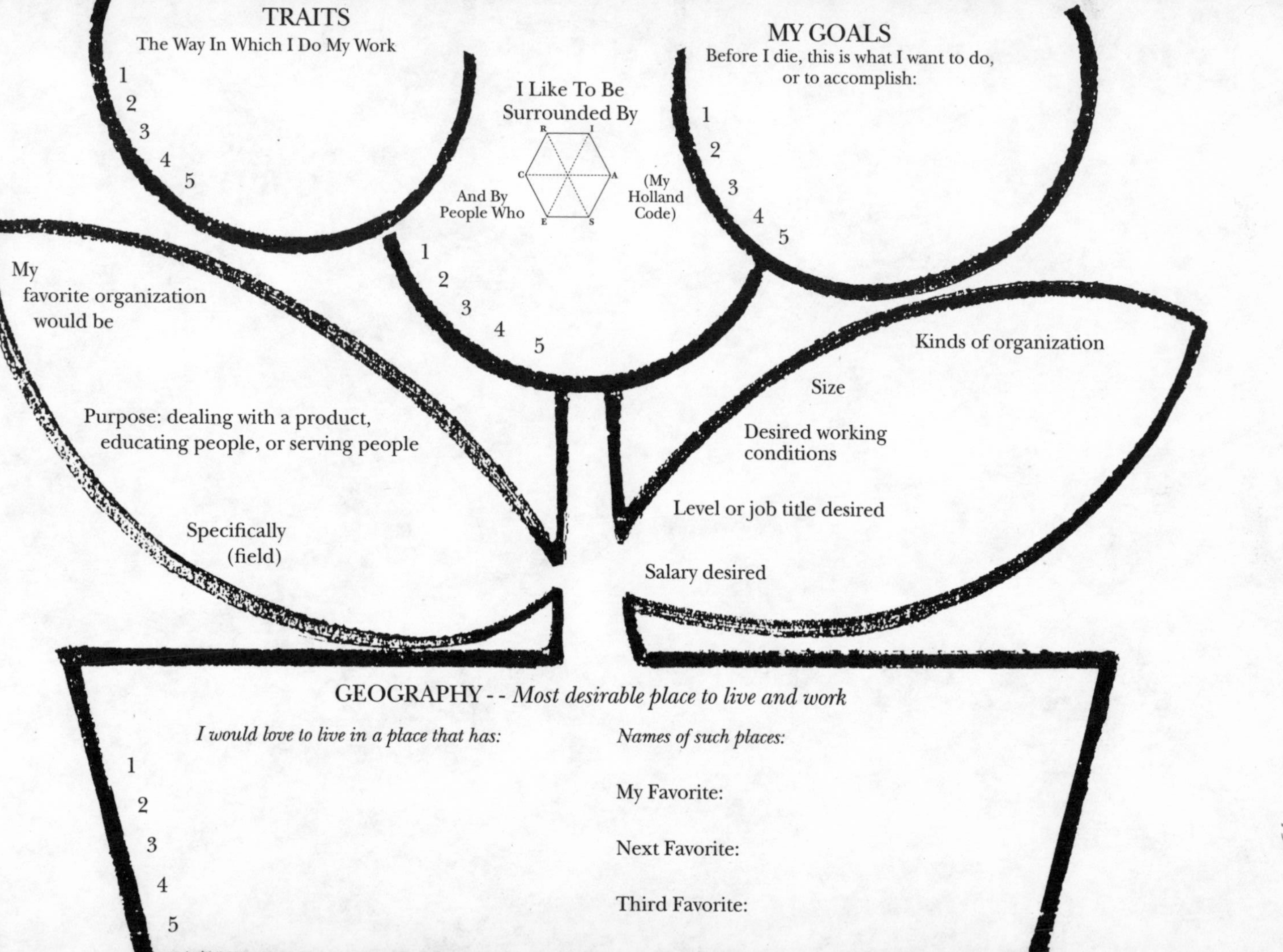
TRAITS
The Way In Which I Do My Work
1
2
3
4
5
I Like To Be
Surrounded By
R
I
C
A
E
S
And By
People Who
(My
Holland
Code)
1
2
3
4
5
MY GOALS
Before I die, this is what I want to do,
or to accomplish:
1
2
3
4
5
My
favorite organization
would be
Purpose: dealing with a product,
educating people, or serving people
Specifically
(field)
Kinds of organization
Size
Desired working
conditions
Level or job title desired
Salary desired
GEOGRAPHY - - Most desirable place to live and work
I would love to live in a place that has:
1
2
3
4
5
Names of such places:
My Favorite:
Next Favorite:
Third Favorite:

II. Researching

How to Research Companies and Places
How to Use Resumes, Agencies & Ads (if you must!)
How to Use the Internet

How To Research Companies or Places

BE NEITHER HAZY NOR LAZY

The surest way to make certain your trip to the library is a total waste of time, is to be *hazy* about what you're trying to find out.

So, please, before you go near a library, write out on a piece of paper, for your own use, "This is the information I am trying to find out *today*: ____________________________." Be specific. Be clear.

For example, do you want to know what the outlook is, in the field that interests you?

Or do you want to know what companies there are, in that field?

Or do you want to find out more about a particular company or organization?

Or do you want to know the names of people within that company or organization?

Or, what?

Think it out ahead of time. Be clear.

Be clear also about why it is important for you to research a company or organization ahead of time. You want to distinguish yourself from all those other job-hunters who walk in on a place and say, "Uh, what exactly do you guys do here?"

Using books -- and contacts -- you want to demonstrate that you cared enough about the place, to learn something about it before you walked in.

WHO DO I TURN TO?

In this section I have listed *some* of the library books which -- as indicated by the experience of career-changers and job-hunters before you -- may prove useful *at one time or another* during the research phase of your career-change or job-hunt.

You may find these resources at your local public library (of course), but don't forget other libraries that may be near you, such as a business library or a local university, college, or community college library.

Some of these books are inexpensive enough for you to purchase, *if you want to*--from your local bookstore (particularly those dealing with job leads). Browse them, first, to see if they are something you want to be able to refer to, again and again.

Some of these books are not inexpensive. In fact, being reference works, they are *hideously* expensive in many cases, so *thank God* for your local library.

Which book to consult? Well of course, the one that helps you with the particular questions you're trying to find answers to.

The books which follow are categorized by the *primary* arena of their information, though each book or resource may have information that spills over into the other categories:

1. **Outlook** (where a particular industry or job-title is going, in the next ten years or so)
2. **Fields** (Descriptions of Occupations or Industries)
3. **Companies** (names, brief or extended information about them)
4. **Individuals** (names, addresses, phone numbers, of people who may serve you as Contacts or Employers)
5. **Vacancies** or Job Leads (where the jobs are, or at least where some people *claim* the jobs are)

As I indicated, your local library should have many if not most of these resources. Ask your local librarian for help. If there is no librarian available, or at least no *helpful* librarian, there are *(mercifully)* indexes/indices to all these directories:

- Klein's *Guide to American Directories;* and
- *Directories in Print.* Gale Research, Inc., 835 Penobscot Bldg., Detroit, MI 48226-4094, which contains over 15,000 current listings of directories, indexed by title or key word or subject (over 3,500 subject headings).

See also:

Encyclopedia of Business Information Sources. Gale Research, Inc., 835 Penobscot Bldg., Detroit, MI 48226-4094. Identifies electronic, print and live resources dealing with 1,500 business subjects. Their companion volume is entitled *Business Organizations, Agencies and Publications Directory,* listing over 24,000 entries, such as federal government advisory organizations, newsletters, research services, etc.

Directory of Special Libraries and Information Centers. Gale Research, Inc., 835 Penobscot Bldg., Detroit, MI 48226-4094. Lists 22,000 research facilities, on various subjects, maintained by libraries, research libraries, businesses, nonprofit organizations, governmental agencies, etc. Detailed subject index, using over 3,500 key words.

And now, to our areas of research:

1. Outlook

Occupational Outlook Handbook. Department of Labor, NTC Publishing Group, 225 W. Touhy Ave., Lincolnwood, IL 60646.

Occupational Outlook Handbook for College Graduates. Superintendent of Documents, U.S. Government.

Petras, Kathryn & Ross, *Jobs '96: By Career, By Industry, By Region.* 1996. Fireside, Rockefeller Center, 1230 Avenue of the Americas, New York, NY 10020. Indicates the outlook, industry by industry. Also lists the leading U.S. companies, associations, directories, and periodicals in each field.

2. Fields

Occupations or Industries

Dictionary of Holland Occupational Codes.

Dictionary of Occupational Titles.

Encyclopedia of Associations, Vol. 1, National Organizations of the U.S.; Vol. 2, Geographic and Executive Indexes; Vol. 3, New Associations and Projects. Gale Research, Inc., 835 Penobscot Bldg., Detroit, MI 48226-4094. Lists 25,000 organizations, associations, clubs and other nonprofit membership groups that are in the business of giving out information. There is a companion series of books: *Regional, State and Local Organizations,* a five-volume set, which lists over 50,000 similar organizations on a regional, state or local level. There is another companion volume, also: *International Organizations.* This lists 4,000 international organizations, concerned with various subjects.

National Trade and Professional Associations of the United States. 29th ed., 1994. Columbia Books, Inc., Publishers, 1212 New York Avenue, N.W., Suite 330, Washington, DC 20005.

Newsletters in Print. Gale Research, Inc., 835 Penobscot Bldg., Detroit, MI 48226-4094. Detailed entry on 10,000 newsletters in various subject fields, or categories. It includes newsletters that are available only online, through a computer and modem.

Standard and Poor's Industry Surveys. Good basic introduction, history, and overview of any industry you may be interested in.

Standard Industrial Classification Manual. 1991. Reprint of material originally published by the U.S. Government Printing Office. Available from: Gordon Press, P.O. Box 459, Bowling Green Station, New York, NY 10003. Gives the Standard Industrial Classification code number for any field or industry -- which is the number used by most business references in their indices.

The Information Please® Business Almanac & Desk Reference, Seth Godin, Editor. Houghton Mifflin Company, 215 Park Ave. So., New York, NY 10003. All kinds of information about industries, with addresses and contacts plus any other business questions you might be curious about (computers, etc.).

U.S. Industrial Outlook. Reprinted from material published by the U.S. Department of Commerce. Available from JIST Works, 720 N. Park Ave., Indianapolis, IN 46202. Covers 350 manufacturing and service industries.

Gives the trends and outlooks for each industry that you may be interested in. Updated annually.

Jobs: What They Are . . . Where They Are . . . What They Pay! by Robert O. Snelling, Sr. and Anne M. Snelling. Fireside, Simon & Schuster Bldg., 1230 Avenue of the Americas, New York, NY 10020. Describes jobs in thirty different fields.

And, for Specific Industries or Fields:

Communications: *Telecommunications Directory.* Gale Research, Inc., 835 Penobscot Bldg., Detroit, MI 48226-4094. Lists over 2,000 national and international firms dealing with communications systems, teleconferencing, videotext, electronic mail, fax services, etc.

Computers: *Information Industry Directory.* Gale Research, Inc., 835 Penobscot Bldg., Detroit, MI 48226-4094. Lists 30,000 computer-based information systems and services, here and abroad. Their companion volume, *Gale Directory of Databases.* Gale Research, Inc., 835 Penobscot Bldg., Detroit, MI 48226-4094, lists trade shows, conventions, users' groups, associations, consultants, etc., worldwide.

Government: In the U.S., the novice government job-hunter assumes that civil service exams introduce a mechanical impartiality to hiring decisions. This is only partially true. If, during your informational interviewing you encounter a federal manager who likes you, and wants to hire you, you can bet your bottom dollar they will do everything they can to guide you through the examination maze -- since any manager worth their salt has long since learned how to creatively use the government's standard operating procedures to their own best advantage. This applies to local and state government positions, as well as federal. For further reading or help:

Krannich, Ronald L., and Krannich, Caryl Rae, *Find a Federal Job Fast!* 4th ed. 1997. Impact Publications, 4580 Sunshine Court, Woodbridge, VA 22192. They have other federal job-hunting aids, as you will discover when they send you their catalog.

Government Job Finder, by Daniel Lauber. 1997. Planning/Communications, 7215 Oak Ave., River Forest, IL 60305. Lists over 2,002 associations, directories, journals, trade magazines, newsletters, computerized job-listings, online services, job-matching services, salary surveys, etc. -- dealing with local, state or federal government work in the U.S. and abroad -- where contacts may be found, or job-leads advertised. Very thorough (see pages 303–308 in that book, especially). Also free updates are available online at: http://jobfindersonline.com.

If you want to work for the Federal government you will have to learn how to fill out a SF-171 form, in many if not most cases. There are guides to help you do this:

Smith, Russ, *The Right SF-171 Writer.* 1994. Impact Publications, 4580 Sunshine Court, Woodbridge, VA 22192.

DataTech's *Quick & Easy 171s.* A software program (for MS-DOS or Windows, only) that produces the SF-171 for Federal job-seekers. Approved by the U.S. Office of Personnel Management. Personal *(single user)* version: $49.95. Order from Impact Publications, 4580 Sunshine Court, Woodbridge, VA 22192.

There is also: *USJOBS Database* (single issue), listing federal jobs nationwide, which you can search by job-title or other parameters. Also has an SF-171 Form Editor, which can turn blank paper into completed SF-171s on your PC. Runs under Windows 3.1. $27.95 from DigiBook Corp., 370 Wall St., Princeton, NJ 08540. Order line: 1-800-734-4371.

United States Government Manual. U.S. Government Printing Office, Stop SSMR, Washington, DC 20402.

Hobbies: *National Recreational Sporting and Hobby Organizations of the U.S.* Columbia Books, Inc., 777 14th St. NW, Washington, DC 20005.

Physical Sciences, Engineering, Biological Sciences: *Directory of Information Resources in the United States.* Washington, DC., Library of Congress.

Research: *Research Center Directory.* Gale Research, Inc., 835 Penobscot Bldg., Detroit, MI 48226-4094. Also: *Research Services Directory.* The two volumes together cover some 13,000 services, facilities, and companies that do research into various subjects, such as feasibility studies, private and public policy, social studies and studies of various cultures, etc.

Statistics: *Statistics Sources.* Gale Research, Inc., 835 Penobscot Bldg., Detroit, MI 48226-4094. Tells you where to find statistics on more than 20,000 specific topics. Key live sources are also featured.

Teaching & Training: *Training and Development Organizations Directory.* Gale Research, Inc., 835 Penobscot Bldg., Detroit, MI 48226-4094. For those of you interested in teaching or training, it lists over 2,500 firms and their areas of interest and expertise.

Public Service Careers: these include such varied occupations as:

- city planner,
- community services officer at a community college,
- gerontology specialist,
- officials dealing with foster parent programs for mentally retarded persons,
- public health officials,
- recreation education,
- social service technician,
- welfare administration,
- workers in the child welfare program,
- workers with the handicapped.

Potential employers for public service occupations or social careers include government (Federal, State, or Local), nonprofit organizations, agencies (independent of state or local government, but often cooperating with them), colleges (particularly community colleges), associations, social welfare agencies, public health departments, correctional institutions, government offices, Job Partnership Training offices, hospitals, rest homes, elementary and secondary schools, parks and recreation agencies, etc.

If you are interested in this general field of social service, you ought to do extensive research, with a heavy emphasis on talking with people actually doing the work you think you would like to do; you will find their names through the national associations in the fields that interest you, also in State departments, and County and City governments (your local reference librarian in your local library can help you locate these associations).

If you know exactly what it is you want to do, but funding is the problem, thorough research on your part will often reveal ways in which funding can be found for positions not yet created; it all depends on your finding a person who knows something about that.

As for what career to choose within this broad category, there are these helps:

Jankowski, Katherine, *The Job Seeker's Guide to Socially Responsible Companies.* 1995. Visible Ink Press™, a division of Gale Research, Inc. 835 Penobscot Bldg., Detroit, MI 48226-4094. An immensely useful book for those who care.

Community Jobs: The Employment Newspaper for the Non-Profit Sector, published by ACCESS: Networking in the Public Interest, 1601 Connecticut Ave., NW, Room 600F, Washington, DC 20009. Lists jobs and internships in nonprofit community organizations. Write directly to them for subscription information.

Peter F. Drucker, *Managing The Non-Profit Organization: Practices and Principles.* HarperCollins Publishers, 10 E. 53rd St., New York, NY 10022. 1990. Very helpful, as is anything from Peter Drucker's pen.

Paul Schmolling, Jr., with William R. Burger and Merrill Youkeles, *Careers in Mental Health: A Guide to Helping Occupations.* Ferguson Publishing Co., 200 West Madison, Suite 300, Chicago, IL 60606.

Mary Scott, *Companies With a Conscience: Intimate Portraits of Twelve Firms That Make a Difference.* Birch Lane Press, New York. 1992.

3. Companies

Large Companies

Company/college/association/agency/foundation *Annual Reports.* Get these directly from the personnel department or publicity person at the company, etc., or from the Chamber or your local library.

The Almanac of American Employers 1996-97. Focuses on the 500 largest, fastest growing, most successful corporate employers; available in most public libraries. Covers companies of 2,500+ employees. Plunkett Research, Ltd., P.O. Drawer 8270, Galveston, TX 77553. 409-765-8530.

America's Fastest Growing Employers: The Complete Guide to Finding Jobs with over 275 of America's Hottest Companies, by Carter Smith with Peter C. Hale. Adams Media, Inc., 260 Center St., Holbrook, MA 02343.

Corporate and Industry Research Reports. Published by R.R. Bowker/Martindale-Hubbell, 121 Chanlon Rd., New Providence, NJ 07974. Can be very helpful.

Corporate Jobs Outlook! A newsletter published every 60 days, available in most public libraries. Covers companies of 500 to 2,500 employees. Plunkett Research, Ltd., P.O. Drawer 8270, Galveston, TX 77553. 409-765-8530.

Corporate Technology Directory. Lists companies by the products they make or the technologies they use. Corporate Technology Information Services, Inc., 12 Alfred St., Suite 200, Woburn, MA 01801-9998.

Directory of American Research and Technology: Organizations Active in Product Development for Business. R.R. Bowker, 121 Chanlon Rd., New Providence, NJ 07974.

Directory of Corporate Affiliations. National Register Publishing Co., Inc.

Dun & Bradstreet's Million Dollar Directory. Very helpful.

Dun & Bradstreet's Million Dollar Directory–Top 50,000 Companies. Very helpful. An abridged version of Dun's *Million Dollar Directory Series.*

Dun & Bradstreet's Reference Book of Corporate Managements.

F & S Indexes (recent articles on firms).

F & S Index of Corporations and Industries. Lists "published articles" by industry and by company name. Updated weekly.

Fitch Corporation Manuals.

Fortune Magazine's 500; they also publish interesting articles during the rest of the year, on major corporations, such as "*America's Most Admired Corporations.*" Visit your local library, and browse back issues.

Hoover's Handbook of American Business 1997, Seventh ed. Publishers: Hoover's, Inc., 1033 La Posada Drive, Suite 250, Austin, TX 78752, 512-374-4500. Profiles of over 500 major U.S. companies. A special section on the companies that have created the most jobs in the last 10 years and those that have eliminated the most jobs. Expensive; see your local library.

Hoover's Company Profiles on CD-ROM. Hoover's, Inc., 1033 La Posada Drive, Suite 250, Austin, TX 78752, 512-374-4500. 2,500 profiles of companies. Includes all the companies in Hoover's books, plus 1,100 more. For Windows or DOS computers.

Hoover's Handbook of World Business 1997. Fourth ed. Hoover's, Inc., 1033 La Posada Drive, Suite 250, Austin, TX 78752, 512-374-4500. 250 profiles of major European, Asian, Latin American, and Canadian companies who employ thousands of Americans both in the U.S. and abroad.

How To Read A Financial Report: Wringing Cash Flow and Other Vital Signs Out of the Numbers, by John A. Tracy, CPA. John Wiley & Sons, Business Law/General Books Division, 605 Third Avenue, New York, NY 10158-0012. Also Chichester, Brisbane, Toronto and Singapore.

Macmillan's Directory of Leading Private Companies.

Moody's Industrial Manual (and other Moody manuals).

Periodicals worth perusing in your public library, in addition to *Fortune,* mentioned above, are *Business Week, Dun's Review, Forbes,* and the *Wall Street Journal.*

Registers of manufacturers for your state or area (e.g., *California Manufacturers Register*).

Standard and Poor's Corporation Records.

Standard and Poor's Industrial Index.

The Adams Jobs Almanac, by the Editors of Adams Media. Adams Media, 260 Center St., Holbrook, MA 02343. Gives a sampling of the major companies in thirty-one industries, together with the kinds of positions they are usually looking for -- when they're looking. Has a state-by-state index of the major employers, plus an introductory section on career outlooks and job-hunting. This same publisher has a *JobBank Series* which you can find in your local bookstore. Currently there are *JobBank* books for: Atlanta, Boston, the Carolinas, Chicago, Dallas-Fort Worth, Denver, Detroit, Florida, Houston, Los Angeles, Minneapolis/St. Paul, New York, Ohio, Philadelphia, Phoenix, St. Louis, San Francisco, Seattle, Tennessee, and Washington D.C. There is also a National JobBank.

Thomas' Register. Thomas Publishing Co. There are 27 volumes in the Thomas register. All the manufacturers there are of 52,000 products and services, plus catalogs, contacts, and phone numbers.

Walker's Manual of Western Corporations. Walker Western Research Co., 1452 Tilia Ave., San Mateo, CA 94402.

Ward's Business Directory, 6 vols. Gale Research, Inc., 835 Penobscot Bldg., Detroit, MI 48226-4094. Updated yearly. Despite the titles, helpful in identifying smaller companies, as well as large.

Small Companies

Hoover's Handbook of Emerging Companies 1997. Fourth ed. Hoover's, Inc., 1033 La Posada Drive, Suite 250, Austin, TX 78752, 512-374-4500. Lists and profiles of 250 smaller, emerging companies with high growth rates. A *sampler* for those seeking employment at smaller companies.

Chamber of Commerce data on an organization or field that interests you (visit the Chamber in the appropriate city or town).

Many public libraries have very efficient database search capabilities, through their computers, and can dig up, copy, and mail to you copies of reports on local companies (for a modest cost). For example, one Pennsylvania job-hunter got the Cleveland (Ohio) Library to send him copies of annual reports on a Cleveland-based company. So, when you get to the point where you're researching organizations, if there's an organization or company that particularly interests you, you might want to try contacting the nearest large public library to that organization's home base, and see what that librarian can turn up for you. (*Please* write and thank her or him, afterward.)

Better Business Bureau report on a particular organization that you may be interested in (call the BBB in the city where the organization is located). These reports sometimes only tell you if there are outstanding, unresolved complaints against a company; if the company has scrambled to settle a complaint in the past, their record will now look pretty good. Still, it's a useful thing to know -- if there are or have been such complaints.

4. Individuals

(As Contacts or Potential Employers)

Consultants and Consulting Organizations Directory. Gale Research, Inc., 835 Penobscot Bldg., Detroit, MI 48226-4094. Lists over 15,000 firms, individuals and organizations engaged in consulting work. Consultants are usually experts in their particular field, and hence may be useful to you in your information search about that job or career-change that you are contemplating.

Dun's Consultants Directory.

Contacts Influential: Commerce and Industry Directory. Businesses in particular market area listed by name, type of business, key personnel, etc. Contacts Influential, Market Research and Development Services, 321 Bush St., Suite 203, San Francisco, CA 94104, if your library doesn't have it.

Standard and Poor's Register of Corporations, Directors and Executives. Key executives in 32,000 leading companies, plus 75,000 directors.

Who's Who in Finance and Industry, and all the other Who's Who books. Useful once you have the name of someone-who-has-the-power-to-hire, and you want to know more about them.

American Society for Training and Development Directory: Who's Who in Training and Development, 1640 King St., Box 1443, Alexandria, VA 22313-2043.

Investor, Banker, Broker Almanac.

American Men and Women of Science.

5. Vacancies or Job Leads

Professional's Job Finder, by Daniel Lauber. 1997. Planning/Communications, 7215 Oak Ave., River Forest, IL 60305. Lists over 3,003 associations, directories, journals, trade magazines, newsletters, computerized job-listings, online services, job-matching services, salary surveys, etc. -- *categorized* very helpfully by fields, industries, and occupations -- where contacts may be found, or job-leads advertised. Very thorough. Also, free updates are available online at: http://jobfindersonline.com.

Non-Profits' and Education Job Finder, by Daniel Lauber. 1997. Planning/Communications, 7215 Oak Ave., River Forest, IL 60305. Lists over 2,222 associations, directories, journals, trade magazines, newsletters, computerized job-listings, online services, job-matching services, foundations, grants, and salary surveys, etc. -- dealing with education and all of the non-profit sector -- where contacts may be found, or job-leads advertised. Also, free updates are available online at: http://jobfindersonline.com.

JOB HUNTER'S SOURCEBOOK: Where to find employment leads and other job search resources, ed. by LeCompte, Michelle. 1996. Gale Research, Inc., 835 Penobscot Bldg., Detroit, MI 48226-4094. A similar exceptional resource, as it tells you how to find sources of information and job-leads for a whole variety of occupations (155, in all). Somebody did their homework well.

The National Job Hotline Directory: Access more than 3,000 employment hotlines 24 hours a day, by Marcia P. Williams and Sue A. Cubbage. McGraw-Hill, Inc., 1221 Avenue of the Americas, New York, NY 10020. The 1998 edition will be with a new publisher.

Caveat: get your hand on the *latest version* of these books in your local bookstore (*or library, if the book is hideously expensive*), and see what up-to-date sources they list, that might know of current jobs. Be painfully aware, before you start, that the sources listed in these books *may not* have any job openings at the time you contact them. If it's a place you're dying to work at, ignore whether or not they have vacancies, and turn to your contacts for help (see the chapters in *Parachute* on "For the Determined Job-Hunter").

HOW TO RESEARCH 'THE PROBLEMS OF AN ORGANIZATION'

Rule No. 1: If it's a large organization that interests you, you don't need to discover the problems of the whole organization. You only need to discover the problems that are bugging *the-person-who-has-the-ultimate-power-to-hire-you.* Conscientious job-hunters always bite off more than they can chew. If they're going to try for a job at the Telephone Company, or IBM or the Federal Government or General Motors or -- like that -- they assume they've got to find out the problems facing that whole organization. *Forget it!* Your task, fortunately, is much more manageable. Find out what problems are bugging, bothering, concerning, perplexing, gnawing at, the-person-who-has-the-power-to-hire-you. This assumes, of course, that you have first *identified* who that person is. Once you have identified her, or him, *find out everything you can about them.* The directories will help. So will the clippings, at your local library. So will any speeches they have given (ask their organization for copies, of same).

If it's a committee of sorts that actually has the responsibility (and therefore the power) to hire you, you will need to figure out who that one individual is (or two) who sways the others. You know, the one whose judgment the others respect. How do you find that out? By using your contacts, of course. Someone will know someone who knows that whole committee, and can tell you who their **real** leader is. It's not necessarily the one who got elected as Chairperson.

Rule No. 2: Don't assume the problems have to be huge, complex, and hidden. The problems bothering the-person-who-has-the-power-to-hire-you may be small, simple, and obvious. If the job you are aiming at was previously filled by someone (i.e., the one who, if you get hired, will be referred to as "your predecessor"), the problems that are bothering the-person-who-has-the-power-to-hire-you may be uncovered simply by finding out through your contacts what bugged your prospective boss about your predecessor. Samples:

"They were never to work on time, took long lunch breaks, and were out sick too often"; OR

"They were good at typing, but had lousy skills over the telephone"; OR

"They handled older people well, but just couldn't relate to the young"; OR

"I never could get them to keep me informed about what they were doing"; etc.

Sometimes, it's as simple as that. Don't assume the problems *have to be* huge and complex. In your research you may be thinking to yourself, "Gosh, this firm has a huge public relations problem; I'll have to show them that I could put together a whole crash P.R. program." That's the huge, complex, and hidden problem that you think the-person-who-has-the-power-to-hire-you *ought to be concerned about.* But, in actual fact, what they are concerned about is whether (unlike your predecessor) you're going to get to work on time, take assigned lunch breaks, and not be out sick too often. Don't overlook the Small, Simple, and Obvious Problems which bug almost every employer.

Rule No. 3: In most cases, your task is not that of educating your prospective employer, but of trying to read their mind. Now, to be sure, you may have uncovered -- during your research -- some problem that the-person-who-has-the-power-to-hire-you is absolutely unaware of. And you may be convinced that this problem is *so crucial* that for you even to mention it will instantly win you their undying gratitude. Maybe. But don't bet on it. Our files are filled with sad testimonies like the following:

"I met with the VP, Marketing, in a major local bank, on the recommendation of an officer, and discussed with him a program I devised to reach the female segment of his market, which would not require any new services, except education, enlightenment, and encouragement. His comment at the end of the discussion was that the bank president had been after him for three years to develop a program for women, and he wasn't about to do it because the only reason, in his mind, for the president's request was reputation enhancement on the president's part . . . "

Interoffice politics, as in this case, or other considerations may prevent your prospective employer from being at all receptive to Your Bright Idea. In any event, you're not trying to find out what *might* motivate them to hire you. Your research has got to be devoted rather to finding out what already does motivate them *when they decide to hire someone for the position you are interested in.* In other words, you are trying to find out What's *Already* Going On In Their Mind. In this sense, your task is more akin to a kind of mind reading than it is to education. (Though some people-who-have-the-power-to-hire are **very** open to being educated. You have to decide whether you want to risk testing this.)

Rule No. 4: There are various ways of finding out what's going on in their mind; don't try just one way.

A. Analyze The Problems Of An Organization That Interests You, By *Thinking* About It:

1. If the organization is expanding, then they need:

   a. More of what they already have; OR
   b. More of what they already have, *but with different style, added skills,* or other pluses; OR
   c. Something they don't presently have: a new kind of person, with new skills doing a new function or service.
2. If the organization is continuing as is, then they need:
   a. To replace people who were fired (find out why; what was lacking:); OR
   b. To replace people who quit (find out what was prized about them); OR
   c. To create a new position. Yes, this happens even in organizations that are not expanding, due to:
      1) Old needs which weren't provided for, earlier, but now must be, even if they have to cut out some other function or position.
      2) Revamping assignments within their present staff.
      3) If the organization is reducing its size, staff, or product or service, then they --
         a) Have not yet decided which staff to terminate, i.e., which functions to give low priority to (in which case **that** is their problem, and you may be able to help them identify which functions are "core-functions"); OR
         b) **Have** decided which functions or staff to terminate (in which case they may need multi-talented people, or generalists able to do several jobs, i.e., functions, instead of just one, as formerly).

B. Analyze The Problems Of The Person Who Has The Power To Hire You, There, By Talking To Him Or Her:

It may be that your paths have accidentally crossed (it happens). Perhaps you attend the same church or synagogue. Perhaps you eat at the same restaurant. In any event, if you *do* ever have a chance to talk to her or him, listen carefully to whatever they may say about the place where they work. The greatest problem every employer faces is finding people who will listen and take them seriously. If you listen, you may find this employer discusses their problems -- giving you firmer grounds to which you can relate your skills.

C. Analyze The Problems Of The Person Who Has The Power To Hire You, By Talking To Their 'Opposite Number' In Another Organization Which Is Similar To The One That Interests You.

If, for some reason, you cannot approach -- at this time -- the organization that interests you (it's too far away, or you don't want to tip your hand yet, or whatever), what you can do is pick a similar organization (or individual) where you are - - and go find out what kind of problems are on their mind. (If you are interested in working for, say, a senator in another state, you can talk to a senator's staff here where you are, first. The problems are likely to be similar.)

D. Analyze The Problems Of The Person Who Has The Power To Hire You, By Talking To The Person Who Held The Job Before You -- Or, Again, Their Opposite Number:

Nobody, absolutely nobody, knows the problems bugging a boss so much as someone who works, or used to work, for them. If they *still* work for them, they may have a huge investment in being discreet (i.e., not as candid as you need). Ex-employees are *not* necessarily any longer under that sort of pressure. Needless to say, if you're trying to get the organization to create a new position, there is no "previous employee." But in some identical or similar organization *which already has this sort of position*, you can still find someone to interview.

E. Analyze The Problems Of The Organization Or The Person Who Has The Power To Hire You, By Talking To Every Contact You Have, In Order To Find Someone Who:

1. Knows the organization that interests you, or knows someone who knows;
2. Knows the-person-who-has-the-power-to-hire-you, or knows someone who knows;
3. Knows who their opposite number would be in a similar/identical organization;
4. Knows your predecessor, or knows someone who knows;
5. Knows your "opposite number" in another organization, or knows someone who knows.

F. Analyze The Problems Of The Organization Or The Person Who Has The Power To Hire You, By Reading Everything You Can Lay Your Hands On:

DO *research in the library*, on the organization, or an organization similar to it; research on the-individual-who-has-the-power-to-hire-you, or on their opposite number in another organization, etc. -- using the resources listed throughout this section, as well as in the Internet section.

POSTSCRIPT ON RESEARCHING:

Ultimately, this business of figuring out the problems *that bother the person who has the power to hire you for the position you want, in the organization that most interests you*, boils down, in the end, to a language-translation problem.

You're trying to take *your* language (i.e., a description of your skills), and translate it into *their* language (i.e., their priorities, their values, their jargon, as these surface within their concerns, problems, etc.). As I have emphasized, most of the-people-who-have-the-power-to-hire-you for the position you want *do not* like the word "problems." It reminds them that they are mortal, have hangups, haven't solved something yet, or that they overlooked something, etc. "*Smartass*" is the street-word normally reserved for someone who comes in and *shows them up*. (This isn't true of *every* employer or manager, but it's true of altogether too many.) Since you're trying to use *their* language, you should probably speak of "an area you probably are planning to move into" or "a concern of yours" or "a challenge currently facing you" or *anything* except: "By the way, I've uncovered a problem you have." Use the word *problems* in your own head, but don't blurt it out during the interview with your prospective employer, *unless you hear them use it first.*

But in your own private thinking, your goal is to be able to speak in the interview of Your Skills *in terms of The Language* of Their Problems.

Well, those are the keys to researching. A lot of hard work, and some good luck.

6. Other Books on Job-Hunting

JOB-HUNTING BOOKS FROM OTHER LEADERS IN THE FIELD

No one book can speak to every reader. While Parachute *has helped millions of people, the truth is that some people are not able to use it. But they may be able to use another book. If you are one of these, I have listed below the primary texts from the other leaders in this field of career planning and job-hunting. You may find that* Parachute *doesn't speak to you, but that one of these other authors does.*

But, down the line, if no *book seems helpful to you in your job-search or career-change dilemma, all is not lost. Consider strongly the possibility of signing up with some reputable career counselor, who can give you the kind of guidance that no book can (see the listings of such, at the end of this Resource Guide).*

The PIE Method for Career Success: A Unique Way to Find Your Ideal Job, by Daniel Porot. JIST Works, Inc., 720 North Park Avenue, Indianapolis, IN 46202. 1996. Daniel and I have taught together for two weeks every summer but one, since 1979. He is a Frenchman, who lives in Geneva, Switzerland. This book, like its author, is brilliantly helpful. No career counselor should fail to read and memorize this book. It is profusely illustrated, and a marvelous 'read.' (For the worried, it *is* in English.)

Sher, Barbara, *Wishcraft: How to Get What You Really Want.* 1983. Ballantine Books, 201 E. 50th St., New York, NY 10022. A very helpful book; our readers love it. *Incidentally, Barbara is a great workshop leader, and if you have a chance to hear her in person, take it! She is smart, witty and helpful.*

Jackson, Tom, *Guerrilla Tactics in the New Job Market* (2nd ed.). 1991. Bantam Books, 1540 Broadway, New York, NY 10036. A very popular and useful book, now revised for the '90s. Tom has some great ideas and insights found in no other author's work.

Figler, Howard E., *The Complete Job-Search Handbook: All the Skills You Need to Get Any Job and Have a Good Time Doing It.* 1988, Revised and Expanded Edition. Henry Holt & Co., Inc., 115 W. 18th St., New York, NY 10011. Identifies the twenty skills the job-hunter needs in order to pull off a job-hunt *successfully.* A very unusual approach to the subject of skills, as well as to the subject of the job-hunt.

Miller, Arthur F., and Mattson, Ralph T., *The Truth About You: Discover What You Should Be Doing with Your Life.* 1977, 1989. Ten Speed Press, Box 7123, Berkeley CA 94707. I like this book a lot. Unfortunately, it's gone out of print. Try your local library.

Career Satisfaction and Success: A Guide to Job and Personal Freedom, by Bernard Haldane. JIST Works, Inc., 720 North Park Avenue, Indianapolis, IN 46202. 1996. Bernard, now 86 years old, has been a leading figure in the career field for over fifty years now, having begun in 1946. This is a re-issue, revised and enlarged, of his most important book.

Gaither, Richard, with Baker, John, *The Wizard of Work: 88 Pages to Your Next Job.* 1995. Ten Speed Press, P.O. Box 7123, Berkeley, CA 94707. A very interesting book, with ideas not found in any other.

Wegmann, Robert and Chapman, Robert, *The Right Place at the Right Time: Finding a Job in the 1990s.* 1987, revised and updated, 1990. Ten Speed Press, Box 7123, Berkeley, CA 94707. I like this book a lot. Unfortunately, it's gone out of print. Try your local library. *Note also that there is another book by these two authors, along with Miriam Johnson:* Work in the New Economy: Careers and Job Seeking into the 21st Century. *1989. Updated. JIST Works, 720 North Park Ave., Indianapolis, IN 46202. Highly recommended, of course. Bob Wegmann's insights in another form.*

Scheele, Adele, *Skills for Success,* Ballantine Books/Random House, 201 E. 50th St., New York, NY 10022. 1981; reprinted 1996. The classic book that asks "what skills are required in order to be successful?"

Krannich, Ronald L., *Change Your Job, Change Your Life! High Impact Strategies For Finding Great Jobs in the 90s.* 1994. This is an updated version of Ron's earlier title, *Careering and Re-Careering For the 90s.* Very thorough. Ron is a prolific writer; he is the author of over thirty books in this field. *U.S. News and World Report* called this one of the two top career books in the country.

Yate, Martin, *Knock 'em Dead: The Ultimate Job Seeker's Handbook.* Revised annually. Adams Media, 260 Center St., Holbrook, MA 02343. Omnipresent in U.S. bookstores, currently, this book should be easy to find. Very popular.

The Guide to Internet Job Searching, by Margaret Riley, Frances Roehm, and Steve Oserman. VGM Career Horizons, a division of NTC Publishing Group, 4255 West Touhy Avenue, Lincolnwood (Chicago), IL 60646-1975. 1996. Known on the Web as 'the Riley guide,' I like this book the best of all those which have been coming out about job-hunting and the Internet. The table of contents includes such topics as "Jobs in Business," "Jobs in the Social Sciences," "International Opportunities," etc. An impressive work, representing hundreds of hours of research on 'the Net.'

Incidentally, the Guide's new website address as of July 7, 1997, is www.dbm.com/jobguide

If you did not find the books you were looking for, in this Research section, there are four kinds of places where you can look further.

(1) Your **local bookstores** -- go to more than one, browse, and see what they have. Disadvantage: you have to buy the book, if you want it. Advantage: They've got the latest most up-to-date edition *(usually -- though not always).* Furthermore, they can order for you almost any book *that is still in print* -- and you'll know *that,* by whether or not it is listed in a reference book most bookstores have, called *Books In Print.* Ask.

(2) Your local **public libraries**, or nearby community college library. If they have a friendly reference librarian, by all means ask to see him or her. They can be worth their weight in gold to you. Tell them your problem or interest, and see what they can dig up. Disadvantage: a library may not have the latest edition of a book (see what edition of *Parachute* they're carrying, for example). Advantage: you can borrow a book for free, and furthermore, the reference librarian often knows of hidden treasures, buried in articles and clippings, which could be the answer to your prayers.

(3) **Mail order**. This is particularly helpful to those who live outside the U.S. There are a number of U.S. mail order places which specialize in career books. Their catalogs are listed on page *271 ff.* Disadvantage: you have to wait to get the book (but if you phone, you can often order them by Federal Express, so sometimes it's *next day* delivery). Advantage: often, you can order it from anywhere in the world, And their listings of career books, tapes, videos and software, are far more extensive than you will find in the average bookstore, or library.

(4) **The Internet**. There are now online bookstores, such as `www.amazon.com`, and Career WEB's online bookstore, from which you can order many of the career books listed here in *Parachute.* This is of particular advantage to our international readers, who find their local bookstores have never heard of most of the books listed here, because they are regarded as "*U.S. books.*" If you are on the Internet, you can now overcome that hurdle, and make them "*worldwide books.*"

How to Use Resumes, Agencies, & Ads
(If You Must)

My favorite comment this year about resumes came from a student graduating from the University of Texas at Austin. *"I can't begin to tell you how grateful I am that you wrote this book. I will be graduating this May and will be gainfully employed by an employer of my choice thereafter. I have the job I want, in the field I love (aviation) while my friends are still sending out resumes! To this day, I have never written nor used such a useless piece of paper! I think I'll put all of my friends out of their misery by telling them to quit wasting time on resumes, and buy them all a copy of your book!"*

Why are his fellow students having so much trouble finding jobs? Well, you remember the track record of resumes, don't you? Only one job-offer tendered and accepted, for every 1470 resumes that are floating around out there in the world of work.

So why don't resumes work better than they do? Why don't employers put more faith in them?

Well, let's start with the word "lying."

As far back as 1992, it was being discovered that 'an unacceptably high' number of 15- to 30-year-olds believed it was okay to lie and cheat at work or school. One-third of them said they were willing to lie on a resume.[1]

This trend is not restricted to the young. People in high places -- executives, superintendents of schools, and the like -- have falsely claimed doctorates, and otherwise lied on their resumes. And been caught.

Thus, experts estimate that one-third to one-half of all job-hunters lie on their resumes.

They lie by: inflating their title or responsibilities, omitting their firings or failures, inflating their results, inflating their credentials, hiding jobs where they did terribly, and a lot of other subterfuges.

If you were an employer, how much faith would you put in a piece of paper where you know there are lies on one-third to one-half of them?

> Resume: An ingenious device that turns a human being into an object (an eight and a half by eleven inches piece of paper). This transformation device is then often used to try and convince people we have never met to invest thousands of dollars in us, by hiring us for a job we have not yet specifically identified. *Michael Bryant*

Still, you're probably determined to use one, so let's look at some things you'll need to keep in mind:

---

1. A survey of 6,873 high school and college students, done by the Josephson Institute of Ethics, reported in *USA Today*, 11/13/92.

A Summary of What We Know About Resumes

RÉSUMÉ **rez-e-mā** n {F. *résumé* fr. pp. of *résumer* to resume, summarize] SUMMARY *specif:* a short account of one's career and qualifications prepared typically by an applicant for a position.

Webster's

Resumes have a lousy track record. A study of employers done a number of years ago discovered that there was one job offer tendered and accepted, for every 1470 resumes that employers received, from job-hunters. Would you take a plane flight if you knew that only one out of every 1470 planes ever made it to its destination?

The few for whom resumes work talk a lot about it; the vast majority for whom resumes don't work, usually keep quiet about it. Hence, the widespread impression that 'this is a method which works for almost everyone.'

If you believe resumes generally work, and you send out loads of resumes, and you don't even get a nibble, you're going to think that something is wrong with *you.* Hence, plummeting self-esteem, thence depression, emotional paralysis, and worse symptoms *often* follow. This has happened to tens of thousands of job-hunters. It has even happened to me. Don't let it happen to you. You have to get back to point #1, above: resumes have a lousy track record. If you don't get even a nibble, that doesn't mean that anything's wrong with you. Something's desperately wrong with resumes . . . as a job-hunting technique.

Those employers who like resumes like them because they enable employers to screen you out *fast* without ever 'wasting their time' on an interview. *Most* employers, or their subordinates, can *screen you out* in approximately thirty seconds, if your resume is sitting in a stack of, say, fifty, on their desk. And if it's in a stack of several hundred, the employer picks up speed and -- we know by actual count -- can screen you out in as little as eight seconds. So, in eight to thirty seconds, *you're gone.* And, with it, any chance for a job there.

In spite of the evidence, almost everyone -- including career counselors and job-hunting books -- will advise you to send out your resume *(or 'curriculum vitae,' c.v. for short)* to a lot of employers, and in answer to a lot of ads for job vacancies. Many people love the *idea* of a resume, no matter how ineffective it is. Never was love more blind. Only 1 in 1470 gets through, remember.

Many employers *hate* resumes. Period. Many others use them, but distrust them, because so many job-hunters lie about their qualifications -- *and are found out.*

Many organizations send no response in answer to resumes. You'll have to guess whether they ever saw your resume, or 'deep-sixed' it, unopened and unread.

Job-hunters will always love resumes, in spite of all the above, because job-hunters *hate* rejection. With resumes, your name gets out there, and though it usually doesn't lead to a job, at least you're not standing there in front of a would-be employer, staring into his or her face while you hear the bad news. With resumes, it's rejection all right. But it doesn't feel so . . . *personal.* Resumes are a nice way to kid ourselves, so that we *feel* we are doing something about our job-hunt, even if -- so far as effectively finding a job is concerned -- we are actually doing next to nothing.

Government/State Employment Agencies

The second job-hunting strategy that we instinctively turn to, in our Neanderthal job-hunting system, is agencies.

Agencies seem like a wonderful idea, when you are unemployed. My goodness, there's actually someone out there who can link employers looking for jobs with very-qualified me. We all like to think that somewhere out there is just such a switchboard, where all the employers and all the job-hunters, in an area, can come to find each other.

Unhappily, no place in this country has even a clue as to where all the jobs are. The best that any place can offer you is a kind of sampling, a sort of smorgasbord, if you will, of some of the jobs that are available, out there.

So, if you want a sampling, you will naturally want to visit an agency. Agencies are of several types: federal/state; private; and those retained by employers. Let's look at them in turn, beginning with The Federal/State Employment Service.

The local State employment office in your town or city is actually part of a nationwide Federal network, called "The United States Employment Service," or USES for short. USES has seen its staff and budget, nationwide, greatly reduced in recent years.

About one-tenth of these offices offer job-search workshops, from time to time -- depending on the demand, and whether or not a counselor is available who knows how to teach such a workshop. Beyond that, they have listings of some of the jobs available in your geographical area -- usually ones that employers have already tried to fill in every other way they can.

According to one study, USES placed only 13.7% of those who sought a job there. This means of course that they failed to find a job for 86.3% of the job-hunters who went there to find a job.

Because it is part of a nationwide network, your local USES or Job Service office should have access to the Interstate Job Bank listings, which will tell you about job opportunities in other states or cities that may be of interest to you. The normal number of these listings runs around 6,000 at any one time; 98% of the USES offices have these listings on microfiche, and 20% of the offices also have a computer hookup. The listings are typically two weeks old before you see them, but many of them are for 'constant hires,' so that may not matter.

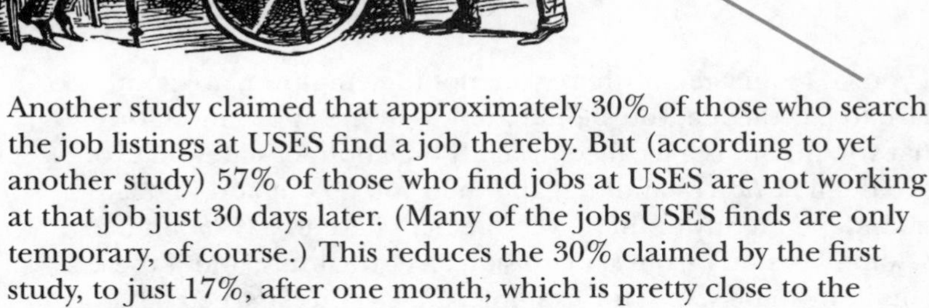

Another study claimed that approximately 30% of those who search the job listings at USES find a job thereby. But (according to yet another study) 57% of those who find jobs at USES are not working at that job just 30 days later. (Many of the jobs USES finds are only temporary, of course.) This reduces the 30% claimed by the first study, to just 17%, after one month, which is pretty close to the 13.7% cited above.

If you go to your State employment office's job listings, be realistic about your chances of finding a job thereby. Your chances are 13 out of 100. Don't put all your job-hunting eggs in this one basket.

Private Employment Agencies

Employment agencies are either for long-term work, or for temporary work. The latter are called 'temporary agencies.'

Some agencies list all kinds of jobs. Most specialize. Typical specialties, among long-term as well as temporary agencies: accountants, office services, data processing, legal, insurance, sales/marketing, underwriting, industrial (assemblers, drivers, mechanics), construction, engineering, management/executives, financial, data processing, nannies (for young and old), and health care/dental/ medical, *among others.* You can find them listed in the Yellow Pages of your local phone book, under such headings as *Employment Agencies; Employment Service–Government, Company, Fraternal, etc.; and Employment–Temporary.* If they specialize, their listing or their ads will usually indicate what their specialties are.

If you go to an agency where you, not the employer, are going to have to pay the fee, you should know that the application form that you fill out is a legal contract. If the contract states that you give them *exclusive* handling, and then you go out and find a job independently of them, you may still have to pay *them* a fee. Beware. Fees vary from state to state. Ask what it is, and if there's a limit. In some states, for example, a fee cannot exceed 60% of one month's salary, i.e., a $15,000-a-year job will cost you $750, payable (usually) in weekly installments of 10% (e.g., $75 on a $750 total). Sometimes in the U.S., such fees are tax deductible, but not if your new job represents a career-change.

Experts allege that the average placement rate for employment agencies is only 5% *of those who walk in the door.* That means a 95% failure rate, right? *Tilt.* Incidentally, you should know that some agencies play games with their figures, so they can *claim* a high placement rate. They boast something like: "95% of all our clients find jobs through our agency." The trick is in whom they consider to be clients. They don't mean all those who come through that door. No, no, no. They make this game work, by accepting as 'clients' only a small percentage of those who walk in the door. And who might these be? You guessed it. The job-hunters that the agency thinks will be easiest to place. *Cute.* Of course they can place 95% of *them!*

Most often, the fees are paid by employers, but sometimes it is the job-hunter who pays. Be sure to ask which is the case. *Naturally,* you want agencies that make no charge to the job-hunter, if you can find them.

While agencies claim to represent employer and job-hunter equally, when push comes to shove (like, when the job listing they have doesn't quite match you) their loyalty will lie with those who pay the bills (which in most cases is the employer), and those who represent repeat business (again, employers). This means that some agencies may try to talk you into taking a job that doesn't fit you at all, just so they can get the employer's business (and fee).

Agencies' usefulness to *career-changers* is very limited. Agency business is primarily a volume business, requiring rapid turnover of clientele, little time given to the individual job-hunter, with their primary focus on the most-marketable job-hunters, especially those on whom they can make a handsome fee. *Career-changers,* who have no previous track record in a particular industry or job, represent huge problems for agencies, which most of the time they are not willing to waste time on.

Agencies Retained by Employers

One of the things that job-hunters rarely understand is the fact that employers are as baffled by our country's Neanderthal job-hunting 'system' as we are, and **don't know how to find decent employees, any more than job-hunters know how to find decent employers.** Therefore, they have certain agencies which they pay to find employees for them. Naturally, such agencies know about vacancies. They're being paid to fill them!

They are commonly referred to as headhunters, body snatchers, flesh peddlers, or talent scouts.

They are historically referred to as executive search firms, executive recruiters, executive recruitment consultants, executive development specialists, management consultants, recruiters. (In the old days, these firms searched only for executives, hence their now-outdated title.)

It's a hazy category. For one thing, yesterday's employment agencies today often prefer to lump themselves into this category. That is because employment agencies typically have to operate under more stringent state or federal regulations than executive search firms do. Their only accountability is that they have to find the exact person with the exact history and exact experience that they are being paid to find!!!

The mission these firms have been given by employers is to hire away from other firms or employers, workers who are already employed, and rising -- executives, salespeople, technicians, data-processing people, or whatever. You will notice it says nothing about their wanting to hire the unemployed.

They are not, therefore, helpful to most job-hunters. But if you research the firms very thoroughly, and find one that deals with your field or specialty, it's always worth sending them your resume -- just in case. Don't count on anything happening, though. You're essentially praying for lightning to strike.[1]

Is there any place out there, set up by employers where employer and job-hunter can meet face-to-face? Well, there are job-fairs in various places around the country, held at various times of the year. Ask your local Chamber of Commerce if they know of any. These are often remarkably unproductive, but some job-hunters have struck pay-dirt by going to them.

On some college campuses, recruiters from various companies show up to interview seniors (and sometimes others) for jobs they have vacant. But it's a very dicey process, and you should by no means count on it. Most often it leads absolutely nowhere.

---

1. There are places that will sell you lists. For example:

Directory of Executive Recruiters, published by Consultant News, Templeton Rd., Fitzwilliam, NH 03447. Published yearly. Lists several hundred firms and the industries served.

Directory of Personnel Consultants by Specialization (Industry Grouping). Published by the National Association of Personnel Consultants, Round House Square, 3133 Mt. Vernon Ave., Alexandria, VA 22305. 1-703-684-0180.

If you want to know more about executive search, there is: John Lucht, *Rites of Passage at $100,000+*, rev. ed. Henry Holt and Co., 115 W. 18th, New York, NY 10011. 800-247-3912. Review by one of our readers: "This book describes in depth the methods of headhunters, what to expect and how to deal with them on an on-going basis. Highly recommended for anyone in middle-management or above. . . ."

Ads In Newspapers

The third job-hunting strategy that we instinctively turn to, in our Neanderthal job-hunting system -- after resumes and agencies -- is want ads.

Want ads are found in your local newspaper -- in the classified section, and/or in the business section, sports section, education section, or Sunday edition. Also, for management or financial job-hunters, ads are to be found in the *Wall Street Journal* (especially Tuesday's and Wednesday's editions).

Some phrases are designed to lure you in, while concealing what the job is really about. Beware! Examples:

"Energetic self-starter wanted" (= You'll be working on commission)
"Good organizational skills" (= You'll be handling the filing)
"Make an investment in your future" (= This is a franchise or pyramid scheme)
"Much client contact" (= You handle the phone, or make 'cold calls' on clients)
"Planning and coordinating" (= You book the boss's travel arrangements)
"Opportunity of a lifetime" (= Nowhere else will you find such a low salary and so much work)
"Management training position" or "Varied, interesting travel" (= You'll be a salesperson with a wide territory)

Within 48–96 hours after an ad appears (the third day is usually the peak), an employer will typically receive from 20 to 1000 or more resumes, and will proceed to systematically *screen out* 95 to 98 out of every 100.

Many classified ads include the employers' phone number, because they want to see if they can *screen you out* over the telephone, without ever having to take the time to see you in person. This is always to your disadvantage. Therefore, most experts say, don't say anything over the phone, except that you want to set up an appointment. One way to avoid being drawn into conversation, designed to screen you out over the phone, is simply to say: "I'm sorry I can't talk now; I'm at work."

A study conducted in two "typical" cities -- one large, one small -- revealed, and I quote, that "85% of the employers in San Francisco, and 75% in Salt Lake City, did not hire any employees through want ads" during a typical year. Yes, that said *any* employees, *during the whole year*.[2] In other words, if you use ads, they only give you access to (at most) 25% of the employers in that city, during the entire year.

As if all of this weren't bad enough, your job-hunting career with ads is further compromised by the fact that some of the ads you see are fakes.

Some employers run fake ads to test the loyalty of their employees (the ad lists only a box number to write to).[3]

Some employment agencies run fake ads, usually listing jobs that have already been filled, in order to draw you in (the old 'bait and switch' process).

Some swindlers run fake ads, pretending they are employers, so that they can get your money (the clue is: the ad gives you a 900 number to call) or get your Social Security number and the number of your driver's license (don't ever give these out over the phone, in response to an ad). With these two numbers alone, from you, they can often take you to the cleaners with some of the con games they've invented.

2. Olympus Research Corporation, "A Study to Test the Feasibility of Determining Whether Classified Ads in Daily Newspapers Are an Accurate Reflection of Local Labor Markets and of Significance to Employers and Job Seekers." 1973. Now out of print.

3. I am citing an actual case here, as my example.

Ads Not In Newspapers

- For Nonprofit Organizations Doing Public or Community Service: ACCESS, Networking in the Public Interest, 1001 Connecticut Ave., N.W., Suite 838, Washington, D.C. 20036. 202-785-4233. Fax: 202-785-4212. Amy Kincaid, Executive Director. Listings of job opportunities in the nonprofit sector, ranging from entry level to Executive positions, are disseminated through two publications: (1) *Community Jobs: The National Employment Newspaper For The Nonprofit Sector;* (2) *Community Jobs/ Northeastern Corridor,* a twice-monthly publication covering Maine to Virginia. ACCESS also provides career development services specifically geared toward the nonprofit job-seeker featuring (for $30) a printout of their database, for the locations and fields that interest you (e.g., animal rights organizations in New York State). Write, call, or fax for details if you are interested in any of their services.

- For Jobs in the Experiential/Adventure (Outdoor) Education Field: *Jobs Clearinghouse.* Association for Experiential Education, 2305 Canyon Blvd., Suite #100, Boulder, CO 80302-5651. 303-440-8844. Fax: 303-440-9581. Timmy Comstedt, Manager. Monthly listings of full-time, part-time, seasonal jobs and internships, in the U.S. and abroad, in the experiential/adventure education field, (3 months for $24, or one issue for $9). Write, call, or fax for details, if you are interested.

- For The Blind: Job Opportunities for the Blind, 1800 Johnson St., Baltimore, MD 21230. 1-410-659-9314, or 1-800-638-7518. Exists to inform blind applicants about positions that are open with public and private employers throughout the country. Maintains a computerized listing. Also, they have cassette instructions on everything for the blind job-seeker. Operated by the National Federation of the Blind in partnership with the U.S. Department of Labor.

- For Jobs Outdoors: Environmental Opportunities, P.O. Box 4379, Arcata, CA, 95518. 707-826-1909. Fax: 707-826-2495. Sanford Berry publishes a monthly newsletter (called *Environmental Opportunities*), listing environmental jobs and internships. Each issue contains sixty to one hundred fulltime positions in a variety of disciplines.

- For Jobs in Horticulture: Ferrell's JOBS IN HORTICULTURE, 8 Terri Dr., Carlisle, PA 17013-9295. 1-800-428-2474. A semi-monthly guide to opportunities. The rate for individuals is $24.95 for six issues (3 months worth). For students, the rate is only $19.95

- For Jobs Overseas: *International Employment Hotline,* a monthly newsletter which lists international employment opportunities. *International Employment Hot line,* Cantrell Corp., Box 3030, Oakton, VA 22124.

- For Government Jobs: *Federal Career Opportunities,* published biweekly by Federal Research Service, Inc., 243 Church St. NW, Vienna, VA 22183. 1-703-281-0200. Each issue is 64 pages, and lists 3,200+ currently available federal jobs, in both the U.S. and overseas.

- For Jobs in Criminal Justice: The *NELS Monthly Bulletin,* National Employment Listing Service, Criminal Justice Center, Sam Houston State Univ., Huntsville, TX 77341. 1-409-294-1592. A nonprofit service providing information on current job opportunities in the criminal justice and social services fields.

- For Jobs in The Christian Church: Intercristo is a national Christian organization that lists over 19,000 jobs, covering hundreds of vocational categories within 1,300 or more Christian service organizations in the U.S. as well as overseas. Their service is called Christian Placement Network. In 1996–1997, 9,000 people used the Network, and one out of every twenty-five of them found a job thereby (which, or course, means that 24 out of 25 *didn't*). But if those odds don't bother you, or the fact that a number of our readers feel that a disproportionate number of listings are in very conservative church settings, then you can contact them at 19303 Fremont Ave. North, Seattle, WA 98133 (phone 1-800-426-1342, or 1-206-546-7330). The cost of being listed there, for three months, is $45.95. If you prefer quicker action, three months on their website (`www.jobleads.org`) costs $59.95, but you get an *instant* listing of jobs that match *your* criteria. From that same website, beginning in 1998, you will be able (for about $130) to sign up for their new Career Assessment Test, which matches you to job-titles in the nonprofit sector (only). *Ann Brooks is their Executive Director.*

The rules for answering ads, *if you must,* are relatively simple:

• Keep your answer brief. You're not trying to sell the employer on the idea that he or she must hire you! That's the purpose of the interview. All you're trying to do, by answering the ad, is to get invited in for an interview.

• In answering an ad, just allude to the specifications *that the ad mentioned or requested;* nothing more! Volunteer no information that could lead the employer to decide not to grant you an interview.

• List your qualifications as a series of points, with perhaps a 'bullet' (like the red dot here) in front of each.

• If the ad mentioned a skill you don't have, like *experienced with motor boats,* you may allude to that specification nonetheless, by saying something like *interested in motor boats.* Of course, that had better be true!

• If the ad requires you to state your salary 'requirements,' you are generally advised by experts to ignore this, because many employers use it as a device to screen you out, without ever having to invite you in for an interview. If you omit any mention of it, the employer may suppose you didn't notice it, and invite you in. However, other experts say, Answer the request, but do so by stating a range, of at least three to five thousand dollars ("*My salary requirements are between fifteen and twenty thousand dollars, depending upon the amount of responsibility I would be given.*")

• If you feel you want to answer the request for your salary requirements, yet you do not wish to state any figure or range, at all, then experts suggest you summarize your past work history to date, with some such phrases as: *I have enjoyed my career, because I have been promoted regularly on the basis of merit, with increased authority each time, and of course with commensurate increases in my salary.*

• You must make certain the spelling in your letter is flawless. "Almost perfect" won't do. Show it to at least two friends, professionals, or members of your family, who are good spellers. If a spelling error is found, *retype* the whole letter.

• Check to make sure the final sentence in your response to that ad keeps the control in your hands. Not: *I'll be looking forward to hearing from you,* but, *I look forward to hearing from you, and will call your office next week to be sure you received this -- the mails being what they are, these days.*

• Be sure to include your phone number, fax number, e-mail number, or any other way that the employer can get ahold of you, to suggest an interview (if indeed this letter of yours elicits that response).

• I advise you not to put stupid things on your envelope, like *Personal and Confidential,* implying this is a letter from the President. Some employers are weary of such strategies, and your letter will get dumped *because* you used it.

• Mail it in. Don't expect much. Remember, on average only two out of each one hundred who answer an ad actually get invited in for an interview.

• Here's a backup strategy for you, however. If you're going to be answering ads more than once, read your local newspaper *daily.* Note particularly the ads you would *like* to respond to, except you don't have the qualifications asked for. It says *"Master's degree required,"* for example, and you have no Master's degree.

• Cut out the ad, save it; if you want to, respond to it. Your letter will probably be ignored. In time, the ad will stop running, usually because the employer will have found the person they are looking for. *But if it runs again,* that's a sign the employer couldn't find a person with all the qualifications they were looking for. Now, you have a chance to write again -- and bargain this time.

• Here's how one job-hunter described her success with this approach: *"The particular ad I answered the first time it ran required at least an associate degree, which I did not have. What I did have was almost ten years' experience in that particular field. When the ad reappeared a month later I sent a letter saying they obviously had not found what they were looking for in the way of a degree, so why not give me a chance; they already had my resume. Well, it worked. I got the interview, I made them an offer that was $6,000 less than they were going to pay a degreed person, but still a $6,000 increase for me, over my prior position. I got the job. Needless to say, everyone was happy. I have recommended this same procedure to three of my friends, and it worked for two out of three of them, also."*

For Further Reading

Richard Lathrop, *Who's Hiring Who?* 12th ed. 1989. Ten Speed Press, Box 7123, Berkeley, CA 94707. This is used more often by our readers than any other book. Richard describes and recommends "a qualifications brief" -- an idea akin to what John Crystal used to propose -- which was, that in approaching an employer you should think of offering him or her a written proposal of what you *will* do in the future, rather than "a resume" of what you did do in the past.

Yana Parker, *The Damn Good Resume Guide.* 1996. Ten Speed Press, Box 7123, Berkeley, CA 94707. Describes, in ten steps, how to write functional and chronological resumes. Employers' comments upon *resumes which actually got people jobs,* are especially helpful. The other most popular resume book (according to our mail). Yana's other resume resources are:

Yana Parker, *The Resume Catalog: 200 Damn Good Examples.* 1996. Ten Speed Press, Box 7123, Berkeley, CA 94707.

Yana Parker, *Blue Collar & Beyond: Resumes for Skilled Trades and Services.* 1995. 125 sample resumes for construction trades, automotive, heavy equipment, warehouse, manufacturing, electronics, services, food and hospitality. Ten Speed Press, Box 7123, Berkeley, CA 94707.

Yana Parker, *Ready-To-Go Resumes* software. 1995. Self-teaching resume templates, with three computer disks for both Macintosh and Windows computers. It is based on her very popular books. Ten Speed Press, Box 7123, Berkeley, CA 94707.

Yana Parker, *Resume Pro: the Professional's Guide.* 1993. Comprehensive manual for professionals in the resume business. Ten Speed Press, Box 7123, Berkeley, CA 94707. There is a companion website of resume advice, at: http://www.damngood.com

David Swanson, *The Resume Solution; How To Write (and Use) A Resume That Gets Results.* 1991. JIST Works, Inc., 720 North Park Ave., Indianapolis, IN 46202-3431. This is a relatively new book on resumes, with tips not to be found in other books. It is very popular. (Dave has been on my staff at my workshops since 1978.)

Tom Jackson, with Ellen Jackson, *The* New *Perfect Resume.* 1996, revised. Anchor Press/Doubleday, Garden City, NY 11530. This is Tom's best-selling book, and with good reason. This edition is completely updated with 100+ resume samples and with internal career advice.

Timothy D. Haft, *Trashproof Resumes: Your Guide to Cracking the Job Market.* 1995. *The Princeton Review,* Random House, Inc., 201 E. 50th St., New York, NY 10022. Geared primarily to college students and recent college graduates. Well done.

There are a *dozens* of additional books on resumes, available at any large bookstore (*Borders, SuperCrown, Barnes & Noble, B. Dalton, and amazon.com, for example*). If the above sampling is not enough for you, see your local bookstore.

Also, there are a number of books out there devoted to *cover letters,* either to go with a resume or by themselves instead of a resume. These include:

Hansen, Katherine, and Hansen, Randall, *Dynamic Cover Letters.* 1996. Ten Speed Press, Box 7123, Berkeley, CA 94707.

Krannich, Ronald L. and Caryl Rae, *Dynamite Cover Letters.* 1992, Impact Publications, 9104-N Manassas Drive, Manassas Park, VA 22111.

William S. Frank, *200 Letters for Job Hunters.* rev. ed. 1993. Ten Speed Press, Box 7123, Berkeley, CA 94707.

Job-Hunting On The Internet

Table of Contents

AN OUTLINE OF THIS CHAPTER

There are five ways in which the Internet can be helpful to job-hunters or career-changers. They are:

#1. As a place for you to search for **vacancies**, listed by employers (often called **job listings**).

#2. As a place to post your **resume**.

#3. As a place to get some job-hunting help or **career counseling**.

#4. As a place to make **contacts** with people, who can help you find information, or help you get in for an interview, at a particular place.

#5. As a place to find **information** or do **research** on fields, occupations, companies, cities, etc.

I have used these five headings (**Job Listings, Resumes, Career Counseling, Contacts,** and **Research**) as the outline for this Guide -- plus a sixth, **Gateway Sites**, that I will explain shortly. But first, let me explain my rating system.

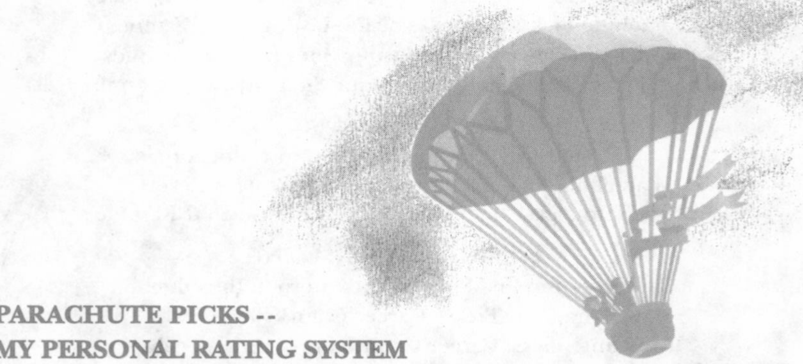

PARACHUTE PICKS -- MY PERSONAL RATING SYSTEM

There are alleged to be 11,000 sites on the Internet that deal with jobs, careers, or job-hunting. The number grows weekly.

I have listed the most useful sites *that I know of* (but, in spite of my spending as many as 7 hours a day on the Internet, I'm just sure there are a lot of good sites that I know nothing about).

All sites listed in this book are better than average, in my opinion.

Of these, I've selected a few that I think are especially good sites *within their category* and given them a Parachute symbol:

 = I think, for job-hunting purposes, this is one of the best sites on the Net, *in its category (the categories are: Gateway Sites, Job-Posting Sites, Resume Sites, Career Counseling Sites, Contacts Sites, and Research Sites)*

And now, let us begin with the large indexes of job-hunting sites on the Net, that I have called "Gateway Sites."

WEB ADDRESSES FOR JOB-HUNTERS AND CAREER-CHANGERS

> Incidentally, this guide is on the Web, at:
>
> `http://www.washingtonpost.com/parachute`
>
> If you think I have omitted an important site, that you discovered and found helpful in your job-hunt, please send your suggestion to an e-mail address, there *(for that purpose, and that purpose only):*
>
> `parachute@washpost.com`

As you enter these addresses into your favorite search engine on the Web, all URLS in this chapter are to be typed, by you, without any spaces whatsoever, from start to finish, even if they spill over on to more than one line in the text here.

GATEWAY SITES

If you were to start from scratch, find your favorite Internet search engine, and ask it to do a search on the keywords: "careers," "jobs," "employment," "resumes," "job listings," "career counseling," and the like, you would turn up a sizeable list.

But you don't need to start from scratch. *Fortunately,* a lot of people have already done this search, for you.

Their results are posted at the following *large, gateway* job-sites:

The Riley Guide

`http://www.dbm.com/jobguide/`

This is the best, by far. If I could only go to one *gateway* job-site on the Web, this would be it. (The URL above, incidentally, is new as of July 7, 1997.)

But there are others, which have done a fine job of putting together summary lists of what's available. We'll start with:

Job Hunt: A Meta-List of Online Job-Services

http://www.job-hunt.org/

You *may* need to increase the memory assigned to your Web browser, first, before mouse-clicking on this site, as this is a *huge* file. Incidentally, this site has *its own* rating system for the career sites it lists.

Emory Colossal List of Career Links

http://www.emory.edu/CAREER/Links.html

This is sponsored by Emory University's career center ("Career Paradise") in Atlanta, Georgia. This site also has its own rating system, called the CareerMeister Rating, on two scales: functionality, and artistic impression. The listings are amusingly described.

Magellan

http://www.mckinley.com/magellan/Reviews/Business/Jobs/index.magellan.html

This search engine's "Career and Employment" section rates its sites in a really helpful way. I like it.

Job Search and Employment Opportunities: Best Bets from the Net

http://www.lib.umich.edu/chdocs/employment/

I don't agree with some of its selections (as "Best"), but it is very comprehensive.

Career Resource Center

http://www.careers.org/index.html

It lists over 11,000 links to jobs, employers, business, education, and career service professionals on the Web, plus 6,000 other career resources (including Australia and New Zealand, Japan, Germany, and United Kingdom as well).

InfoSeek Guide -- Jobs & Careers

http://guide-p.infoseek.com/business/

This search engine's "Jobs & Careers" section lists "similar pages" for each item. Great idea.

Yahoo! Employment

http://www.yahoo.com/Business_and_Economy/Employment/

These search engines change their navigation about every three minutes. If this doesn't take you to where you want to go, go to their home page, and select.

Point's Top 5% -- Careers & Jobs

http://point.lycos.com/reviews/database/buca.html

This is one of those sites that tries to choose "the best" in each category. Their criteria for choosing the top 5 percent related to "Careers and Jobs" depend on: content, presentation, and experience. You, of course, want the top 5 percent to be based on "effectiveness in finding a job." Keep this difference in mind as you explore this list.

And that concludes my listing of the large *gateway* sites for job-hunting on the Internet. Now, visit the one or ones you are curious about; when you are done, you can then choose any of the five sections that I have divided this guide into. As I said earlier, there are five ways in which the Internet can be helpful to job hunters or career changers. They are:

#1. As a place for you to search for **vacancies**, listed by employers (often called **job listings**).

#2. As a place to post your **resume**.

#3. As a place to get some job-hunting help or career **counseling**.

#4. As a place to make **contacts** with people, who can help you find information, or help you get in for an interview, at a particular place.

#5. As a place to find **information** or do **research** on fields, occupations, companies, cities, etc.

Let us look at each of these, in turn.

1 JOB LISTINGS

JOB LISTINGS ON THE INTERNET

We come here to the sites that make many job-hunters salivate: the promise of access to millions of *vacancies, help-wanted ads*, or *job listings,'* listed on the Internet by employers. Indeed, one Web site kept track of its visitors and found that the largest number of those visitors -- 33% -- went to the job listings, as compared with 26% to the next most popular area there -- salary surveys -- and just 13% to the place where they could put their resume online.

Job listings! What a lovely sound! *A new place to meet employers.* Thousands of job opportunities, listed on the Internet! Ah, yes. How true! But just keep in mind two teensy tiny little problems as you explore these job listings.

HOW EFFECTIVE?

My personal estimate of the effectiveness of Job Posting Sites on the Internet: **one percent**, if the job you're looking for is not computer-related; **40 percent** if it is. That is, out of every one hundred computer people who search job listings on the Internet, 40 of them will find a job as a result. I think 60 will not. And out of every 100 non-computer people who search job listings on the Internet, one of them will find a job as a result. I think 99 will not.

The first is this: people's naive vision of the Internet is that it offers one central, unified place, where you can find a list of all available jobs in your own geographical region, if not in the whole country. Unfortunately, the reality is that we currently have 11,000 sites on the Internet dealing with jobs or careers. So, if you want to find out what jobs are posted on the Internet, you have to go to hundreds if not thousands of different sites to find that out. Yuk!

What you will not believe, until it happens to you, is that it is possible to hunt through all these listings on the Internet, and *still* not find one job that interests you -- unless of course, you're in the computer field, in which case the Internet is essentially like striking it rich. How can this be? How can you strike out so dramatically? Well, that brings us to our second problem: the infamous *hidden job market.*

What that phrase means is that employers, generally speaking, prefer every other method of filling vacancies that there is, before they will resort to want-ads or job listings. For many if not most of them, want-ads or job listings are their *court of last resort,* used only after all other methods have failed. You can see this in the diagram on the right, starting at the bottom.

(We job-hunters, of course, prefer to start at the top of this diagram, and work down. That is why our job-hunting system in this country is so *Neanderthal.* We prefer to job-hunt in exactly the reverse order that employers do.)

But, back to the diagram, if employers can fill their job vacancies without resorting to want-ads or job listings, they will; in 80% of all cases, they succeed. Hence the familiar statistic, for *decades*: "80% of all jobs are never advertised." Never advertised on the Internet, nor anywhere else.

What all this means for you is this: by all means browse these job-listings. You may find just the opportunity you are looking for. But don't get discouraged if you don't. Only 20% of all available jobs in this country ever get advertised, by employers. The rest wait for you to find other ways of finding them.

Just post these words above your computer, and keep them ever in mind if you've spent hours surfing through page after page of job listings, and have found *nothing* that interests you:

**"There are tons of jobs out there,
that the Web knows nothing about!"**

The way a typical job-hunter likes to hunt for a job (starts here)

6 "I will place an ad to find someone."

Newspaper Ads

Resumes

5 "I will look at some resumes which come in, unsolicited."

Employment Agency for Lower Level Jobs

4 "I want to hire someone for a lower level job, from a stack of potential candidates that some agency has screened for me."

This is called 'a private employment agency,' or - - if it is within the company - - 'the human resources department,' formerly the 'personnel department.' Incidentally, only 15% of all organizations have such an internal department.

Search Firm for Higher Level Jobs

3 "I want to hire someone for a higher level job, from among outstanding people who are presently working for another organization; and I will pay a recruiter to find this outstanding candidate for me."

The agency, thus hired by an employer, is called 'a search firm' or 'headhunter'; only employers can hire such agencies.

A Job-Hunter Who Offers Proof

"I want to hire someone who walks in the door and can show me samples of their previous work."

2 "I want to hire someone whose work a trusted friend of mine has seen and recommends."

That friend may be: mate, best friend, colleague in the same field, or colleague in a different field.

From Within

Employer's Thoughts:

1 "I want to hire someone whose work I have seen." (Promotion from within of a full-time employee, or promotion from within of a part-time employee; hiring a former consultant for a regular position (formerly on a limited contract); hiring a temp for a regular position; hiring a volunteer for a regular position.)

The way a typical employer prefers to fill vacancies (starts here)

Our Neanderthal Job-Hunting System

PARACHUTE PICKS: VACANCIES OR JOB LISTING SITES (MULTIPLE)

To begin with, there are some sites that have put a number of job posting *search-engines* all on one page. We start with:

JobBank USA MetaSEARCH

http://www.jobbankusa.com/search.html

It will give you 20 or more employment search engines, for vacancies, all on one page. An outstanding site!

SEARCH.COM

http://www.search.com/

This site will give you 17 or more employment search engines that have job listings, all on one page. Another very good site, in this category.

Internet Job Surfer

http://www.rpi.edu/dept/cdc/jobsurfer/

This is a site maintained by Rensselaer Polytechnic Institute. It has an impressively lengthy list of commercial organizations that provide job databases or resume listings (or other services). The organizations are indexed alphabetically. Many other countries are included. And the list was updated as of the very date I visited the site.

Connect

http://www.cabrillo.cc.ca.us/connect/docs/Jobs.html

That stands for: **C**alifornia **O**ccupational **N**ews **N**etwork **E**mploying **C**omputerized **T**elecommunications. It has a fine listing of job boards and other places to find job listings, including (of course) California-oriented sites. I like this site, and found it helpful.

Infoseek Guide -- Company Job Offerings

http://guide-p.infoseek.com

It lists over 1,000 companies and gives you the ability to search all 1,000 sites at once, with a keyword of your own choosing -- though somewhat limited outside technology/business sites. "Teacher" turned up only 7 sites, "writer" turned up 156, nationwide.

100hot

http://www.100hot.com/

It will give you a mixture of company sites and job listing sites, including international sites.

Excite -- Job Directories Reviews

http://www.excite.com/Reviews/Business/Jobs/Job-Directories/index.html

It rates the various sites thus listed, in an interesting way.

Point Top 5%

http://www.pointcom.com/reviews/database/buca.html

It will give you a number of sites, *some* of which deal with job listings.

Lycos/A2Z Job Classifieds

http://a2z.lycos.com/

A limited listing, in my opinion.

ZD Net Jobs Database

http://www.zdnet.com/zdi/jobs/jobs.html

This site is tied to the Monster Board (see below) and is sometimes very difficult to get into. If you have trouble, try later at night.

PARACHUTE PICKS: VACANCIES OR JOB LISTING SITES (INDIVIDUAL)

Multiple listings aside, you will want to familiarize yourself with some of the better known individual sites, *which get listed again and again in various career indices.* You will already have come across many of these, if you used any of the multiple-site pages listed previously. As you view the sites below, keep in mind that *many* of them offer more than just *job listings.*

America's Job Bank

http://www.ajb.dni.us/

This site is maintained by the Dept. of Labor, U.S. Employment Service. It links 1,800 state Employment Service offices in the U.S., and typically lists approximately 250,000 jobs. A wonderful site, if job listings are what you are looking for -- allowing you to sort available jobs by a first, second, third, and last priority (e.g., state, city, title, salary, and/or field).

Career Path

http://www.careerpath.com/

It claims (legitimately, I think) to be "the most visited job-related site on the Internet," with nearly 3 million *searches* per month. It lists *some or all of* the current week's and previous Sunday's *help wanted* ads from at least 22 major newspapers in the U.S. Consequently, on a typical day, you can search over 130,000 help wanted ads, and they add 250,000 new ads per month. I think this is a very useful site, *if* classified ads are what you are looking for.

CareerPost

http://www.washingtonpost.com/wp-adv/classifieds/careerpost/front.htm

This site has job listings taken from the last two Sunday editions of *The Washington Post.*

Career Magazine

http://www.careermag.com/db/cmag_postsearch_form

Now, I think this is a very interesting site. Every day it downloads, and indexes, all the job listings from the major Internet *jobs newsgroups*, and then offers keyword sifting through those listings, according to your skills, title, and preferred location. It also offers more information about employers than most online resources. Be forewarned, however, you can still strike out.

JobTrak

http://www.jobtrak.com/

This site lists over 2,100 new job listings each day -- for college students, graduates, and alumni. In fact, you must list the campus you are on, and get a password, before you can access the job listings. Since I'm not on a campus, and have forgotten every password anyone ever gave to me, naturally I can't evaluate the job listings at this site. "*I'm on the outside, looking in . . .*"

JobNet

http://www.westga.edu/~coop/jobs.html

This is a collection of resources from the Web, Usenet News, Gopher, and Listserve. I happen to like it, because it has jobs from the parts of the job-market so often ignored at other job listing sites (e.g., "outdoor careers," "training," and the like).

The World Wide Web Employment Office

http://www.harbornet.com/biz/office/annex.html

This is a very interesting site, as it lists job posting sites by field or occupation, and this means *a wide spectrum* of fields, unlike some other sites I could name. This site has links not only to the U.S. but to other countries as well.

JobWeb/Catapult Employment Centers

http://www.jobweb.org/catapult/jobsall.htm

Part of JobWeb, this site is maintained by the National Association of Colleges and Employers. Inside or outside of academia, it has a nice list of job search resources, including "Other Directories of Employment Resources," listed by geographical region.

LDOL CareerNet Want Ads

http://www.ldol.state.la.us:80/career1/hp_wanta.htm

This CareerNET Resource and Development Center, sponsored by the Louisiana Department of Labor, is one of my favorite sites. Here you will find an impressive list of job listings (heavily weighted toward Louisiana, naturally), but check out "Jobs by Field."

PARACHUTE PICKS: VACANCIES OR JOB LISTING SITES (FAMOUS)

Now *some* of the sites we just looked at are well-known; but there are others that are even more famous. The problem with *these* that I am about to share with you is that, so far as job listings are concerned, many if not most of them have a big Achilles heel: namely, lots of listings -- but across a relatively narrow spectrum of the 12,000+ occupations that are out there. Mostly just jobs in technology, business, and academia. You will look in vain for very many listings for teachers, artists, craftspeople, etc., etc. Internet *experts* like to say, "Yes, I know, I know; but the situation is changing." Indeed it is, but having roamed these sites for two years now, I'd have to say change toward listing more of the 12,000+ occupations that are "out there" is occurring at a speed that makes a glacier look like a greyhound.

Now, I'm going out of my way to accidentally offend a good many people, because of my concern about *you.* I don't want you to let these sites throw you into a depression. And believe me, they can -- if you *think* they work for everyone else except *you.*

Take my word for it, some of these sites have a wonderful interface, but often you will feel like Dorothy and her friends when they were first ushered into the chambers of the Wizard of Oz: wonderful stuff up front, but take care to look behind all that smoke and mirrors. Often you can't. You can't tell what they have behind the curtain. Just remember this: no matter how many listings they claim to have, do not take it personally if you don't find *anything* in the area you're looking for. The problem is not with you; the problem is with the Internet, and the limited spectrum of the job-market that it (thus far) covers.

Having said that about these sites' job listings, let me add that these sites do many other things besides job listings (and often do them very well). Okay, here goes.

CareerMosaic

`http://www.careermosaic.com/cm/usenet.html`

This is an immensely famous job site, but as far as job listings are concerned, I struck out again and again when I looked (in various geographical regions) for anything but technical or computer jobs. Don't get discouraged if there is nothing here in your field.

The Online Career Center

`http://www.occ.com/`

This site, sponsored by a non-profit association of leading corporations, is another immensely famous job site, and (like Career Path, earlier, and The Monster Board below) also claims to be "the Internet's first and most frequently accessed career center." It is heavily weighted toward technical and computer-related jobs, and when you go to "Search by Industry," they give you home pages of companies rather than individual job listings. It does have a good listing of Career Fairs and Events. And, of course, if you're looking for a computer-related or technical job, you may find this site very helpful.

The Monster Board Career Search

http://www.monster.com/pf/mb/client/ui/search/jobserch.htm

This also claims to be "the premier career site on the World Wide Web," with over 750,000 visitors per month. The site claims over 50,000 listings, with 1,500 new ones being added each week; it also features a career center, and resume listings as well. It still seems to me to suffer from the same problems as so many other sites: lots of listings, but in a relatively narrow portion of the total job market. Don't get discouraged if there is nothing here that interests you.

Career Resource Center -- Jobs

http://www.careers.org/01_jobs.html

This site lists over 11,000 links to jobs, employers, business, education and career service professionals on the Web, plus 6,000 other helpful career resources (which includes Australia and New Zealand, Japan, Germany, and the United Kingdom as well). Unfortunately, job-posting-wise, it is more of a sampler than anything else. Of course, its samples may be what you're looking for. Still, don't get discouraged if there is nothing here that interests you.

CareerWeb -- Jobs

http://www.cweb.com/jobs/

This is another "often-cited" site, but it has the same problem as so many other sites: not enough listings. For example, when I tried it, it only listed 33 accountant/banking/financial services jobs in the entire country. Don't get discouraged if there is nothing here that interests you.

E-Span Job Search

http://www.espan.com/job

They bill themselves as "Your Online Employment Connection." It's another famous site, but -- again -- seems to me to be heavily oriented toward technology/computer-related jobs. But if that's your cup of tea, go to it!

The Black Collegian JASS

http://www.black-collegian.com/jobsg.html

JASS means "Job Assistance Selection Service." This site, unfortunately, lists companies more than "Job Opportunities," and even this is more of a sampler than anything else. You are left to figure out whether or not the company needs anyone.

PARACHUTE PICKS: VACANCIES OR JOB LISTING SITES (PARTICULAR KINDS OF JOBS)

The Law Employment Center

http://www.lawjobs.com

If you are a lawyer looking for work, this is emphatically the site to visit. It's sponsored by the *Law Journal*, and has an *alive* feeling that some of the other job listing sites lack.

Academe This Week -- Job Openings

http://chronicle.merit.edu/.ads/.links.html

This site gives you the job listings in the current issue of the *Chronicle of Higher Education.* If it's faculty or research positions or other college or university jobs that you are looking for, this is the site to visit. (It also has some listings that are outside academe.)

Galaxy -- Employment -- Academic

http://galaxy.einet.net./GJ/employment.html

This is another good source of job listings in academia.

Government jobs are to be found at a number of sites, including the following four:

The Federal Jobs Digest

http://www.jobsfed.com/fedjob4.shtml

They list from 2,000 to 4,000 active vacancies on a typical day. The site is absolutely up to the minute, and this is clearly *the place* to visit, if you're looking for a job with the federal government. Has helpful salary charts for various grade levels. Only one minor caveat: they do need secretaries ("Secreterial" *[sic]* was misspelled twice on the main menu, on the three times I visited this site).

FedWorld Federal Jobs Search

http://www.fedworld.gov/jobs/jobsearch.html

This is an official U.S. government site, and has very similar listings to those found in *Federal Jobs Digest*, above, except that you must tap on *each* listing here, in order to find out where the job is and other details. I prefer the *Federal Jobs Digest* interface to this.

OPM's USAjobs

http://www.usajobs.opm.gov/

This is another of the U.S. Government's official sites for jobs and employment information. On my first visit to this Web site I was dismayed to note it had been a month since it was last updated -- according to their own admission. On my most recent visit, while it was now up to date, I was dismayed to discover it had a slim selection in a number of job categories. Again, I prefer the *Federal Jobs Digest.*

Federal Jobs Central
http://www.fedjobs.com/

You have to be a subscriber to access the job listings on this site. (Hourly online subscription begins at $45 for one hour.) They also publish *Federal Career Opportunities*, a bi-weekly printed listing of federal jobs that is mailed to you (at $39 for six issues) -- plus other tools (at a price) for the federal jobs hunter.

Cool Works
http://www.coolworks.com/showme/

Leisure jobs in national parks, resorts, cruise ships, camps, plus volunteering, are to be found here.

Summer Jobs World-Wide
http://www.summerjobs.com/do/where

The site to come to if you're looking for a summer job.

Peterson's Summer Programs for Kids/Teens
http://www.petersons.com/summerop/ssector.html

The site to come to if you're looking for a summer program and you're a kid.

JobTrak Job Fair Calendar
http://www.jobtrak.com/cfc/show.html

This site is for those who want to go face to face with employers.

Monster Board Career Fair Info
http://199.94.216.77/careerfair.html

Likewise, I'm sure.

JobSmart -- Upcoming Career Fairs
http://jobsmart.org/resource/fairs/jobfairs.htm

Still another career fair/job fair site.

PARACHUTE PICKS: VACANCIES OR JOB LISTING SITES (ELSEWHERE ON THE NET)

There are many other Web sites featuring *Job Listings/Ads/Openings/Vacancies/Jobs Available.* Just type the word "jobs" into your favorite search engine.

In addition to the Web, there are Usenet Newsgroups on the Internet that have job listings/want ads. Lists of them can be found at the following three sites:

Yahoo! Jobs on Newsgroups
http://www.yahoo.com/Business_and_Economy/Employment/Jobs/Usenet

Jobs Offered Newsgroups
http://darkwing.uoregon.edu/~liwang/newsjob.html

CareerMag Search Job Listings -- Newsgroups
http://www.careermag.com/db/cmag_postsearch_form

Then there are bulletin board services (called BBSs), which used to be primarily, if not exclusively, *outside* the Web. Now, many of them can be accessed directly through the Web; a wonderful list of these has been compiled by a man named Richard Mark, on a very pretty site, which can be found at:

Richard Mark's SBI
http://dkeep.com/sbi.htm

Another complete list of BBSs both within and outside the Web, can be found at *Harry's Job Search BBS & Internet Hot List* (compiled by a remarkable man, the pioneering Harold Lemon):
Harry's Job Search BBS & Internet Hot List
http://www.job-hunt.org/jobs-bbs.html

Finally, if you search every job listing there is, on all the above sites (shouldn't take more than 4 weeks), and you discover nothing, zip, nada, that interests you, and you're *truly* desperate, there is a list of Employment Agencies to be found at:
HandiLinks To Employment Agencies
http://www.ahandyguide.com/cat1/e/e126.htm

But of course, in many cases, your local Yellow Pages might serve you just as well, or better.

(If you try all these job-listing sites, and still can't find a job, see page *146ff.*)

2 YOUR RESUME

Many job-hunters think this should be the very best use of the Internet for a job-hunter: being able to post your resume. Oh, my, oh my! Let's recall some simple truths, here: *a resume is a resume is a resume.* As readers of *What Color Is Your Parachute?* know, it usually is not a very effective job-hunting tool; normally, for every 1,470 resumes floating around out there in the world of work, only one job-offer is tendered and accepted.

And, I'm sorry to report, it doesn't get much better just because it's online. While it is obvious that some job-hunters' resumes do get seen by employers on the Internet, and do lead to a job, it is also obvious that in a depressingly-large number of cases, *nothing* happens. Zero. Zip. Nada.

What's the problem here? Why doesn't your resume get more results, *online?* Well, for a resume to work online, some employer:

- has got to be *desperate* to find someone like you,
- has got to be at the point, in their search for someone like you, that they are reduced to reading resumes,
- has got to then go online,
- has got to accidentally stumble across the site where you posted your resume, and then
- has got to take the time and trouble to read it, and then
- has got to take the time and trouble to print it out, in all its blah ASCII sameness.

Not only is this a big *pain in the neck* to employers, but there are *at least* 10 million U.S. employers (not to mention other countries) who don't even *think* of the Internet when it's time to hire. Not even *think* of the Internet?? Yes, believe it or not, the CEOs of some very *large* corporations, still haven't got a computer anywhere in sight in their office or in their secretary's office. Just an old faithful *IBM Selectric.* Down through the twentieth century, it has always been true: *job-hunters* flock to a new technology or job-hunting aid, but a comparatively much smaller proportion of *employers* do.

So, in many if not most cases, your beautiful resume is just sitting there on the Internet. And sitting there. And sitting there. And sitting there.

HOW EFFECTIVE?

My personal estimate of the effectiveness of Resume sites on the Internet: **less than one half of one percent**, if the job you're seeking is not computer-related; **20 percent** effectiveness, if it is. That is: out of every 100 computer people who post their resume on the Internet, 20 of them will find a job as a result. I think 80 will not. And out of every 100 non-computer people who post their resume on the Internet, less than 1 of them will find a job as a result. 99 of them will not.

But, you're going to put your resume on the Internet, at either a Web or newsgroup site, anyway, aren't you? Sure, you are! It may not get you a job, but your friends will be impressed, when you tell them what you've done! *You?! On the Internet?! Wow!*

There are a number of guides online which tell you exactly *how* to do this, and exactly *where* to do this. They'll tell you the rules about scanning, and the rules about keywords, and so forth. These guides are listed below in the Parachute Picks of resume sites.

Just one caveat: do remember that posting your resume online is the equivalent of nailing your resume to a tree in the town square -- where every employer, solid citizen, salesperson, con-artist, pervert, and drunk can see it, and copy down whatever he (or she) wants from it, for follow-up. *Think about it!*

Gary Morris -- of the **Union College Career Development Center** Web site (`http://apollo.union.edu/CDC/CDC.html`) -- suggests that if you are posting your portfolio or resume to a public area (such as a Web site) or an online resume database, security should always be a consideration. Gary advises his students to "never include personal or contact information in the body of your resume for safety and security purposes."

I would say that you may want to give your phone number *('cause this is most employers' favorite way of contacting job-hunters)*, plus your e-mail address, but **not** your street address, nor business address, nor names of past employers or references *online.* You can always mail this information to an interested employer or recruiter *after* they have contacted you by phone or e-mail.

One final word about resumes *online:* since your resume is going to look *very bland* in plain old ASCII, stripped of all its lovely formatting and the "nice look" of the original, Martin Kimeldorf suggests that one sentence you may want to add at the end of your posted resume, is: "An attractive and fully formatted hard copy version of this document is available upon request."

PARACHUTE PICKS:
SITES TO HELP YOU WRITE A RESUME

JobSmart

`http://jobsmart.org/tools/resume/index.htm`

This site features the best overall summary about resumes on the Internet, that I have seen, written by Clara Horvath and Yana Parker. If I were interested in putting my resume on the Internet, and if I could visit only one resume site for guidance and help, this would surely be it. Yana is the author of the popular *Damn Good Resume Guide* series, while Clara teaches classes in this subject. They have a sample list of places on the Internet to post your resume, free and for-fee.

Joyce Lain Kennedy

http://www.wiley.co.uk/Promotions/Kennedy/ActualMaterial.html

If you want to know how to write an electronic resume, Joyce Lain Kennedy is the most popular syndicated careers columnist in America, and the author of several books on electronic job-hunting. She has become an expert on Internet job-hunting. Unfortunately, this site only gives us a sample of her insights. It does tell us, however, that she emphasizes the importance of keywords in electronic resumes.

Career Center Job Search Gopher

gopher://merlin.hood.edu:9999/11gopher_root:%5bcareer_center.job_search%5d

Speaking of which, an excellent long list of specific keywords for various professions can be found at this *gopher* site (assuming your Internet Service Provider gives you access to *gopherspace*).

Resumix ResumeBuilder

http://www.resumix.com/resume/resume-form.html

If you want to actually build your resume online, there's a site that will lead you step-by-step through the compiling of a "plain vanilla" resume, and then format it for you, and submit it. The site is maintained by Resumix, Inc.

Intellimatch - - "Watson"

http://riga.intellimatch.com/watson/owa/w3.logon

Well, to begin with, this is another one of those sites that *boasts* ("Internet's #1 Service for Matching Job Seekers & Employers"). They call their resume system "Watson" or the "Power Resume." Like Resumix, above, this system will lead you step-by-step (it takes an hour) through the putting together of your resume -- and then formats it in the HTML language that a Website reads so well. But, be aware that the list of skills that they offer you, to use in your resume, is actually a list of *knowledges* -- akin to the "keywords" that some of the sites above talk about -- and this is not exactly the same thing as "skills." (See *The 1997 What Color Is Your Parachute?*)

This site's unique feature: they say they will then match your resume to their employer database, to see if there is an intelligent match (hence "IntelliMatch"). Sounds great, and many reviewers have warmly saluted this *idea.* The idea *is* great. The problem is in the execution of it. As of the time I talked with them (10/9/96), they reported 50,000 resumes in their database, but only 100 employers. That's because, while they don't charge you, the job-hunter, they do charge each employer (the basic package costs an employer $5,000).

PARACHUTE PICKS: SITES WHERE YOU CAN POST YOUR RESUME

When you've got your resume all done, one way or another, and want to post it on the Internet, there are good lists of resume posting sites at the following locations:

The World Wide Web Employment Office

http://www.harbornet.com/biz/office/annex.html

This is an excellent site, as it lists resume sites by field or occupation, covering a wide spectrum of fields. Outstanding! It is also a resume site itself (fee-based) -- you can link your resume (posted elsewhere) to their site for $10/yr, or put it on their site (if it is not posted anywhere yet) for $40/yr. As I mentioned elsewhere in this book, this site is unusual in another way: it has links not only to the U.S. but to other countries as well.

Tripod - - Where to Send Your Resume

http://www.tripod.com/work/resume/linklist.html

When last I visited, it only listed 22 resume sites; *but*, where it is different from other lists, is that it evaluates each site, *very* realistically. Hence, naturally I like it -- a lot.

Yahoo! Resume Services

http://www.yahoo.com/Business_and_Economy/Companies/Employment/resume_services/

It lists 80 or more resume sites.

JobHunt Resume Banks

http://www.job-hunt.org/resume.shtml

It listed 36 resume sites, last time I visited; it is very up-to-date.

JobSmart Descriptions of Major Resume Banks

http://jobsmart.org/internet/resbanks.htm

It lists a *sampler* of free sites (it lists six, in great detail) and for-fee sites (five, in great detail).

Yahoo! jobs newsgroups

http://www.yahoo.com/Business_and_Economy/Employment/Jobs/Usenet/

Leaving the Web, there are the Usenet Newsgroups on the Internet where resumes can also be posted. Yahoo! has lists of these, at the above site. You will note that not everything on Yahoo!'s list is devoted to resumes (it calls them "jobs wanted" or "requests for employment" when they are). The remainder on this list are actually job listings by employers (you can detect this when it calls them "jobs offered" or "jobs available").

Remember, if you post your resume on *all* of these sites, and absolutely *nothing* happens, do not take it personally. Reread (five times) my overall evaluation of resume sites, that appeared on pages 128–129. In a nutshell: it ain't you; it's the system.

(If you try putting your resume on the Net, and after a time still can't find a job, see page *146ff.*)

3 CAREER COUNSELING

CAREER COUNSELING SITES ON THE INTERNET

Well, I'm happy to report that there are some very interesting career centers on the Web. Most of them belong to universities and colleges.

I wish I could say the same for the *non-collegiate* commercial career counseling centers on the Web and elsewhere -- but having roamed a number of such places online, myself, for upwards of two years now -- *and* having talked to other *Web-savvy* career counselors around the nation to gather *their* impressions, I must report that we have found the situation downright depressing.

What one would *hope* to find on the commercial sites, are:

- detailed answers to the questions raised by job-hunters, running a couple of paragraphs or on up to a page or so;
- written by *truly competent* career-counselors;
- at no cost to the job-hunter;
- and without the career counselor or counseling center trying to sell additional services and products -- often *expensive* services (*hidden agendas*).

The reality is sometimes far from this. In fact, my various colleagues around the country feel that some of the career advice online is absolutely awful. As I have read some of the "answers" to job-hunters' questions on the Web, my hair has turned gray (but then, I'm 70 years old -- maybe my hair turned gray for other reasons). To be sure, the Web is wonderful. But, the fact that inept job-hunting advice is on the Web in living color doesn't magically make that advice un-inept. *Caveat emptor!*

Having said that, let me add: I think this picture has improved *tremendously* in the last half year or so, and I'm much encouraged by what I see. Some really good people have been coming online lately. Mary-Ellen Mort's site, *JobSmart,* is a case in point.

I think the situation will continue to improve.

HOW EFFECTIVE?

My personal estimate of the effectiveness of career counseling sites on the Internet: **10 percent**. That is, out of every 100 people who seek career counseling on the Internet, 10 of them will find a job thereby, due to the coaching that they pick up there. I think 90 will not.

PARACHUTE PICKS: CAREER COUNSELING SITES

To begin with, there are some *gateway* sites that list career counseling sites on the Internet. The two I like the best are:

Catapult Career Office

http://www.jobweb.org/catapult/homepage.htm

It has a list of college career counseling offices that have sites on the Internet, sorted by country (the United Kingdom, the United States, Canada, and Australia) and region -- within the United States, anyway. It's not thorough: I know of many colleges that are on the Web, but are not on this list. Still, it's a good place to begin.

RPI Career Resource

http://www.rpi.edu/dept/cdc/homepage.html

This site, maintained by Rensselaer Polytechnic Institute, also has a good list of career counseling sites, at least for the United States.

As for individual sites, you might want to begin, first of all, by going back and looking at some of the famous sites that I mentioned under "Job Listings." Many of them have career counseling as well -- career advice, career articles, lists of helpful books for the job-hunter, and that sort of thing. Others worth noting:

JobSmart

http://jobsmart.org/

This is a *great,* relatively new career counseling site, and one of my favorites, developed by Mary-Ellen Mort, for California.

Career Paradise

http://www.emory.edu/CAREER/

This site, hosted by the career center at Emory University in Atlanta, was created 1/4/96, with lots of impudent humor -- attributable to John H. Youngblood, who was its Webmaster from then until 8/24/96. Unfortunately, he has moved on and now some of the information, such as that on the "Colossal List of Career Links," is somewhat out of date. Still, what it does have is helpful, and this site has a fine summary of the career planning process.

The CareerNET Resource and Development Center

http://www.ldol.state.la.us:80/career1/ldolcp.htm

If you want a nice list of career books before you go down to the bookstore or library, this site, sponsored by the Louisiana Department of Labor, has such a list, often with extensive outlining and critique of each book.

The Career Action Center

http://www.careeraction.org/

Formerly located in Palo Alto, this Center is one of the most famous career counseling places in the U.S. The Center has recently moved, but its Web site hasn't changed.

PARACHUTE PICKS: CAREER COUNSELING MANUALS OR BOOKS

Now, aside from career counseling centers, the Internet can offer you elementary career counseling or job-hunting manuals. Here are some interesting sites, in that regard:

Creative Job Search

http://www.des.state.mn.us/cjs/cjs_site/cjs-home.htm

This site, maintained by the Minnesota Department of Economic Security, has put together the equivalent of a job-search manual, on their "Creative Job Search" page. Mark this: these authors really understand what *skills* are (refreshing, on the Internet). Employment applications, interviews, etc., are also covered.

Career Services at the University of Waterloo

http://www.adm.uwaterloo.ca/infocecs/CRC/manual-home.html

The career center at the University of Waterloo has put together a thorough detailed description to guide you through your job-hunt; its self-assessment manual is one of the best on the Internet.

Job Search Guide: Strategies for Professionals

http://www.cabrillo.cc.ca.us/connect/docs/jobsearch.html

An amazingly thorough 74-page introduction to the job search is put out by the **United States Employment Service**, at this site; the manual can be printed out on your home printer.

PARACHUTE PICKS: MISCELLANEOUS CAREER COUNSELING HELPS

Myers-Briggs (personality typing newsgroup archive)

http://sunsite.unc.edu/personality/

The Myers-Briggs *instrument* is all the rage in Career Counseling these days. It is not on the Internet. But there is a personality-type test online ("The Keirsey Temperament Test") which you fill out online, whence it automatically scores itself, and gives you a Myers-Briggs–like code. It is to be found at this newsgroup's list about "personality typing systems" (this does not refer to a computer keyboard).

Myers-Briggs FAQ: A Summary of Personality Typing

http://sunsite.unc.edu/personality/faq-mbti.html

If you want more of an explanation of Personality Typing, plus a brief summary of the sixteen personality types, go to this site.

The Holland Game

http://www.phlab.missouri.edu/~cppcwww/holland.html

Readers of *What Color Is Your Parachute?* who like the "Party Exercise" that I invented (based on John Holland's RIASEC system) will find it, sans *diagram,* but with the same wording, at this University of Missouri site.

Informational Interviewing

http://danenet.wicip.org/jets/jet-9407-p.html

This important technique, serving as an alternative to the traditional job-hunt, is explained and discussed at this site.

4 CONTACTS

SITES ON THE INTERNET WHERE YOU CAN MAKE CONTACTS

I think this is the next-to-most-helpful use of the Internet in job-hunting because, in its essence, *all job-hunting is a search for people contacts* -- that is, for links between you and an employer, or between you and clients. Contacts are the name of the game (at least in *creative* job-hunting).

Through the Internet, you can contact people all over the globe.

If you know who you want to reach, you can do it instantly, without waiting five days for a letter to get there -- by using e-mail.

If you don't know who (or whom) you want to reach, you can locate people through:

- **gopher sites** ("Gopher" is a menu-driven system of getting information; it pre-dates the Web, but its sites are accessible through your Web browser.)
- **newsgroups** (A "newsgroup" is like a discussion group that meets on an electronic bulletin board -- devoted to some field of interest -- where each of you leaves messages for one another on that bulletin board. These newsgroups are located on a part of the Internet called *Usenet,* and are accessible through your Web browser here *if* your Internet service provider gives you *Usenet access.*)
- **e-mailing lists** (Also called "mailing lists," these are discussion groups like *Usenet,* except that every message from every member on the list is automatically sent to your e-mail address. You don't have to go anywhere to get the messages -- they come to you.)
- **chat rooms** (There are also *"chat-rooms"* on the Internet and on commercial services such as *America Online,* where you "meet with" other people, online, and have a chat with each other in real time -- via your keyboard input.)

In sum, the number of contacts you can make online, is absolutely mind-boggling. Any faraway place that interests you, you'll likely find a contact online. Any question you need an answer to, you'll likely find someone online who knows the answer. Any organization where you need to know how to meet "the-person-who-has-the-power-to-hire," you'll likely find someone on line who knows somebody who . . .

You will want to remember, of course, that anyone you contact on the Internet should be approached -- as in *real* life -- respectfully, politely, courteously, and with keen awareness on your part that this is a very busy person, who may or may not be able to respond. If they do give you any help, e-mail thank-you notes should *always* be sent to them, *promptly* (within three days) for the help they gave you.

HOW EFFECTIVE?

My personal estimate of the effectiveness of going online, in getting a job: **20 percent** -- that is, out of every 100 people who make contact with people on the Internet, 20 of them will find a job as a result. I think 80 will not.

PARACHUTE PICKS: SITES TO MAKE CONTACTS

Finding Newsgroups or Mailing Lists

http://www.synapse.net/~radio/finding.htm

As I mentioned above, one of your best bets for finding contacts is to discover a newsgroup or e-mailing list, centered around the field of interest in which you are trying to find a contact. This site here, run by Synapse Internet, has a good list of such places, and how to find them.

The Contact Center Network -- Directory

http://www.contact.org/sample/dir.htm

This excellent site lists over 8,000 organizations, publications, nonprofits, and community organizational interests. You can browse around the world, by country, or by keyword. Great site!

Publicly Accessible Mailing Lists

http://www.neosoft.com/internet/paml/

Finding contacts by interest field can also be done on this site, maintained by NeoSoft™. It has a wonderful list that can be accessed by subject, name, or title.

555-1212.com

http://www.555-1212.com/

Once you know the name of a contact, you of course want to be able to find them. This site links to a number of *directories,* all on one page (it's a *long* page -- be sure to scroll down). You'll find some nifty features, including "a reverse directory." It includes on its page, three directories that I find particularly useful, myself. They are:

Switchboard

http://www.switchboard.com/

This site looks for *complete* addresses and phone numbers. In my experience, it finds people that some of the other directories know nothing about. It has saved my life, more than once.

WhoWhere?

http://www.whowhere.com/

Well, I can't always find what I want here. But what it does, it does exceedingly well. It searches not only for an individual's address, phone number, and/or e-mail address, but it will even search a phone number to see who it belongs to. (Scary!) It lists *companies* on the Net, and in the Yellow Pages, as well -- in case you're trying to reach someone at a particular company.

Four11

http://www.Four11.com/cgi-bin/Four11Main?fonesearch&FormId=

Just type in the name of the person and the state they live in, and this program *may* turn up their address, zipcode, and phone number. However, it *sometimes* omits streets, just when I want them most. And, like all these search directories, it can turn up *dozens* of similar names in large metropolitan areas -- and sometimes the addresses are outdated or wrong.

My overall advice, if you're looking for a specific person by name, as a potential contact: be *sure* to use all three of these programs. Sometimes two of them will miss, but the third will tell you exactly what you want to know.

Use http://www.555-1212.com/ if all three of them fail.

5 RESEARCH

INFORMATION OR RESEARCH SITES ON THE INTERNET

All job-hunting is a search for information. And the Internet is a superlative place to find information, without the limitations that a normal public library would have. You can access the Internet on holidays, you can access it 24 hours a day, and you don't have to even leave the house.

The amount of information you can find on the Internet today is mind-boggling. But be aware of this before you start: when you're doing job-hunting research on the Internet, you can find so many interesting sidepaths, that it can divert you from your job-hunt or career-change for weeks, *all the while giving you the illusion that you are hard at work on it. "Hey, what do you mean I'm not working very hard on my job-hunt? I spent three hours yesterday surfin' the Net."*

It's the sidepaths that can kill you. In the past month, while surveying job-hunting sites, I found the following alluring sidepaths: I suddenly grew curious about the names of the Seven Dwarves. *Found that, easily.* I then wanted to know the words to an old song. *Found that, easily.* Wanted to know what films a certain actor had appeared in, throughout his career. *Found that, easily.* I remembered that a member of my family was going to school in Australia. *Easily found* a map of the campus, a map of the town, and an academic calendar for next year, all of which I could print out *in living color.*

Fascinating. Eating up the hours. But as I said: these sidepaths can kill you -- leaving you no time for your actual job-hunt. If you're going to do any of your job-hunting on the Internet, bring carloads of self-discipline. I mean: carloads.

HOW EFFECTIVE?

The effectiveness of online research in getting a job? Well, **that depends** of course on what kind of information you're looking for, how essential it is for your job-hunt or career-change that you find this piece of information, etc., etc. In other words, it's impossible to say. We can, however, say this about job-hunting on the Internet & World Wide Web: it can be a great adjunct to your job-hunt, *if rightly used.*

PARACHUTE PICKS: RESEARCH SITES: STANDARD REFERENCE WORKS

I mean things like: *dictionaries, encyclopedias, access to libraries on the Internet,* and the like.

LDOL CareerNet Reference

http://www.ldol.state.la.us:80/career1/hp_refer.htm

This site has a good list of reference works, including ERIC, CARL, Usenet Search, an Online Dictionary of Computing, Internet Public Library, a congressional bill-tracking database, directories to nonprofit organizations, etc. Extremely useful.

Yahoo! Reference

http:www.yahoo.com/Reference/

Yahoo! also has a list of reference works, but I found it easier to find *job-hunting-related works* on the CareerNet site, above.

SunSITE LibWeb

http://sunsite.berkeley.edu/Libweb/

This Berkeley Digital Library SunSITE has a good list of libraries that are online, in the U.S. and throughout the world. They, in turn, have many resources on their own individual online sites.

PARACHUTE PICKS: RESEARCH SITES: OCCUPATIONAL FIELDS

The Occupational Outlook Handbook

http://stats.bls.gov/ocohome.htm

This is the place to begin, *of course,* in researching particular occupational fields. It is the Bureau of Labor Statistics' official handbook.

Bureau of Labor Statistics' Projections

http://stats.bls.gov/news.release/ecopro.toc.htm

You may wish to supplement the Outlook Handbook with figures and articles concerning the projected future of particular occupations. In that case, this is the site to visit.

JobTrak College/Major Index

http://www.jobtrak.com/docs/collegelist.html

If you want a list of possible fields for you to consider, hundreds of them are listed here. If, further, you want to take a course of study or a degree program in any of these fields, this site lists which universities, colleges or two-year colleges offer such majors.

AT&T Toll-Free Internet Directory

http://www.tollfree.att.net/dir800/

If the above list is too narrow for you, and you want more choices, there is another way to generate ideas of fields you might be interested in -- and that is, by going through the Yellow Pages and looking at the Yellow Page *categories.* Such categories are roughly equivalent to "fields." You can find them at this site (choose "Browse by Category" once you're there).

Yahoo! Professional Organizations

http://www.yahoo.com/Economy/Organizations/Professional/

If you want to explore a particular field (or fields) further, you want to go to their *Associations,* or *Professional Associations,* and many of them are listed here.

Job Databases by Professional Societies/ Other Institutions

http://www.rpi.edu/dept/cdc/society/

You can also find such a list of such Associations or *Professional Societies* on this site.

The Argus Clearinghouse: Business & Employment

http://www.clearinghouse.net/cgi-bin/chadmin/viewcat/Business__Employment?Kywd++

If you want *articles* related to particular fields, this is the site to visit (it's called "Internet Job Surfer").

JobSmart Salary Info

http://jobsmart.org/tools/salary/index.htm

For some job hunters, no research of a particular occupation is complete until they've found out what it pays. For them, and for you, the best list of salary surveys on the Net (hands down!) is at this site. It has over 120 of them.

Pencom Career Center

http://www.pencomsi.com/careerhome.html

This site also deals with salary research. It offers an interactive salary guide, as well as other 'goodies': nationwide job listings, and articles on particular careers.

PARACHUTE PICKS: RESEARCH SITES: COMPANIES, ORGANIZATIONS, OR BUSINESSES

Once you've researched an occupational field, or occupation, you will of course want information on particular companies, organizations, or businesses in your chosen field. To help you in this task, a number of Internet search engines and directories have compiled lists of company directories for you:

Yahoo! Company Directories

http://www.yahoo.com/Business_and_Economy/Companies/Directories/

Here's the beginning of some help. You'll probably need additional directories, though, such as the three which follow.

Accufind Business/Corporate Resource Sites

http://nln.com/business.htm

This site has a very helpful bunch of directories for you to try.

100hot

http://www.100hot.com/

More lists of directories and companies.

Excite's Company Reviews

http://www.excite.com/Reviews/Business/Companies/index.html

More lists of directories and companies. Needless to say, these four sites, cited here, have some *overlap*. But each one knows things the others don't.

Mansfield U. Business/Economics Reference

http://www.mnsfld.edu/~library/mu-biz.html

Once you know the name of an organization or company, you'll of course want to be able to research it. To get you started, Mansfield University's library online has a wonderful collection of *Business and Economics References* -- Business Yellow Pages, Canadian Statistics, Hoover's, Edgar (SEC database), etc.

Starting Point-Business

http://www.stpt.com/busine.html

Starting Point also has a great collection of Commercial Directories at this site.

Business Job Finder

http://www.cob.ohio-state.edu/dept/fin/osujobs.htm

For those interested in business careers, or careers in finance, accounting, or management, The Fisher College of Business at Ohio State has this "Business Job Finder" just for you.

LookupUSA

http://www.abii.com/

And now, to get really detailed. This site, sponsored by American Business Information, Inc., lists 88 million households and 11 million businesses. They can give you a full company profile with key executives, number of employees, sales volume, lines of business, fax numbers, and more. A profile is available, by phone call, for $3.

IBM InfoMarket

http://www.infomarket.ibm.com/

This site has information on more than 10 million companies. But if you want a detailed report, it will cost you.

Dun & Bradstreet

http://www.dbisna.com/dbis/product/secure.htm

Well of course *they* have information about companies, more than 10 million of them. But, again, if you want anything detailed, these reports will be for a price.

Big Book on WashingtonPost.com

http://www.washingtonpost.com/wp-adv/bigbook

As far as *locating* a business is concerned, once you know its name, there are *huge* telephone directories on the Web, which are searchable by name. This one will not only give you the address, but also draw you a map showing you where the business is located. Only drawback: the maps are not always accurate, key streets are not named at times *unless you zoom all the way in*, and sometimes the addresses are as much as a year out of date. (Bad news if the place moved in the last 12 months.) Still it's a good start.

BigYellow

http://www.bigyellow.com/

NYNEX has another such directory, helpful in locating the phone number and address of a particular business, anywhere in the country.

See also the directories listed under contact sites on pages *137–138*.

PARACHUTE PICKS: RESEARCH SITES: SPECIAL POPULATIONS OR SPECIAL PROBLEMS

If you have a special problem or special population in mind, give it to your favorite search engine, and see what it turns up. I have listed a sampler of the *kind* of things to be found on the Internet, in this regard.

Resources for Minorities

VJF Internet Resources for Minorities

http://www.vjf.com/pub/docs/jobsearch.html

Your search engine will find such things as this site belonging to **Virtual Job Fair's**, "The Global Village: Resources for Minorities on the Internet." First rate.

Resources for Women

WWWomen

http://www.wwwomen.com/

Your search engine will find such things as this site which calls itself "The Premier Search Directory for Women Online."

Pleiades Women's Directory

http://www.pleiades-net.com/lists/orgs.html

Your search engine will find such things as this site belonging to **Pleiades Network**. They call it the "Women's Directory."

FeMiNa

http://www.femina.com/

A number of good resources for women are also listed on this site.

Resources for Gays and Lesbians

Lavender Pages

http://www.lavenderpages.com/

Your search engine will find such things as this site. It is a San Francisco Bay Area resource, listing over 1,200 businesses and organizations for the lesbian, gay and bisexual community -- not just in San Francisco. Very comprehensive.

Bach Personnel

http://www.best.com/~bach/

Your search engine will also find personnel agencies "targeted at, but not limited to, the gay and lesbian community." This is a well-known one in San Francisco.

Resources for the Elderly

Social Security Administration

http://www.ssa.gov/pubs/10069.html

Your search engine will find such sites as this one, dealing with Social Security and retirement. Among other things, this site has useful information about benefits, and advice about how and when to retire.

Resources for People with Disabilities

The Job Accommodation Network

http://janweb.icdi.wvu.edu/kinder/

Your search engine will find such sites as this one, which gives information particularly related to the Americans with Disabilities Act.

Resources for Those Seeking Work with Nonprofits

Nonprofit Resources Catalog

http://www.clark.net/pub/pwalker/General_Nonprofit_Resources/

Your search engine will find a lot of sites dealing with nonprofits. What is unusual, I think, about these sites, is that they are almost all uniformly excellent. But, in my estimation, this site has the best list, an outstanding one maintained by Phillip A. Walker.

The Contact Directory to Nonprofits

http://www.contact.org/sample/dir.htm

This site has some wonderful lists, categorized by field, state, and country (the directory is worldwide).

Magellan

http://www.mckinley.com/

This site also has an excellent list.

Good Works

http://www.tripod.com/work/goodworks/search.html

This site, maintained by Tripod, Inc., and aimed at young adults moving from college into the workplace, has a list of nonprofits doing good in the community.

Ralph Nader -- Essential Information

http://www.essential.org/

Created by Ralph Nader's organization, this site, called "Essential Information," likewise has a section called Good Works, which provides access to the book by that title, and lists some actual job listings.

4Work

http://www.4work.com/

Here you will find job listings from various business and not-for-profit organizations, internships, youth positions, and volunteer work. This site has what looks at first sight like a nifty search tool: by registering your name, e-mail address, keywords, and geographic specifications, you are automatically updated via e-mail whenever a new job listing occurs, that matches your specifications of what you are looking for. That's the good news. The bad news is that their listings seem limited, *to say the least.* The first time I visited this site, it had a *heavy* emphasis on opportunities in Colorado. The second time I visited this site, things looked a little *broader.* Let's hope that trend continues.

Resources for Those Seeking Self-Employment

Working Solo

http://www.workingsolo.com/

Your search engine will find such sites as this one, a "site for independent entrepreneurs," that lists 1,200 business resources for those seeking self-employment. Great site!

Small Business Administration

http://www.sbaonline.sba.gov/

Let us not forget the obvious friend of self-employed businesspersons, the U.S. Small Business Administration, which has *a very helpful* site here, loaded with information.

Yahoo! Small Business Information

http://www.yahoo.com/Business_and_Economy/Small_Business_Information/

Here you can find all kinds of information of interest to the small businessperson, such as stuff about intellectual property (copyrights, etc.) or anything else that you're curious about.

Business Resource Center

http://www.greatinfo.com/business_cntr/bus_res.html

All kinds of resources for the self-employed can be found at The Information Center's site. It leads you to MoneyHunter, a site for seeking investment for your enterprise -- and other interesting places.

Excite Business Reviews

http://www.excite.com/Reviews/Business/

This search engine has another list of helpful resources for the self-employed.

Resources for Those Interested in Volunteering or in Internships

4Work

http://www.4work.com/

Your search engine will find such sites as this one. I mentioned it earlier. It is of interest here because it has some helpful resources dealing with volunteering and internships.

Resources for Those Seeking Temp Work

Temp Access

http://www.tempaccess.com/agenlist.html

Your search engine will find such sites as this one. They have here a particularly good listing of all the temporary agencies in the U.S. that are online. Very useful!

The Red Guide

http://www.panix.com/~grvsmth/redguide/

Speaking of temporary agencies, New York City has a truly exemplary use of what the Web could be. It's called the Red Guide, and is found here. Let me tell you what I like about it. They have created here a site where people who have worked for temporary agencies in NYC can write in afterwards, about their experience with those agencies. (Choose "Review Database.") Wish we had this kind of use of the Web throughout the whole country! For temp agencies. For companies. For everything.

Conclusion: If You Don't Find a Job

Well, that is the end of our guide to job-hunting on the Internet. If all of this pays off for you, and you get the job you most desire, *great!* But, if it doesn't, please don't take it personally. Remember the words of Margaret Riley, everybody's favorite expert on electronic job-hunting: "The Internet is merely an added dimension to the traditional job search, and it is not necessarily an easy dimension to add." And let me add: It *doesn't* pay off for huge numbers of people.

Let me show you what I mean:

Reports from the Field: The Experience of Actual Job-Hunters Concerning Their Resumes (and Job Listings) On the Internet This Year

Jobhunter #1. *I have not had any positive reaction to any of my listings of my resume online. The one exception was a headhunter who asked for my resume. You will get a lot of offers from strange companies or people looking for things that I would describe as pyramid schemes.*

Jobhunter #2. *It was a waste of my time . . . not a single reply!*

Jobhunter #3. *I haven't gotten any responses online. My impression is that if you're not in the computer field, you can pretty much forget finding work online.*

Jobhunter #4. *I found the Internet to be very limited, even for computer employment (which is what I do). Even the "Entry-Level" newsgroup is full of jobs requiring previous experience. Most of the employer listings seem to be looking for another Albert Einstein with just as many years of experience.*

Jobhunter #5. *I didn't actually get my job from the Net, though I made a pass at it. But in the end, I probably reverted to old habits rather than pursuing the job search on the Net the way I said I would. At the same time, the Net definitely played a part in my job hunt, as I pursued many of my contacts via e-mail -- much better than making "cold" telephone calls, once I'd gotten an e-mail address for a contact in a company (for some reason, a much easier thing than getting direct phone numbers). If I had it to do over again, I would probably do more to take advantage of the Net . . .*

Jobhunter #6. *I found seeking work online was worthwhile, but I'm in computer programming. After watching the listings for a few weeks, I saw a posting in mid-December which I answered with an e-mailed cover letter and resume. I heard back within a few hours, indicating they would be in touch when they scheduled interviews. While waiting to hear back, I saw another posting for which I considered myself qualified (Note: only two listings that fitted me at all, in four weeks). I answered this one, but never heard back. However, the first one did call me back four weeks later, to set up an appointment, and they offered me the job two weeks after that. I started three weeks after that. But notice how long this process took. While you connect quickly on the Internet, the employment process still moves at a snail's pace "out there." You'll need patience. Big time patience.*

Jobhunter #7. *I feel that online job lists should be viewed with the same healthy skepticism that we offer to want ads. That is, there are many scams, there are comparatively few jobs outside high tech, the government, and academe, and the qualifications sought are either high or highly specialized. Thus, one should not spend any greater time online than he or she would spend looking at the want ads. There is more hype than substance for the so-called average job seeker.*

If you're job-hunting on the Internet, and nothing turns up for you, that's because the Internet (currently) just presents us with the old job-hunting system in a new dress. That system didn't work very well before the Internet, and it doesn't work very well now. But, of course, you want to try it anyway.

My advice is: budget only a certain amount of your total job-hunting time to *the Internet part of your job-search* (I'd say 15% of your time, *max*). Keep tabs on yourself, and if after two weeks you discover that the Internet is *all* you are doing with your life, disconnect, give your modem to a friend, and go back to job-hunting *the old way:* the way people job-hunted before the computer was discovered.

But follow *the creative method of job-hunting,* puh-leaze. The rules are simple: *Know your best and most enjoyable transferable skills. Know what kind of work you want to do, what field you would most enjoy working in. Talk to people who are doing the work you want to do, in that field. Find out how they like the work, how they found their job. Do some research, then, in your chosen geographical area on those organizations which interest you, to find what they do and what kinds of problems/challenges they or their industry are wrestling with. Then identify and seek out the person who actually has the power to hire you at each organization, for the job you want; use your personal contacts -- everyone you know -- to get in to see him or her. Show this person with the power to hire you how you can help them with their problems/needs/challenges; and how you would stand out as "one employee in a hundred." Don't take turndown or rejection personally. Remember, there are two kinds of employers out there: those who will be bothered by your handicaps -- age, background, inexperience, or whatever they are -- and those who won't be, and will hire you, so long as you can do the job. If you get rejected by the first kind of employer, keep persevering, until you find the second.*

In all of this, cut no corners, take no shortcuts.

For Further Reading

If you feel you could use more help than this book has given you, go to your local bookstore and get the following:

The Guide to Internet Job Searching by Margaret F. Riley, Frances Roehm, and Steve Oserman (Foreword by Tom Jackson), VGM Career Horizons, a division of NTC Publishing Group, Lincolnwood, Illinois, 1996. *An extraordinary work. An update was in the works, as we went to press. The authors plan to update it, regularly.*

Also this Riley Guide, as it is called, can be found online -- at the new URL (as of July 7, 1997) of: `http://www.dbm.com/jobguide`.

III. Job-Hunting Tips for Special Populations

Job-Hunting and High School Students, including Summer Jobs
Job-Hunting and College Students
Job-Hunting and Women
Job-Hunting and Executives
Job-Hunting and Retirement
Job-Hunting and Ex-Military
Job-Hunting and Clergy
Job-Hunting and The So-Called 'Handicapped'
Job-Hunting and Minorities
Job-Hunting and Gays and Lesbians
Job-Hunting and Immigrants to the U.S.
Job-Hunting and 'People in Recovery'
Job-Hunting and Ex-Offenders

JOB
LAND

Job-Hunting Tips for Special Populations

The main body of *Parachute* tells you 98% of what you need to know, in order to successfully conduct your job-hunt. However, for those of you who are in one of the groups listed below, I do have some further comments and counsel.

High School Students

And Job-Hunting

If you are a high school graduate (or student) looking for work, you already know that you face especial difficulties during your job-hunt. You *can* overcome these difficulties. But you do need to be aware of what they are.

To begin with the bad news, in the U.S. only 18% of executives would hire a high school graduate for an entry-level job, according to a recent survey.[1] One employer (Nynex), for example, had to test 60,000 applicants to fill 3,000 job vacancies. When another employer (BellSouth) tested technician applicants, only 8 out of every 100 passed.

What's the problem? Bad work habits, say 78% of all employers.[2] That means U.S. high school graduates as a whole, often have a most unfortunate reputation for failing to show up regularly, balking at doing tasks they consider 'beneath them,' failing to accomplish assigned tasks, arguing that as long as they just keep busy they are doing their job, and failing to go 'the extra mile.'

What's the problem? It's also: reading, writing, and 'rithmetic. In 1945, the written vocabulary of a 6- to 14-year-old American was 25,000 words. Today it is only 10,000. The average young adult in the U.S. is reading at only a 2.6 level of English proficiency, while current jobs require a proficiency, on average, of 3.0 (*going up to 3.6 by the year 2000, experts say*).

And, finally, in the area of skills, 90% of all employers feel that high school graduates "do not know how to solve complex problems."

So, if you are still in high school, **get these skills** -- reading, writing, math, keyboarding (computers), and knowing how to solve problems -- while you are still there. Also, learn what good work habits are, even if you have to go and interview every manager of fast-food places within ten miles -- asking them the question: what is the mark of a really good employee here? what is the mark of a really bad employee here? Make a list of what they say are good work habits, and follow that list slavishly at whatever job you take thereafter.

If you are already *out* of high school, consider seriously going to night school at your local high school or community college, and picking up the skills listed in the previous paragraph, if you don't already have them.

If you are having difficulty finding work, then you must read, mark, learn and inwardly digest the chapter in *Parachute* called "The Determined Job-Hunter," and *do* the Quick Job-Hunting Map here in this *Workbook.*

The rules you must follow in your job-hunt are easy to master, since they are the same for you as they are for everyone: *Know your skills. Know what kind of work you want to do. Talk to people who are doing it. Find out how they like*

---

1. Reported in *USA Today,* 3/27/96.

2. According to a 1991 Harris Poll, reported in *USA Today,* 5/1/92.

the work, how they found their job. Do some research, in your chosen geographical area, on organizations which interest you, to find what they do and what kinds of problems they or their industry are wrestling with. Then identify and seek out the person who actually has the power to hire you there, for the job you want; use your contacts to get in to see him or her. Show this person with the power to hire you how you can help them with their problems; and how you would stand out as 'one employee in a hundred.' In all of this, cut no corners, take no shortcuts.

Remember this *above all:* all employers divide into two groups: those who will be bothered by the fact you are of high school age, and those who won't be -- and will hire you, so long as you can do the job. Your task is to find the second group of employers, and just thank the first very politely for their time.

For Further Reading

The Guide To Basic Skills Jobs: 2nd ed., *Vols. 1 and II.* 1993. RPM Press, Inc., P.O. Box 31483. Tucson, AZ 85751. 602-886-1990. A catalog of viable jobs for individuals with only basic work skills and/or limited education and/or limited general aptitudes -- such as persons with physical impairments, limited English proficiency, migrant workers, welfare recipients, persons with mental illness, etc. The database is *broken out* from the *D.O.T.*, but a concise, easy-to-use classification system is added. This volume identifies over 5,000 major occupations which require no more than an eighth grade level of education, and no more than one year of specific vocational preparation. Based upon research originally done by occupational analysts at North Carolina State University, and U.S.E.S. *Immensely useful book* for any of the above populations.

Hayes, Charles D., *Proving You're Qualified: Strategies for Competent People without College Degrees.* 1995. Autodidactic Press, P.O. Box 872749, Wasilla, AL 99687. The title says it all; very useful book.

Otto, Luther B., *Helping Your Child Choose A Career.* 1997 (Revised Edition). JIST Works, Inc., 720 N. Park Ave., Indianapolis, IN 46202. The classic, in this field of career books for the young.

Barkley, Nella, *How to Help Your Child Land The Right Job (without being a pain in the neck).* 1993. Workman Publishing Company, Inc., 708 Broadway, New York, NY 10003.

For summer jobs in the U.S. or elsewhere, there are directories for high school or college students. They are updated annually, and the year of their revision often appears in their title:

Beusterien, Pat, ed., *Summer Employment Directory of the United States.* Peterson's Guides, P.O. Box 2123, Princeton, NJ 08543.

Hatchwell, Emily, ed., *Directory of Summer Jobs in Britain.* Peterson's Guides, P.O. Box 2123, Princeton, NJ 08543.

Woodworth, David, ed., *Directory of Overseas Summer Jobs.* Issued in annual revisions. Peterson's Guides, P.O. Box 2123, Princeton, NJ 08543.

College Students

And Job-Hunting

College is no longer just for 18-year-olds. Some 42% of college students today are over the age of 24, according to the National Center for Education Studies. *(Source: ReCareering Newsletter, March-April 1995)*

If you are a college graduate looking for work, you already know that you face especial difficulties during your job-hunt. You *can* overcome these difficulties. But you do need to be aware of what they are.

The major problem is the false belief that there is a job out there that goes with the degree. *After all, don't corporate recruiters just come on campus during your senior year, and clamor for you to come work for them?* Well, no, they don't. In the U.S., for example, only one in three graduates has a job waiting for them at graduation time. At some colleges or universities, that figure was only one in ten.[3]

In most cases, therefore, you are going to have to take charge of your own job-hunt. The race for the best jobs belongs not to the strong, but to those who take initiative, are persistent, and know how to conduct their job-hunt themselves.

Summer jobs or internships may stand you in good stead, as you go through college. Remember that one out of seven students, in some sections of the country, get their job at the place where they interned.[4] So, internships might be an important part of your planning during the four years. There is a company called Back Door Experiences, which has a comprehensive guidebook for those seeking a short-term work experience (internship, seasonal job, program abroad, etc.). Cost is $30. For a free information packet you can write the author, Michael Landes, at 1414 Arbutus Ave., Chico, CA 95926-2660. 916-343-3867, 800-552-PATH.

If you are still having difficulty finding work, then you must read, mark, learn and inwardly digest the chapter in *Parachute* called "The Determined Job-Hunter," and *do* the Quick Job-Hunting Map here in this *Workbook*.

The rules you must follow in your job-hunt are easy to master, since they are the same for you as they are for everyone: *Know your skills. Know what kind of work you want to do. Talk to people who are doing it. Find out how they like the work, how they found their job. Do some research, in your chosen geographical area, on organizations which interest you, to find what they do and what kinds of problems they or their industry are wrestling with. Then identify and seek out the person who actually has the power to hire you there, for the job you want; use your contacts to get in to see him or her. Show this person with the power to hire you how you can help them with their problems; and how you would stand out as 'one employee in a hundred.'* In all of this, cut no corners, take no shortcuts.

Remember this *above all:* all employers divide into two groups: those who will be bothered by the fact you are a recent college graduate, and those who won't be -- and will hire you, so long as you can do the job. Your task is to find the second group of employers, and just thank the first very politely for their time.

---

3. *USA Today*, 5/1/92

4. *San Francisco Chronicle*, 5/27/92

For Further Reading

Figler, Howard, *Liberal Education and Careers Today.* Ferguson Publishing Co., 200 West Madison, Suite 300, Chicago, IL 60606. 1989. Very helpful, as is anything from Howard's pen.

Scheele, Adele, *Beating the Good Student Trap.* Simon and Schuster/ Kaplan, 1230 Avenue of the Americas, New York, NY 10020. 1997.

If you are interested in jobs or careers that are outdoors, there is:

Stientstra, Tom, and Schlueter, Robyn, *Sunshine Jobs: Career Opportunities Working Outdoors.* Live Oak Publications, P.O. Box 2193, Boulder, CO 80306. 303-447-1087. 1997. Careers you haven't even thought of.

Landes, Michael, *The Back Door Guidebook.* Ten Speed Press, P.O. Box 7123, Berkeley, CA 94707. 1997. 1000 programs are listed, dealing with off-the-beaten-path, ongoing/short-term/work/learn/travel adventures throughout the world. You can contact the author directly at: Back Door Experiences, P.O. Box 177, Chico, CA 95927-0177. Phone: 1 800 552-PATH.

Books on summer jobs are listed at the end of the previous section.

Women

And Job-Hunting

If you are a woman looking for work, you already know that you face especial difficulties during your job-hunt. You *can* overcome these difficulties. But you do need to be aware of what they are.

The advice for women who go job-hunting is the same as it is for men:

If you are having difficulty finding work, then you must read, mark, learn and inwardly digest the chapter in *Parachute* called "The Determined Job-Hunter," and *do* the Quick Job-Hunting Map here in this *Workbook.*

The rules you must follow in your job-hunt are easy to master, since they are the same for you as they are for everyone: *Know your skills. Know what kind of work you want to do. Talk to people who are doing it. Find out how they like the work, how they found their job. Do some research, in your chosen geographical area, on organizations which interest you, to find what they do and what kinds of problems they or their industry are wrestling with. Then identify and seek out the person who actually has the power to hire you there, for the job you want; use your contacts to get in to see him or her. Show this person with the power to hire you how you can help them with their problems; and how you would stand out as 'one employee in a hundred.'* In all of this, cut no corners, take no shortcuts.

Remember this *above all:* all employers divide into two groups: those who will be bothered by the fact you are a woman, and those who won't be -- and will hire you, so long as you can do the job. Your task is to find the second group of employers, and just thank the first very politely for their time.

Once hired, women do face five unique problems.

(1) **Salary** is a major one. Women are notoriously underpaid, even when of equal experience and training to men in the same company or firm. There are several strategies for dealing with this inequity.

- Some women go into a field belonging predominantly to men, where salary inequities are generally rarer.

• Some women go into a new field, where the salary is more likely to be equitable.

• Some search for unusual job-titles, as -- again -- they are then more likely to be paid an equitable wage.

• Some women prefer to negotiate for a higher salary before they even accept the job offer. And indeed you *can* increase the salary offered you, *if* you know something about salary negotiation, before you go in for the job interview. Be *sure* and study pages 208 ff, in *Parachute*.

(2) Related to salary is the problem of **child-care**. For the working poor, child-care costs often represent at least one fifth of their income, which of course reduces the *net* amount of their already-low paycheck by at least that much.

(3) The third problem is **getting promoted**. You have to figure out who the decision-makers are, concerning any promotion you may be qualified for. You have to educate them, whether with a yearly report to your immediate supervisor, copy to the decision-makers, detailing your accomplishments for the year -- or whatever may occur to you. It also helps to volunteer to work on committees or in other departments, so you get experience in many areas there at your place of business. It helps to ask for feedback from co-workers and your supervisor, as to how you could do the work better. It helps if you *ask* for more responsibility, particularly those kinds where there is a definite contribution to the profit or loss side of your place of business. About all else, ask for what you want, gently, kindly, persistently. Robin Wolaner, vice president of Time Publishing Ventures, was quoted in the press recently as saying that early in her career "I kept expecting people to give me things because I deserved it. Then I realized you had to raise your hand." Mark this well!

(4) The fourth problem for women after they get the job, is that of **the invisible *'glass ceiling.'*** This now well-known phrase refers to the difficulty women have, in getting promoted beyond a certain point. At lower levels, women are not running into as much trouble getting promoted as they used to. But when they get to higher levels, the going gets much tougher, as their head hits *the glass ceiling!* This explains why so many women are gravitating eventually to small organizations, or forming their own companies. The National Association of Women Business Owners estimates that there are over 7.7 million businesses in the U.S. owned by women.

(5) The fifth and final problem facing women especially is that of **sexual harassment** or abuse in the workplace.

• While harassment in this crazy topsy-turvy world can sometimes be inflicted by women managers on the men or women they work with, or by males on males, the vast majority of harassment is done by males to females: and the harassment ranges from subtle to yucky to gross to demonic. This is particularly likely in 'the blue-collar world,' or any job where men are the dominant job-holders.

• The crux of the problem lies in *some* men's ignorance, some men's meanness, some men's *power* needs, and some men's assumption that women basically think like they do. As for the latter, no! no! men and women do not think alike, as John Gray has been spending some years convincing the world. *Men are from Mars, Women are from Venus.*

• Evidence: 75% of men in the workplace find sexual advances from the opposite sex *flattering*, while 75% of women in the workplace find them *offensive.*[5]

• Further evidence: many good-hearted men regard an offer to help a woman colleague or client, particularly outside of working hours, as innocent; whereas many good-hearted women are deeply suspicious of such offers, often due to prior experience with such offers from bad-hearted men, who intended it as a prelude to seduction.

Now, if you are a woman and someone in your workplace is overtly harassing you, sexually or otherwise, making your life truly miserable, you have three courses of action open to you:

• The first is to pray he or she will go away. Sometimes they will. It helps if you give a nice unambiguous "No" to any sexual propositions -- veiled or overt -- and a nice firm, "I'm going to pretend this conversation never took place" in response to any crude language. Silence is not golden. If you have kept silent, please when next you go home, practice in front of a mirror if you must, "I will not keep silent. I will tell this person, No, no, no. I will not keep silent." If you can't bring yourself to break your silence, then I urge you to do whatever you need to do, with therapy, group work, or whatever, to build up your self-confidence. If you have already said No, and it hasn't changed a thing, then plan on leaving. Incidentally, when women are asked why they did not protest harassment on the job, their universal reply is: "Because I couldn't afford to risk losing the job." Sometimes that's because they love the work, and the pay is fabulous. More often than not, however, this clinging to their present job-turned-bad arises from their lack of confidence in their ability to go find another job of equal merit. In other words, their problem is lack of knowledge about the job-hunt. Go fix *that* lack of knowledge, and you will be better able to decide what to do about the harassment. Study this book. You *must* realize that you do have the ability to find another job of equal merit, and without harassment.

• The second course of action is to file a lawsuit. It is an idea which is becoming increasingly attractive, especially if you have witnesses to the offending behavior, and a lawyer who is experienced with these kinds of cases. The only thing you must recognize is that such a lawsuit sometimes takes *forever,* and I mean *forever.* As I write, the Equal Employment Opportunity Commission in the U.S. has a backlog of 97,000 cases.[6] Count the cost, also: I have counseled three women whose lawsuit, some years ago, dramatically affected their present employability. Future employers may see you as 'a troublemaker.' You can mitigate this, perhaps, before you file, by trying to

---

5. According to a survey done in the U.S., in 1992.

6. If you decide to file a suit, you must consult a lawyer *experienced in such matters.* You may also wish to read articles such as "Getting Justice Is No Easy Task," in the May 13, 1996 issue of *Business Week.* Look it up in the archives at your local library, or online (the *Business Week* site on America Online).

find out if any of your co-workers have endured such harassment, and getting them to enter into the lawsuit with you -- so that it is more of a group action. Needless to say, if you're planning on retiring, or going into business for yourself, or if you plan on going to work for some new employer -- female or male -- who will regard you as a heroine on account of this lawsuit, then this last point is moot.

• The third course of action open to you, as I mentioned earlier, is to leave. Don't tell yourself, *"Hey, it's a good job and I like everything else about it, so I'll just put up with the sexual innuendos, leers, or abuse."* No, no:

A 'good job' with sexual harassment present
is by definition *a bad job.*

My advice to you, for what it's worth, is that if you are being harassed, and you decide not to file a suit, *don't* trade your self-esteem just for a paycheck. Make plans -- even long-range plans -- to leave, if your tormentor doesn't leave first! Prepare the groundwork *now* by increasing your command of the job-hunt. Devour this book. Do all the exercises. Really sharpen your job-hunting skills. And when you're confident about your ability to go find another job, go find it.

For Further Reading

The WomanSource Catalog & Review: Tools for Connecting the Community of Women, edited by Ilene Rosoff. Celestial Arts, P.O. Box 7123, Berkeley, CA 94707. 1995. Countless resources for women; an immensely helpful book.

Petrocelli, William, and Repa, Barbara Kate, *Sexual Harassment on the Job: What it is and how to stop it.* Nolo Press, 950 Parker St., Berkeley, CA 94710-9867. 1995. Very enlightening and helpful.

McCann, Nancy Dodd, and McGinn, Thomas A., *Harassed: 100 Women Define Inappropriate Behavior in the Workplace.* Business One Irwin, Homewood, IL 60430. 1992. Discusses one situation after another, and then tells what percentage of the women in their survey felt this situation represented harassment. Men who haven't kept up with the changing sensitivities of the '90s will find this *very* enlightening.

Nivens, Beatryce, *Careers for Women without College Degrees.* McGraw-Hill Book Company, 11 West 19th St., New York, NY 10011. 1988. Has some useful information about the skills required for some typical occupations that a woman might be considering. She has also written: *How To Change Careers.* 1990. The Putnam Publishing Group, 390 Murray Hill Pkwy., Dept. B, East Rutherford, NJ 07073.

Scheele, Adele, *Career Strategies for the Working Woman,* Simon and Schuster/Fireside, 1230 Avenue of the Americas, New York, NY 10020. 1994.

Caroline Bird, *Lives of Our Own: Secrets of Salty Old Women.* Houghton Mifflin, 1995.

Executives

And Job-Hunting

Well, you may have quit or you may have been let go. If the latter, be aware that if you are a U.S. executive or manager in your middle years or beyond, working in an organization of 20 or more employees, and you feel you were let go because of your age -- even if it was in the midst of a downsizing -- you may have a discrimination case under a U.S. law called the Age Discrimination in Employment Act (ADEA).

Merely saying, "I *feel* I was let go because of my age" isn't sufficient. You need evidence. So, keep a record of *any* statements made to you by your superiors that substantiate your claim and your *feelings* ('we need younger blood in here,' or 'we could get two college graduates for what we are paying you,' etc.). Poor performance ratings, suddenly, after years of good ones -- with no reason -- may also substantiate your claim. If you have such evidence, and you decide you do want to pursue legal remedies, a stamped self-addressed envelope sent to the National Employment Lawyers Association, 600 Harrison St., #535, San Francisco, CA 94107 will get you names of attorneys who practice employment law. Hie thee to one of them, evidence in hand, and see what they think.

If this route is of no interest to you, as well it may not be for any number of good reasons, and you just want to get on with your next job-hunt, be aware that because of your age and other factors you will face some subtle difficulties during your upcoming job-hunt. You *can* overcome these difficulties. But you do need to be aware of what they are. And, how to overcome them.

The first is, there are a lot of other executives who are job-hunting at the same time you are. The current mania for downsizing, mergers and so forth, has hit white-collar workers *hard.* There are a lot of middle- to upper-level managers out there, who suddenly find themselves looking for work after twenty years at a place. That's why the average job-search period for executives, recently, was 6.8 months.[7]

Secondly, the length of your job-search will likely be related to your age, and the amount of salary that you are seeking. One large outplacement firm kept records and discovered that if an executive was 25–34 years of age, the average length of their job-hunt was about 20 weeks, but if over 55 years in age, it took almost 30 weeks. They further discovered that for those seeking an annual salary of $40,000 to $75,000, the average length of their job-hunt was about 25 weeks, while for those seeking more than $100,000, the average length of their job-hunt was almost 30 weeks.[8] That's what you *may* be up against.

---

7. According to Drake Beam Morin Inc., for the year 1990.

8. Reported in the *National Business Employment Weekly,* in the 8/27/89 edition. Statistics were for the year 1989.

However, these statistics reflect the manner in which executives go job-hunting. Many are completely baffled by this process, and have *no idea* how to go job-hunting -- except to rely almost exclusively on the sending out of resumes. That route always has a bad track record, and may account for why the average job-hunt of executives takes so long. A better job-hunting method would equal a shorter time out of work, in many, many cases.

If you are having difficulty finding work, then you must reconsider *how* you are conducting your job-hunt. Do read, mark, learn and inwardly digest the chapter in *Parachute* called "The Determined Job-Hunter," and *do* the Quick Job-Hunting Map here in this *Workbook.*

The rules you must follow in your job-hunt are easy to master, since they are the same for you as they are for everyone: *Know your skills. Know what kind of work you want to do. Talk to people who are doing it. Find out how they like the work, how they found their job. Do some research, in your chosen geographical area, on organizations which interest you, to find what they do and what kinds of problems they or their industry are wrestling with. Then identify and seek out the person who actually has the power to hire you there, for the job you want; use your contacts to get in to see him or her. Show this person with the power to hire you how you can help them with their problems; and how you would stand out as 'one employee in a hundred.'* In all of this, cut no corners, take no shortcuts.

Remember this *above all:* all employers divide into two groups: those who will be bothered by your age or by the fact that you were laid off in a downsizing or merger, and those who won't be -- and will hire you, so long as you can do the job. Your task is to find the second group of employers, and just thank the first very politely for their time.

When you are being interviewed, be aware that in the U.S. the ADEA forbids the employer to ask your age.

For Further Reading

Burton, Mary Lindley, and Wedemeyer, Richard A., *In Transition: From the Harvard Business School Club of New York's Career Management Seminar.* HarperBusiness, 10 E. 53rd St., New York, NY 10022. 1991.

For Networking

There are various organizations dedicated to networking among executives -- employed or unemployed.

Forty Plus, described in detail on page 267 is one such organization; it has branches all around the country, and Canada.

Exec-U-Net *(25 Van Zant St., Suite 15-3 Norwalk, CT 06855. 203-851-5180. David B. Opton, Executive Director)* is another such organization. It sends its members every two weeks a list of nearly 400 new unadvertised positions (many of them apparently from recruiters). Membership, however, is limited to executives who make (or used to make) over $75,000 a year. Its fee is around $110, for three months membership (six issues).

Out there, also, are "executive counseling firms," which *claim* extensive networks, that they will happily place at the service of their clients *(for a very large fee, up front).* If you are tempted to go to such a place, be sure to read (*three times*) the section on pages 244–252 You *can* 'lose your shirt' at such places, and get *nothing* in return.

Note: my mentioning a resource is for information purposes only, to make you aware of the *kinds of things* that are available *out there;* it is not a recommendation or endorsement of that place.

Retirement

And Job-Hunting

'Retirement' has become a nebulous concept. It used to mean *not working*-- sitting on the front porch, or on the beach, or taking a cruise -- but in general enjoying a life of leisure. However, a recent *Gallup Poll/USA Today* survey turned up the fact that 70% of baby boomers said they expect to work after they 'retire,' whether that is at age 65 or earlier.[9] So now, 'retirement' often means simply a time for a *career change,* if one doesn't continue at what one has always been doing.

Incidentally, the number of people in the U.S. who retire annually is nearly 2 million, and the median age (of retirement) currently is age 62. In fact, one-third of all retirees do so by age 55.[10]

Of course, not *everyone* works after they 'retire.' For many, retirement *is* retirement. They drop out of the workforce, and half of them, according to a relatively recent study,[11] are satisfied with that situation, while one-quarter are very unhappy over the fact that they aren't working. (In point of fact, one out of three retired men does return to the workforce, usually within two years.)[12] *The remaining one-quarter not accounted for above, are people who are simply unable to work, presumably because of their health.*

In the U.S., if you are a retiree receiving Social Security, and have decided to go looking for work, your desire to work will be complicated by the Social Security requirements, which amount to a kind of *disincentive* to work. In 1996, the law is this: once you are 62 years of age, and through the time you are 64, you lose $1 of Social Security benefits for every $2 earned above $8,280; once you are 65 and through the time you are 69, you lose $1 of benefits for every $3 earned above $12,500.

In 1997, this latter limit rises to $13,500; in 1998, to $14,500; in 1999, to $15,500; in the year 2000, to $17,000; in 2001, to $25,000; and in the year 2002, to $30,000.

The limit for the 62–64 year age range remains *indexed* to the cost of living for each year, so the changes there should be comparatively slight.

In any and all of these years, if you are past your 70th birthday, you can earn without limit, and you will lose none of your benefits no matter how much you earn.

---

9. *USA Today,* 4/29/96.

10. *Monthly Labor Review,* July 1992, "Trends in retirement age by sex, 1950-2005."

11. Reported in *The New York Times,* 4/22/90.

12. Reported in *American Demographics,* 12/90. Statistics for women in retirement were not covered in the article.

> These Social Security rules and limits do get changed by Congress and time, so be sure not to take my word for any of this, but check with your local Social Security office to find out if this has changed between the time I write this and the time you read this; and remember, you're still subject to the regular employment taxes, on what you earn, just like everyone else.

If you want to work primarily (or solely) to supplement your retirement income, the foregoing may be a disincentive. On the other hand, if you want to work for the pure joy of working, the economic disincentive will probably not faze you. *And,* you can always volunteer your time without cost to the place where you are dying to serve.

If you do decide to job-hunt, you may face particular difficulties because of your age, as you know. You can overcome those difficulties, of course, but to do so you must read, mark, learn and inwardly digest the chapter in *Parachute* called "The Determined Job-Hunter," and *do* the Quick Job-Hunting Map here in this *Workbook.*

The rules you must follow in your job-hunt are easy to master, since they are the same for you as they are for everyone: *Know your skills. Know what kind of work you want to do. Talk to people who are doing it. Find out how they like the work, how they found their job. Do some research, in your chosen geographical area, on organizations which interest you, to find what they do and what kinds of problems they or their industry are wrestling with. Then identify and seek out the person who actually has the power to hire you there, for the job you want; use your contacts to get in to see him or her. Show this person with the power to hire you how you can help them with their problems; and how you would stand out as 'one employee in a hundred.'* In all of this, cut no corners, take no shortcuts.

Remember this above all: all employers divide into two groups: those who will be bothered by your age, and those who won't be -- and will hire you, so long as you can do the job. Your task is to find the second group of employers, and just thank the first very politely for their time.

For Further Reading

If you want some guidance about possible places to retire to, in the U.S., there are these resources:

Richard Boyer and David Savageau, *Places Rated Almanac: Your Guide to Finding the Best Places to Live in North America.* rev. ed. 1993. Prentice-Hall, 15 Columbus Circle, New York, NY 10023. A marvelous book. Immensely helpful for anyone weighing where to move next. All 343 metropolitan areas are ranked and compared for living costs, job outlook, crime, health, transportation, education, the arts, recreation, and climate. Has numerous helpful diagrams, charts, and maps, showing (for example) earthquake risk areas, tornado and hurricane risk areas, the snowiest areas, the stormiest areas, the driest areas, and so on. Highly recommended. A knockout of a book.

Savageau, David, *Retirement Places Rated.* 3rd ed. 1990. Prentice Hall Press, 15 Columbus Circle, New York, NY 10023. 151 top retirement areas ranked and compared for costs of living, housing, climate, personal safety, services, work opportunities, and leisure living. Highly recommended. Tremendously useful. He updates it periodically.

If you want to know what retired people do, by way of work, after retirement, the classic on this subject is:

Bird, Caroline, *Second Careers: New Ways to Work After 50.* 1992. Little, Brown and Company, Time Warner Bldg., 1271 Avenue of the Americas, New York, NY 10020. The subject of this book is not what 'seniors' *ought* to do after age 50, but what in fact they *do* do . . . and why. This book is her 'report to the nation' of her analysis of some 36,000 questionnaires sent in by readers of *Modern Maturity* Magazine. Highly recommended.

Ex-Military

And Job-Hunting

If you are an ex-military person who has decided to look for work outside the military, in the general workplace, you already know that you will have some problems convincing the world you know *anything* except how to wage war. You *can* convince them, but it will take work.

Your major problem is that you speak a different language from those out there in the world. You have been living in a sub-culture within our general culture, and this sub-culture is in many respects like the general job-market, *except* that it has its own unique vocabulary. It is *crucial* that you sit down and inventory the skills you have been using during your time in the military. Take especial care to take your skills and fields of knowledge out of the military *jargon*, and translate them into language that is understood in the general marketplace.

There are three aids to help you do this:

The first is 'The Quick Job-Hunting Map' at the beginning of this workbook.

Secondly, each service's personnel manuals has a section where military jobs and tasks are cross-coded to the civilian *Dictionary of Occupational Titles.*

Thirdly, there is a two-volume Military Occupation Training Data series, available from Defense Manpower Data Center, 1600 Wilson Blvd., Suite 400, Arlington VA 22209, which does the same thing.

If you are or were an officer, you should know that the Retired Officers Association (TROA), 201 N. Washington Street, Alexandria, VA 22314-2529, 703-838-8117, has an Officer Placement Service which maintains a comprehensive job-search library, a computerized placement service, and resume critiques for their members. It is, unfortunately, open only to officers, and only to those who become members of TROA.

Officer or not, your salvation depends on the same creative job-hunting -- and career-changing -- methods as anyone else.

If you are having difficulty finding work, then you must read, mark, learn and inwardly digest the chapter in *Parachute* called "The Determined Job-Hunter," and *do* the Quick Job-Hunting Map here in this *Workbook.*

The rules you must follow in your job-hunt are easy to master, since they are the same for you as they are for everyone: *Know your skills. Know what kind of work you want to do. Talk to people who are doing it. Find out how they like the work, how they found their job. Do some research, in your chosen geographical area, on organizations which interest you, to find what they do and what kinds of problems they or their industry are wrestling with. Then identify and seek out the person who actually has the power to hire you there, for the job you want; use your contacts to get in to see him or her. Show this person with the power to hire you how you can help them with their problems; and how you would stand out as 'one employee in a hundred.'* In all of this, cut no corners, take no shortcuts.

Remember this *above all:* all employers divide into two groups: those who will be bothered by the fact you were in the military, and those who won't be -- and will hire you, so long as you can do the job. Your task is to find the second group of employers, and just thank the first very politely for their time.

For Further Reading

Schlachter, Gail Ann, and Weber, R. David, *Financial Aid for Veterans, Military Personnel, and Their Dependents 1990–1991.* 1990. Reference Service Press, 1100 Industrial Road, Suite 9, San Carlos, CA 94070. Outlines over 1,000 programs open to veterans and their dependents. See if there is an updated version, by the time you read this.

Clergy

And Job-Hunting

If you are an ordained person who has decided to look for work outside the church, in the general workplace, you already know that you will have some problems convincing the world you know *anything* except theology. As a matter of fact, you *can* convince them, but it will take work.

Your major problem is that you speak a different language from those out there in the world. Like the military (above), you have been living in a subculture within our general culture, which describes your skills and work-experience in its own unique vocabulary. It is *crucial* that you sit down and inventory the skills you have been using during your time in the church, and that you take especial care to *translate* your skills and fields of knowledge out of the clerical *jargon* and into language that is understood in the general marketplace.

You must read, mark, learn and inwardly digest the chapters in *Parachute* called "For the Determined Job-Hunter," and *do* the Quick Job-Hunting Map here in this *Workbook.*

The rules you must follow in your job-hunt are easy to master, since they are the same for you as they are for everyone: *Know your skills. Know what kind of work you want to do. Talk to people who are doing it. Find out how they like the work, how they found their job. Do some research, in your chosen geographical area, on organizations which interest you, to find what they do and what kinds of problems they or their industry are wrestling with. Then identify and seek out the person who actually has the power to hire you there, for the job you want; use your contacts to get in to see him or her. Show this person with the power to hire you how you can help them with their problems; and how you would stand out as 'one employee in a hundred.'* In all of this, cut no corners, take no shortcuts.

Remember this *above all:* all employers divide into two groups: those who will be bothered by the fact you were in the clergy, and those who won't be -- and will hire you, so long as you can do the job. Your task is to find the second group of employers, and just thank the first very politely for their time.

For Further Reading

In case you want further reading, or counseling, the books and counselors who look at job-hunting and career-changing particularly from a religious point of view are to be found at the end of The Epilogue, on page *238 ff*

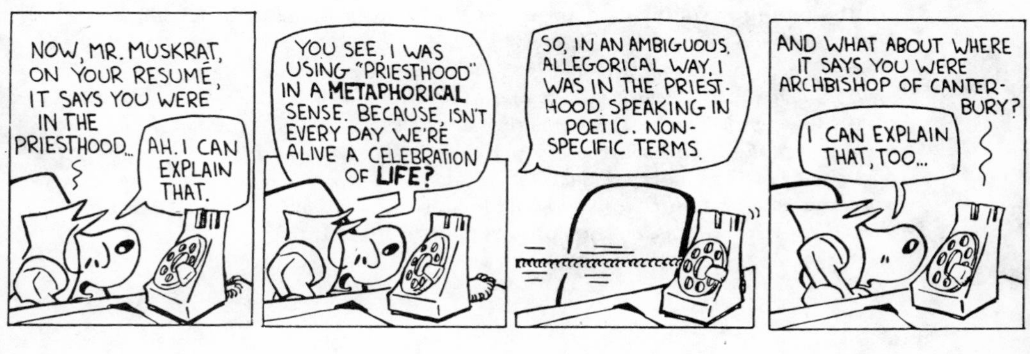

The So-Called Handicapped

And Job-Hunting

If you are a person with a handicap or disability, and are looking for work, you already know that you face especial difficulties during your job-hunt. You *can* overcome these difficulties. But you do need to be aware of what they are.

The first is that of *language.* There is much debate in our culture about how to describe those of us who have disabilities or handicaps. This debate is founded on the belief that *language* enshrines prejudice, and that if we can change the language we can change the prejudice. I understand the logic of this, but am dumbfounded at how obstinate prejudice is, in the face of *all* attempts to alter it. I have reluctantly come to the conclusion that changing *language* does not change the human *heart.* Hence, I think *politically correct* language is misguided, as it has turned the whole matter of disability into a joke: *physically-challenged,* etc.

I think you can call yourself whatever you wish. I liked a wonderful senior deaf and blind woman who was interviewed in the national press this past year. She said, "I'm not *disabled* -- like a car. I'm *handicapped* -- as in golf."

There are, of course, employers who are prejudiced, irrespective of what language you use to describe yourself. If you have a physical, mental, emotional, or other disability, and are looking for work, *of course* you are going to run into them. It helps if you remember this above all: all employers divide into *two* groups: those who will be bothered by your disability, and those who won't be -- and will hire you, so long as you can do the job.

Your task is to find the second group of employers, and just thank the first very politely for their time, plus secure any referrals they may be able to suggest.

If you are having difficulty finding work, then you must read, mark, learn and inwardly digest the chapter in *Parachute* called "The Determined Job-Hunter," and *do* the Quick Job-Hunting Map here in this *Workbook.*

The rules you must follow in your job-hunt are easy to master, since they are the same for you as they are for everyone: *Know your skills. Know what kind of work you want to do. Talk to people who are doing it. Find out how they like the work, how they found their job. Do some research, in your chosen geographical area, on organizations which interest you, to find what they do and what kinds of problems they or their industry are wrestling with. Then identify and seek out the person who actually has the power to hire you there, for the job you want; use your contacts to get in to see him or her. Show this person with the power to hire you how you can help them with their problems; and how you would stand out as 'one employee in a hundred.'* In all of this, cut no corners, take no shortcuts.

For Further Reading

I would like to list here all the resources available to you in your job-hunt, but this has proved to be a list that is too long for this *Workbook.* The list is available as a separate booklet, together with some extended advice on my part as to how you conduct interviews, and so forth; you can order it from the publisher if you want further help. It may also be in your local bookstore. It is:

Bolles, Richard N., *Job-Hunting Tips For The So-Called Handicapped or People Who Have Disabilities. A Supplement to What Color Is Your Parachute?* 1991. Order from Ten Speed Press, Box 7123, Berkeley, CA 94707. 61 pp. $4.95.[13]

Titles published since my booklet, include:

Azrin, Nathan H., and Besalel, Victoria A., *Finding A Job.* Ten Speed Press, P.O. Box 7123, Berkeley, CA 94707. 1982. Listed on page 46 in my booklet. (You can always try your local library, of course, to see if they have a copy.)

Helpful titles *newly-published* since my booklet, include:

Jeffrey Allen's *Successful Job Search Strategies for the Disabled: Understanding the ADA.* 1994. John Wiley & Sons, Inc., 605 Third Ave., New York, NY 10158.

Gail Ann Schlachter & R. David Weber, *Financial Aid for the Disabled and Their Families, 1996-1998.* 1996. Reference Service Press, Suite 9, 1100 Industrial Rd., San Carlos CA 94070-4131.

There is a wonderful bookstore in Vancouver, Washington, called *The Disability Bookshop,* which has a fantastic catalog of materials for the so-called 'handicapped.' Run by Helen Hecker, R.N., she reviews hundreds of books, and presents the best of them in her catalog, updated monthly. It is accessible online, at: `http://www.netm.com/mall/infoprod/twinpeak/helen.htm`. You can also contact her at P.O. Box 129, Vancouver, WA 98666-0129. 360-694-2462. Fax: 360-696-3210. e-mail: 73743.2634@compuserve.com. Orders (only): 1-800-637-2256.

Minorities

And Job-Hunting

If you are a member of some minority group looking for work, you already know that you may face especial difficulties during your job-hunt. You *can* overcome these difficulties. But you do need to be aware of what they are.

The principal one is the mental view that others have, by which they see the whole world in terms of 'tribes.' I call this mental view *tribalism,* and I regard it as the root of most of the troubles throughout the world: cf. Ireland, Bosnia, Iraq, the Middle East, Liberia, Somalia, Russia, and -- *of course* -- the U.S. So long as whites remain dominant among employers, here, *tribalism* and its bastard offspring, *prejudice,* is something you have to take into account.

---

13. If you wish to save this money, you can consult your local library to see if it has a copy of the booklet, *or* a copy of the 1990 or 1991 editions of *Parachute,* since this stuff first appeared as an Appendix in the back of those editions.

If you are having difficulty finding work in the face of such prejudice, then you *must* read, mark, learn and inwardly digest the chapters in *Parachute* called "For the Determined Job-Hunter," and *do* the Quick Job-Hunting Map here in this *Workbook.*

The rules you must follow in your job-hunt are easy to master, since they are the same for you as they are for everyone: *Know your skills. Know what kind of work you want to do. Talk to people who are doing it. Find out how they like the work, how they found their job. Do some research, in your chosen geographical area, on organizations which interest you, to find what they do and what kinds of problems they or their industry are wrestling with. Then identify and seek out the person who actually has the power to hire you there, for the job you want; use your contacts to get in to see him or her. Show this person with the power to hire you how you can help them with their problems; and how you would stand out as 'one employee in a hundred.'* In all of this, cut no corners, take no shortcuts.

Remember this *above all:* all employers divide into two groups: those who will be bothered by the fact you belong to a minority, and those who won't be -- and will hire you, so long as you can do the job. Your task is to find the second group of employers, and just thank the first very politely for their time.

For Further Reading

The Big Book of Minority Opportunities, 6th ed. 1997. Ferguson Publishing Co., 200 West Madison, Suite 300, Chicago, IL 60606. Lists over 4,000 organizations that have special programs to help minorities.

Minority Organizations: A National Directory. 1997. Ferguson Publishing Co., 200 West Madison, Suite 300, Chicago, IL 60606. An annotated directory of 5,800 African-American, Hispanic, Native American, and Asian or Pacific Islander organizations.

The Black Resource Guide. 10th ed., 1992. Black Resource Guide, Inc., 501 Oneida Pl., NW, Washington, DC 20011. A comprehensive list of over 3,000 black resources or organizations in the U.S.

Gays & Lesbians

And Job-Hunting

If you are a gay or lesbian looking for work, and want to be 'up front' about this, you already know that you will face especial difficulties during your job-hunt. You *can* overcome these difficulties.

Over the past decade or two, 'the Gay movement' in the U.S. and elsewhere in the world has made tremendous strides in gaining acceptance for their members within the broader society. Nonetheless, this is still 'but a drop in the bucket.' Vast antagonism to homosexuals still remains, making your orientation a definite handicap when you approach many employers, looking for a job.

Of course you can go looking for companies known to be the best places for you to work. There is, for example, a book by Ed Mickens, called *The 100*

Best Companies for Gay Men and Lesbians, Pocket Books, Simon & Schuster, 1994.

Further, if you are in the San Francisco area or want to be, there is a Personnel Agency whose mission is "to increase employment opportunities targeted, but not limited to, the Gay and Lesbian Community." They are at 2358 Market St., near Castro, in San Francisco, CA 94114. Their phone is 415-626-4663, and they also have a site on the Internet: http://www.best.com/~bach/

But if you want to conduct a broad search, and simply choose a company that is your preferred place to work, without knowing anything about their prejudice or lack of prejudice, your reception is less certain.

If you are having difficulty finding work in the face of such prejudice, then you *must* read, mark, learn and inwardly digest the chapters in *Parachute* called "For the Determined Job-Hunter," and *do* the Quick Job-Hunting Map here in this *Workbook.*

The rules you must follow in your job-hunt are easy to master, since they are the same for you as they are for everyone: *Know your skills. Know what kind of work you want to do. Talk to people who are doing it. Find out how they like the work, how they found their job. Do some research, in your chosen geographical area, on organizations which interest you, to find what they do and what kinds of problems they or their industry are wrestling with. Then identify and seek out the person who actually has the power to hire you there, for the job you want; use your contacts to get in to see him or her. Show this person with the power to hire you how you can help them with their problems; and how you would stand out as 'one employee in a hundred.'* In all of this, cut no corners, take no shortcuts.

Remember this *above all:* all employers divide into two groups: those who will be bothered by the fact that you are a gay or lesbian, and those who absolutely won't, and will hire you if you are able to do the job. Your task is to find the second group of employers, and just thank the first very politely for their time.

For Further Reading

The Alyson Almanac: The Fact Book of the Lesbian and Gay Community, Boston, Alyson Publications, Inc., 40 Plympton St., Boston, MA 02118. 1993. Has a section on laws and attitudes, state by state and in over 100 countries.

The Gay and Lesbian Address Book, by the editors of *Out* Magazine, Perigree, published by Berkley Publishing Group, 200 Madison Ave., New York, NY 10016. 1995. Lists all kinds of organizations and individuals.

Career and Life Planning with Gay, Lesbian, and Bisexual Persons, by Susan Gelberg and Joseph T. Chojnacki. American Counseling Association, 1-800-ACA-648, or 301-470-4ACA. 1996

The Corporate Closet: The Professional Lives of Gay Men in America, by James D. Woods with Jay H. Lucas. The Free Press, a division of Macmillan, Inc., 866 Third Ave., New York, NY 10022. 1994. Discusses all the different issues about how to conduct oneself in the workplace: the asexual professional, dodging the issue, playing it straight, etc.

Immigrants

And Job-Hunting

If you are newly arrived in the U.S., and are looking for work, you already know that you face especial difficulties during your job-hunt. You *can* overcome these difficulties. But you do need to be aware of what they are. And, how to overcome them.

Most of what you need to know, on both counts, can be learned in two ways. First of all, by talking to other immigrants, who have been here longer than you have, and have already 'learned the ropes.' And secondly, by reading *Parachute* thoroughly.

You will discover the chief job-hunting handicaps you need to overcome are your level of education, and your fluency (or lack of fluency) in English. See the earlier section on "High School Students and Job-Hunting."

If you are having difficulty finding work, then you must read, mark, learn and inwardly digest the chapters in *Parachute* called "For the Determined Job-Hunter," and *do* the Quick Job-Hunting Map here in this *Workbook*.

The rules you must follow in your job-hunt are easy to master, since they are the same for you as they are for everyone: *Know your skills. Know what kind of work you want to do. Talk to people who are doing it. Find out how they like the work, how they found their job. Do some research, in your chosen geographical area, on organizations which interest you, to find what they do and what kinds of problems they or their industry are wrestling with. Then identify and seek out the person who actually has the power to hire you there, for the job you want; use your contacts to get in to see him or her. Show this person with the power to hire you how you can help them with their problems; and how you would stand out as 'one employee in a hundred.'* In all of this, cut no corners, take no shortcuts.

Remember this *above all:* all employers divide into two groups: those who will be bothered by the fact you are newly arrived in this country, and those who won't be -- and will hire you, so long as you can do the job. Your task is to find the second group of employers, and just thank the first very politely for their time.

For Further Reading

Friedenberg, Joan E., Ph.D., and Bradley, Curtis H., Ph.D., *Finding a Job in the United States.* 1988, 1986. NTC Publishing Group, 4255 W. Touhy Ave., Lincolnwood, IL 60646-1975. A guide for immigrants, refugees, limited-English-proficient job-seekers, foreign-born professionals -- anyone who is seeking work in the United States. It contains job information based on the successful experience of job-seekers, plus advice from the U.S. Department of Labor. Includes information about American job customs and laws related to immigration, as well as a systematic plan for job-hunting.

Also, Stephen Rosen, Chairman of the Science and Technology Advisory Board, 575 Madison Ave., 22nd Floor, New York, NY 10022-2585, 212-940-6415, specializes in working with newly arrived immigrants with a science, engineering, or professional background -- his specialty is Russian immigrants, in particular. For people in the New York City area, he runs a 12-session program called Scientific Career Transitions, for which there is no charge.

People In Recovery

And Job-Hunting

If you are a person with a previous history of substance abuse, and you are now 'in recovery' and are looking for work, you already know what I'm going to say: you may face especial difficulties during the hiring interviews. You *can* overcome these difficulties. But in order to do so, you must read, mark, learn and inwardly digest the chapters in *Parachute* called "For the Determined Job-Hunter," and *do* the Quick Job-Hunting Map here in this *Workbook*.

The rules you must follow in your job-hunt are easy to master, since they are the same for you as they are for everyone: *Know your skills. Know what kind of work you want to do. Talk to people who are doing it. Find out how they like the work, how they found their job. Do some research, in your chosen geographical area, on organizations which interest you, to find what they do and what kinds of problems they or their industry are wrestling with. Then identify and seek out the person who actually has the power to hire you there, for the job you want; use your contacts to get in to see him or her. Show this person with the power to hire you how you can help them with their problems; and how you would stand out as 'one employee in a hundred.'* In all of this, cut no corners, take no shortcuts.

Remember this *above all:* all employers divide into two groups: those who will be bothered by the fact you are in recovery, and those who won't be -- and will hire you, so long as you can do the job. Your task is to find the second group of employers, and just thank the first very politely for their time.

For Further Reading

Tanenbaum, Nat, and Eric A., *The Career Seekers: A Program for Career Recovery.* 1988. This book is for people who are actively practicing any 12-step program, or are in counseling for co-dependency; but its principles apply to all who see themselves as 'recovering people.' A useful supplement to *Parachute.* Order from Nat Tanenbaum, 21 Timberlane Circle, Pisgah Forest, NC 28768, 704-884-2995.

Whitfield, M.D., Charles L., *A Gift to Myself.* 1990. Health Communications, Inc., 3201 SW 15th St., Deerfield Beach, FL 33442. Deals with root emotional issues often blocking job-hunters in recovery.

Ex-Offenders

And Job-Hunting

Currently, more than 5.1 million people in the U.S. are behind bars or on parole or probation.

If you are an ex-offender, and are looking for work, *of course* you are going to face especial difficulties during the hiring interviews, because of your history. You *can* deal with this problem, though you may need help.

If you decide you want to work on getting a college degree while you are in prison, get your hands on a book by John Bear and Mariah Bear, called *College Degrees by Mail 1997: 100 Accredited Schools that Offer Bachelor's, Master's, Doctorates and Law Degrees by Home Study.* 1997. Ten Speed Press, Box 7123, Berkeley, CA 94707. It has an Appendix entitled, "Advice for People in Prison."

Once you're out, and job-hunting, the Federal/State Employment Offices can often be of particular assistance to ex-offenders. All offices can provide for bonding of ex-offenders, if needed to obtain employment. They also have information on tax breaks for employers who hire ex-offenders. The larger offices even have Ex-Offender Specialists.

There is also *The Fortune Society,* 39 W. 19th St. (between 5th & 6th Avenues), New York, NY 10011. 212-206-7070. JoAnne Page, Executive Director. This Society works primarily with people who can come to their office, but they can also direct ex-offenders to the *Prisoners' Assistance Directory,* developed by the ACLU; the *Directory of Programs Serving Families of Adult Offenders,* published by the U.S. Department of Justice; *Post-Release Assistance Programs for Prisoners,* published by McFarland & Co., Inc.; and the *Guide to Community Services,* a publication of the Community Resource Network -- all of which will list resources for the area of the country in which you wish to find employment. The Society publishes the *Fortune News,* which is sent to you if you send them a contribution.

If all else fails, contact your local Chamber of Commerce or United Way, to see if they can tell you which community service organizations work with ex-offenders in your town or city.

If, in spite of all these resources, you are still having trouble finding work, then you *must* read, mark, learn and inwardly digest the chapters in *Parachute* called "For the Determined Job-Hunter," and *do* the Quick Job-Hunting Map here in this *Workbook.*

The rules you must follow in your job-hunt are easy to master, since they are the same for you as they are for everyone: *Know your skills. Know what kind of work you want to do. Talk to people who are doing it. Find out how they like the work, how they found their job. Do some research, in your chosen geographical area, on organizations which interest you, to find what they do and what kinds of problems they or their industry are wrestling with. Then identify and seek out the person who actually has the power to hire you there, for the job you want; use your contacts to get in to see him or her. Show this person with the power to hire you how you can help them with their problems; and how you would stand out as 'one employee in a hundred.'* In all of this, cut no corners, take no shortcuts.

Remember this *above all:* all employers divide into two groups: those who will be bothered by your incarceration, and those who won't be -- and will hire you, so long as you can do the job. Your task is to find the second group of employers, and just thank the first very politely for their time.

For Further Reading

The Correctional Educator, Annual Employment Issue, published by the Correctional Education Company, $15 for this special issue. Errol Craig Sull, President, 370 Franklin St., Buffalo, NY 14202. 716-849-0247. Fax: 716-845-5393. $79 for five issues annually. Sample copy sent on request. Also: *The Ex-Inmate's Complete Guide to Successful Employment,* by Errol Craig Sull. $29.95 plus $5.00 Shipping & Handling.

American Correctional Association, 8025 Laurel Lakes Ct., Laurel, MD 20707-5075. 301-206-5059 or 800-825-2665. Publishes: "As Free As An Eagle."

Interstate Publishers, P.O. Box 50, Danville, IL 61834-0050. 217-446-0500 or 800-843-4774. Publishes a parole planning manual called "From the Inside Out."

Open Inc., P.O. Box 566025, Dallas TX 75356-6025. 214-271-1971. Offender Preparation and Education Network. Publishes "99 Days & a Get-up," and "Man, I Need a Job!"

Manatee Publishing, 4835 North O'Conner St., #134435, Irving, TX 75062. Publishes: "Getting Out and Staying Out."

Want More Resources?

If you want more books than are included in the preceding sections, there are three places where you can look:

(1) Your **local bookstores** -- go to more than one, browse, and see what they have. Disadvantage: you have to buy the book, if you want it. Advantage: they've got the latest most up-to-date edition *(usually -- though not always).* Furthermore, they can order for you almost any book *that is still in print* -- and you'll know *that,* by whether or not it is listed in a reference book most bookstores have, called *Books In Print.* Ask.

(2) Your local **public libraries**, or nearby community college library. If they have a friendly reference librarian, by all means ask to see him or her. They can be worth their weight in gold to you. Tell them your problem or interest, and see what they can dig up. Disadvantage: a library may not have the latest edition of a book (see what edition of *Parachute* they're carrying, for example). Advantage: you can borrow a book for free, and furthermore, the reference librarian often knows of hidden treasures elsewhere in the library, buried in articles and clippings, which could be the answer to your prayers.

(3) **Mail order.** This is particularly helpful to those who live outside the U.S. There are a number of U.S. mail order places which specialize in career-related or job-hunting books for special populations. Their catalogs are listed in the section for Career Counselors, beginning on page *271ff.* Disadvantage: you have to wait to get the book, though if you phone, you can often order them by Federal Express, so sometimes it's *next day* delivery. Advantage: often you can order it from anywhere in the world, and their listings of career books, tapes, videos and software, are far more extensive than you will find in the average bookstore, or library.

IV. Special Problems

When You Want To Start Your Own Business

Moving

Working Overseas

What to Do, If Your Job-Hunt Drags On and On: How to Deal with Rejection and Depression

When You Want To Start Your Own Business

Self-Employment
Working for Yourself
Working at Home
Being An Independent Contractor
Being An Inventor
Becoming a Free-Lancer
Running A Franchise

Sure, you've thought about it, a million times. Hasn't everyone? Every time you're tied up in traffic going to or from work. You've toyed with the idea of not having to go to an office or other place of business, but of running your own business, keeping all the profits for yourself, being your own boss, making your own product or selling your own services, maybe out of your own home. It's called 'the world's fastest commute,' or 'going downstairs, instead of downtown.'[1]

Great idea! *But,* so far as you are concerned, nothing's ever come of it. Until now. Now, you're out of work, or you're fed up with your job, and you're thinking to yourself: *Maybe it's now, or never. Maybe I ought to just* do *it.*

WHAT KIND OF BUSINESS DO YOU WANT TO START?

You need to begin, of course, by deciding **what** kind of business you want to be in. Perhaps you haven't the foggiest notion.

Or, perhaps you know exactly *what,* because you've been thinking about it for *years,* and may even have been *doing* it for years -- only, in the employ of someone else. If you are now thinking about doing this on your own, whether it be business services, or consultancy, or repair work, or some kind of craft, or the making of some kind of product, or teaching, or offering of home services such as childcare or delivery by night.

---

1. Coined by Robert E. Calem in *The New York Times,* 4/18/93.

The next question you need to decide is just exactly **where** you're going to be doing it. Some self-employment ideas will require an outside place. For example, your dream may be: *I want a horse ranch, where I can raise and sell horses.* Or *I want to run a bed-and-breakfast place.* Stuff like that.

Some businesses are *independent of site.* It is possible to define a business -- given the telephone, fax machine, e-mail, and the Internet -- which could be run from a ski resort or wherever your preferred environment in the whole world is -- whether out in nature, or at your favorite vacation spot, or even in some other country. You can put them anywhere.

The only rule is, be *sure* to go talk to other people who have already done what you are contemplating *or something like it.* Pick their brains for everything they're worth. No need for you to step on the same *landmines* that they did.

WORKING OUT OF YOUR OWN HOME

Most people, however, when starting their own businesses, prefer to begin by running them out of their home if they possibly can. They can thus save money, overhead, rent, and cut down on many other expenses.

Three hundred years ago, of course, nearly everybody worked this way. They worked at home or on their farm. Only when the industrial revolution came, did the idea of working *away from* home become the rule.

In recent times, however, the idea of working at home has been finding new life, due to congestion on the highways, and the development of new technologies. If you can afford them, the telephone,[2] a fax machine, a computer with a modem, e-mail, online services and/or the Internet, mail order houses, and the like, all have combined to make a home business feasible, as never before.

It's called *self-employment,* or being *an independent contractor,* or *free-lancing* or *contracting out your services.*[3]

If you're thinking about doing this, working out of your own home, apartment, or condo, you would be joining the more than 23.8 million home-based workers who already do this in the U.S., plus the estimated 25 million additional workers who are *thinking* about doing it.

But you need to begin by being aware of the problems you will face, so that you will know in advance how to deal with them.

---

2. This family includes cellular telephones, 'call-forwarding' -- the technology where people call your one fixed telephone number, and then get automatically forwarded to wherever you have told the phone company you currently are -- and voice/electronic mail.

3. If you decide to launch yourself on this path, be sure to talk to people who have been free-lancers, until you know the name of every pitfall and obstacle in *free-lancing.* Where do you find such people? Well, free-lancers are *everywhere.* Independent screenwriters, copy writers, artists, songwriters, photographers, illustrators, interior designers, video people, film people, consultants, and therapists, are only *some* examples of the type of people who must free-lance, in the very nature of their job. Talk with enough of them, even if they're not free-lancing in the same business you have in mind, until you learn all the pitfalls of free-lancing.

THE THREE MAJOR PROBLEMS OF HOME BUSINESSES

(1) The first major problem of home businesses, according to experts, is that on average home-based workers *(in the U.S. at least)* only earn 70% of what their full-time office-based equals do. So, you must think carefully whether you could make enough money to survive -- *or even prosper.*

(2) The second major problem of home businesses is that it's often difficult to maintain the balance between business and family time. Sometimes the *family* time gets short-changed, while in other cases the demands of family (particularly with small children) may become so interruptive, that the *business* gets short-changed. So, do investigate thoroughly, ahead of time, *how* you would go about doing this *well.* There are books that can help.

(3) Lastly, a home business puts you into a perpetual job-hunt. Oh, I know, the *theory* about becoming self-employed is that you will thus be able to avoid the job-hunt. And, in the technical sense, you do. But you still have to hunt, and hunt, and hunt for new clients or customers -- who are, in a sense, new *employers* (that is because they *pay* you for the work you are doing). If you are going to be running your own business, you will have to *continually* beat the bushes for new clients or customers -- who will be in fact your short-term -- or long-term -- employers. I mention this, because some of us, when unemployed, are attracted to the idea of starting our own business because this seems like an ideal way to cut short their job-hunt. The irony is, that your own business makes you in a very real sense a *perpetual* job-hunter.

Of course, the dream of most self-employed people is to ultimately become so well known, and so in demand, that clients or customers will be literally beating down your doors -- and you will be able to stop this endless job-hunt. They will come hunting for *you.* But that only happens to a *relative* minority, and your realistic self needs to know that, from the beginning.

The greater likelihood is that you will *always* have to beat the bushes for employers/clients. It may get easier as you get better at it, or it may get harder, if economic conditions take a severe downturn. But it may well be the one aspect of your work that you will *always* cordially dislike.

If you avoid the task of finding new customers *like the plague,* you're probably going to find "*your own business*" is just a glamorous synonym for '*starving.*' I know *many* self-employed people to whom this has happened, and it happened precisely for this reason -- because they couldn't stomach going out to beat the bushes for clients or customers. If that's true for you, you should plan to start out by *hiring, co-opting, or getting someone to volunteer* part-time, to do this for you -- someone who, in fact, 'eats it up.' There are such, out there; you will have to find and link up with one of them.

WHEN YOU DON'T KNOW WHAT KIND OF BUSINESS YOU WANT TO START

Maybe you like the idea of working for yourself. Maybe you love the idea of running your own business. But maybe you haven't the foggiest notion of what kind of business to start. *Minor little detail!*

There are several steps you can take, to nail this down.

First, read. There are oodles of books out there that are *filled* with ideas for home businesses. Browse your local library, or bookstore. If none of the books you look at have any ideas that grab you, businesses that you might consider are: offering home deliveries of local restaurants' dinners, or home delivery of grocery orders from any downtown supermarket. Evening delivery services of laundry, etc. Daytime or evening office cleaning services and/or home cleaning services. Home repairs, especially in the evening or on weekends, of TVs, radios, audio systems, laundries, dishwashers, etc. Lawn care. Care for the elderly in their own homes. Childcare in their own homes. Pick up and delivery of things (even personal stuff, like cleaning) at the office. Automobile care or repair services, with pickup and delivery. Offering short-term business consultancy in various fields. Other successful businesses these days deal with leisure activities.

Secondly, look around your own community, and ask yourself what services or products people seem to need the most. Or what service or product already offered in the community could stand a lot of *improving*? There may be something there that *grabs* you.

The underlying theme to 90% of the businesses that are *out there* these days is *things that save time.* It's what single parents, families where both parents work, and singles who have overcrowded lives, most want.

Third, consider mail order. If you find no needs within your own community, you may want to broaden your search, to ask what is needed in this country -- or the world. After all, mail order businesses can be started *small* at home, and catalogs can be sent *anywhere.* If this interests you, read up on the subject. Also, for heaven's sakes, go talk to other mail order people (for names, just look at the catalogs you're already likely receiving).

Fourth, dream. In evaluating any ideas that you pick up, the first thing you ought to look at are your dreams. What have you always dreamed about doing? Since childhood? Since last week? Now is the time to dust off those dreams.

And please don't pay any attention, for now, to whether those dreams represent *a step up* for you in life, or not. Who cares? Your dreams are yours. You may have been dreaming of earning *more* money. But then again, you may have been dreaming of doing work that you really love, even if it means a lesser salary or income than you have been accustomed to. Don't *judge* your dreams, and don't let anyone else judge them either.

WHEN YOU'VE INVENTED SOMETHING

If you are inclined toward invention or tinkering, you might want to start by improving on an idea that's already *out there.* Start with something you like, such as bicycles. You might experiment with making -- let us say -- a folding-bicycle. Or, if you like to go to the beach, and your skills run to sewing, you might think about making and selling beach towels with weights sewn in the corners, against windy days.

If you've already invented something, and it's been sitting in your drawer, or the garage, but you've never attempted to duplicate or manufacture it before, now might be a good time to try. Think out very carefully just how you are going to get it manufactured, advertised, and marketed, etc. There are firms out there which claim to specialize in promoting inventions such as yours, for a fee. However, according to the Federal Trade Commission, in a study of 30,000 people who paid such promoters, not a single inventor ever made a profit after giving their invention to such firms.[4] If you want to gamble some of your hard-earned money on such firms, consider whether you might better drop it at the tables in Las Vegas. I think the odds are *better* there.

You're much better off, *of course,* doing your own research as to how one gets an invention marketed. Through the copyright office, and your library, locate other inventors, and ask if they were successful in marketing their own invention. When you find those who were, pick their brains for everything they're worth. Of course one of the first things they're going to tell you is to go get your invention copyrighted or trademarked or patented.

FRANCHISES

If nothing else appeals, you may want to consider a franchise. Franchises exist because some people want to have their own business, but don't want to go through the agony of starting it up. They want to *buy in* on an already established business, and they have the money in their savings with which to do that (or they know where they can get a bank loan). And they don't care if the business in question is not *in the home* (though some franchises can be done from your home, the majority require an outside site).

Fortunately for you, if this interests you, there are a lot of such franchises. In the U.S., for example, there are more than 2,100 franchised businesses, with more than 478,000 outlets, employing more than 6 million people. Your library or bookstore should have books that list many of these, in this country and elsewhere.

In the U.S., the overall failure rate for franchises is less than 4%.[5] You want to keep in mind that some *types* of franchises have a failure rate *far* greater than that. The ten *riskiest* small businesses, according to experts, are local laundries and dry cleaners, used car dealerships, gas stations, local trucking firms, restaurants, infant clothing stores, bakeries, machine shops,

---

4. *San Francisco Chronicle,* 1/26/91.

5. Ray Bard and Sheila Henderson, *Own Your Own Franchise,* Addison Wesley, 1987, p.1.

grocery or meat stores, and car washes -- though I'm sure there will be some new nominees for this list, by the time you read this. *Risky* doesn't mean you can't make them succeed. It only means the odds are greater than they would be with other small businesses.

You want to keep in mind also that some individual franchises are *terrible* -- and that includes well-known names. They charge too much for you to *get on board,* and often they don't do the advertising or other commitments that they promised they would. You can be left a whole lot poorer, and gnashing your teeth.

There isn't a franchising book that doesn't warn you eighteen times to go talk to people who have *already* bought that same franchise, before you ever decide to go with them. And I mean *several* people, not just one. Most experts also warn you to go talk to *other* franchises in the same field, not just the kind you're thinking about signing up with. Maybe there's something better, that your research will uncover.

If you are drawn to the idea of a franchise, because you are in a hurry, and you don't want to do any homework first, *'cause it's just too much trouble,* you will deserve what you get, believe me. That way lies madness.

YOUR OWN BUSINESS OR FRANCHISE: WHAT ARE YOUR CHANCES OF 'MAKING A GO' OF IT?

If you investigate the odds of succeeding at your own business -- whether it be at home or downtown, whether it be of your own devising or is a franchise -- the first thing you will come across are some *intimidating* statistics. Hidden in them is not just bad news, but also some good news.

U.S. Statistics

The following figures are for the U.S., but similar statistics probably can be found in every industrialized country of the world. Currently, in the U.S., 10,200,000 people -- or one out of every twelve people in the workforce -- have started their own business. *But,* at least 65% of all new businesses fail within their first five years of operation -- that's more than one out of every two. A well-known statistic, and the only debate you'll get on it from experts is whether or not the figure is *too low.* 96,100 businesses went bankrupt in 1992.[6] So, if you want to go into business for yourself, there's a great risk that it's going to go belly-up[7] *early on.* That is, as they say, the bad news.

The good news is that *if* you survive this early-on period, things start to look up. The risk decreases. There are two evidences for saying this:

First, only about 25% of new businesses fail *in any given year*; so, taking it on just a year-to-year basis, you have a 75% chance of *not* going belly-up *that* year.[8] Secondly, there are about 28 *old* businesses in the U.S. for every new business that starts up. So, the national bankruptcy/failure rate -- taking *all* businesses into account -- is *much* lower than most people think. In one year recently, out of each 10,000 businesses in the U.S., only 120 failed.[9] That means that 9,880 out of each 10,000 businesses survived.

What these statistics add up to, is that *if* you can make it through the first few years in your home business, you'll probably survive thereafter.

That leaves the BIG question: how *do* you survive those first few difficult years? The answer is: *Research. Homework. Interviewing people.* Before you commit yourself to this new thing, you need to find out something. That *something* can be summarized in the following formula:

---

6. *San Francisco Chronicle,* Thursday, 1/21/93, p. C1.

7. If any of my readers outside the U.S. do not understand the slang phrase "belly-up," other more familiar synonyms would be: bankrupt, out of business, kaput.

8. These figures are from David Birch's *Job Creation In America.* The Free Press, 866 Third Ave., New York, NY 10022. 1987. David is an excellent researcher, and knows more about small businesses than anyone else in the country that I know of; I recommend this book, highly. It describes at length where the new jobs are coming from, and how our smallest companies put the most people to work.

9. 1986, the most recent year for which I have statistics.

A, MINUS B, EQUALS C

By way of introduction to this subject, in the past twenty-five years I have found it *mindboggling* to discover how many people start a new business, at home or elsewhere, without ever going to talk to anybody else in the same kind of business.

One job-hunter told me she started a homemade candle business, without ever talking to anyone else who had tried a similar endeavor. Her business went belly-up within a year and a half. She concluded: no one should go into such a business. I concluded: she hadn't done her homework, before she started.

To avoid her fate, here are the rules for homework you *must* do, before starting your own home business -- or any kind of new venture. Please *memorize* them:

A – B = C

1. You write out exactly what kind of business you are thinking about starting.

2. You identify towns or cities that are at least twenty-five miles away, and you try to get their phone books, addresses of their Chambers of Commerce, etc.

3. By using the phone book and the Chambers, you try to identify names of three businesses in those towns, that are identical or similar to the business you are thinking of starting. You journey to that town or city, and talk to the founder/owner of same.

4. When you talk to them, you ask them what pitfalls or obstacles they ran into. You ask them how they overcame them. You ask them what skills or knowledges do they think are necessary to running this kind of business successfully. You make a list of the latter. When you've finished talking to all three owners, you put together a list of the skills and knowledges they agreed on, as necessary to running the business. We'll call this list "A."

5. Back home you sit down and inventory your own skills and knowledges, perhaps using Chapters 5 and 6 in this book. We'll call this list "B."

6. Finally, you subtract "B" from "A," and this results in a list we will call "C." That's the list of the skills or knowledges you don't have, but must find -- either by taking courses, or by getting volunteers with those skills, or by hiring someone with those skills.

Why twenty-five miles away? Well, actually, that's a minimum. You want to interview businesses which, *if they were in the same town* with you, would be your rival. And if they were in the same town with you, wouldn't likely tell you how to get started. After all, they're not going to train you just so you can then take business away from them.

But, when a guy, a gal, or a business is twenty-five miles away -- even better, fifty miles away -- you're not as likely to be perceived as a rival, and therefore they're much more likely to tell you what you want to know about their own experience, and how *they* got started, and where the landmines are hidden.

Doubtless at this point you would like an example of this whole process. Okay. Our job-hunter is a woman who has been making harps for some employer, but now is thinking about going into business for herself, not only *making* harps at home, but also *designing* harps, with the aid of a computer. After interviewing several home-based harpmakers and harp designers, and finishing her own self-assessment, her chart of **A – B = C** came out looking like the next page.

If she decides to try her hand at becoming an independent harpmaker and harp designer, she now knows what she needs but lacks: *computer programming, knowledge of the principles of electronics, and accounting.* Column **C.** These she must either go to school to acquire for herself, OR enlist from some friends of hers in those fields, on a volunteer basis, OR go out and hire, part-time.

These are the essential steps for any new enterprise that you are considering: A – B = C. If you want to start up more than one venture, you need to interview people *in each line of work* to find out A – B = C for both jobs.

You may also want to talk to people who have juggled two (or more) careers, at the same time.

HOW CAN YOU DO A – B = C, IF YOU'VE THOUGHT OF A BUSINESS OR CAREER THAT NO ONE'S EVER HEARD OF BEFORE

No matter how inventive you are, you're probably *not* going to invent a job that *no one* has ever heard of, before. You're only going to invent a job that *most* people have never heard of, before. But the likelihood is *great* that someone, somewhere, in this world of endless creativity, has already put together the kind of job you're dreaming about. Your task: to find her, or him, and interview them thoroughly. And then. . . . well, you know the drill: **A – B = C.**

A − B = C

Skills and Knowledges Needed to Run This Kind of Business Successfully	Skills and Knowledges Which I Have	Skills and Knowledges Needed, Which I Do Not Have, and Which I Will Therefore Have to Get Someone to Volunteer, or I Will Have to Go Out and Hire
Precision-working with tools and instruments	Precision-working with tools and instruments	
Planning and directing an entire project	Planning and directing an entire project	
Programming computers, inventing programs that solve physical problems		Programming computers, inventing programs that solve physical problems
Problem solving: evaluating why a particular design or process isn't working.	Problem solving: evaluating why a particular design or process isn't working.	
Being self-motivated, resourceful, patient, and persevering, accurate, methodical, and thorough	Being self-motivated, resourceful, patient, and persevering, accurate, methodical and thorough	
Thorough knowledge of: Principles of electronics	*Thorough knowledge of:*	*Thorough knowledge of:* Principles of electronics
Physics of strings	Physics of strings	
Principles of vibration	Principles of vibration	
Properties of woods	Properties of woods	
Computer programming		Computer programming
Accounting		Accounting

If there isn't someone doing *exactly* what you are dreaming of, there is at least someone who is *close.* This is how you find them:

WHEN NO ONE HAS DONE WHAT YOU WANT TO DO

You can always find someone who has done something that at least *approximates* what you want to do. The rules are:

1. Break down your projected business or career into its parts.

2. Then take any two of those parts at a time. See what kind of person that describes.

3. Find out the names of such persons, preferably two or more.

4. Go see, phone, write, him or her; you will learn a great deal, that is relevant to your dream.

5. They, in turn, may be able to give you a lead to someone whose business is even closer to what it is you want to do. And then you can go interview them. And so on, and so forth.

For example, let's suppose your dream is -- here we take a ridiculous case -- to use computers to monitor the growth of plants at the South Pole. And suppose you can't find anybody who's ever done such a thing. The way to tackle this seemingly insurmountable problem, is to break the proposed business down into its parts, which -- in this case -- are: *computers, plants,* and *the Antarctic.*

Then you try combining any two parts, together, to define the person or persons you need to talk to. In this case, that would mean finding someone who's *used computers with plants here in the States,* or someone who's *used computers at the Antarctic,* or someone who has *worked with plants at the Antarctic,* etc. You go talk to them, and along the way you may discover there *is* someone who has used computers to monitor the growth of plants at the South Pole. Then again, you may not. In any event, you will learn most of the pitfalls that wait for you, by hearing the experience of those who are in *parallel* businesses or careers.

Thus, it is *always* possible -- with a little blood, sweat, and imagination -- to find out what **A** – **B** = **C** is, for the business you're trying to design.

NEW WAYS TO WORK

Well, we've about covered now some new ways to work. If you're at a turning point in your life, all of these are worth weighing and considering.

Of course, none of the strategies in this section are actually *new* ways to work. They are only *new to you.* Even so, it takes a lot of guts to try something new *for you* in today's economy. It's easier, however, if you keep three rules in mind:

1. There is always some risk, in trying something new. Your job is not to avoid risk -- there is no way to do that -- but to make sure ahead of time that the risks are *manageable.*

2. You find this out before you start, by first talking to others who have already done what you are thinking of doing; then you evaluate whether or not you still want to go ahead and try it.

3. Have a Plan B, already laid out, *before you start,* as to what you will do if it doesn't work out; i.e., know where you are going to go, next. Don't wait, *puh-leaze!* Write it out, now. *This is what I'm going to do, if this doesn't work out:*____

These rules always apply, no matter where you are in your life: just starting out, already employed, unemployed, in mid-life, recovering after a crisis or accident, facing retirement, or whatever. Do take them very seriously.

If you're sharing your life with someone, sit down with that partner or spouse and ask what the implications are *for them* if you try this new thing. Will it require all your joint savings? Will they have to give up things? If so, what? Are they willing to make those sacrifices? And so on.

If you aren't out of work, you will need to debate the wisdom of quitting your job before you start up the new company, or business. And what do the experts say, here? In a word, they say, if you have a job, *don't* quit it. Better by far to move *gradually* into self-employment, doing it as a moonlighting activity first of all, while you are still holding down that regular job somewhere else. That way, you can test out your new enterprise, as you would test a floorboard in an old run-down house, stepping on it cautiously without at first putting your full weight on it, to see whether or not it will support you.

If your investigation revealed that it takes good accounting practices in order to turn a profit, and you don't know a thing about accounting, you go out and hire a (part-time) accountant *immediately* -- or, if you absolutely have no money, you talk an accountant friend of yours into giving you some volunteer time, for a while.

It is up to you to do your research thoroughly, weigh the risks, count the cost, get counsel from those intimately involved with you, and then if you decide you want to do it (whatever *it* is), go ahead and try -- no matter what your well-meaning but pessimistic acquaintances may say.

You only have one life here on this earth, and that life (under God) is *yours* to say how it will be spent, or not spent.

For Further Reading

New books dealing with all kinds of self-employment come out *monthly.* But below are the *kind* of books you will find at your local bookstore or public library:

Paul and Sarah Edwards, *Finding Your Perfect Work: The New Career Guide to Making a Living, Creating a Life.* A Jeremy P. Tarcher/Putnam Book, 200 Madison Avenue, New York, NY 10016. 1996. The book features an alphabetical directory of self-employment careers. They advertise this as "The What Color Is Your Parachute for the Next Decade." *That's the fifth book I've seen, with that claim.*

Paul and Sarah Edwards, *Working from Home: Everything You Need to Know about Living and Working under the Same Roof.* 3rd ed. J.P. Tarcher, Inc., 200 Madison Avenue, New York, NY 10016. Now revised and expanded. 440 pages. Has a long section on computerizing your home business, and on telecommunicating.

Barbara Brabec, *Homemade Money: Your Homebased Business Success Guide:* 4th ed. Betterway Books, 1507 Dana Avenue, Cincinnati, OH 45207. 1992. A very fine book, with an A to Z business section, and a most helpful summary of which states have laws regulating (or prohibiting) certain home-based businesses; it is updated regularly. Barbara also publishes a newsletter, *National Home Business Report.* If you wish more information, you can ask for her catalog, by writing to National Home Business Network, P.O. Box 2137, Naperville, IL 60567.

Lynie Arden, *The Work-at-Home Sourcebook.* 5th ed. 1994. Live Oak Publications, P.O. Box 2193, 1515 23rd St., Boulder, CO 80306.

Homeworking Mothers, a quarterly newsletter for women who want to start their own businesses and work from their homes. Mother's Home Business Network, Box 423, East Meadow, NY 11554.

There is also *Working Moms Network,* an organization that provides networking and resource information to "moms" throughout the U.S. Working Moms Network, P.O. Box 2413, Yakima, WA 98907-2413. 509-965-2827. Nancy L. Soules, Director.

Nicholas, Ted, *How To Form Your Own Corporation Without A Lawyer For Under $75.00.* Upstart Publishing Company, Dearborn Financial Publishing, Inc., 155 N. Wacker Dr., Chicago, IL 60606-1719. For mail orders, write: Nicholas Direct, Inc., 1511 Gulf Blvd., P.O. Box 877, Indian Rocks Beach, FL 34635. 1996. This is a classic in the field, with over a million copies sold, through fifteen revisions.

Barbara Notarius and Gail Sforza Brewer, *Open Your Own Bed & Breakfast.* 2nd ed. John Wiley & Sons, Inc., Business/Law/General Books Division, 605 Third Ave., New York, NY 10158-0012. 1992.

Jeffrey Maltzman, *Jobs in Paradise: The Definitive Guide to Exotic Jobs Everywhere.* Perennial Library, HarperCollins, 10 East 53rd Street, New York, NY 10022. 1993. Describes jobs at lakes, rivers, coasts and beaches, snow & skiing, tropical islands, mountains, deserts, and so forth. You will probably not want to look so much at the *jobs* described here, as at the *categories,* to help you think out just what *kind* of place you might like to be a telecommuter from. As a place to *start* some informational interviewing, this is a great book -- *if* you're interested in working exactly where you'd also like to spend your leisure time.

Richard C. Levy, *The Inventor's Desktop Companion: A Guide to Successfully Marketing and Protecting Your Ideas.* Visible Ink Press, a division of Gale Research Inc., 835 Penobscot Bldg., Detroit, MI 48226-4094. 1991. From securing a patent for it, to selling it, a very complete compendium.

Fred Grissom & David Pressman, *The Inventor's Notebook.* Nolo Press, 950 Parker St., Berkeley, CA 94710. 1987. A manual to help you keep records about your invention.

Lynie Arden, *101 Franchises You Can Run From Home,* John Wiley & Sons, Professional and Trade Division, 605 Third Ave., New York, NY 10158-0012. 1990.

Franchise Opportunities Handbook, 22nd ed., Sterling Publishing Co., Inc., 387 Park Ave. S., New York, NY 10016. 1991. This is a reprint of the 22nd edition of *Franchise Opportunities Handbook,* issued by the U.S. Government Printing Office. An immensely thorough book, together with a good introductory section about how to investigate a franchise.

Erwin J. Keup, *Franchise Bible: A Comprehensive Guide.* 2 vol. The Oasis Press®/PSI Research, 300 N. Valley Dr., Grants Pass, OR 97526. 1991. Mr. Keup is a lawyer who has specialized in franchise law and franchise consulting for the past 32 years. He covers 'buying an existing business,' as well as franchises. Also, if you have a successful business already, he discusses the pros and cons of turning it into a franchise.

Ray Bard and Sheila Henderson, *Own Your Own Franchise: Everything You Need to Know about the 160 Best Opportunities in America.* A Stonesong Press Book, Addison-Wesley Publishing Co., Inc., Route 128, Reading, MA 01867. 1987.

Robert Laurance Perry, *The 50 Best Low-Investment, High-Profit Franchises.* 1990. Prentice-Hall, Order Dept., 200 Old Tappan Road, Old Tappan, NJ 07675. 1-800-223-2348. Since there is a disturbing trend in franchises these days toward higher and higher start-up fees, up in the $150,000 category or higher, Perry attempts to list ones which people can afford; most of them are less than $20,000, some less than $5,000.

The 220 Best Franchises to Buy. Philip Lief Group's Editors, Bantam Books, 1540 Broadway, New York, NY 10036. 1993. A sourcebook for evaluating the best franchise opportunities.

There are also books that may help you out of the financial thicket, such as James D. Schwartz's *"ENOUGH" A Guide to Reclaiming Your American Dream.* Labrador Press, distributed by RE/MAX International, Inc., 5445 DTC Pkwy., Suite 1200, Englewood, CO 80111. 1992.

Moving

WHEN YOU WANT A CHANGE OF SCENERY AND A NEW PLACE TO LIVE

Our ancestors were nomads. We are the descendants of our ancestors. Surveys reveal that the average person in the U.S. moves eleven times between birth and death. Sometimes that's within the same town; other times it's to a faraway place. Similar patterns of mobility often occur in other countries, as well.

There are three reasons why you might want to move:

(1) Some family member -- say, your ailing or aging mother and father -- may need you, and you decide to move in order to be near them.

(2) You like where you're living, but *you just can't find any work* -- decent-paying work, anyway -- there. It seems as though every job there is filled, numbered, and has a waiting list besides. You've decided you've *got* to move, if you're to find employment. Alternatively, it's too expensive to live where you are, and you want to move somewhere in the country where housing is cheaper, and a family can get by on less.

(3) You can find work where you are, *but* you have reached the point where you decide that *where you live* is more important to you than any other consideration. Maybe you're living in some city, town, or rural area that you detest more, every day you are there. Finally you decide you can't stand it any longer. You've only one life to live, on this earth, and you want to spend the rest of it in a place you really enjoy. This realization can occur when you're twenty, forty, or sixty. If you're retiring, you may particularly want a place where it's always warm, or a place where you can always ski, or whatever. *(Incidentally, nearly four in ten 'baby boomers' who turned fifty in 1996 say they plan to move when they retire, half of these to a different state in the U.S.*[1]*)*

WHEN YOU KNOW EXACTLY WHERE YOU'RE MOVING

If it's to be with your family, then of course you know the place.

If it's to be with friends you know well, who will support and help you get settled there, then -- again -- you know the place.

If it's your dream city, you've been there on visits before, and now you want to move there permanently, then you know the place.

1. *USA Today*, 5/13/96.

In all of these cases, where you *know* where you're going (and you know who's going with you), you need no advice from me. Except about job-hunting, once you get there; in which case, read *Parachute.*

WHEN YOU DON'T KNOW WHERE TO MOVE TO

But there are those other times, when you need or want to move, but have no idea where to move to.

We're back to our first considerations.

What's most on your mind? Jobs, or *a wonderful place?*

Let's look at these two scenarios, taking jobs first:

AND FINDING A JOB IS THE FIRST THING ON YOUR MIND

If jobs are the first thing on your mind, in deciding to move, you have two ways to go.

One is to move where the unemployment rate is low for *all* jobs. In the U.S., your local Federal/State employment office can usually give you the current statistics about all 50 States. You look for the States with the lowest unemployment rate. Currently, the 10 with the lowest rate (where they're desperate for workers) are:

> *Nebraska (the lowest unemployment rate in the nation: only 2.39%),* South Dakota (2.82%), *North Dakota (3.14%),* Iowa (3.28%), *Utah (3.36%),* Minnesota (3.45%), *Wisconsin (3.67%),* Colorado (3.84%), *New Hampshire (3.89%),* and Delaware (4.11%).[2]

- Get a detailed map of each State that interests you, and pick one or more metropolitan areas in those States, so you can call or write to their Chambers of Commerce (pick up your phone and ask *Information* for their phone numbers, in each city).
- Ask those Chambers for all the information they have in writing about businesses which deal with your trade or specialty, and you ask that these lists be sent to you.
- Send them a thank-you note *the day* the stuff arrives, *please.* You may need to contact them again later, perhaps when you're actually in the area, and it will help *you* a lot if *they* can say, *"Oh yes, you're that nice person who sent us a thank-you note when we sent you our materials. First thank-you note we've gotten in three years."* Chances are, they will bend over *backwards* to help you.

If jobs are the first thing on your mind, in deciding to move, there is a second way to go. And that is, to find out what places in the country have a particular need *for your kind of skills.*

This is hard to do in the case of some jobs -- like that of a writer, say, but easier to do if you are a craftsperson or practice a particular trade.

2. The Bureau of Labor Statistics.

• In the latter case, go to your local library, and ask the librarian to help you find a trade association directory, or directories.

• Look up the association that deals with your occupation, and jot down the address, phone, fax number, and e-mail address of their national headquarters.

• Fax, write, or phone them and ask if they know where the demand is greatest, in that industry, nationwide. Jot down what they say.

• If they say they don't know, ask who might know. Get said person(s)' address and phone numbers. Contact them.

• If the answer ultimately turns out to be '*several places*,' then you can fall back on the books listed at the end of this section -- such as Richard Boyer's and David Savageau's *Places Rated Almanac* -- to decide which of those is your first choice, which is your second, etc.

• Once you move there, you may feel very stranded and lonely at first.

• If going into a new geographical area is a totally new experience for you, and you have no friends there, just remember there are various ways of meeting people, making friends, and developing contact rather quickly.

• The key is, *find people who share some interest or enthusiasm of yours.*

• There are also athletic clubs, Ys, churches, charitable and community organizations, where you can present yourself and meet people, from the moment you walk in the doors.

• You will soon develop many acquaintances, and some beginning friendships, and the place won't seem so lonely after all.

• Also, visit or write your high school or college before you set out for this new town and find out what graduates live in the area that you are going to be visiting for the first time: they are your friends already, because you went to the same school.

• Once you get there, you will want to talk to key individuals *who can suggest other people you might talk to, as you try to find out what organizations interest you.* You will want to define these key individuals in your distant city ahead of time and let them know you are coming. Your list may include all the people listed above, plus Chamber of Commerce executives, city manager, regional planning offices, appropriate county or state offices in your area of interest, the Mayor, and high-level management in particular companies that look interesting from what you've read or heard about them.

• When you "hit town," you will want to remember the City Directory, the Yellow Pages of your phone book, etc. You *may* want to put a modest-sized advertisement in the paper once you are in your chosen geographical area saying you would like to meet with other people who are following the job-hunting techniques of *What Color Is Your Parachute?* That way you'll form, or join, a kind of 'job-hunters anonymous,' where you can mutually support one another in your hunt.

• One successful job-hunter described how all of this research about *place* can lead as well to information about *jobs*:

"Suppose I arrived cold in some city, the one place in all the world I want to live -- but with no idea of what that city might hold as a match and challenge for my 'personal-talent bank.' I have an economic survey to make, yes; but I also have an equally or more important personal survey to accomplish.

So, I meet pastors, bankers, school principals, physicians, dentists, real estate operators, et al. I would be astonished if opportunities were not brought to my attention, together with numerous offers of personal introduction to key principals. All I would be doing is forging links (referrals) in a chain leading to some eventual jobs. *The referral is the key.*"

IF FINDING A WONDERFUL PLACE IS THE FIRST THING ON YOUR MIND

When you haven't a clue as to where to move, you just want it to be *wonderful,* there are, this time, *three* ways you can go.

• First of all, you can interview all your friends and acquaintances, to ask them what places *they* have loved the most, in the U.S. or in whatever country you live. And *why.* This task can be a lot of fun. And then, out of all the *candidate cities or towns* they propose, choose two or three places that really interest you, for further investigation.

• Alternatively, you can turn to books. In the U.S., there are quite a number of them that rate various cities and towns according to *factors* that may be important to you, such as *weather, crime, educational system, recreational opportunities,* etc. The best of these, by a long shot, is Richard Boyer's and David Savageau's aforementioned *Places Rated Almanac,* listed at the end of this section on *Moving.*

If you live in another country, you may find similar resources for your own country; visit a large bookstore, and ask. One word of caution: do remember, in all these books, that a computer was usually used to sum up, and rate, all the factors. You may find that *the whole* is less than the sum of its *parts* -- i.e., it has the factors you want, but you're less than enchanted with how *it all came together* in the case of this particular place you're thinking about.

• Thirdly, you can do the geographical exercises in *The Quick Job-Hunting Map*, at the beginning of this Resource Guide, which tells you how to do a thorough-going analysis of all the places you have ever lived, in terms of *factors* -- and then how you come up with *names* of places that combine all the factors that were ever important to you in any town or city from your past.

• In the end, you want to try to come up with three names, because if your first choice doesn't pan out for some reason, you will have a backup, and also a backup to your backup.

WHEN YOU WANT TO 'GO RURAL'

It may be you will discover, as you go about this task, that your idea of *paradise* is to 'go rural' -- to move, at last, to 'the country'. Sometimes it's the desire for a simpler life; sometimes, it's the desire for a less expensive cost of living. Whatever the reasons, if this is your vision, take this vision seriously. You only have one life to live, on this earth.

• Just be sure to investigate it *thoroughly*, even as I was just cautioning you, in the case of urban places. "Look before you leap" is always a splendid caution, and it means -- in this particular case -- that if there's a place that sounds good to you, *be sure* to go visit it as a tourist before you up and move there.

• *Go there*, and talk to *everyone*. Get the good side, and the bad. Interview anyone you know, who has moved from urban to rural, and ask them what they like most about the move, *and what they miss the most about their former locale.*

• Then weigh what you learn.

Fortunately, there are a number of resources, books and such, that you can use to explore rural life, if it interests you. They are listed at the end of this section.

EXPLORING THE FARAWAY PLACE OF YOUR CHOICE

Well, let us suppose that one way or another, you've picked a place.

• It *is* crucial to go visit there, if you possibly can, rather than just letting your choice rest on the fact that the place looks good in a book. You may *hate* this place, on sight. How nice to learn that, *early on.* So, figure out how to get there.

• Do you have a vacation coming to you, that would fall within the time period between now and when you must finally have a job there? Could you visit it on that vacation?

• Could you take a summer job there?

• Go there on leave?

• Get sent to a convention there?

• Get appointed to a group or association that meets there? Think it through.

• And finally, when you're ready to go visit that town or city *in person*, try to line up contacts and interviews *ahead of time*, before you go there. See the next section, below, to learn how you uncover possible job-leads.

• If you have trouble lining up contacts, see if that town or city has any church, synagogue, or national organization that you belong to *here*. Write, tell them of your local affiliation, and ask for their help in finding the kind of people you're trying to connect with.

• If you have a spouse or partner, who will be going with you, they should be doing the same kind of research, and setting up their own interviews. In addition to interviewing about jobs, you will want to explore (of course) the issues of apartment vs. house, of rental vs. buying, and the like.

• Back home again, you will want to weigh what you have learned, and weigh whether or not the place still interests you; and whether any of the jobs you looked at, interest you.

WHAT TO DO WHEN YOU CAN'T GO THERE, ANY TIME SOON, TO VISIT OR INTERVIEW

If your finances are tight, it may not be possible for you to go to visit your new chosen destination, at least in the immediate future. In which case, you want to research the place, as best you can, from a distance:

How do you do this, while still remaining in your present location. More specifically, how do you find out about *jobs*, at a distance?

There are *ways*.

• If your chosen city or town has a local newspaper, *subscribe,* even while you are still living *here*. Read the whole paper, when it comes, however long delayed. Look particularly for: news of companies that are *expanding*, news of *promotions* or *transfers* (that creates vacancies *down below* in 'the company store'), and the like.

• If you can get the Chamber of Commerce there, or someone you know there, to send you their phone book, particularly the Yellow Pages, by all means do so.

• You first want to discover some organizations that, at a distance, look interesting to you.

• Then you want to research them, at a distance, as much as you can.

• It will help if you can regard the city or town where you presently are, as a kind of *parallel city* to the town or city you are interested in. In which case, some of your research can be done where you are, and then its learnings transferred. For example, suppose you wanted to use your interests in psychiatry, plants, and carpentry, in your future career. In the city where you presently are, you would try to learn how to combine these three. You might learn, right where you are, that there is a branch of psychiatry which uses plants in the treatment of deeply withdrawn patients, and these plants have to be put, of course, in wooden planters. Now, having learned that where you presently are, you would then explore your chosen city or town to see what psychiatric facilities they have there, and which ones -- if any -- use plants in their healing program. Thus can you conduct your research where you are, and then transfer its learnings to the place where you want to be.

• In doing your research of organizations that interest you, it is perfectly permissible for you to write to the library in your target city, asking for information that may be only there. If the librarian is too busy to answer, then use one of your contacts there to find out. "Bill (or Billie), I need some information that I'm afraid only the library in your town has. Specifically, I need to know about company x." Or whatever.

• Develop contacts, even at a distance, as much as you can.

• Ask your friends where you currently live, if they know of anyone who lives in that city or town. Use these names *only if* they know the employer to whom you are writing.[3]

• If you went to college, find out if any graduates of that college live in this chosen city or town of yours. (Contact the alumni office of your college, and ask.)

• Also any church, synagogue, or national organization you belong to, that has a presence in that city or town, may yield true helpfulness to you, *if you know what it is you want to know.* Write or phone them, and tell them that you're one of their own and you need some information. *"I need to know who can tell me what nonprofit organizations there are in that city, that deal with x."* "I need to know how I can find out what corporations in town have departments of mental hygiene." *Or, whatever.*

• If you decide to approach the places which interest you, first of all by mail, you will want to research each organization so that you know *who* to address the letter to, *by name.* Get the name spelled absolutely accurately, and double-check. Nothing turns off a prospective employer like your misspelling her or his name.

• Your letter will carry a lot more weight if you can mention, in it, the name of contacts that you have developed, as outlined above.

• As for whether or not you should enclose a resume with your initial contact letter, experts' opinions vary widely. *Everything* depends on the nature of the resume, and the nature of the person you are sending it to. With some employers I know, the sight of a resume is *death* to any future rapport between you and this person. It will *ensure* that your letter is merely tossed aside. Other employers like to see resumes. It's hard to predict what you should do.

• Personally, I think a well-composed letter summarizing all you would say in a resume, may be your best bet; with a closing paragraph indicating that your resume is available, should they wish it.

---

3. Unless -- the job-hunter's nightmare -- your mutual "friend"/contact has *misrepresented* how close he or she is to your target employer, and as a matter of fact said employer can't stand the sight of this "mutual friend." *It has happened.* It is to die. Asking a question beforehand, of the "mutual friend," like "How *well* do you know him -- or her?" may help avoid this.

• Once you've turned up some promising job prospects, you will *have* to go there, to that town or city, in almost all cases, for the actual job interview(s). And if this is your first visit to the place, try to go there a week or so ahead of your interviews, so you can look the place over, and decide *Do I really want to move here?* It's a little late to do on-site explorations, but, hey, better late than never!

HOW HARD SHOULD I WORK AT THIS?

We kept score with one man's job-hunt. He was researching a distant place. While still at a distance, by means of diligent research he turned up 107 places that seemed interesting to him. Over a period of some time, he sent a total of 297 letters to them. He also made a total of 126 phone calls to that city. When he was finally able to go there in person, he had narrowed the original 107 that looked interesting, down to just 45. He visited all 45, while there. Having done his homework on himself thoroughly and well, -- and having obviously conducted *this* part of his search in an extremely professional manner, he received 35 job offers. When he had finished his survey, he went back to the one job he most wanted -- and accepted it.

No one can argue that you should be dealing with numbers of this magnitude. But this may at least give you some idea of *how hard you may need to work* at this. Certainly, we're not just talking about five letters and two phone calls. We're talking about rolling up your sleeves, and being *very thorough.*

DOES ALL OF THIS REALLY WORK?

Well, that's a legitimate question. Obviously, thousands if not millions of people have moved to new cities and towns, and found not only work but joyful work there. Obviously, also, many people have moved to new towns or cities and have not been able to find work. Much, much depends upon *the method* they use in their job-search. If you follow diligently the process described in *Parachute,* in the chapter called, "For the Determined Job-Hunter," you will vastly increase your chances of success. Here is how one job-hunter described the whole process, and the way in which it worked for him:

"In 1990, my wife and I took a trip out to the Southwest from our home in Annapolis, Maryland, to see the Grand Canyon and sights like that. We both fell in love with the Southwest, and said, "Wouldn't it be great if I could get a job out here as a highway engineer, and maybe we could work with the Native Americans." Back in Annapolis, I purchased Parachute *and read it with extreme interest. So I started some network planning, and scheduled another upcoming trip to Arizona in February of 1992, planning to visit various engineering offices and check out living conditions.*

"Meanwhile, I visited the U.S.G.S. Headquarters in Reston, Virginia. On the way out, I noticed an ad on the bulletin board for 'Highway Engineer - Bureau of Indian Affairs, Gallup, New Mexico.' Naturally, I applied for the job but received notice that the position had been cancelled. Disappointed, my wife and I decided to each spend a day in prayer. On the following day I received a call from that office in Gallup inform-

ing me there was another position for Highway Planner now open; was I still interested? Still interested?!

"Using your advice, I called the Bureau in Gallup and got the names of the bosses of the various divisions or sections that would impinge upon my application. I sent in the application to the person by name who was the chief decision-maker. In February of 1992 we carried out the trip I had been planning, now including a visit to Gallup. We visited headquarters there, though they weren't yet ready to formally interview, since not all applicants had yet been screened. However, it was a useful visit, and on returning, I wrote Thank You notes to all the people I had met, and hoped for the best.

"In March I received another phone call, asking for further information; I used this to invite myself out for an actual interview, at my expense. My offer was accepted, I was out there in two days, the interview went well, and I received official notice to report for work in May. We were ecstatic! And we found a house in Gallup, through a friend in Annapolis who had a friend in Gallup, who knew of a co-worker who was moving out.

"In short, ours is a wonderful story. Who would think a 66 year old man could leave one job and move into another full-time job, at a salary almost equal to his present one, in a place 2600 miles away, that he and his wife truly love! What a blessing! And what you said has stuck with me all this time: I've remembered to write my Thank You notes."

For Further Reading

Well, you want to move, you've figured out your preferred *geographical factors,* but you don't know the name of the place, or places yet -- eh? There are helps:

Richard Boyer and David Savageau, *Places Rated Almanac: Your Guide to Finding the Best Places to Live in North America.* Prentice-Hall, Order Dept., 200 Old Tappan Road, Old Tappan, NJ 07675. 1-800-223-2348. A marvelous book. Immensely helpful for anyone weighing where to move next. All 343 metropolitan areas are ranked and compared for living costs, job outlook, crime, health, transportation, education, the arts, recreation, and climate. Has numerous helpful diagrams, charts, and maps, showing (for example) earthquake risk areas, hurricane and tornado risk areas *(you did see the movie* Twister *didn't you?)*, the snowiest areas, the stormiest areas, the driest areas, and so on. Don't leave home without it.

David Savageau, *Retirement Places Rated.* 3rd ed. 1990. Prentice-Hall, Order Dept., 200 Old Tappan Road, Old Tappan, NJ 07675. 1-800-223-2348. Although purportedly about retirement, it is useful information for anyone. Compares 151 top geographical areas in the U.S.

Norman D. Ford, *50 Healthiest Places to Live and Retire in the U.S.*, Mills & Sanderson, 41 North Rd., Suite 201, Bedford MA 01730-1021.

Lee & Saralee Rosenburg, *50 Fabulous Places to Raise Your Family,* Career Press, 1-800-CAREER-1.

Jill Andresky Fraser, *The Best U.S. Cities for Working Women.* Plume Books, New American Library, 1633 Broadway, New York, NY 10019. 1986.

There is a firm which uses a specialized questionnaire to help a person or family locate three places in the U.S. that fit their expressed personal desires about a place to live. It is run by Andrew Schiller, M.S., a professional geographer, who is thoroughly familiar with *Parachute.* The firm's name is *Relocation Research,* P.O. Box 53391, Knoxville, TN 37950. Write or call, for price: 800-278-9884.

If you are interested in the rural life, there are these resources:

William L. Seavey runs a business called *Greener Pastures Institute,* which publishes a newsletter (sample back issue: $5). He has also written a book which tells you the basic resources for moving to the country or a small town. Its name is *Moving to Small Town America,* 1996, Dearborn Financial Publishers, 800-829-7934. Bill's address is: Greener Pastures Institute, 6301 S. Squaw Valley Rd., Suite 1383, Pahrump, NV 89048-7949, 800-688-6352.

John F. Edwards, *Starting Fresh: How to Plan for a Simpler, Happier, and More Fulfilling New Life in the Country.* Prima Publishing, Sierra Gardens, Suite 130, Roseville, CA 95661. 1988.

Frank Levering and Wanda Urbanska, *Simple Living.* Viking Penguin, 375 Hudson St., New York, NY 10014. 1992.

The Caretaker Gazette, published by Gary C. Dunn, 1845 NW Deane St., Pullman, WA 99163-3509. 509-332-0806. $24 for a one-year subscription (six issues), outside the U.S., $30. The only up-to-date source for property caretaking in the world. Landowners, who are searching for caretakers advertise in this *Gazette.* People who want to be caretakers, in a particular place, advertise here. Caretaking is an inexpensive way for you to experience life in a specific geographic area, particularly rural ones. *While the majority of the jobs listed are in the U.S., a number of international positions are also included.* A map on the front page of each issue indicates where the employment opportunities are. The March/April 1997 issue, by way of example, had 74 job listings in 34 states and eight other countries.

Marilyn and Tom Ross, *Country Bound!™ Trade Your Business Suit Blues For Blue Jean Dreams™.* Communication Creativity, P.O. Box 909, Buena Vista, CO 81211. 1992.

Working Overseas

WHEN YOU WANT TO WORK OVERSEAS

I will assume here that we are talking about job-hunters in the U.S. who want to work in Europe, Africa, Asia, Canada, or South America. However, the same principles apply to those of you who live in other places than the U.S., and want to move here.

First of all, be sure you're not going overseas simply because you're fed up with this country, and think some other place will be the Utopia you've always dreamed about. Of course it may be. But it is much more likely it will not be. Even if (big *if*) you do not find the same things there that irritate you about the U.S., I guarantee you that you will find a whole pack of new things that irritate you.

Regarding the mechanics of going overseas: many people assume you find an overseas job by packing a bag, buying a ticket and passing out resumes once you reach your foreign destination. The reality is that work-permit requirements and high unemployment often make finding jobs in other countries difficult, or impossible. For example, if you were to study employment classifieds in, say, a newspaper from London, England, you would at first sight think you had found some grand opportunities for yourself. *Unfortunately,* these are in most cases job opportunities open only to British nationals or citizens of EEC nations.

What is true in England is true elsewhere. Your U.S. citizenship will actually preclude you from working in a foreign country -- even Canada -- unless your employer can prove that a local national is unavailable to take the job, and can subsequently secure a work permit for *you.*

BEGIN AT HOME

Your wisest approach is to begin your job-hunt for an overseas job while you are still here in the U.S. How do you go about it?

Well, first of all, research the country or countries that interest you, as to living conditions, conditions of employment, et cetera.

Talk to everyone you possibly can who has in fact been overseas, most especially visitors to, or former citizens of, that country or countries that interest you. A nearby large university will probably have such faculty or students *(ask)*. Companies in your city which have overseas branches *(your library should be able to tell you which they are)* should be able to lead you to people also -- possibly to the names and addresses of personnel who are still "over there" to whom you can write for the information you are seeking.

Alternatively, try asking every single person you meet for the next week (at the supermarket checkout, at your work, at home, at church or synagogue, etc.) if they know someone who used to live overseas and now lives here in your city or town. You may be amazed at how many normal looking people are actually world travelers.

By doing research with such people, you will learn a great deal. Find out what they liked and didn't like, about the country which interests you. Find out what they know about the conditions for working over there.

LISTINGS OF JOB OPENINGS

Next, you need to research what kinds of job possibilities exist in that country. Every *successful* overseas search starts with *some* sources of information on "who's hiring now." *Which* sources you access, and how you make use of them, will greatly affect your chances of landing an overseas assignment.

What do I mean? Well, for openers, beware of such sources as employment agencies that promise to find you an overseas job for an advance fee. 98% of their clients *do not* find an overseas job. This fleecing industry has flourished for years, with a few individuals often running scores of companies under an assortment of names. Such companies regularly go out of business or file for bankruptcy *once they've fleeced enough suckers.*[1]

Beware also of directories advertised in newspapers, etc., as *listing overseas employers.* Many, though not all, of these job listings are out of date and tend to report on "who *was* hiring" rather than "who is hiring *now.*"

You can still make effective use of any such directory by taking care that *if* you contact an organization listed therein, you include a cover letter which requests that your resume be kept on file 'for further consideration *if there are no current openings'.* As I have emphasized elsewhere in this book, pure dumb luck -- which means, having your name in 'the right place at the right time' -- often plays a crucial role in finding most jobs. Since you can't get *over there,* at the moment, you will have to rely more heavily on resumes here than I would normally advise, to keep your name in the right place. In the case of overseas employment, the more employers who have your resume, the better.

Rather than the kind of resources mentioned above, I think your best bet for job leads are authoritative directories such as those listed under *For Further Reading* below. Also, in your job-search do not forget that the U.S. Government is a heavy overseas employer. Understandably, in the post-USSR world, with the end of the cold war, there are numerous cutbacks going on

---

1. Write to Stuart Alan Rado, 1500 West 23rd St., Sunset Island #3, Miami Beach, FL 33140, if you wish to know more.

overseas. Nonetheless, this possibility is still well worth exploring. *How* you explore it, is described in the books listed under *Further Reading.*

BACKUP STRATEGIES

If you run into an absolute stone wall in your search for an overseas job, there are two backup strategies for you to consider. The first is to seek an international internship.

The second strategy begins with the fact that many companies operating in this country, both domestic and foreign-owned, *have branches overseas.* Thus, *sometimes* your ticket to getting overseas may be to start working here in the U.S. for such a company, hoping they will eventually send you overseas. It *does* happen. And if it happens, they will likely take care of the visa and work permit red tape, pick up your travel bill, and provide other helpful benefits.

Unfortunately, however, you can't *count* on their ever sending you overseas. Many such firms now prefer to use nationals in the country in question, rather than sending U.S. citizens abroad. In other words, if you take employment with a U.S. firm that has overseas work, hoping that they will send you overseas, understand from the beginning that it's a big fat gamble. *You* have to decide whether you're willing to take that gamble, or not.

If you decide to do either of the above strategies, you'll find the names of such organizations by going to your local library and asking the reference librarian to help you find such directories as these: *Principal International Businesses,* published by Dun's Marketing Service; *International Directory of Corporate Affiliations,* published by Corporate Affiliations Information Services, of the National Register Publishing Company; and *International Organizations, revised annually,* published by Gale Research, Inc.

Lastly, contact every friend you have who already lives overseas -- even if it's not in the country that is your target. Ask for their counsel, advice, help, and prayers. They went before you; hopefully they can now be your guide, and door-opener.

One final word about hunting for an overseas job: above all, be patient. The search for an overseas job takes *more* time than looking for a job in this country. Don't expect to be in an exotic foreign capital within 90 days. Perseverance is the key.

For Further Reading

International Employment Hotline, Box 3030, Oakton, VA 22124. Published monthly by Will Cantrell since 1980, this highly reputable newsletter provides job-search advice and names and addresses of employers currently hiring for international work in government, nonprofit organizations, and private companies. A six-month subscription is $26, one year is $39.

ISS Directory of Overseas Schools, by International Schools Services. 500 profiles of overseas schools in 120 countries, with contact names and addresses, teaching staff positions; useful for teachers looking for overseas employment. Available from Worldwise Books, P.O. Box 3030, Oakton, VA 22124.

International Business Travel and Relocation Directory, 6th ed. Gale Research,

Inc., 835 Penobscot Bldg., Detroit, MI 48226-4094. It presents all the relevant details for every country in the world.

Sanborn, Robert, Ed.D., *How To Get A Job in Europe: The Insider's Guide.* 2nd ed. Surrey Books, 230 E. Ohio St., Suite 120, Chicago, IL 60611. 1993. Includes tips on how to find a job in the New Europe.

Chambers, Dale, *Passport to Overseas Employment: 100,000 Job Opportunities Abroad.* Prentice-Hall, Order Dept., 200 Old Tappan Road, Old Tappan, NJ 07675. 1-800-223-2348. 1990. Deals with overseas study programs, international careers, temporary employment, airlines and cruises, embassies and consulates, United Nations, and volunteer programs.

Richard Zinks, *Overseas Exotic Jobs.* Zink International Career Guidance, P.O. Box 587, Marshall, MI 49068-0587. 616-789-2334.

Griffith, Susan, *Work Your Way Around the World.* 6th ed. Peterson's Guides, P.O. Box 2123, Princeton, NJ 08543. 1993.

Green, Mary, and Gillmar, Stanley, *How to Be an Importer and Pay for Your World Travel.* 2nd ed. Ten Speed Press, Box 7123, Berkeley, CA 94707. 1993.

Frances Bastress, *The New Relocating Spouse's Guide to Employment: Options & Strategies in the U.S. and Abroad.* 4th ed. 1993. Impact Publications, 9104-N Manassas Drive, Manassas Park, VA 22111.

For teachers wishing to work overseas, the Department of Defense publishes a pamphlet, with application, entitled *Overseas Employment Opportunities for Educators.* Write to U.S. Department of Defense Dependent Schools, Recruitment and Assignments Section, Hoffman Bldg. I, 2461 Eisenhower Ave., Alexandria, VA 22331-1100, for the pamphlet/application.

Your library should also have books such as Angel, Juvenal, *Dictionary of American Firms Operating in Foreign Countries* (World Trade Academy Press).

And to research overseas public companies which sell stock in this country, the Securities Exchange Commission will have their Form 6-K, which they filed in order to be able to sell that stock.

If you want more books about overseas work (or study), write to Worldwise Books, P.O. Box 3030, Oakton, VA 22124, and/or Writer's Digest Books, 1507 Dana Ave., Cincinnati, OH 45207, and ask for their catalogs.

What To Do If Your Job-Hunt Drags On and On

Dealing with Rejection and Depression

WHY WE GET DEPRESSED WHEN UNEMPLOYED

Most of us are good at doing difficult things, as long as we only have to do them for a short time.

We can walk (quickly) through an area with a bad stench. We can put up with a three-day cold.

We can stand to miss one meal.

We can hold our breath for thirty seconds.

We can run a hundred-yard dash.

We can endure a bad relationship, as long as it doesn't last more than one week.

But we really don't like it when things go on for too long. That starts to get us down.

That, of course, is our situation when we are unemployed. A period of unemployment that lasts only two weeks -- hey, *no problem!* But if it drags on and on and on, many of us start to get depressed.

And how likely is it, that it will drag on and on?

Well, let's look at some statistics.

U.S. Statistics

Unemployment is pretty much the same the world around. But the U.S. keeps *statistics* about it all.

And so we know that in the U.S. one out of every five or six workers is unemployed at *some* time during each year. Of those who are unemployed in any given month:

35 out of every 100 of them have been out of work less than five weeks;

28 out of every 100 have been out of work between five and fourteen weeks;

13 out of every 100 have been out of work between fifteen and twenty-six weeks; and

24 out of every 100 have been out of work twenty-seven weeks or longer; and/or have stopped looking altogether.[1]

Which means, of course, that if you were 'downsized,' 'made redundant,' 'laid off,' 'fired,' or quit, there is a 35% chance that you will find work within five weeks.

But, the odds are twice as great -- 65% -- that your job-hunt will take longer, maybe *much* longer. (It can range up to two years, in worst-case scenarios.)

If it drags on for any length of time, it can put us into a real depression.

FOR TRULY DEEP DEPRESSIONS

Now what do we mean by *depression*? Well, the word is commonly used in two different senses: the *diagnostic* sense, as used by psychiatrists or therapists; and the looser, everyday meaning, as it is used out there on the streets.

Thus, when we are unemployed and we meet somebody out on the streets and say, *"I feel depressed,"* we usually mean: *'I've got the blues.'* We mean: *"I feel sad."* We mean: *"I'm not my usual self."* We mean: *"I feel down, because it's hard to stay upbeat or optimistic in this situation."* We mean: *"I'm in a funk."* This feeling of being *depressed* is our emotional response to *this one particular situation.* Once we have found a job, it lifts, and we start feeling happy and upbeat once again.

Psychiatrists and therapists, however, see a very different kind of depression, daily, in their offices.

---

1. Statistics based, in part, on the February 1992 issue of the Monthly Labor Review, published by the U.S. Department of Labor, Bureau of Labor Statistics; and, in part, on the figures for discouraged workers for that same time period; and, in part, on a paper by the late Bob Wegmann, entitled, "How Long Does Unemployment Last?"

This is an *illness,* which the person has usually lived with for a long time. It varies in its force and weight, sometimes seeming on a par with a cold, sometimes seeming on a par with double-pneumonia. It does not go away just because our life gets 'better.' When *this* kind of depression is upon us, it often feels like it is going to totally crush our spirit, and extinguish our life. Feelings of utter worthlessness, thoughts of suicide, often attend it. It is what has often been called 'the dark night of the soul.'[2]

Many brave souls have endured this 'dark night of the soul' for years, with astounding courage -- through sheer guts, through faith, through therapeutic treatments and medicines that hold the illness partly, or mostly, or completely, at bay.

It is estimated by experts that in the U.S. alone some 10 million Americans are experiencing this illness during a typical year.[3] And of course some of them are unemployed. But if we are subject to *this* kind of depression, it usually has antedated our period of unemployment, and is something we have wrestled with for years -- though our unemployment may turn it into a 'visitation' that is much deeper than usual.

If we go into *this* kind of a deep depression at the time of our unemployment, it is important to keep in mind that such an illness is not a character defect, something we could shrug off 'if only we were stronger characters.' No, no. Measles are not a character defect; neither is *this* illness.

> **de•pres•sion** \di-'presh-ən\ n (1): a state of feeling sad : DEJECTION (2): a psychoneurotic or psychotic disorder marked esp. by sadness, inactivity, difficulty in thinking and concentration, a significant increase or decrease in appetite and time spent sleeping, feelings of dejection and hopelessness, and sometimes suicidal tendencies (3): a reduction in activity, amount, quality, or force (4): a lowering of vitality or functional activity.
>
> *Webster's*

---

2. This term is sometimes used by mystics to mean something slightly different: when the soul feels, falsely, as though it had been abandoned by God. This is, however, not that different from *depression,* where false feelings (like, *worthlessness*) abound.

3. A patient's guide to Depression is available from Depression, P.O. Box 8547, Silver Spring, MD 20907, free. You may also call 1-800-358-9295, to ask for it. For further reading, I refer you to: *The Good News About Depression: New Medical Cures & Treatments That Can Work for You.,* by Mark S. Gold, M.D. 1988. Bantam Books, 1540 Broadway, New York, NY 10036. There is also: *Depression, the Mood Disease,* by Francis Mark Mondimore, M.D. rev. ed. 1993. Available from the Johns Hopkins University Press, 2715 N. Charles St.,, Baltimore, MD 21218, 1-800-537-5487.

There is also 'computer-aided psychotherapy,' as discussed in Julian Simon's book, *Good Mood,* 1993, Open Court Publishing Co., Carus Publishing, Suite 2000, 332 S. Michigan Ave., Chicago, IL 60604-9968. The software program, *Overcoming Depression,* can be obtained from Malibu Artificial Intelligence Works, 25307 Malibu Rd., Malibu, CA 90265. 800-497-6889.

To begin with, depression may have a physical basis.

It can be caused or made worse by such physical causes as a thyroid disorder, or a lack of serotonin in our brain, or the side-effects of medications we may be taking for other ailments, etc.

So, if your depression feels very deep, it is your first duty to yourself and your loved ones to check out this possibility, by getting yourself immediately to a qualified physician and asking them to do blood tests on you, to see if something physical is causing this, or making it worse.

> If you are depressed *and* feeling suicidal, you need to go see a psychiatrist, therapist, or doctor *today.* Suicidal thoughts, or intentions, indicate that your depression has become a medical emergency, *akin to* a heart attack; *don't* mess around with such thoughts, thinking, "Oh, it'll go away." Act! Go report it to someone who can give you some medicine or help, immediately. Many areas now have a 'Suicide Hot-Line.' Your local hospital should be able to give you the number. Call. Also, look in *The Yellow Pages* of your local telephone directory, under "Suicide Prevention Counselors."

If your depression is of lesser degree, but still numbing, and if investigation doesn't turn up any physical basis for it, then you need to consider the possibility that it is caused by factors in your situation, present or past, and the feelings they engendered -- particularly feelings of anger.

This, again, is not a character defect, but is rooted in our very nature as human beings. I think of it as comparable to a clogged drainage pipe. We human beings, like a pipe, are meant to have experiences, feel the emotions they engender, and then let those feelings drain out of us, as through a clear-running pipe.

But if the emotions don't drain off, if they get stored up, then things start to back up in our system, as in a clogged pipe. I think of *some kinds* of depression as the results of that backup.

The remedy is clear. We need to unclog that pipe, so that we may get on with our life, victoriously. And, *talking* about our experiences, present or past, plus the feelings they aroused within us, is the way we go about unclogging that pipe.

So, if you are depressed, *start talking.* Talk about anything that is bothering you, past or present, and talk about it first of all with your partner, mate, family, or friends. If that doesn't help, then you ought to get yourself to an experienced therapist, and I'd say preferably one who has had therapy themselves. *(Ask.)*

Now, having said this about the illness, I want to return to the *unlearned* sense in which we, when unemployed, use the term, in common everyday street talk. As I said, this is more about the situation we find ourselves in, for a time. It's when we're unemployed, and we wake up one morning thinking, "I feel *blue,*" or "I'm in a *funk,*" or "I'm *really* not enjoying life just now."

As I said, I think of this as *unemployment depression.*

THE FOUR ROOTS OF 'UNEMPLOYMENT DEPRESSION'

There are four roots to unemployment depression, as it seems to me. These are: (1) emotional; (2) mental; (3) spiritual; and (4) physical. Each of the four *contributes* toward the feelings of depression. In this sense, depression is like a river, fed by these four tributaries.

Hence, we need remedies which deal with these four.

THE EMOTIONAL ROOT OF UNEMPLOYMENT DEPRESSION

We get depressed because we feel angry. If we are out of work because we were 'let go,' and especially if it came out of the blue, or was done in a shabby way, we may justifiably feel a great deal of anger about the whole thing.

It's rejection, and we hate it.

If we go looking for work, and can't find anything, after getting turned down at the 307th place, we may feel very angry.

Again, it's rejection, and we hate it.

And if, above all, we didn't expect any of this, then we're suffering from what I call:

Nobody likes to be rejected. Not at work. Not during the job-hunt. We *hate* it.

All of this anger, unresolved, doesn't just fade away with time; it often turns into depression, as I mentioned above.

Need I mention that we would probably drop our anger quickly if it were relatively easy to find another job, doing basically the thing we love at the same level of responsibility and at the same salary, or greater, in the same town, with an even better boss. But, given our Neanderthal job-hunting system, it is not. It is not easy to find such jobs even when they exist.

Hence, much of the blame for our anger should lie at the door of this so-called job-hunting '*system*'-- which leaves us feeling devalued and discarded by our society for weeks, months, and sometimes years. Our anger is justified and understandable, in the beginning.

But if it keeps on and on, then that's another story. And if our anger is directed not against the job-hunting system in this country, but against our ex-employers, that's the beginning of trouble. I see this often, as people who have been let go discuss the place where they used to work: *'I'll never forgive them. They've ruined the rest of my life.'*

Of course, the only way our former employers can actually ruin the rest of our lives is if *we* help them out, by holding on to our anger forever. This *will* wreck the rest of our lives. I have seen it happen many many times in the lives of the unemployed.

We forget an ancient truth: that when anger becomes a burning fire within us, that fire gradually consumes not its object, but its host. Certainly it doesn't achieve its desired effect upon the objects of our anger. They are sleeping soundly, while it is we who are lying awake at night. No, anger consumes its host not its object, and it does this by giving birth within us to irritability, withdrawal, loneliness, broken relationships, divorce (often), and sometimes (rarely) suicide. After a period of time, this anger commonly segues into depression.

Remedies

- *Your basic need is to face forward, toward your future, not backward, toward your past. Staying rooted in your anger keeps you facing toward the past.*
- *Talk out the anger with someone who is a good listener, understanding, and compassionate: partner, mate, friend, or therapist.*
- *If you have a lot of anger still left, so you feel you'd like to punch someone (your ex-employer comes to mind),* don't. *Punch a pillow instead. A big pillow. Or your mattress. Punch it hard.*
- *If you are a man or woman of faith, hand over your anger to God. Then set your face toward the future.*

THE MENTAL ROOT OF UNEMPLOYMENT DEPRESSION

We get depressed because we feel powerless. For months, years, maybe decades, we have thought of ourselves in terms of *that job* at *that place*. It gave our life its coherence, it gave us our daily routine, it gave us our identity. *"Who are you?"* "Oh, I'm a foreman at the General Motors plant down the road." We may have been saying *that* for years. But when we are let go, that era comes to an end. What do we say now? *"Who are you?"* "Well, I don't really know, any more." Of course, we get depressed.

This often spirals into our spending much of our time each day, every day, brooding about what is *wrong*. What is wrong with people, what is wrong with our life, what is wrong with our situation, what is wrong with anything and everything. In our conversation with friends or family, we focus our attention on what we didn't like about the conversation...or *them*. In a movie or play, we focus on what we didn't like about it. When we travel, we focus on what we didn't like about each place we visited. This habit of mind focusses always on other people's failings, on what is not the way we want it to be, on what is (from our point of view) missing. We get more depressed.

We always get more depressed when we feel powerless. Obsessing on what's wrong with everything, is a good way to feel more and more powerless.

Remedies

• *Remember this simple truth: you always have power -- the power to change how you view your situation, and thus to alter your situation, in the days ahead.*

• *Spend time learning to think about yourself in a new way. Do the Workbook in this book, called* The Quick Job-Hunting Map, *so as to learn to think of yourself -- not in terms of a job-title, but in terms of gifts. "I am a person who. . . ."*

• *Spend time thinking about what you'd like to do with the rest of your life. Make it a time of philosophical and spiritual renewal for you.*

• *If you would avoid staying depressed, it is crucial to focus your attention on happy things.*[4] *Adopt a more lenient view of the world as it is, not as you would have it. And, as Baltasar Gracián said,*[5] *"Get used to the failings of your friends, family, and acquaintances . . ." And your bosses. And your co-workers.*

• *Don't stay by yourself all the time. Spend time with friends and loved ones, in conversation, cuddling, drives in the country, exercise, taking walks, singing, listening to beautiful music, sitting in front of the fireplace (hopefully with a fire burning in it). If you have no fireplace, sit in front of a burning candle, with your loved one.*

THE SPIRITUAL ROOT OF UNEMPLOYMENT DEPRESSION

We get depressed because we feel life is meaningless. You will likely feel depressed while unemployed if you view this experience of being laid-off, and having to spend a long time finding a new job, as essentially a random, senseless and meaningless event in your life.

At a medical symposium which I attended many years ago, a doctor was reviewing the puzzle of healing. Two patients, he said, of the same age and with the same medical history, would undergo the same operation. Yet, one would heal rapidly, while the other's healing was long delayed. Doctors had no idea why this was so. They set up a study at a major New York hospital, to see if they could identify what factors explained this difference.[6] Using a computer, they decided to compare *everything* about the patients who healed quickly, with those same factors -- or to be more exact, the *absence* of those same factors -- in the patients who healed slowly. And so they began to ask the computer their questions.

4. Especially helpful is Barbara Ann Kipfer's *14,000 things to be happy about.* Workman Publishing Company, 708 Broadway, New York, NY 10003. 1990.

5. Baltazar Gracián, *The Art of Worldly Wisdom: A Pocket Oracle.* Doubleday/Currency, Publishers. 1992. Baltazar was a Spanish writer who lived in the 1600s.

6. I have, incidentally, tried to go back and identify that study, with the help of others as well; but we have been basically unsuccessful in this search. I am left only with a clear memory of *the findings,* as they were reported by that doctor at that symposium.

Were those who healed quickly characterized by *optimism,* while those who healed slowly were not? No, said the computer; that wasn't the answer.

Were those who healed quickly characterized by *some kind of religious faith,* while those who healed slowly were not? No, said the computer; that wasn't the answer.

And so it went.

What the answer finally turned out to be was this: those who healed quickly felt there was some meaning to every event that happened to them in their lives, even if they did not understand what that meaning was, at the present time; while those who healed slowly felt that most events which happened to them had no meaning; they were merely random or senseless. Hence, if both patients were being operated on for cancer, the one who viewed the cancer as having some meaning in the larger scheme of things, for their life, healed quickly; while the one who viewed the cancer as a senseless and meaningless interruption in their life, healed slowly.

We may apply all of this to being let go, at work. Being fired or terminated is rarely the outrageous, meaningless event that it at first seems to be. The last time I was fired, the firing occurred shortly before noon, and at 3 o'clock that same afternoon I had an appointment with my dentist, to have some drilling done on my teeth. '*What a wonderful day this is turning out to be!*' I thought, with rich irony.

Anyway, my dentist was a wise man, quite a bit older than I, and when I told him of my plight, he said some words I have never forgotten: "Someday," he said, "you will say this was the best thing that ever happened to you. I don't expect you to believe a word I am saying now, but wait and see. I have seen this happen in so many people's lives, that I know it will come true for you."

Of course, he was absolutely right. I now indeed say, that firing was the best thing that ever happened to me, for it caused me to rethink my whole life and what I wanted to contribute to the world. It caused *Parachute* to be born. Light was born out of darkness.

According to Gallup Polls since 1960, about 94% of the population in the U.S. believe in *some* concept of God.[7] When they find themselves summarily dismissed from a job that they may have held for *years,* many find their faith in God a bulwark of strength that helps them through this very difficult period, daily.

But, if you are a man or woman of faith, you must rest assured also of this truth: nothing which happens to you is meaningless. If unemployment drags on and on, there is a meaning to it, even if you can't figure out what it is, at this time.

To feel there is no rhyme or reason to anything that happens to you in life, will leave you feeling depressed.

---

7. Reported in George Gallup's *The People's Religion: American Faith in the 90s.* Macmillan & Co., Order Dept., 201 W. 103rd St., Indianapolis, IN 46290. 1989. In addition to reporting that 94% of us believe in God, the Gallup polls also discovered that 90% of us pray, 88% of us believe God loves us, and 33% of us report we have had a life-changing religious experience; and these figures have remained pretty unvarying during the last thirty years of opinion polls conducted by the Gallup Organization.

Remedies

• *If your job-hunt is dragging on and on, change your job-hunting strategy. Read, and devour Chapters 5, 6, 7 in* Parachute. *Try some new job-hunting behaviors, and methods.*

• *Think of your life as like a tapestry, being woven by God on an enchanted loom.*[8] *Every bobble of the shuttle has intention, every thread is important, every event in your life has meaning.*

• *Sit down and write out stories about your past years, when you were going through dark times. Write down what meaning you now see in those events.*

• *Don't feel abandoned by God, just because this happened to you. Hold high the truth that God does not save the believer from hard times. Hard times come to believer and non-believer alike. Above all, avoid the plaintive plea, "Why me?"*

• *Search for a higher concept of God. Consider this parable. Imagine that you have, in your dining room, a fine wooden chair, which one day has its back broken off completely -- I mean, into smithereens -- by someone in the house. You run down the street, to call a carpenter who lives nearby. He comes and examines the chair. He pronounces the back unrepairable. "But," he says, "I think I could make a fine wooden stool out of the remainder of the chair, for you." And so he spends much time, shaping, polishing and sanding it, and fashioning out of the former chair a fine stool, more resplendent than anything you have ever dreamed. He inlays it with gold, and soon it is the treasure of your house.*

• *Let me underline a couple of key points in this parable. First of all, the carpenter did not break the chair. Someone else did that. But the carpenter came quickly, and with all his art and powers, to see if he could not only repair it, but make of it something even finer than it had been before. And, he labored mightily, to that end.*

• *And so, a higher concept of God holds that God does not create our unemployment or any of the calamities in our life. God gives us all free-will, and it is our fellow human beings who misuse that free will and thus create our calamities. But though God has given freedom of choice to us all, yet He steps in as soon as someone else has misused their freedom of will in our lives. Like the carpenter, the Lord comes instantly, with all His art and powers, to not only repair our life, but to make of it something even finer than it had been before -- not a physical thing, like the stool inlaid with gold, but a work on the spiritual level that corresponds to the stool, in splendor. And thus no event in our lives remains meaningless. Some higher purpose is always worked out, therein.*

• *Do not limit your faith only to what you can feel. If you can't feel God's presence during these hard times, that does not mean a thing. Feelings often fail to correspond to reality. We can be in a fog that obscures our vision. Walk by faith.*

---

8. The reference to the *loom,* which follows, comes by analogy to Sir Charles Sherrington's description of the brain: *"It is as if the Milky Way entered upon some cosmic dance. Swiftly the brain becomes an enchanted loom where millions of flashing shuttles weave a dissolving pattern, always a meaningful pattern though never an abiding one; a shifting harmony of subpatterns."*

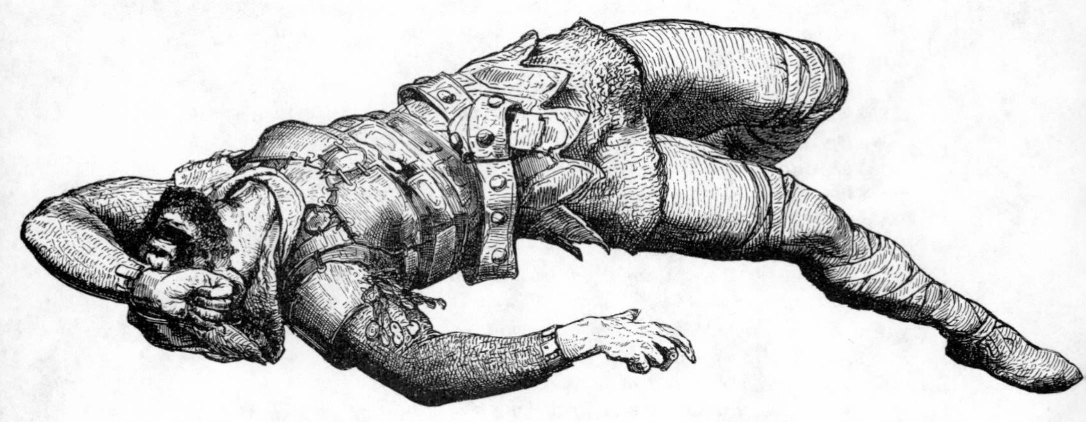

THE PHYSICAL ROOT OF UNEMPLOYMENT DEPRESSION

We get depressed because we are physical creatures. You will feel depressed if you are short on your sleep, or your body is otherwise run-down.

The world never looks bright or happy to people who are *very short of sleep.*

The world never looks bright or happy to people who are *feeling depressed.*

It is therefore easy to confuse the two feeling-states. What you may imagine is depression may in fact be simply the feelings that come from sleep-deprivation.

I said we get depressed because we are physical creatures. This involves other things, as well.

As physical creatures, we need to keep a roof over our heads, food on the table, and clothes on our back. In the U.S. over 30% of *all adults* describe their financial situation as typically 'shaky' anyway -- whether they are working or not. And naturally, when we become unemployed a much higher percentage of us would describe our financial situation as 'shaky' -- inasmuch as many of us just live from paycheck to paycheck. The longer this 'hand-to-mouth' existence goes on, the more depressed you are likely to feel.

Remedies

• *It has been amazing to me, in the past, to see very-depressed job-hunters turn into happier, more upbeat people, just by catching up on their sleep. Turn off the TV by 10 o'clock, and go to bed! You'll soon feel better; sometimes,* much *better.*

• *Try to keep regular hours, going to bed at the same time every night.*

• *Avoid things that can keep you awake, like caffeine, once dinner is finished. Reduce alcohol consumption to one drink at most, per day.*

• *If you lie awake for more than 30 minutes,* get up *and read, write, or meditate until you get sleepy. Don't do this in bed. Use the bed only for sleeping and love-making.*

• *In addition to the sleep thing, there are other things that need to be done to keep yourself physically fit while unemployed.*[9] *When I was myself unemployed I found it important to:*

• *Get out in sunlight as much as possible, or sit under bright lights in one's apartment or house, especially during the winter (it is a well-known fact that many people get particularly depressed during winter, because they need light, and especially sunlight; the affliction is called S.A.D.);*

• *Get regular exercise, involving a daily walk;*

• *Drink plenty of water each day (I try for at least eight glasses of water a day -- this seems silly, but it is often very important);*

• *Eat balanced meals, with plenty of fiber. One must not pig out just on junk food in front of the telly; if ever one has thought about cutting down on fats (meats, dairy products), sugar, baked goods, and caffeine, now is an excellent time to do it;*

• *Eliminate sugar as much as possible from the diet;*[10]

• *Take supplementary vitamins daily (no matter how often doctors and nutritionists may tell us that we already get plenty, just from our daily food);*

• *And all that other stuff that our mothers always told us to do.*

• *If you're real short of money, take a 'stop-gap' job -- any honest work, whatsoever, that brings in some money while you continue your job-hunt. Look at 'temp agencies,' in particular, to see if there is one in your town or city that specializes in temporarily placing people with your background and skills. They're in the Yellow Pages, under "Employment Agencies." Look for the word 'temporary' in their title, or ad.*

• *Finally, you may want to use this time to think about what your essential needs are in life, and perhaps embrace a simpler life with less 'things' and more time spent with loved ones and friends. This 'voluntary simplicity' may be just what your soul is craving.*

---

9. Of course, these principles make sense equally when one has found a job.

10. The sugar/depression connection is a matter that has been well-established, and were I feeling depressed the first thing I would eliminate from my diet would be sugar. See *Sugar Blues,* by William Dufty. Warner Books, Inc., 1271 Avenue of the Americas, New York, NY 10020. 1993. Available in bookstores, health-food stores, and your local library.

PERSPECTIVE

When all these things are said and done, all roots diagnosed, all remedies pursued, unemployment depression may still remain -- especially if your job-hunt just keeps draggin' on and on. You've tried everything, you've done *The Map*, you've devoured the chapter on "The Determined Job-Hunter." You've prayed. You've done it all. What then?

The key at such a time, it seems to me, is to keep some kind of perspective about it all. You know, like when you're in the middle of a thunderstorm, and it looks like it will never let up. But you know it will, and you draw cheer from that thought.

Even so, while we are unemployed I think it is important to realize that life, by its very nature, consists in a series of *alternating* periods:

Life is sometimes somber; life is sometimes joyous.
Life is sometimes difficult; life is sometimes easy.
Life is sometimes tawdry; life is sometimes beautiful.
Life is sometimes worse; life is sometimes better.
Life finds us sometimes struggling; life finds us sometimes well off.
Life is sometimes sickness; life is sometimes health.
Life is sometimes depressing; life is sometimes elating.
Life is sometimes sorrow; life is sometimes happiness.
Life is sometimes death; life is sometimes resurrection.
Life sometimes casts us down; life sometimes exalts us.
Life is sometimes a battle; life is sometimes glorious.

It's an alternating rhythm -- a sort of *death and resurrection, death and resurrection*. Over and over again.

Hence this period, when you've been fired or let go, when you've been treated badly, when you're having a hard time with the job-hunt, is one of the periods we inevitably go through in life.

But life is an alternating rhythm. This difficult depressing time will eventually yield to the contrasting theme of joy and happiness, in due time. You need to know this, and thus put this period of your life in perspective.

After three months, do some other things besides your job-hunt. Seek out a career counselor for help. Go out, get active, volunteer someplace, take a college course, be a blessing to this Earth even though you don't yet have a job. In good time, the alternating rhythm will come.

V. How to Find Your Mission in Life

God and One's Choice of Vocation

Introduction

As I started writing this section, I toyed at first with the idea of following what might be described as an "all-paths approach" to religion. But, after much thought, I decided not to try that. This, because I have read many other writers who tried, and I felt the approach failed miserably. An "all-paths" approach to religion ends up being a "no-paths" approach, even as a woman or man who tries to please everyone ends up pleasing no one. It is the old story of the "universal" vs. the "particular."

Those of us who do career counseling could predict, ahead of time, that trying to stay universal is not likely to be helpful, in writing about religion. We know well from our own field that truly helpful career counseling depends upon defining the **particularity** or uniqueness of each person we try to help. No employer wants to know only what you have in common with everyone else. He or she wants to know what makes you unique and individual. As I have argued throughout this book, the identification and inventory of your uniqueness or *particularity* is crucial if you are ever to find meaningful work.

This particularity invades and carries over to *everything* a person does; it is not suddenly "jettisonable" when he or she turns to religion. Therefore, when I or anyone else writes about religion I believe we **must** write out of our own particularity -- which *starts,* in my case, with the fact that I write, and think, and breathe as a Christian -- as you might expect from the fact that I have been an ordained Episcopalian minister for the last forty-three years. Understandably, then, this article speaks from a Christian perspective. I want you to be aware of that, at the outset.

Balanced against this is the fact that I have always been acutely sensitive to the fact that this is a pluralistic society in which we live, and that I owe a great deal to my readers who may have religious convictions quite different from my own. It has turned out that the people who work or have worked here in my office with me, over the years, have been predominantly of other faiths, mainly Jewish. Furthermore, **Parachute's** more than 5 million readers have not only included Christians of every variety and persuasion, Mormons, Christian Scientists, Jews, members of the Baha'i faith, Hindus, Buddhists, adherents of Islam, but also believers in 'new age' religions, secularists, humanists, agnostics, atheists, and many others. I have therefore tried to be very courteous toward the feelings of all my readers, *while at the same time* counting on them to translate my Christian thought forms into their own thought forms. This ability to thus translate is the indispensable *sine qua non* of anyone who wants to communicate helpfully with others, these days.

In the Judeo-Christian tradition from which I come, one of the indignant Biblical questions is, "Has God forgotten to be gracious?" The answer was a clear No. I think it is important *for all of us* also to seek the same goal. I have therefore labored to make this section gracious as well as helpful.

R. N. B.

How to Find Your Mission in Life

God and One's Choice of Vocation

How I Came To Write This

Some time ago, a woman asked me how you go about finding out what your Mission in life is. She assumed I would know what she was talking about, because of a diagram which appears a number of times in one of my other books, The Three Boxes of Life:

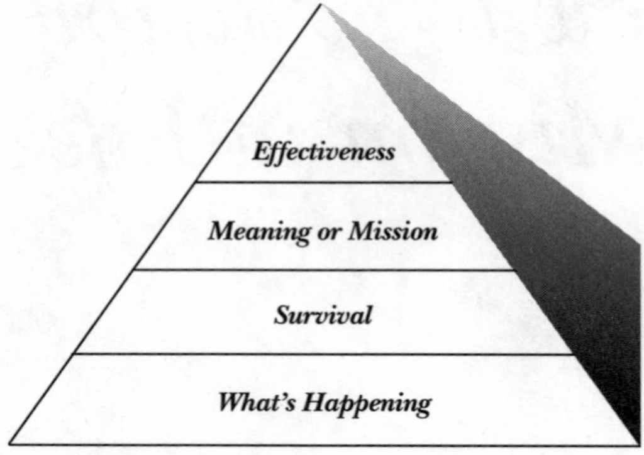

The Issues of the Job-Hunt

As this diagram asserts, the question of one's Mission in life arises naturally as a part of many people's job-hunt.

She told me that what she was looking for was not some careful, dispassionate, philosophical answer, where every statement is hedged about with cautions and caveats -- "It may be . . .' or " It seems to me . . ." Nor did she want to know why *I thought what I did, or* how *I learned it, or what Scriptures* support *it. "I want you to just speak with passion and conviction," she said, "out of what you most truly feel and believe. For it is some vision that I want. I am hungry for a vision of what I can be. So, just speak to me of what you most truly feel and believe about our mission in life. I will know how to translate your vision into my own thought forms for my own life, when I reflect afterwards upon what you have said. But I want you to talk about this now with passion and conviction -- please."*

And so, I did. And I will now tell you what I said to her.

The Motive for Finding A Sense of Mission in Life

We begin with the fact that, according to fifty years of opinion polls conducted by the Gallup Organization, 94% of us believe in God, 90% of us pray, 88% of us believe God loves us, and 33% of us report we have had a life-changing religious experience (*The People's Religion: American Faith in the 90s.* Macmillan & Co. 1989).

It is hardly surprising therefore, that so many of us are searching these days for some sense of mission. Career counselors are often afraid to give help or guidance here, for fear they will be perceived as trying to talk people into religious belief. It is a groundless fear. Clearly, the overwhelming majority of U.S. job-hunters and career-changers already have their religious beliefs well in place.

But, we want some guidance and help in this area, because we want to *marry* our religious **beliefs** with our **work**, rather than leaving the two -- our religion and our work -- compartmentalized, as two areas of our life which never talk to each other. We *want* them to talk to each other and uplift each other.

This marriage takes the particular form of a search for a Sense of Mission because of our conviction that God has made each of us unique, even as our fingerprints attest. We feel that we are not just another grain of sand lying on the beach called humanity, unnumbered and lost in the 5 billion mass, but that God caused us to be born and put here for some unique reason: so that we might contribute to Life here on earth something no one else can contribute in quite the same way. At its very minimum, then, when we search for a sense of Mission we are searching for reassurance that the world is at least a little bit richer for our being here; and a little bit poorer after our going.

Every keen observer of human nature will know what I mean when I say that those who have found some sense of Mission have a very special joy, "which no one can take from them." It is wonderful to feel that beyond eating, sleeping, working, having pleasure and *it may be* marrying, having children, and growing older, you were set here on Earth for some special purpose, *and* that you can gain some idea of what that purpose is.

So, how does one go about this search?

I would emphasize, at the outset, two cautions. First of all, though I will explain the steps that seem to me to be involved in finding one's Mission -- based on the learnings I have accumulated over some sixty years, I want to caution you that these steps are not the only Way -- by any means. Many people have discovered their Mission by taking other paths. And you may, too. But hopefully what I have to say may shed some light upon whatever path you take.

My second caution is simply this: you would be wise not to try to approach this problem of "your Mission in life" as primarily an **intellectual** puzzle -- for the mind, and the mind alone, to solve. To paraphrase Kahlil Gibran, *Faith* is an oasis in the heart that is not reached merely by the journey of the mind. It is your will and your heart that must be involved in the search as well as your mind. To put it quite simply, it takes the total person to learn one's total Mission.

It also takes the total disciplines of the ages -- not only modern knowledge but also ancient thought, including the wisdom of religion, faith, and the spiritual matters. For, to put it quite bluntly, the question of Mission inevitably leads us to God.

The Main Obstacle in Finding Your Mission in Life: Job-Hunting Compartmentalized from Our Religion or Faith

Mission challenges us to see our job-hunt in relationship to our faith in God, because *Mission* is a religious concept, from beginning to end. It is defined by Webster's as "a continuing task or responsibility that one is destined or fitted to do or specially called upon to undertake," and historically has had two major synonyms: *Calling* and *Vocation.* These, of course, are the same word in two different languages, English and Latin. Regardless of which word is used, it is obvious upon reflection, that a Vocation or Calling implies *Someone who calls,* and that a destiny implies *Someone who determined the destination for us.* Thus, unless one opts for a military or governmental view of the matter, the concept of Mission with relationship to our whole life lands us inevitably in the lap of God, before we have even begun.

There is always the temptation to try to speak of this subject of *Mission* in a secular fashion, without reference to God, as though it might be simply "a purpose you choose for your own life, by identifying your enthusiasms, and then using the clues you find from that exercise to get some purpose you can choose for your life." The language of this temptation is ironic because the substitute word used for "Mission" -- *Enthusiasm* -- is derived from the Greek, '*en theos,*' and literally means "God in us."

It is no accident that so many of the leaders in the job-hunting field over the years -- the late John Crystal, Arthur Miller, Ralph Mattson, Tom and Ellie Jackson, Bernard Haldane, Arthur and Marie Kirn, and myself -- have been people of faith. If you would figure out your Mission in life, you must also be willing to think about God in connection with your job-hunt.

The Secret of Finding Your Mission in Life: Taking It in Stages

The puzzle of figuring out what your Mission in life is, will likely take some time. It is not a *problem* to be solved in a day and a night. It is a *learning process* which has steps to it, much like the process by which we all learned to eat. As a baby we did not tackle adult food right off. As we all recall, there were three stages: first there had to be the mother's milk or bottle, then strained baby foods, and finally -- after teeth and time -- the stuff that grown-ups chew. Three stages -- and the two earlier stages were not to be disparaged. It was all Eating, just different forms of Eating -- appropriate to our development at the time. But each stage had to be mastered, in turn, before the next could be approached.

The Three Stages of Mission: What We Need to Learn

By coincidence, there are usually three stages also to learning what your Mission in life is, and the two earlier stages are likewise not to be disparaged. It is all "Mission" -- just different forms of Mission, appropriate to your development at the time. But each stage has to be mastered, in turn, before the next can be approached. And so, you may say either of two things: You may say that you have *Three Missions in Life.* Or you may say that you have *One Mission in Life, with three parts to it.* But there is a sense in which you must discover what those three parts are, each in turn, before you can fully answer the question, "What is my Mission in life?" Of course, there is another sense in which you never master any of these stages, but are always growing in understanding and mastery of them, throughout your whole life here on Earth.

As it has been impressed on me by observing many people over the years (admittedly through *Christian spectacles*), it appears that the three parts to your Mission here on Earth can be defined generally as follows:

(1) *Your first Mission here on Earth* is one which you share with the rest of the human race, but it is no less your individual Mission for the fact that it is shared: and it is, **to seek to stand hour by hour in the conscious presence of God, the One from whom your Mission is derived**. *The Missioner before the Mission,* is the rule. In religious language, your Mission here is: *to know God, and enjoy Him forever, and to see His hand in all His works.*

(2) Secondly, once you have begun doing that in an earnest way, *your second Mission here on Earth* is also one which you share with the rest of the human race, but it is no less your individual mission for the fact that it is shared: and that is, **to do what you can, moment by moment, day by day, step by step, to make this world a better place, following the leading and guidance of God's Spirit within you and around you.**

(3) Thirdly, once you have begun doing that in a serious way, *your third Mission here on Earth* is one which is uniquely yours, and that is:

a) **to exercise that Talent which you particularly came to Earth to use -- your greatest gift, which you most delight to use,**
b) **in the place(s) or setting(s) which God has caused to appeal to you the most,**
c) **and for those purposes which God most needs to have done in the world.**

When fleshed out, and spelled out, I think you will find that there you have the definition of your Mission in life. Or, to put it another way, these are the three Missions which you have in life.

The Two Rhythms of the Dance of Mission: Unlearning, Learning, Unlearning, Learning

The distinctive characteristic of these three stages is that in each we are forced to *let go* of some fundamental assumptions which the world has *falsely* taught us, about the nature of our Mission. In other words, throughout this quest and at each stage we find ourselves engaged not merely in a process of *Learning.* We are also engaged in a process of *Un*learning. Thus, we can restate the above three Learnings, in terms of what we also need to *un*learn at each stage:

• We need in the first Stage to *un*learn the idea that our Mission is primarily to keep busy *doing* something (here on Earth), and learn instead that our Mission is first of all to keep busy being something (here on Earth). In Christian language (and others as well), we might say that we were sent here to learn how *to be* sons of God, and daughters of God, before anything else. "*Our Father, who art in heaven . . .*"

• In the second stage, "Being" issues into "Doing." At this stage, we need to *un*learn the idea that everything about our Mission must be *unique* to us, and learn instead that some parts of our Mission here on Earth are *shared* by all human beings: e.g., we were all sent here to bring more gratitude, more kindness, more forgiveness, and more love, into the world. We share this Mission because the task is too large to be accomplished by just one individual.

• We need in the third stage to *un*learn the idea that that part of our Mission which is truly unique, and most truly ours, is something Our Creator just *orders* us to do, without any agreement from our spirit, mind, and heart. (On the other hand, neither is it something that each of us chooses and then merely asks God to bless.) We need to learn that God so honors our free will, that He has ordained our unique Mission be something which we have some part in choosing.

• In this third stage we need also to *un*learn the idea that our unique Mission must consist of some achievement which all the world will see, -- and learn instead that as the stone does not always know what ripples it has caused in the pond whose surface it impacts, so neither we nor those who watch our life will always know *what we have achieved* by our life and by our Mission. *It may be* that by the grace of God we helped bring about a profound change for the better in the lives of other souls around us, but it also may be that this takes place beyond our sight, or after we have gone on. And we may never know what we have accomplished, until we see Him face-to-face after this life is past.

• Most finally, we need to *un*learn the idea that what we have accomplished is our doing, and ours alone. It is God's Spirit breathing in us and through us which helps us to do whatever we do, and so the singular first person pronoun is never appropriate, but only the plural. Not "*I* accomplished this" but "*We* accomplished this, God and I, working together . . ."

That should give you a general overview. But I would like to add some random comments on my part about each of these three Missions of ours here on Earth.

Some Random Comments About Your First Mission in Life

Your first Mission here on Earth is one which you share with the rest of the human race, but it is no less your individual Mission for the fact that it is shared: and that is, **to seek to stand hour by hour in the conscious presence of God, the One from whom your Mission is derived**. The Missioner before the Mission, is the rule. In religious language, your Mission is: to know God, and enjoy Him for ever, and to see His hand in all His works.

Comment 1: How We Might Think of God

Each of us has to go about this primary Mission according to the tenets of his or her own particular religion. But I will speak what I know out of the context of my own particular faith, and you may perhaps translate and apply it to yours. I will speak as a Christian, who believes (passionately) that Christ is the Way and the Truth and the Life. But I also believe, with St. Peter, "that God shows no partiality, but in every nation any one who fears him and does what is right is acceptable to him." (Acts 10:34-35)

Now, Jesus claimed many unique things about Himself and His Mission; but He also spoke of Himself as the great prototype for us all. He called himself "the Son of Man," and He said, "I assure you that the man who believes in me will do the same things that I have done, yes, and he will do even greater things than these . . ." (John 14:12)

Emboldened by His identification of us with His life and His Mission, we might want to remember how He spoke about His Life here on Earth. He put it in this context: **"I came from the Father and have come into the world; again, I am leaving the world and going to the Father."** (John 16:28)

If there is a sense in which this is, in even the faintest way, true also of our lives (and I shall say in a moment in what sense I think it is true), then instead of calling our great Creator "God" or "Father" right off, we might begin our approach to the subject of religion by referring to the One Who gave us our Mission and sent us to this planet not as "God" or "Father" but -- *just to help our thinking* -- as: **"The One From Whom We Came and The One To Whom We Shall Return**," when this life is done.

If our life here on Earth be at all like Christ's, then this is a true way to think about the One who gave us our Mission. We are not some kind of eternal, pre-existent *being*. We are **creatures**, who once did not exist, and then came into Being, and continue to have our Being, only at the will of our great Creator. But as creatures we are both body and soul; and although we know our body was created in our mother's womb, our soul's origin is a great mystery. Where it came from, at what moment the Lord created it, is something we cannot know. It is not unreasonable to suppose, however, that the great God created our *soul* before it entered our body, and in that sense we did indeed stand before God before we were born; and He is indeed **"The One From Whom We Came and The One To Whom We Shall Return."**

Therefore, before we go searching for "what work was I sent here to do?" we need to establish or in a truer sense *reestablish* -- contact with this **"One From Whom We Came and The One To Whom We Shall Return."** Without this reaching out of the creature to the great Creator, without this reaching out of *the creature with a Mission* to *the One Who Gave Us That Mission*, the question ***what** is my Mission in life?* is void and null. The *what* is rooted in the *Who;* absent the Personal, one cannot meaningfully discuss The Thing. It is like the adult who cries, "I want to get married," without giving any consideration to *who* it is they want to marry.

Comment 2: How We Might Think of Religion or Faith

In light of this larger view of our creatureliness, we can see that *religion* or *faith* is not a question of whether or not we choose to (*as it is so commonly put*) "have a relationship with God." Looking at our life in a larger context than just our life here on Earth, it becomes apparent that some sort of relationship with God is a given for us, about which we have absolutely no choice. God and we **were and are** related, during the time of our soul's existence before our birth and in the time of our soul's continued existence after our death. The only choice we have is what to do about **The Time In Between**, i.e., what we want the nature of our relationship with God to be during our time here on Earth and how that will affect the *nature* of the relationship, then, after death.

One of the corollaries of all this is that by the very act of being born into a human body, it is an inevitable that we undergo a kind of *amnesia* -- an amnesia which typically embraces not only our nine months in the womb, our baby years, and almost one-third of each day (sleeping), but more importantly any memory of our origin or our destiny. We wander on Earth as an amnesia victim. To seek after Faith, therefore, is to seek to climb back out of that amnesia. Religion or faith is **the hard reclaiming of knowledge we once knew as a certainty**.

Comment 3: The First Obstacle to Executing This Mission

This first Mission of ours here on Earth is not the easiest of Missions, simply because it is the first. Indeed, in many ways, it is the most difficult. All can see that our life here on Earth is a very physical life. We eat, we drink, we sleep, we long to be held, and to hold. We inherit a physical body, with very physical appetites, we walk on the physical earth, and we acquire physical possessions. It is the most alluring of temptations, *in our amnesia*, to come up with just a *Physical* interpretation of this life: to think that the Universe is merely interested in the survival of species. Given this interpretation, the story of our individual life could be simply told: we are born, grow up, procreate, and die.

But we are ever recalled to do what we came here to do: that without rejecting the joy of the Physicalness of this life, such as the love of the blue sky and the green grass, we are to reach out beyond all this to **recall** and recover a *Spiritual* interpretation of our life. *Beyond* the physical and *within* the physicalness of this life, to detect a Spirit and a Person from beyond this Earth who is with us and in us -- the very real and loving and awesome Presence of the great Creator from whom we came -- and the One to whom we once again shall go.

Comment 4: The Second Obstacle to Executing This Mission

It is one of the conditions of our earthly amnesia and our creatureliness that, sadly enough, some very *human* and very *rebellious* part of us *likes* the idea of living in a world where we can be our own god -- and therefore loves the purely Physical interpretation of life, and finds it *anguish* to relinquish it. Traditional Christian vocabulary calls this "**sin**" and has a lot to say about the difficulty it poses for this first part of our Mission. All who live a thoughtful life know that it is true: our greatest enemy in carrying out this first Mission of ours is indeed *our own* heart and our own rebellion.

Comment 5: Further Thoughts About What Makes Us Special and Unique

As I said earlier, many of us come to this issue of our Mission in life, because we want to feel that we are unique. And what we mean by that, is that we hope to discover some "specialness" intrinsic to us, which is our birthright, and which no one can take from us. What we, however, discover from a thorough exploration of this topic, is that we are indeed special -- but only because God thinks us so. Our specialness and uniqueness reside in Him, and His love, rather than in anything intrinsic to our own *being*. The proper appreciation of this distinction causes our feet to carry us in the end not to the City called Pride, but to the Temple called Gratitude.

> What is religion? Religion is the service of God out of grateful love for what God has done for us. The Christian religion, more particularly, is the service of God out of grateful love for what God has done for us in Christ.
>
> Phillips Brooks, author of
> *O Little Town of Bethlehem*

Comment 6: The Unconscious Doing of The Work We Came To Do

You may have *already* wrestled with this first part of your Mission here on Earth. You may not have called it that. You may have called it simply "learning to believe in God." But if you ask what your Mission is in life, this one was and is the precondition of all else that you came here to do. Absent this Mission, and it is folly to talk about the rest. So, if you have been seeking faith, or seeking to strengthen your faith, you have -- willy nilly -- already been about *the doing of the Mission you were given.* Born into **This Time In Between**, you have found His hand again, and reclasped it. You are therefore ready to go on with His Spirit to tackle together what you came here to do -- the other parts of your Mission.

Some Random Comments About Your Second Mission in Life

Your second Mission here on Earth is also one which you share with the rest of the human race, but it is no less your individual mission for the fact that it is shared: and that is, **to do what you can moment by moment, day by day, step by step, to make this world a better place -- following the leading and guidance of God's Spirit within you and around you.**

Comment 1: The Uncomfortableness of One Step at a Time

Imagine yourself out walking in your neighborhood one night, and suddenly you find yourself surrounded by such a dense fog, that you have lost your bearings and cannot find your way. Suddenly, a friend appears out of the fog, and asks you to put your hand in theirs, and they will lead you home. And you, not being able to tell where you are going, trustingly follow them, even though you can only see one step at a time. Eventually you arrive safely home, filled with gratitude. But as you reflect upon the experience the next day, you realize how unsettling it was to have to keep walking when you could see only one step at a time, even though you had guidance in which you knew you could trust.

Now I have asked you to imagine all of this, because this is the essence of the second Mission to which *you* are called -- and *I* am called -- in this life. It is all very different than we had imagined. When the question, "*What is your Mission in life?*" is first broached, and we have put our hand in God's, as it were, we imagine that we will be taken up to *some mountaintop*, from which we can see far into the distance. And that we will hear a voice in our ear, saying, "Look, look, see that distant city? That is the goal of your Mission; that is where everything is leading, every step of your way."

But instead of the mountaintop, we find ourself in *the valley* -- wandering often in a fog. And the voice in our ear says something quite different from what we thought we would hear. It says, "**Your Mission is to take one step at a time, even when you don't yet see where it all is leading, or what the Grand Plan is, or what your overall Mission in life is. Trust Me; I will lead you.**"

Comment 2: The Nature of This Step-by-Step Mission

As I said, in every situation you find yourself, you have been sent here to do whatever you can -- moment by moment -- that will bring more gratitude, more kindness, more forgiveness, more honesty, and more love into this world.

There are dozens of such moments every day. Moments when you stand -- as it were -- at a spiritual crossroads, with two ways lying before you. Such moments are typically called "**moments of decision.**" It does not matter what the frame or content of each particular decision is. It all devolves, in the end, into just two roads before you, *every time.* **The one** will lead to *less* gratitude, *less* kindness, *less* forgiveness, *less* honesty, or *less* love in the world. **The other** will lead to *more* gratitude, *more* kindness, *more* forgiveness, *more* honesty, or *more* love in the world. Your Mission, each moment, is to seek to choose the latter spiritual road, rather than the former, *every time.*

Comment 3: Some Examples of This Step-by-Step Mission

I will give a few examples, so that the nature of this part of your Mission may be unmistakably clear.

You are out on the freeway, in your car. Someone has gotten into the wrong lane, to the right of *your* lane, and needs to move over into the lane you are in. You *see* their need to cut in, ahead of you. **Decision time.** In your mind's eye you see two spiritual roads lying before you: the one leading to less kindness in the world (you speed up, to shut this driver out, and don't let them move over), the other leading to more kindness in the world (you let the driver cut in). **Since you know this is part of your Mission, part of the reason why you came to Earth, your calling is clear. You know which road to take, which decision to make.**

You are hard at work at your desk, when suddenly an interruption comes. The phone rings, or someone is at the door. They need something from you, a question of some of your time and attention. **Decision time.** In your mind's eye you see two spiritual roads lying before you: the one leading to less love in the world (you tell them you're just too busy to be bothered), the other leading to more love in the world (you put aside your work, decide that God may have sent this person to you, and say, "Yes, what can I do to help you?"). **Since you know this is part of your Mission, part of the reason why you came to Earth, your calling is clear. You know which road to take, which decision to make**.

Your mate does something that hurts your feelings. **Decision time.** In your mind's eye you see two spiritual roads lying before you: the one leading to less forgiveness in the world (you institute an icy silence between the two of you, and think of how you can punish them or otherwise get even), the

other leading to more forgiveness in the world (you go over and take them in your arms, speak the truth about your hurt feelings, and assure them of your love). **Since you know this is part of your Mission, part of the reason why you came to Earth, your calling is clear. You know which road to take, which decision to make**.

You have not behaved at your most noble, recently. And now you are face-to-face with someone who asks you a question about what happened. **Decision time.** In your mind's eye you see two spiritual roads lying before you: the one leading to less honesty in the world (you lie about what happened, or what you were feeling, because you fear losing their respect or their love), the other leading to more honesty in the world (you tell the truth, together with how you feel about it, in retrospect). **Since you know this is part of your Mission, part of the reason why you came to Earth, your calling is clear. You know which road to take, which decision to make**.

Comment 4: The Spectacle Which Makes the Angels Laugh

It is necessary to explain this part of our Mission in some detail, because so many times you will see people wringing their hands, and saying, "*I want to know what my Mission in life is,*" all the while they are cutting people off on the highway, refusing to give time to people, punishing their mate for having hurt their feelings, and lying about what they did. And it will seem to you that the angels must laugh to see this spectacle. *For these people wringing their hands,* their Mission was right there, on the freeway, in the interruption, in the hurt, and at the confrontation.

Comment 5: The Valley vs. The Mountaintop

At some point in your life your Mission may involve some grand *mountaintop experience,* where you say to yourself, "This, this, is why I came into the world. I know it. I know it." *But until then,* your Mission is here in *the valley,* and the fog, and the little callings moment by moment, day by day. More to the point, it is likely you cannot ever get to your mountaintop Mission unless you have first exercised your stewardship faithfully in the valley.

It is an ancient principle, to which Jesus alluded often, that if you don't use the information the Universe has already given you, you cannot expect it will give you any more. If you aren't being faithful in small things, how can you expect to be given charge over larger things? (Luke 16:10,11,12; 19:11–24) If you aren't trying to bring more gratitude, kindness, forgiveness, honesty, and love into the world each day, you can hardly expect that you will be entrusted with the Mission to help bring peace into the world or anything else large and important. If we do not live out our day-by-day Mission in the valley, we cannot expect we are yet ready for a larger *mountaintop* Mission.

Comment 6: The Importance of Not Thinking of This Mission As 'Just A Training Camp'

The valley is not just a kind of "training camp." There is in your imagination even now an invisible *spiritual* mountaintop to which you may go, if you wish to see where all this is leading. And what will you see there, in the imagination of your heart, but the goal toward which all this is pointed: **that Earth might be more like heaven. That human's life might be more like God's**. That is the large achievement toward which all our day by day Missions *in the valley* are moving. This is a *large* order, but it is accomplished by faithful attention to the doing of our great Creator's **will** in little things as well as in large. It is much like the building of the pyramids in Egypt, which was accomplished by the dragging of a lot of individual pieces of stone by a lot of individual men.

The valley, the fog, the going step-by-step, is no mere training camp. The goal is real, however large. "**Thy Kingdom come, Thy will be done, on Earth, as it is in heaven**."

Some Random Comments About Your Third Mission in Life

Your third Mission here on Earth is one which is uniquely yours, and that is:

a) **to exercise that Talent which you particularly came to Earth to use -- your greatest gift which you most delight to use**
b) **in those place(s) or setting(s) which God has caused to appeal to you the most,**
c) **and for those purposes which God most needs to have done in the world.**

Comment 1: Our Mission Is Already Written, "in Our Members"

It is customary in trying to identify this part of our Mission, to advise that we should ask God, in prayer, to speak to us -- and **tell us** plainly what our Mission is. We look for a voice in the air, a thought in our head, a dream in the night, a sign in the events of the day, to reveal this thing which is otherwise *(it is said)* completely hidden. Sometimes, from just such answered prayer, people do indeed discover what their Mission is, beyond all doubt and uncertainty.

But having to wait for the voice of God to reveal what our Mission is, is not the truest picture of our situation. St. Paul, in Romans, speaks of a law "written in our members," -- and this phrase has a telling application to the question of **how** God reveals to each of us our unique Mission in life. Read again the definition of our third Mission (above) and you will see: the clear implication of the definition is that God has **already** revealed His will to us concerning our vocation and Mission, by causing it to be **"written in our members.**" We are to begin deciphering our unique Mission by studying our talents and skills, and more particularly which ones (or One) we most rejoice to use.

God actually has written His will *twice* in our members: *first in the talents* which He lodged there, and secondly *in His guidance of our heart,* as to which talent gives us the greatest pleasure from its exercise (**it is usually the one which, when we use it, causes us to lose all sense of time**).

Even as the anthropologist can examine ancient inscriptions, and divine from them the daily life of a long lost people, so we by examining **our talents** and **our heart** can *more often than we dream* divine the Will of the Living God. For true it is, our Mission is not something He **will** reveal; it is something He **has already** revealed. It is not to be found written in the sky; it is to be found written in our members.

Comment 2: Career Counseling: We Need You

Arguably, our first two Missions in life could be learned from religion alone -- without any reference whatsoever to career counseling, the subject of this book. Why then should career counseling claim that this question about our Mission in life is its proper concern, *in any way?*

It is when we come to this third Mission, which hinges so crucially on the question of our Talents, skills, and gifts, that we see the answer. If you've read the body of this book, before turning to this Epilogue, you know without my even saying it, how much the identification of Talents, gifts, or skills is the province of career counseling. Its expertise, indeed its *raison d'etre,* lies precisely in the identification, classification, and (forgive me) "prioritization" of Talents, skills, and gifts. To put the matter quite simply, career counseling knows how to do this better than any other discipline -- **including** traditional religion. This is not a defect of religion, but the fulfillment of something Jesus promised: "When the Spirit of truth comes, He will guide you into all truth." (John 16:12) Career counseling is part (we may hope) of that promised late-coming truth. It can therefore be of inestimable help to the pilgrim who is trying to figure out what their greatest, and most enjoyable, talent is, as a step toward identifying their unique Mission in life.

If career counseling needs religion as its helpmate in the first two stages of identifying our Mission in life, religion repays the compliment by clearly needing career counseling as **its** helpmate here in the third stage.

And this place where you are in your life right now -- facing the job-hunt and all its anxiety -- is the perfect time to seek the union within your own mind and heart of both career counseling (as in the pages of this book) and your faith in God.

Comment 3: How Our Mission Got Chosen: A Scenario for the Romantic

It is a mystery which we cannot fathom, in this life at least, as to why one of us has this talent, and the other one has that; why God chose to give one gift -- and Mission -- to one person, and a different gift -- and Mission -- to another. Since we do not know, and in some degree cannot know, we are certainly left free to speculate, and imagine.

We may imagine that before we came to Earth, our souls, *our Breath, our Light,* stood before the great Creator and volunteered for this Mission. And God and we, together, chose what that Mission would be and what particular gifts would be needed, which He then agreed to give us, after our birth. Thus, our Mission was not a command given preemptorily by an unloving Creator to a reluctant slave without a vote, but was a task jointly designed by us both, in which as fast as the great Creator said, "**I wish**" our hearts responded, "**Oh, yes**." As mentioned in an earlier Comment, it may be helpful to think of the condition of our becoming human as that we became amnesiac about any consciousness our soul had before birth -- and therefore amnesiac about the nature or manner in which our Mission was designed.

Our searching for our Mission now is therefore a searching to recover the memory of something we ourselves had a part in designing.

I am admittedly a hopeless romantic, so of course I like this picture. If you also are a hopeless romantic, you may like it too. There's also the chance that it just may be true. We will not know until we see Him face-to-face.

Comment 4: Mission As Intersection

There are all different kinds of voices calling you to all different kinds of work, and the problem is to find out which is the voice of God rather than that of society, say, or the superego, or self-interest. By and large a good rule for finding out is this: the kind of work God usually calls you to is the kind of work (a) that you need most to do and (b) the world most needs to have done. If you really get a kick out of your work, you've presumably met requirement (a), but if your work is writing TV deodorant commercials, the chances are you've missed requirement (b). On the other hand, if your work is being a doctor in a leper colony, you have probably met (b), but if most of the time you're bored and depressed by it, the chances are you haven't only bypassed (a) but probably aren't helping your patients much either. Neither the hair shirt nor the soft birth will do. **The place God calls you to is the place where your deep gladness and the world's deep hunger meet.**

Fred Buechner
Wishful Thinking -- A Theological ABC

Comment 5: Examples of Mission As Intersection

Your unique and individual mission will most likely turn out to be a mission of Love, acted out in one or all of three arenas: either in the Kingdom of the Mind, whose goal is to bring more Truth into the world; or in the Kingdom of the Heart, whose goal is to bring more beauty into the world; or in the Kingdom of the Will, whose goal is to bring more Perfection into the world, through Service.

Here are some examples:

"My mission is, out of the rich reservoir of love which God seems to have given me, to nurture and show love to others -- most particularly to those who are suffering from incurable diseases."

"My mission is to draw maps for people to show them how to get to God."

"My mission is to create the purest foods I can, to help people's bodies not get in the way of their spiritual growth."

"My mission is to make the finest harps I can so that people can hear the voice of God in the wind."

"My mission is to make people laugh, so that the travail of this earthly life doesn't seem quite so hard to them."

"My mission is to help people know the truth, in love, about what is happening out in the world, so that there will be more honesty in the world."

"My mission is to weep with those who weep, so that in my arms they may feel themselves in the arms of that Eternal Love which sent me and which created them."

"My mission is to create beautiful gardens, so that in the lilies of the field people may behold the Beauty of God and be reminded of the Beauty of Holiness."

Comment 6: Life As Long As Your Mission Requires

Knowing that you came to Earth for a reason, and knowing what that Mission is, throws an entirely different light upon your life from now on. You are, generally speaking, delivered from any further fear about how long you have to live. You may settle it in your heart that you are here until God chooses to think that you have accomplished your Mission, or until God has a greater Mission for you in another Realm. You need to be a good steward of what He has given you, while you are here; but you do not need to be an anxious steward or stewardess.

You need to attend to your health, *but you do not need to constantly worry about it.* You need to meditate on your death, *but you do not need to be constantly preoccupied with it.* To paraphrase the glorious words of G. K. Chesterton: **"We now have a strong desire for living combined with a strange carelessness about dying. We desire life like water and yet are ready to drink death like wine**." We know that we are here to do what we came to do, and we need not worry about anything else.

Final Comment: A Job-Hunt Done Well

If you approach your job-hunt as an opportunity to work on this issue as well as the issue of how you will keep body and soul together, then hopefully your job-hunt will end with your being able to say: "Life has deep meaning to me, now. I have discovered more than my ideal job; I have found my Mission, and the reason why I am here on Earth."

For Further Reading

Most, though not all, of the following resources are written from a Judaic-Christian viewpoint, but they should be suggestive and helpful for people of any faith, as you mentally translate these texts into your own thought-forms and concepts of your faith:

Kise, Jane A.G., and Stark, David, and Hirsh, Sandra Krebs, *LifeKeys: Discovering Who You Are, Why You're Here, What You Do Best.* Bethany House Publishers, 11300 Hampshire Ave. South, Minneapolis, MN 55438. 1996. A course, integrating the Myers-Briggs Type Indicator, and Scripture.

Haldane, Bernard, and Haldane, Jean M., *Gifts: Dependable Strengths for Your Future; With A Theology of Work.* Dependable Strengths Institute, 1402 Third Ave., #1330, Seattle, WA 98101. 1997.

Buford, Bob, *Half-Time: Changing Your Game Plan from Success to Significance.* 1994. Zondervan Publishing House, Grand Rapids, MI 49530. Bob has authored a follow-up to *Half-Time,* called *Game Plan.* Same publisher. 1997.

Blanchard, Ken, *We Are the Beloved: A Spiritual Journey.* 1994. Zondervan Publishing House, Grand Rapids, MI 49530. By the co-author of *The One Minute Manager.*

Lewis, Roy, *Choosing Your Career, Finding Your Vocation: A Step by Step Guide for Adults and Counselors.* 1990. Integration Books, Paulist Press, 997 Macarthur Blvd., Mahwah, NJ 07430. Particularly helpful for mid-life issues.

Blanchard, Tim, *A Practical Guide to Finding and Using Your Spiritual Gifts.* 1983. Tyndale House Publishers, Inc., Box 80, Wheaton, IL 60189.

Edwards, Lloyd, *Discerning Your Spiritual Gifts.* 1988. Cowley Publications, 28 Temple Place, Boston, MA 02111.

Roskind, Robert, *In The Spirit of Business: Applying the Principles of* A Course in Miracles *to Business.* 1992. Celestial Arts, P.O. Box 7123, Berkeley, CA 94707.

A Center for the Practice of Zen Buddhist Meditation, *That Which You Are Seeking Is Causing You to Seek.* Available from the Center, P.O. Box 91, Mountain View, CA 94042. 1990. A *great* title, and a very interesting book, written -- of course -- from the Buddhist point of view, with one of the contributors being a woman who was at that time dying from cancer. (She has passed away, since.)

Mattson, Ralph, and Miller, Arthur, *Finding a Job You Can Love.* 1982. Thomas Nelson Publishers, Nelson Place at Elm Hill Pike, Nashville, TN 37214. The most useful, I think, of all the books in this section. It is now out-of-print at the moment, but (while copies last) you can procure a copy directly from Arthur Miller, at 203-868-0317.

Kreinberg, Luke, *The Book of Goals.* 1994. First Step Publishing, P.O. Box 1092, Mill Valley, CA 94942. I know a woman who was able to turn her life around by taking large goals for her life, and breaking them down into smaller, more manageable projects or tasks. Soon she -- who had told herself she wasn't accomplishing anything with her life -- was deriving a great deal of benefit from a new-found sense of accomplishment. This book aims to help you with a number of journal pages, where you can take the same steps that she took: breaking larger life goals down into simpler *steps.*

For Counseling

All counselors in these centers are sincere; many are also very skilled. If you run into a clerical counselor who is sincere but inept, you will probably discover that the ineptness consists in an inadequate understanding of the distinction I mention in the next section -- namely, the distinction between career **assessment** -- roughly comparable to taking a snapshot of people as they are in one frozen moment of time -- vs. career **development** -- which is roughly comparable to teaching people how to take their own motion pictures of themselves, from here on out.

Having issued this caution, however, I will go on to add that at some of these centers, listed below, are some simply *excellent* counselors who fully understand this distinction, and are well trained in that empowering of the client, which is what career *development* is all about.

We begin with counseling centers founded primarily to help **clergy** (though in most cases not restricted just to them). No profession has developed, or had developed for it, so many resources to aid in career assessment as has this profession.

THE OFFICIAL INTERDENOMINATIONAL CAREER DEVELOPMENT CENTERS

The Career and Personal
Counseling Service
St. Andrew's Presbyterian
College, Laurinburg,
NC 28352
919-276-3162
Also at: 4108 Park Rd.,
Suite 200,
Charlotte, NC 28209
704-523-7751
Elbert R. Patton, Director

The Career and Personal
Counseling Center
Eckerd College
St. Petersburg, FL 33733
813-864-8356, Ext. 356
John R. Sims, Director

The Center for Ministry
8393 Capwell Dr., Suite 220
Oakland, CA 94621-2123
510-635-4246
Robert L. Charpentier, Director

Lancaster Career
Development Center
561 College Ave.
Lancaster, PA 17603
717-397-7451
L. Guy Mehl, Director

North Central Career
Development Center
516 Mission House Lane
New Brighton, MN 55112
612-636-5120
Kenneth J. McFayden, Ph.D.,
Director

Northeast Career Center
407 Nassau Street
Princeton, NJ 08540
609-924-9408
Roy Lewis, Director

Career Development
Center of the Southeast
531 Kirk Rd.
Decatur, GA 30030
404-371-0336
Earl B. Stewart, D. Min., Director

Midwest Career
Development Service
1840 Westchester Blvd.,
Westchester, IL 60154
708-343-6268
Also at: 1520 Old Henderson Rd.,
Suite 102B,
Columbus, OH 43221-3616
614-442-8822
Also at: 754 N. 31st St.,
Kansas City, KS 66110-0816.
Ronald Brushwyler, Director

Southwest Career
Development Center
Box 5923
Arlington, TX 76005
817-640-5181
Jerry D. Overton
Director-Counselor

Center for Career
Development and Ministry
70 Chase St.
Newton Center, MA 02159
617-969-7750
Stephen Ott, Director.

Clergy wishing to stay within the parish ministry, but wanting help with the search, will want to know about:

Mead, Loren B., and Miller, Arthur F., and Ayers, Russell C., and Bolles, Richard N., *Your Next Pastorate: Starting the Search.* Order #AL122 from The Alban Institute, Inc., 4125 Nebraska Ave., N.W., Washington, DC 20016.

And now, on to centers which are open to anyone, and do career counseling from a spiritual point of view:

ALSO DOING CAREER COUNSELING FROM A RELIGIOUS POINT OF VIEW

(*These are listed by general geographical location, from West Coast to East Coast, North to South)*

People Management Group International, 924 First Street, Suite A, **Snohomish, WA** 98290. 206-563-0105. Arthur F. Miller, Jr., Chairman.

Bernard Haldane, 2821 2nd Ave., Suite 1002, **Seattle, WA** 98121. 206-448-0881. A pioneer in the clergy career management and assessment field, Bernard teaches *(totally independently of the agency which bears his name)* seminars and training of volunteers (particularly in churches) to do job-search counseling.

Career Development and Vocational Testing Services, 2515 Park Marina, Suite 203-B, **Redding, CA** 96001. 916-246-2871.

Lizbeth Miller, M.S., 3880 S. Bascom Ave., Suite 202, **San Jose, CA** 95124. 408-486-6763. Affiliated with the Christian Counseling Center.

Lifework Design, 448 S. Marengo Ave., **Pasadena, CA** 91101, 818-577-2705. Kevin Brennfleck, M.A., and Kay Marie Brennfleck, M.A., Directors.

Harlan H. Shippy, M.Div., Ph.D., Counseling Ministries, 8035 La Mesa Blvd., **La Mesa, CA** 91941-6434. 619-462-2277.

Occupational and Career Services, Inc., 3311 N. 44th St., Suite 120, **Phoenix, AZ** 85018. 602-840-9084. Julie A. Schwartz, M.S., C.R.C.

Olson Counseling Services, 8720 Frederick, Suite 105, **Omaha, NE** 68124, 402-390-2342. Gail A. Olson, P.A.C.

Ministry of Counseling and Enrichment, 1333 N. 2nd St., **Abilene, TX** 79601, 915-675-8131. Mary Stedham, Director.

New Life Institute, Box 1666, **Austin, TX** 78767, 512-469-9447. Bob Breihan, Director.

Institute of Worklife Ministry, 2650 Fountainview Drive, Suite 444, **Houston, TX** 77057, 713-266-2456. Diana C. Dale, Director.

Life/Career Planning Center for Religious, 10526 W. Cermak Rd., Suite 111, **Westchester, IL** 60153, 708-531-9228. Dolores Linhart, Director. Doing work with Roman Catholics.

Life Stewardship Associates, 6918 Glen Creek Dr., SE, **Dutton, MI** 49316, 616-698-3125. Ken Soper, M.Div., M.A., Director.

Professional Pastoral Counseling Institute, Inc., 8035 Hosbrook Rd., Suite 300, **Cincinnati, OH** 45236. 513-771-5990. Judy Kroger, Counselor.

Career Resources, 2323 Hillsboro Rd., Suite 508, **Nashville, TN** 37212. 615-297-0404. Jane C. Hardy, Principal.

RHM Group, P.O.Box 271135, **Nashville, TN** 37227, 615-391-5000. Robert H. McKown.

Career Achievement, NiS International Services, 1321 Murfreesboro Road., Suite 610, **Nashville, TN** 37217, 615-367-5000. William L. (Bill) Karlson, Harry McClure, Manager.

Mid-South Career Development Center, 2315 Fisher Place, **Knoxville, TN** 37920, 615-573-1340. W. Scott Root, Director.

Dan Miller, The Business Source, 7100 Executive Center Drive, Suite 110, **Brentwood, TN** 37027. 615-373-7771.

Career and Personal Counseling Center, 1904 Mt. Vernon St., **Waynesboro, VA** 22980, 703-943-9997. Lillian Pennell, Director.

Center for Growth & Change, Inc., 6991 Peachtree Ind. Blvd., Suite 310, **Norcross, GA** 30092, 404-441-9580. James P. Hicks, Ph.D., L.P.C., Director.

Career Pathways, 601 Broad St., **Gainesville, GA** 30501, 800-722-1976. Lee Ellis, Director. Offers career-guidance from a Christian point of view, through the mails -- based on questionnaires and various instruments or inventories which they send you.

Call to Career, 8720 Georgia Ave., Suite 802, **Silver Spring, MD** 20910. 301-961-1017. Cheryl Palmer, M.Ed., NCC, NCCC, President.

Judith Gerberg Associates, 250 West 57th St., **New York, NY** 10107, 212-315-2322. Judith Gerberg.

VI. If You Decide You Need A Career Counselor

How to Choose a Career Counselor,

LOOK BEFORE YOU LEAP:

There are two basic types of career counselors.

One type's primary expertise is in the area called 'career development' or 'career assessment.' They help people figure out what they want to do with their lives, by way of career choice, etc. They *may* know very little about the actual job-hunting process.

The other type almost always also knows something about 'career development' or 'career assessment,' but their *primary* expertise is in the job-search process.

Some of these follow the *traditional* approach: resumes and interviewing. If you have already given up on that traditional approach, then this is not the counselor for you.

Others follow the *creative* process of job-hunting, described in Chapter 5, in this book. This is the kind you want.

All counselors, of either type, divide into a) sincere and good at what they do; or b) sincere and inept; or c) wolves in sheep's clothing, ready to take you to the cleaners (or to the shearing).

No one has a list of counselors who are sincere and good at what they do, either in this country or in any other part of the world.

if you decide you need one

You have to go find them yourself, and this is particularly true if you live outside a major city or you live outside the United States. You *can* do it. It's just going to take some work. And before you begin, you need to keep some principles in mind:

What you're looking for in them, besides a firm grasp of the whole job-hunting process at its most creative and effective level, is that they be someone you feel true *rapport* with. You *like* them. You *trust* them.

You've got to do your own homework, or research, here, and your own interviewing, in your own geographical area, or you will deserve what you get.

No one but you knows whether or not you're going to get along with a particular career counselor. Maybe he's a wonderful man, but unhappily he reminds you of your Uncle Harry. You've always **hated** your Uncle Harry. No one knows that, but you. Or maybe the counselor is a wonderful woman, but unhappily . . . *well, you get the point.*

No one can do this research for you. Because the real question is not "Who is best?" but "Who is best **for you**?" Those last two words demand that it be you who 'makes the call.'

Now, what do you want? First of all, you want **names**.

You want to find the names of at least **three** career counselors in your community.

Where do you find names?

First, from your friends: ask if any of them have ever used a career counselor. And if so, what is that counselor's name; and what did they think of them.

Secondly, from the *Sampler* toward the rear of this section of *The Resource Guide*. See if there are any names near you. They may know how you find out the other names in your community.

Try also your telephone book's local Yellow Pages, under such headings as: *Aptitude and Employment Testing, Career and Vocational Counseling, Personnel Consultants* and (if you are a woman) *Women's Organizations and Services.* You will discover that even the Yellow Pages can't keep up with the additional groups that spring up daily, weekly, and monthly -- including job clubs and other group activities. The most comprehensive list of these, in the U.S., is to be found in the *National Business Employment Weekly*, on its pages called "Calendar of Career Events." It is an extensive listing. Available on newsstands, $3.95 per issue; or, order an issue directly from: National Business Employment Weekly, P.O. Box 300, Princeton, NJ 08543. Their phone is: 800-JOB-HUNT, or 800-562-4868.

Then you want **talk**.

You want to go talk with all three of them, and decide which of the three (if any) you want to hook up with.

You're going to be doing comparison shopping.

You visit in person each of the three places you have chosen. Don't try to do this over the telephone, *please!* There is so much more you can tell, when you're looking the person straight in the eyes. Note well: if this is a firm, trying to sell you a package, they will almost certainly give you the initial interview for free. On the other hand, if it's an individual counselor, who charges by the hour, you *are* going to have to pay them for this exploratory hour, or part of an hour -- even if it's only five or ten minutes. Do not expect that individual counselors can afford to give you this exploratory interview for nothing! If they did that, and got a lot of requests like yours, they would never be able to make a living. You do have the right, however, to inquire *ahead of time* how much they are going to have to charge you for the exploratory interview.

When you are face-to-face with the firm or with the individual counselor, you ask *each* of them the same questions, listed on the form below. (Keep a little pad or notebook with you, so you can write their answers down.) When you get home, study all their answers, compare the three, and see if any of them interests you.

MY SEARCH FOR A GOOD CAREER COUNSELOR

Questions I will Ask Them	Answer from counselor #1	Answer from counselor #2	Answer from counselor #3
1. What is your program?			
2. Who will be doing it? And how long have you been doing it?			
3. What is your success rate?			
4. What is the cost of your services?			
5. Is there a contract?			

Remember, you don't have to choose any of the three counselors, if you didn't really care for any of them. If that is the case, then choose three new counselors, dust off the notebook, and go out again. It may take a few more hours to find what you want. But the wallet, the purse, the job-hunt, the life, you save will be your own.

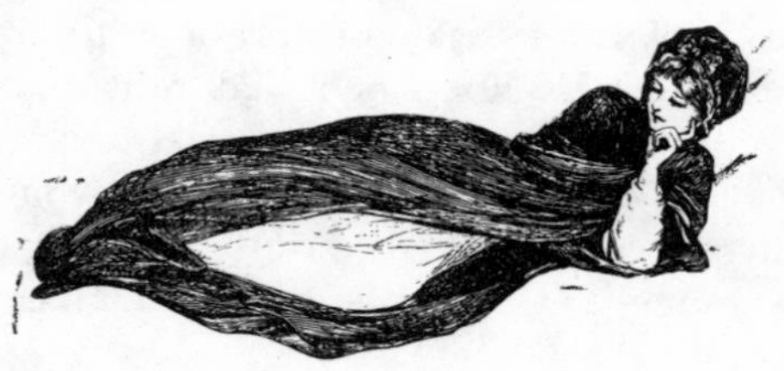

Back home now, after visiting the three places you chose for your comparison shopping, you have to decide: a) whether you want none of the three, or b) one of the three (and if so, which one). Look over your notes on all three places. Compare those places. The simple fact is: there is no definitive way for you to determine a career counselor's expertise. It's something you'll have to smell out, as you go along. But here are some clues:

BAD ANSWERS

• If they give you the feeling that everything will be done for you, by them (including interpretation of tests, and decision making about what this means you should do, or where you should do it) -- rather than you having to do all the work, with their basically assuming the role of coach,

(15 bad points)

You want to learn how to do this for yourself; you're going to be job-hunting again, you know.

• If they say they are not the person who will be doing the program with you, but deny you any chance to meet the counselor you would be working with,

(75 bad points)

You're talking to a salesperson. Avoid any *firm that has a salesperson.*

• If you do get a chance to meet the counselor, but you don't like the counselor as a person,

(150 bad points)

I don't care what their expertise is, if you don't like them, you're going to have a rough time getting what you want. I guarantee it. Rapport is everything.

• If you ask how long the counselor has been doing this, and they get huffy or give a double-barreled answer, such as: "I've had eighteen years' experience in the business and career counseling world,"

(20 bad points)

What that may mean is: seventeen and a half years as a fertilizer salesman, and one-half year doing career counseling. Persist. "How long have you been with this firm, and how long have you been doing formal career counseling, as you are here?"

You might be interested to know that some executive or career counseling firms hire yesterday's clients as today's new staff. Such new staff are sometimes given training only after they're "on-the-job." They are practicing on you.

• If they try to answer the question of their experience by pointing to their degrees or credentials,

(3 bad points)

Degrees or credentials tell you they've passed certain tests of their qualifications, but often these tests bear more on their expertise at career assessment than on their knowledge of creative job-hunting.

• If, when you ask about their success rate, they say they have never had a client that failed to find a job, no matter what,

(15 bad points)

They're lying. I have studied career counseling programs for over twenty years, have attended many, have studied records at State and Federal offices, and I have hardly ever seen a program that placed more than 86% of their clients, tops, in their best years. And it goes downhill from there. A prominent executive counseling firm was reported by the Attorney General's Office of New York State to have placed only 38 out of 550 clients (a 93% failure rate).[1] *If they make it clear that they have had a good success rate, but if you fail to work hard at the whole process, then there is no guarantee you are going to find a job, give them three stars.*

• If they show you letters from ecstatically-happy former clients, but when you ask to talk to some of those clients, you get stone-walled.

(45 bad points)

I quote from one job-hunter's letter to me: "I asked to speak to a former client or clients. You would of thought I asked to speak to Elvis. The Counselor stammered and stuttered and gave me a million excuses why I couldn't talk to some of these 'satisfied' former clients. None of the excuses sounded legitimate to me. We went back and forth for about thirty minutes. Finally, he excused himself and went to speak to his boss, the owner. The next thing I knew I was called into the owner's office for a more 'personal' sales pitch. We spoke for about 45 minutes as he tried to convince me to use his service. When I told him I was not ready to sign up, he became angry and asked my Counselor why I had been put before 'the committee' if I wasn't ready to commit? The Counselor claimed I had given a verbal commitment at our last meeting. The owner then turned to me and said I seemed to have a problem making a decision and that he did not want to do business with me. I was shocked. They had turned the whole story around to make it look like it was my fault. I felt humiliated. In retrospect, the whole process felt like dealing with a used car salesman. They used pressure tactics and intimidation to try to get what they wanted. As you have probably gathered, more than anything else this experience made me angry."

---

1. For further details, go to your local library and look up "Career Counselors: Will They Lead You Down The Primrose Path?" by Lee Guthrie, in the December 1981 issue of *Savvy* Magazine, pp. 60ff.

• If they claim they only accept 5 clients out of every hundred who apply, and your name will have to be put before 'The Committee' before you can be accepted.

(1000 bad points)

This is one of the oldest tricks in the book. You're supposed to feel 'special' before they lift those thousands of dollars out of your wallet. Personally, the minute I heard this at a particular agency or service, I would run for the door and never look back.

• If you ask what is the cost of their services, and they reply that it is a lump sum that must all be paid "up front" before you start or shortly after you start, either all at once or in installments,

(100 bad points)

For twenty-five years I've tried to avoid saying this, but I have grown weary of the tears of job-hunters who 'got taken.' So now I say it without reservation: if the firm charges a lump sum for their services, rather than allowing you to simply pay for each hour as you go, go elsewhere. Every insincere and inept counselor or firm charges a lump sum. So, of course, do a few *sincere and good counselors and firms. Trouble is: you won't know which kind you've signed up with, until they've got all your money. The risk is too great, the cost is too high. If you really like to gamble that much, go to Las Vegas. They give better odds.*

• If they asked you to bring in your partner or spouse with you,

(45 bad points)

This is a well-known tactic of some of the slickest salespeople in the world, who want your spouse or partner there so they can manipulate one or the other or both of you to reach a decision on the spot, while they have you in their 'grasp.'

• If they ask you to sign a contract,

(1000 bad points)

With insincere and inept firms or counselors, there is always a written contract. And you must sign it, before they will help you. (Often, your partner or spouse will be asked to sign it, too.) The fee normally ranges from $1000 on up to $10,000 or more. You may think the purpose of that firm's contract is that they are promising you something, that they can be held to. Uh-uh! *More often, the main purpose of the contract is to get you to promise them something. Like, your money. Don't . . . do . . . it.*

You will sometimes be told that, "Of course, you can get your money back, or a portion of it, at any time, should you be dissatisfied with the career counselor's services." Nine times out of ten, however, you are told this verbally, and it is not in the written contract. Verbal promises, without witnesses, are difficult if not impossible for you to later try to enforce. The written contract is binding.

Sometimes the written contract will claim to provide for a partial refund, at any time, until you reach a cut-off date in the program, which the contract specifies. Unfortunately, many crafty fraudulent firms bend over backwards to be extra nice, extra available, and extra helpful to you until that cut-off point is reached. So, when the cut-off point for getting a refund has been reached, you let it pass because you are very satisfied with their past services, and believe there will be many more weeks of the same. Only, there aren't. At fraudulent firms, once the cut-off point is passed, the career counselor becomes virtually impossible for you to get ahold of. Call after call will not be

returned. You will say to yourself "What happened?" Well, what happened, my friend, is that you paid up in full, they have all the money they're ever going to get out of you, and now they don't want to give you any more time.

You may think I am exaggerating: I mean, can there possibly be such mean men and women, who would prey on job-hunters, when they're down and out. Yes, ma'am, and yes, sir, there are. That's why you have to do this preliminary research so thoroughly.

I quote from the late Robert Wegmann, former director of the UHCL Center for Labor Market Studies: "One high-charging career counseling firm went bankrupt a few years ago. They left many of their materials behind in their former office. A box of what they abandoned has come into my possession. Going through the contents of the box has been fascinating.

"Particularly interesting are several scripts used to train their salespeople. The goal of the sales pitch is to convince the unemployed (or unhappily employed) person that he or she can't find a good job alone, but can do it with professional help. Hiring us, they argue, is just like hiring a lawyer . . .

"Then, at the end of the pitch, comes the 'takeaway.' The firm may not accept your money, you are warned! There will have to be a review board meeting at which your application is considered. Only a minority of applicants are accepted. The firm only wants the right kind of clients.

"That's the pitch. But the rest of the documents tell a very different story. In fact, the firm is running a series of sales contests with all the 'professionalism' of a used car lot . . .

"These salespeople were paid on commission. The higher the sales the higher the percentage of the customer's fee they got to keep.

"There are sales contests. The winner receives a handsome green Master's jacket. Each monthly winner qualifies for a Grand Master's Tournament, with large prizes. . .

"So take this one piece of advice. . . . If someone offers to help you find a great job as long as you'll pay several thousand dollars in advance, do as follows:

"A. Find door

"B. Walk out same

"C. Do not return."

Over the last twenty years, I have had to listen to grown men and women cry over the telephone, all because they signed a contract. Most often they were executives, or senior managers, who never had to go job-hunting before, and unknowingly signed up with some executive counseling firm that was fraudulent, or at least on the edge of legality.

If you want to avoid their tears in your own job-search, don't sign anything--ever.[2]

---

2. If you are **dying** to know more, and your local library has back files of magazines and newspapers (on microfiche, or otherwise) there was a period when bad firms and counselors came under heavy fire (1978-1982) and you can look up some of the articles of that period, as well as those articles which have appeared more recently, to wit:

"A Consumer's Guide to Retail Job-Hunting Services," Special Report, reprinted from the *National Business Employment Weekly;* available from National Business Employment Weekly Reprint Service, P.O. Box 300, Princeton, NJ 08543-0300. 1-800-730-1111. $8 by mail; $12.95 by fax. A *very* thorough series of articles on the industry, and its frauds, which names *names,* and gives the addresses of Consumer protection agencies in each state, to whom you may complain. **Required reading** for anyone who wants to avoid getting 'burned.'

"'Employment counselors' costly, target of gripes," *The Arizona Republic,* 10/8/89.

"Career-Counseling Industry Accused of Misrepresentation," *New York Times,* 9/30/82.

"Consumer Law: Career Counselors and Employment Agencies" by Reed Brody, *New York Law Journal,* Feb. 26, 1982, p. 1. Reed was Assistant Attorney General of the State of New York, and more recently Deputy Chief of the Labor Bureau within that State's Department of Law; in this capacity he became the leading legal expert in the country, on career counseling malpractices, though unfortunately (for us) he now works overseas in Europe, in another profession.

"Career Counselors: Will They Lead You Down the Primrose Path?" by Lee Guthrie, *Savvy* Magazine, 12/81, p. 60ff.

"Franklin Career Search Is Accused of Fraud In New York State Suit," *Wall Street Journal,* 1/29/81, p. 50.

"Job Counseling Firms Under Fire For Promising Much, Giving Little," *Wall Street Journal,* 1/27/81, p. 33.

Of course, you're tempted to skip over all this research and visiting and questioning, aren't you? *"Well, I'll just call up one place, and if I like the sound of them, I'll sign up. I'm a pretty good judge of character."* Right. I hear many a sad tale from people who had this over-confidence in their ability to detect a phony, and then found out too late that they had been *taken,* by slicker salespeople than they had ever run into before. As they tell me their stories, they *cry* over the telephone. My reply usually is, "I'm sorry indeed to hear that you had a very disappointing experience; that is very unfortunate, But -- as the Scots would say -- "Ya dinna do your homework. Often you could easily have discovered whether a particular counselor was competent or not, before you ever gave them any of your money, simply by asking the right questions during your preliminary research."[3]

Alternatively, people try to avoid all this research by saying, "Well, I'll just see who Bolles recommends." That takes a leap, because I never recommend *any* agency or counselors -- though some try to claim I do. *(Rockport Institute in Maryland is one example that comes to mind; I just read them, yesterday, claiming this on the Internet.)* In this book, now and in the past, all that I ever list are '*examples*' of the type of agencies out there, and I do this purely as a public service to my readers. But, such an inclusion in this book does *not* constitute an endorsement or recommendation by me -- as I have been at great pains to make clear for the past twenty-five years. Never has. Never will.

Faced with this silence on my part, some readers, then, have *tried to read between the lines.* I can give you an example. Because I allude to the wisdom of *the man* Bernard Haldane in this book, some readers have assumed that this means *the agency* which bears his name must be recommended by me. Nope. Nada. Never.

The man is the oldest figure in this field -- he is eighty-six -- and was the original fountainhead in the '40s and '50s of many ideas that help job-hunters today. He is justly venerated, and as I just said to him when we were together recently, I appreciate all that he has contributed over the past 50 years.

But *the agency* which bears his name is another kettle of fish, entirely. Bernard gave up ownership of that agency years ago. And, for my part, I have neither gone to that agency *(as some of their counselors have claimed)* nor recommended them.

So, in sum: *don't* try to 'read between the lines.'

Go do your own homework.

Ask searching questions of *anyone* you are thinking of signing up with. And remember, my advice -- for what it's worth: don't sign up with *anyone* who offers you a contract, or charges other than by the hour.

GOOD ANSWERS

Fortunately there are career counselors who charge by the hour. With them, there is no written contract. You sign nothing. You pay only for each hour as you use it, according to their set rate. Each time you keep an appointment, you pay them at the end of that hour for their help, according to that rate. Period. Finis. You never owe them any money. You can stop seeing them at any time, if you feel you are not getting the help you wish.

What will they charge? You will find, these days, that the best career counselors (and some of the worst, too) will charge you whatever a really good therapist or marriage counselor charges per hour, in your geographical area. Currently, in large metropolitan areas, that runs around $100 an hour, sometimes more. In suburbia or rural areas, it may be much less -- $40 an hour, or so.

That fee is for individual time with the career counselor. If you can't afford that fee, ask whether they also run groups. If they do, the fee will be much less. And, in one of those delightful ironies of life, since you get a chance to listen to problems which other job-hunters in your group are

A Sampler

This is not a complete directory of anything. It is exactly what its name implies: a **Sampler**. Were I to list all the career counselors *out there,* we would end up with an encyclopedia. Some states, in fact, have *encyclopedic* lists of counselors and businesses, in various books or directories, and your local bookstore or library should have these, in their *Job-Hunting Section,* under such titles as "How to Get A Job in . . ." or "Job-Hunting in . . ."

Most of the places listed in this **Sampler** are listed at their own request, simply as places for you to begin your investigation with -- nothing more.

Many truly *helpful* places are *not* listed here. If you discover such a place, which is very good at helping people with *Parachute* and creative job-hunting or career-change, do send us the pertinent information. We will ask them, as we do all the listings here, a few intelligent questions and if they sound okay, we will add that place to next year's edition.

We do ask a few questions because our readers want counselors and places which claim some expertise in helping them finish their job-hunt, *using this book.* So, if they've never even heard of *Parachute,* we don't list them. On the other hand, we can't measure a place's expertise at this long distance, no matter how many questions we ask.

Even if listed here, you must do your own sharp questioning before you decide to go with anyone. If you don't take time to research two or three places, before choosing a counselor, you will deserve whatever you get (or, more to the point, *don't* get). So, please, *do your research.* The purse or wallet you save, will be your own.

Yearly readers of this book will notice that we do remove people from this Sampler, without warning. Specifically, we remove (without further notice or comment): ➡

having, the group will often give you more help than an individual session would. Not always; but often. It's always ironic when *cheaper* and *more helpful* go hand in hand.

If the career counselor in question does offer groups, there should (again) never be a contract. The charge should be payable at the end of each session, and you should be able to drop out at any time, without further cost, if you decide you are not getting the help you want.

There are, incidentally, some career counselors who run free (or almost free) job-hunting workshops through local churches, synagogues, chambers of commerce, community colleges, adult education programs, and the like, as their community service, or pro bono work (as it is technically called). I have had reports of such workshops from a number of places in the U.S. and Canada. They surely exist in other parts of the world as well. If money is a big problem for you, in getting help with your job-hunt, ask around to see if such workshops as these exist in your community. Your Chamber of Commerce will likely know, or your church or synagogue.

The listings which follow are alphabetical within each state, except that

A Sampler, continued

Places which have moved, and don't bother to send us their new address. If you are listed here, we expect you to be a professional at *communication.* When you move, your first priority should be to let us know, *immediately.* As one exemplary counselor just wrote: "You are the first person I am contacting on my updated letterhead . . . hot off the press just today!" So it should always be. A number of places get removed every year, precisely because of their poor communication skills, and their sloppiness in letting us know where they've gone to. *Other causes for removal:*

Places which have disconnected their telephone, or otherwise suggest that they have gone out of business.

Places which our readers lodge complaints against, with us, as being either unhelpful or obnoxious. The complaints may be falsified, but we can't take that chance.

Places which change their personnel, and the new person has never even heard of *Parachute,* or creative job-search techniques.

Places which misuse their listing here, claiming in their brochures, ads, or interviews, that they have some kind of 'Parachute Seal of Approval' -- that we feature them in *Parachute,* or recommend them or endorse them. This is a big 'no-no.' A listing here is no more of a recommendation than is a listing in the phone book.

College services that we discover (belatedly) serve only '*Their Own.*'

Counseling firms which employ salespeople as the initial 'in-take' person that a job-hunter meets.

If you discover that any of the places listed in this Sampler falls into any of the above categories, you would be doing a great service to our other readers by dropping us a line and telling us so. (P.O. Box 379, Walnut Creek, CA 94597.)

counselors listed by their name are in alphabetical order according to their *last* name. To make this clear, only their last name is in **bold** type.

What do the letters after their name mean? Well, B.A., M.A. and Ph.D. you know. However, don't assume the degree is in career counseling. Ask. N.C.C. means "Nationally certified counselor." There are about 20,000 such in the U.S. This can mean *general counseling expertise,* not necessarily career counseling. On the other hand, N.C.C.C. does mean "Nationally certified career counselor." There are currently about 850 in the U.S. Other initials, such as L.P.C. -- "Licensed professional counselor" -- and the like, often refer to State licensing. There are a number of States, now, that have some sort of regulation of career counselors. In some States it is mandatory, in others it is optional. But, *mostly,* this field is unregulated.

In the early days, say twenty years ago, we used to list quite a bit of information about each place: fees, services, hours, etc. Unfortunately, as requests grew that places be listed, we had to abbreviate the information in the listings. Among the other things **not** listed here: their fax, their e-mail, their website (if they have one). Not only "space considerations" but "personal philosophy" enters in, here. I intend to list only counselors whom you can go to see face to face. Listing those who can be approached more impersonally, say through websites or through e-mail, would involve worldwide listings, and of course would *balloon* this list to the size of a telephone book.

Incidentally, some of the places listed in the Sampler offer group career counseling, some offer testing, some offer access to job-banks, etc. You have their phone number, here. Call, and ask.

One final note: generally speaking, the places listed in the Sampler counsel *anybody.* A few, however, may have restrictions unknown to us *("we counsel only women," etc.).* If they aren't able to help you, your phone call wasn't wasted, *so long as* you then go on to ask them "who else in the area can you tell me about, who helps with job-search, and are there any (among them) that you think are particularly effective?"

If you are looking for places which specialize in doing career counseling from a religious point of view, these are listed separately on page 239ff. However, many of the counselors listed below are also people of faith.

ALABAMA

(There is a new area code in Alabama, 334, which may affect some of the numbers below.)

Career Decisions, 638 Winwood Dr., Birmingham, AL 35226. 205-822-8662, or 205-870-2639. Carrie Pearce Hild, M.S.Ed., Career Counselor and Consultant.

Maureen J. **Chemsak**, NCC, NCCC, LPC, Director of Counseling and Career Services, Athens State College, 300 North Beaty St., Athens, AL 35611. 205-233-8285 or 205-830-4610.

Enterprise State Junior College, P.O. Box 1300, Enterprise, AL 36331. 205-347-2623 or 393-ESJC. Nancy Smith, Director of Guidance Services.

Interchange, 2 Perimeter Park S., Suite 200W, Birmingham, AL 35243. 205-324-5030. Michael Tate, Vice-President.

ALASKA

Career Transitions, 4241 B St., Suite 306, Anchorage, AL 99503. 907-561-5445. Deeta Lonergan, Director.

ARIZONA

(There is a new area code in Arizona, 520, which may affect some of the numbers below.)

Career/Life Planning Services, SummerSmith Inc., 4740 E.Sunrise Dr., #323, Tucson, AZ 85718. 520-529-1565. Janet Summers, MEd., President.

Debra Davenport Associates, Center for Creative Living, 6945 E. Cochise Rd., Suite 138, Scottsdale, AZ 85253. 602-368-9801. Debra Davenport, M.A., L.C.C.

Occupational and Career Services, Inc., 3311 N. 44th St., Suite 120, Phoenix, AZ 85018. 602-840-9084. Julie A. Schwartz, M.S., C.R.C.

Southwest Institute of Life Management, 11122 E. Gunshot Circle, Tucson, AZ 85749. 602-749-2290. Theodore Donald Risch, Director.

ARKANSAS

Donald **McKinney,** Ed.D., Career Counselor, Rt. 1, Box 351-A, DeQueen, AR 71832. 501-642-5628.

CALIFORNIA

(Note: some 310 area codes, listed below, will change to 562 no later than February 1, 1997.)

Alumnae Resources, 120 Montgomery St., Suite 1080, San Francisco, CA 94104. 415-274-4700.

Judy Kaplan **Baron Associates,** 6046 Cornerstone Ct. West, Suite 208, San Diego, CA 92121. 619-558-7400. Judy Kaplan Baron, Director.

Astrid **Berg**, M.S., Career and Life Planning, P.O. Box 1686, Capitola, CA 95010. 408-462-4626.

Dwayne **Berrett**, M.A., RPCC, Berrett & Associates, 1551 E. Shaw, Suite 103, Fresno, CA 93710. 209-221-6543.

Beverly **Brown**, M.A., N.C.C.C., N.C.C. 809 So. Bundy Drive, #105, Los Angeles, CA 90049. 310-447-7093.

Career Action Center, 10420 Bubb Rd., Suite 100, Cupertino, CA 95014-4150. 408-253-3200. Betsy Collard, Director, Strategic Development, Linda Surrell, Manager, Counseling Services. *A tremendously impressive career center, one of the most comprehensive in the U.S., with a large number of job listings (81,000) and other resources, including individual counseling, workshops, books, videos, etc.*

Career and Personal Development Institute, 690 Market St., Suite 402, San Francisco, CA 94104. 415-982-2636. Bob Chope.

Career Decisions, 760 Market St., Suite 925, San Francisco CA 94102-2304. 415-296-7373. Mark Pope, Ed.D., NCC, NCCC.

Career Development Center, John F. Kennedy University, 1250 Arroyo Way, Walnut Creek, CA 94596. 510-295-0610. Susan Geifman, Director. *Open to the public. Membership or fee.*

Career Development Life Planning, 3585 Maple St., Suite 237, Ventura, CA 93003. 805-656-6220. Norma Zuber, N.C.C.C., M.S.C., & Associates.

Career Dimensions, Box 7402, Stockton, CA 95267. 209-957-6465. Fran Abbott.

Career Directions, 215 Witham Road, Encinitas CA 92024. 619-436-3994. Virginia Byrd, M.Ed., Work/Life Specialist, Career Management.

Career Planning Center/Business Action Center, 1623 S. La Cienega Blvd., Los Angeles, CA 90035. 310-273-6633.

Career Strategy Associates, 1100 Quail Street, Suite 201, Newport Beach, CA 92660. 714-252-0515. Betty Fisher.

Center for Career Growth and Development, P.O. Box 283, Los Gatos, CA 95031. 408-354-7150. Steven E. Beasley.

Center for Creative Change, 3130 West Fox Run Way, San Diego, CA 92111. 619-268-9340. Nancy Helgeson, M.A., MFCC.

The **Center for Life and Work Planning,** 1133 Second St., Encinitas, CA 92024. 619-943-0747. Mary C. McIsaac, Executive Director.

Stephen **Cheney-Rice**, M.S., 2113 Westboro Ave., Alhambra, CA 91803-3720. 818-281-6066, or 213-740-9112.

Constructive Leisure, Patsy B. Edwards, 511 N. La Cienega Blvd., Los Angeles, CA 90048. 310-652-7389.

Consultants in Career Development, 2017 Palo Verde Ave., Suite 201B, Long Beach, CA 90815. 310-598-6412. Dean Porter and Mary Claire Gildon.

Cricket Consultants, 502 Natoma St., P.O. Box 6191, Folsom, CA 95763-6191. 916-985-3211. Bruce Parrish, M.S., CDMS.

Cypress College, Career Planning Center, 9200 Valley View St., Cypress, CA 90630. 714-826-2220, Ext. 120.

Margaret L. **Eadie,** M.A., A.M.Ed. Career Consultant, 1000 Sage Pl., Pacific Grove, CA 93950. 408-373-7400.

Experience Unlimited Job Club. There are 35 Experience Unlimited Clubs in California, found at the Employment Development Department in the following locations: Anaheim, Corona, El Cajon, Escondido, Fremont, Fresno, Hemet, Hollywood, Lancaster, Monterey, North Hollywood, Oakland, Ontario, Pasadena, Pleasant Hill, Redlands, Ridgecrest, Riverside, Sacramento (Midtown and South), San Bernardino, San Diego (also East and South), San Francisco, San Mateo, San Rafael, Santa Ana, Santa Cruz, Santa Maria, Simi Valley, Sunnyvale, Torrance, Victorville, and West Covina. Contact the club nearest to you through your local Employment Development Department (E.D.D.).

Mary Alice **Floyd,** M.A., N.C.C., Career Counselor/ Consultant, Career Life Transitions. 3233 Lucinda Lane, Santa Barbara, CA 93105. 805-687-5462.

Futures . . . , 103 Calvin Place, Santa Cruz, CA 95060. 408-425-0332. Joseph Reimuller.

Marvin F. **Galper,** Ph.D., 4036 Third Ave., Suite 204, San Diego, CA 92103. 619-295-4450.

Judith **Grutter**, M.S., N.C.C.C., G/S Consultants, P.O. Box 7855, South Lake Tahoe, CA 96158. 916-541-8587.

The Guidance Center, 1150 Yale St., Suite One, Santa Monica, CA 90403. 310-829-4429. Anne Salzman, Career Counselor and Psychologist.

H.R. Solutions, Human Resources Consulting, 390 South Sepulveda Blvd., Suite 104, Los Angeles, CA 90049. 310-471-2536. Nancy Mann, President/Consultant.

Jewish Vocational Services, 6505 Wilshire Blvd., Suite 303, Los Angeles, CA 213-655-8910.

Patrick L. **Kerwin**, NCC, NCCC. Kerwin & Associates, Career Counseling, 1347 N.Allen Avenue, Glendale, CA 91201. 818-840-0366.

Life's Decisions, 1917 Lowland Ct., Carmichael CA 95608. 916-486-0677. Joan E. Belshin, M.S., N.C.C.C.

Peller **Marion**, 388 Market St., Suite 500, San Francisco, CA 94111. 415-296-2559.

Lizbeth **Miller**, M.S., 3880 S. Bascom Ave., Suite 202, San Jose, CA 95124. 408-559-1115.

Susan W. **Miller,** M.A., 6363 Wilshire Blvd., Suite 210, Los Angeles CA 90048. 213-651-5514.

Montgomery & Associates, Career Development Services, 2515 Park Marina Dr., Suite 203B, Redding, CA 96001-2831. 916-246-2871. Gale Montgomery, Director.

M. Robert **Morrison**, Ph.D., C.R.C., California Counselors, 327 Laurel Street, San Diego, CA 92101. 619-544-0844.

New Ways to Work, 785 Market St., Suite 950, San Francisco CA 94103-2016. 415-995-9860 fax: 415-995-9867. Primarily publishes job-hunting aids these days, rather than seeing clients: Looking for Work: A Bay Area Guide to Employment Resources. $5.00 plus tax.

Saddleback College, Counseling Services and Special Programs, 28000 Marguerite Pkwy., Mission Viejo, CA 92692. 714-582-4571. Jan Fritsen, Counselor.

George H. **Schofield**, 1529 Hearst Ave., Berkeley, CA 94703. 510-704-9406. Specializes in working with people who are 'stuck.'

Olivia Keith **Slaughter**, LEP, Sunshine Plaza, 71 301 Highway 111, Suite 1, Rancho Mirage, CA 92270. 619-568-1544.

Stoodley & Associates, 1434 Willowmont Ave., San Jose, CA 95118. 408-448-3691. Martha Stoodley, M.S., M.F.C.C., President.

Transitions Counseling Center, 171 N. Van Ness, Fresno, CA 93701. 209-233-7250. Margot E. Tepperman, L.C.S.W.

Turning Point Career Center, University YWCA, 2600 Bancroft Way, Berkeley, CA 94704. 510-848-6370. Winnie Froehlich, M.S., Director.

Caroline **Voorsanger,** Career Counselor for Women, 1650 Jackson St., #608, San Francisco, CA 94115. 415-567-0890.

Patti **Wilson,** P.O. Box 35633, Los Gatos, CA 95030. 408-354-1964.

Women at Work, 50 N. Hill Ave., Pasadena, CA 91106. 818-796-6870.

COLORADO

(There is a new area code in Colorado, 970, which may affect some of the numbers below:)

Accelerated Job Search, 4490 Squires Circle, Boulder, CO 80303. 303-494-2467. Leigh Olsen, Counselor.

CRS Consulting, 425 W. Mulberry, Suite 205, Fort Collins, CO 80521. 970-484-9810. Marilyn Pultz.

Patricia **O'Keefe,** M.A., 350 Cook St., Denver, CO 80206. 303-393-8747.

Life Work Planning, 4306 19th St., Boulder, CO 80304. 303-449-9603. Lauren T. Murphy, Career Development Counselor.

Betsy C. **McGee**, The McGee Group, 2485 W. Main, Suite 202, Old Downtown Littleton, CO 80120. 303-794-4749.

Resource Center, Arapahoe Community College, 2500 West College Dr., P.O. Box 9002, Littleton, CO 80160-9002. 303-797-5805.

Women's Resource Agency, 1018 N. Weber, Colorado Springs, CO 80903. 719-471-3170.

YWCA of Boulder County Career Center, 2222 14th St., Boulder, CO 80302. 303-443-0419. A full-service career center, fees on a sliding scale. Counseling, testing, support groups, workshops. Natalie Parker, NCCC, Career Services Manager.

CONNECTICUT

(There is a new area code in Connecticut, 860, which may affect some of the numbers below:)

Accord Career Services, The Exchange, Suite 305, 270 Farmington Ave., Farmington, CT 06032. 800-922-1480, or 860-674-9654. Tod Gerardo, M.S., Director.

Career Choices/RFP Associates, 141 Durham Rd., Suite 24, Madison, CT 06443. 203-245-4123.

Career Services Inc., 94 Rambling Rd., Vernon, CT 06066. 860-871-7832. Jim Cohen, Ph.D., C.R.C.

Fairfield Academic and Career Center, Fairfield University, Dolan House, Fairfield, CT 06430. 203-254-4220.

Jamieson Associates, 61 South Main Street, Suite 101, West Hartford, CT 06107-2403. 860-521-2373. Lee Jamieson, Principal.

The Offerjost-Westcott Group, 263 Main St., Old Saybrook, CT 06475. 203-388-6094. Russ Westcott.

Bob **Pannone**, M.A., N.C.C.C., Career Specialist, 768 Saw Mill Road, West Haven, CT 06516. 203-933-6383.

People Management International Ltd., Ltd., 8B North Shore Rd., New Preston CT 06777. 203-868-0317 fax: 203-868-9776. Arthur Miller, founder and principal.

Releasing Your Original Genius™, The Center for Healing, 998 Farmington Ave., Suite 207, West Hartford, CT 06107. 860-561-2142. Lorraine P. Holden, MSW, Career/Life Planning Consultant.

Vocational and Academic Counseling for Adults (VOCA), 115 Berrian Rd., Stamford, CT 06905. 203-322-8353. Ruth A. Polster.

J. Whitney Associates, 11092 Elm St., Rocky Hill, CT 06067. 860-721-0842. Jean Whitney, Career Manager.

DELAWARE

Brandywine Psychotherapy Center, 2500 Grubb Road, Suite 240, Wilmington, DE 19810. 302-475-1880. Also at J-27 Omega Professional Center, Newark, DE 19713. 302-454-7650. Kris Bronson, Ph.D.

YWCA of New Castle County, Women's Center for Economic Options, 233 King St., Wilmington, DE 19801. 302-658-7161.

DISTRICT OF COLUMBIA

Community Vocational Counseling Service, The George Washington University Counseling Center, 718 21st St. NW, Washington, DC 20052. 202-994-4860. Robert J. Wilson, M.S., Asst. Director for Educational Services.

George Washington University, Center for Career Education, 2020 K Street, Washington, DC 20052. 202-994-5299. Abigail Pereira, Director.

FLORIDA

(There is a new area code in Tampa, 941, and a new area code in Miami, 954, plus a new area code in northern Florida, 352, which may affect some of the numbers below:)

Barbara **Adler**, Ed.D., Career Consulting, 203 North Shadow Bay Dr., Orlando, FL 32825-3766. 407-249-2189.

The **Career and Personal Counseling Center,** Eckerd College, 4200 54th Ave. South, St. Petersburg, FL 33711. 813-864-8356. John R. Sims.

Career Moves, Inc., 5300 North Federal Highway, Fort Lauderdale, FL 33308. 305-772-6857. Mary Jane Ward, M.Ed., NCC, NCCC.

Center for Career Decisions, 6100 Glades Rd., #210, Boca Raton, FL 33434. 561-470-9333. Linda Friedman, M.A., N.C.C., N.C.C.C., Director.

Chabon & Associates, 1665 Palm Beach Lakes Blvd., Suite 402, West Palm Beach, FL 33401. 407-640-8443. Toby G. Chabon, M.Ed., N.C.C., President.

The Challenge: Program for Displaced Homemakers, Florida Community College at Jacksonville, 101 W. State St., Jacksonville, FL 32202. 904-633-8316. Rita Patrick, Project Coordinator.

Crossroads, Palm Beach Community College, 4200 Congress Ave., Lake Worth, FL 33461-4796. 407-433-5995. Pat Jablonski, Program Manager.

Focus on the Future: Displaced Homemaker Program, Santa Fe Community College, 3000 N.W. 83rd St., Gainesville, FL 32606. 904-395-5047. Nancy Griffin, Program Coordinator. Classes are free.

Larry **Harmon**, Ph.D., Career Counseling Center, Inc., 2000 South Dixie Highway, Suite 103, Miami, FL 33133. 305-858-8557.

Ellen O. **Jonassen**, Ph.D., 10785 Ulmerton Rd., Largo, FL 34648. 813-581-8526.

Life Designs, Inc., 7860 SW 55th Ave. #A, South Miami, FL 33143, *or at* 19526 East Lake Dr., Miami, FL 33015. 305-665-3212. Dulce Muccio Weisenborn.

New Beginnings, Polk Community College, Station 71, 999 Avenue H, NE, Winter Haven, FL 33881-4299 (Lakeland Campus). 813-297-1029.

The Women's Center, Valencia Community College, 1010 N. Orlando Ave., Winter Park, FL 32789. 407-628-1976.

WINGS Program, Broward Community College, 1000 Coconut Creek Blvd., Coconut Creek, FL 33066. 305-973-2398.

GEORGIA

(There is a new area code in Atlanta, 770, which may affect some of the numbers below:)

Atlanta Outplacement and Career Consulting, 1150 Lake Hearn Drive, N.E., Suite 200, Atlanta, GA 30342. 404-250-3232. Harvey Brickley, Consultant.

Emmette H. **Albea**, Jr., M.S., LPC, NCCC, 2706 Melrose Drive, Valdosta, GA 31602. 912-241-0908.

Career Quest/Job search Workshop, St. Ann, 4905 Roswell Rd., N.E., Marietta, GA 30062-6240. 770-552-6402. Tom Chernetsky. Features instruction on Internet job-hunting.

D & B Consulting, 3390 Peachtree Road N.E., Suite 900, Atlanta, GA 30326. 404-240-8063. Deborah R. Brown, MSM, MSW, Career Consultant.

Jewish Vocational Service, Inc., 4549 Chamblee Dunwoody Road, Dunwoody GA 30338-6120, 770-677-9440, Anna Blau, Director.

St. Jude's Job Network, St. Jude's Catholic Church, 7171 Glenridge Dr., Sandy Springs, GA 30328. 404-393-4578.

Mark **Satterfield**, 720 Rio Grand Dr., Alpharetta, GA 30202. 770-640-8393.

HAWAII

Career Discovery, 1441 Kapiolani Blvd., Suite 2003, Honolulu, HI 96814. 808-739-9494. Nancy Hanson, M.A., NCCC.

IDAHO

Transitions, 1970 Parkside Dr., Boise, ID 83712. 208-368-0499. Elaine Simmons, M.Ed.

ILLINOIS

(There is a new area code in Chicago: 630, which may affect some of the numbers below.)

Alumni Career Center, University of Illinois Alumni Association, 322 South Green St., Suite 204, Chicago, IL 60607-3544. 312-996-6350. Barbara S. Hundley, Director; Claudia M. Delestowicz, Associate Director. Full Service Career Center open to the community.

Career Path, 1240 Iroquois Ave., Suite 510, Naperville, IL 60563. 630-369-3390. Donna Sandberg, M.S., NCC., Owner/Counselor.

Career Workshops, 5431 W. Roscoe St., Chicago, IL 60641. 312-282-6859. Patricia Dietze.

Jean **Davis,** Adult Career Transitions, 1405 Elmwood Ave., Evanston, IL 60201. 708-492-1002.

The **Dolan Agency**, 2745 East Broadway, Suite 102, Alton, IL 62002. 618-474-5328. J. Stephen Dolan, M.A., C.R.C., Rehabilitation and Career Consultant.

Barbara Kabcenell **Grauer**, M.A., N.C.C., 1370 Sheridan Road, Highland Park, IL 60035. 708-432-4479.

Grimard Wilson Consulting, 111 N. Wabash Ave., Suite 1006, Chicago, IL 60602. 312-201-1142. Diane Grimard Wilson, M.A.

Harper College Career Transition Center, Building A, Room 124, Palatine, IL 60067. 708-459-8233. Mary Ann Jirak, Coordinator.

David P. **Helfand**, Ed.D., N.C.C.C., 250 Ridge, Evanston, IL 60202. 708-328-2787. David, incidentally, is the author of a book entitled *Career Change: Everything You Need to Know to Meet New Challenges and Take Control of Your Career.*

Living by Design, Oak Brook & Oak Park, IL. 106 S. Oak Park Ave., Suite 203, Oak Park, IL 60302. 708-386-2505. Barbara Upton, MSW, Career/Life Planner.

Midwest Women's Center, 828 S. Wabash, Suite 200, Chicago, IL 60605. 312-922-8530.

Moraine Valley Community College, Job Placement Center, 10900 S. 88th Ave., Palos Hills, IL 60465. 708-974-5737.

Right Livelyhood$, 23 W. 402 Green Briar Drive, Naperville, IL 60540. 708-369-9066. Marti Beddoe, Career/ Life Counselor; or 312-281-7274, Peter LeBrun.

The Summit Group, P.O. Box 3702, Peoria, IL 61612-3702. 309-274-4100. John R. Throop, D. Min., President.

Widmer & Associates, 1510 W. Sunnyview Dr., Peoria, IL 61614. 309-691-3312. Mary F. Widmer, President.

INDIANA

Career Consultants, 107 N. Pennsylvania St., Suite 400, Indianapolis, IN 46204. 317-639-5601. Al Milburn, Career Management Consultant.

Sally **Jones**, Program Coordinator/Developer, Indiana University, School of Continuing Studies, Owen Hall, Room 202, Bloomington IN 47405. 812-855-4991.

KCDM Associates, 10401 N. Meridian St., Suite 300, Indianapolis, IN 46290. 317-581-6230. Mike Kenney.

John D. **King & Associates,** Career Counseling and Consulting, 205 N. College, Suite 614, Bloomington, IN 47404. 812-332-3888.

William R. **Lesch**, M.S., Career & Life Planning, Health Associates, 9240 N. Meridian St., Suite 292, Indianapolis, IN 46260. 317-844-7489.

IOWA

Rosanne **Beers**, Beers Consulting, 5505 Boulder Dr., West Des Moines, Iowa 50266. 515-225-1245.

Jill **Sudak-Allison**, 3219 SE 19th Court, Des Moines, IA 50320. 515-282-5040.

University of Iowa, Center for Career Development and Cooperative Education, 315 Calvin Hall, Iowa City, IA 52242. 319-335-3201.

Gloria **Wendroff**, Secrets to Successful Job Search, 703 E. Burlington Ave., Fairfield, IA 52556. 515-472-4529.

Suzanne **Zilber**, 801 Crystal St., Ames, IA 50010. 515-232-9379.

LOUISIANA

Career Planning and Assessment Center, Metropolitan College, University of New Orleans, New Orleans, LA 70148. 504-286-7100.

MAINE

Susan L. **Arledge**, Life-Planning /Career Consultant, 50 Exeter St., Portland, ME 04102. 207-761-7755.

Career Perspectives, 75 Pearl Street, Suite 204, Portland, ME 04101. 207-775-4487. Deborah L. Gallant.

Heart at Work, 78 Main St., Yarmouth, ME 04096. 207-846-0644. Barbara Sirois Babkirk, M.Ed., N.C.C., L.C.P.C., Licensed Counselor and Consultant.

Johnson Career Services, 34 Congress St., Portland ME 04101. 207-773-3921. R. Ernest Johnson.

Women's Worth Career Counseling, 18 Woodland Rd., Gorham, ME 04038. 207-892-0000. Jacqueline Murphy, Counselor.

MARYLAND

Career Perspectives, 510 Sixth St., Annapolis, MD 21403. 410-280-2299. Jeanne H. Slawson, Career Consultant.

Careerscope, Inc., One Mall North, Suite 216, 1025 Governor Warfield Pkwy., Columbia, MD 21044. 410-992-5042 or 301-596-1866. Constantine Bitsas, Executive Director.

Career Transition Services, 3126 Berkshire Rd., Baltimore MD 21214-3404. 410-444-5857. Michael Bryant.

College of Notre Dame of Maryland, Continuing Education Center, 4701 N. Charles St., Baltimore, MD 21210. 410-532-5303.

Goucher College, Goucher Center for Continuing Studies, 1021 Dulaney Valley Rd., Baltimore, MD 21204. 410-337-6200. Carole B. Ellin, Career/Job-Search Counselor.

Anne S. **Headley**, M.A., 7100 Baltimore Ave., Suite 208, College Park, MD 20740. 301-779-1917.

Kensington Consulting -- Career Planning and Psychological Consultation, 8701 Georgia Ave., Suite 406, Silver Spring, MD 20910. 301-587-1234. David M. Reile, Ph.D., NCCC, Barbara H. Suddarth, Ph.D., NCCC.

Maryland New Directions, Inc., 2220 N. Charles St., Baltimore, MD 21218. 410-235-8800. Rose Marie Coughlin, Director.

Irene N. **Mendelson**, NCCC, BEMW, Inc., Counseling and Training for the Workplace, 7984 D Old Georgetown Rd., Bethesda, MD 20814-2440. 301-657-8922.

Prince George's Community College, Career Assessment and Planning Center, 301 Largo Rd., Largo, MD 20772. 301-322-0886. Margaret Taibi, Ph.D., Director.

TransitionWorks, 10964 Bloomingdale Dr., Rockville, MD 20852-5550. 301-770-4277. Stephanie Kay, M.A., A.G.S., Principal. Nancy K. Schlossberg, Ed.D., Principal.

MASSACHUSETTS

Boston Career Link, 281 Huntington Ave., Boston, MA 02115. 617-536-1888.

Changes, 29 Leicester St., P.O. Box 35697, Brighton, MA 02135. 617-783-1717. Carl Schneider. Career counseling and job hunt training. Individual or group therapy for job hunters. Carl is one of the most service-to-people counselors that we have in this Sampler. He's been in here for many years now.

Career Link, Career Information Center, Kingston Public Library, 6 Green Street, Kingston, MA 02364. 617 585 0517. Free videos, audiocassettes, and books on job search, plus computerized career guidance (SIGI), public access computer, and workshops. Sia Stewart, Director of the Library.

Career Management Consultants, Thirty Park Ave., Worcester, MA 01605. 508-853-8669. Patricia M. Stepanski, President.

Career Resource Center, Worcester YWCA, 1 Salem Square, Worcester, MA 01608. 508-791-3181.

Career Source, 185 Alewife Brook Pkwy., Cambridge, MA 02138. 617-661-7867. *This place inherited the Radcliffe Career Services Office's library, after that Office closed permanently.* Career Source also offers career counseling.

Center for Career Development & Ministry, 70 Chase St., Newton Center, MA 02159. 617-969-7750. Stephen Ott, Director.

Center for Careers, Jewish Vocational Service, 105 Chauncy St., 6th Fl., Boston, MA 02111. 617-451-8147. Lee Ann Bennett, Coordinator, Core Services.

Jewish Vocational Service, Mature Worker Programs, 333 Nahanton St., Newton, MA 02159. 617-965-7940.

Linkage, Inc., 110 Hartwell Ave., Lexington MA 02173. 617-862-4030. David J. Giber, Ph.D.

Wynne W. **Miller,** 15 Cypress St., Suite 205, Newton Center, MA 02159-2242. 617-527-4848. Career counseling oriented toward finding meaning and mission.

Murray Associates, P.O. Box 312, Westwood, MA 02090. 617-329-1287. Robert Murray, Ed.D., Licensed Psychologist.

Neville Associates, Inc., 10 Tower Office Park, Suite 416, Woburn, MA 01801. 617-938-7870. Dr. Joseph Neville, Career Development Consultant.

Smith College Career Development Office, Drew Hall, 84 Elm Street, Northampton, MA 01063. 413-585-2570. Career counseling services to the community. Jane Sommer, Associate Director.

Suit Yourself International, Inc., 115 Shade St., Lexington, MA 02173-7724. 617-862-6006. Debra Spencer, President.

Wellness Center, 51 Mill St., Unit 8, Hanover, MA 02339. 617-829-4300. Janet Barr.

MICHIGAN

Careerdesigns, 22 Cherry St., Holland, MI 49423. 616-396-1517. Mark de Roo.

Hill & Hill Consulting, Inc., 555 South Shore E., Frankfort, MI 49635. 616-352-6018. Barbara H. Hill, President. *This resource was formerly in Warren, Ohio.*

Lansing Community College, 2020 Career and Employment Development Services, PO Box 40010, Lansing, MI 48901-7210. 517-483-1221 or 483-1172. James C. Osborn, Ph.D., L.P.C., Director, Career and Employment Services.

New Options: Counseling for Women in Transition, 2311 E. Stadium, Suite B-2, Ann Arbor, MI 48104. 313-973-0003. Phyllis Perry, M.S.W.

Oakland University, Continuum Center for Adult Counseling and Leadership Training, Rochester, MI 48309. 313-370-3033.

University of Michigan, Center for the Education of Women, 330 East Liberty, Ann Arbor, MI 48104. 313-998-7080.

MINNESOTA

Richard E. **Andrea**, Ph.D., Titan Office Park, Suite 202A, 1399 Geneva Ave., Oakdale, MN 55119. 612-738-6600.

Associated Career Services, 3550 Lexington Ave. N., Suite 120, Shoreview, MN 55126. 612-787-0501.

Career Dynamics, Inc., 8400 Normandale Lake Blvd., Suite 1220, Bloomington, MN 55437. 612-921-2378. Joan Strewler, Psychologist.

Human Dynamics, 3036 Ontario Rd., Little Canada, MN 55117. 612-484-8299. Greg J. Cylkowski, M.A., founder.

Prototype Career Services, 626 Armstrong Ave., St. Paul, MN 55102. 800-368-3197. Amy Lindgren, and Julie Remington, Counseling psychologists.

Stanley J. **Sizen**, Vocational Services, P.O.Box 363, Anoka, MN 55303. 612-441-8053.

Southwest Family Services, 10267 University Ave. North, Blaine, MN 55434. 612-825-4407. Kathy Bergman, M.A., LP. Career planning services.

Working Opportunities for Women, 2700 University Ave., #120, St. Paul, MN 55114. 612-647-9961.

MISSISSIPPI

Mississippi State University, Career Services Center, P.O. Box P, Colvard Union, Suite 316, Mississippi State, MS 39762-5515. 601-325-3344.

Mississippi Gulf Coast Community College, Jackson County Campus, Career Development Center, P.O. Box 100, Gautier, MS 39553. 601-497-9602. Rebecca Williams, Manager.

MISSOURI

Career Center, Community Career Services, 110 Noyes Hall, University of Missouri, Columbia, MO 65211. 314-882-6803.

Career Management Center, 8301 State Line Rd., Suite 202, Kansas City, MO 64114. 816-363-1500. Janice Y. Benjamin, President. Janice is also co-author of *How to Be Happily Employed in Kansas City, 4th ed.*

Women's Center, University of Missouri-Kansas City, 5100 Rockhill Rd., 104 Scofield Hall, Kansas City, MO 64110. 816-235-1638.

MONTANA

Career Transitions, 321 E. Main, Suite 215, Bozeman, MT 59715. 406-587-1721. Estella Villasenor, Executive Director. Darla Joyner, Assistant Director.

NEBRASKA

Career Management Services, 5000 Central Park Dr., Suite 204, Lincoln, NE 68504. 402-466-8427. Vaughn L. Carter, President.

Olson Counseling Services, 8720 Frederick, Suite 105, Omaha, NE 68128. 402-390-2342. Gail A. Olson, P.A.C.

Student Success Center, Central Community College, Hastings Campus, Hastings, NE 68902. 402-461-2424.

NEVADA

Greener Pastures Institute, 6301 S. Squaw Valley Rd., Suite 1383, Pahrump, NV 89048-7949, 800-688-6352. Bill Seavey.

NEW HAMPSHIRE

Individual Employment Services, 90-A Sixth St., P.O. 917, Dover, NH 03820. 603-742-5616. James Otis, Employment Counselor.

NEW JERSEY

Adult Advisory Service, Kean College of New Jersey. Administration Bldg., Union, NJ 07083. 908-527-2210.

Adult Resource Center, 100 Horseneck Road, Montville, NJ 07045. 201-335-6910.

Arista Concepts Career Development Service, P.O. Box 2436, Princeton, NJ 08540. 609-921-0308. Kera Greene, M.Ed.

Beverly **Baskin**, M.A., Baskin Business & Career Services, 6 Alberta Drive, Marlboro, NJ 07746-1202. 800-300-4079. Offices also in Woodbridge, and Princeton.

Behavior Dynamics Associates, Inc., 34 Cambridge Terrace, Springfield, NJ 07081. 201-912-0136. Roy Hirschfeld.

Career Options Center, YWCA Tribute to Women and Industry (TWIN) Program, 232 E. Front St., Plainfield, NJ 07060. 908-756-3836, or 908-273-4242. Janet M. Korba, Program Director.

Jerry **Cohen**, M.A., NCC, NCCC, Chester Professional Bldg., P.O. Box 235, Chester, NJ 07930. 908-879-4404.

Loree **Collins,** 3 Beechwood Rd., Summit, NJ 07901. 908-273-9219.

Douglass College, Douglass Advisory Services for Women, Rutgers Women's Center, 132 George St., New Brunswick, NJ 08903. 908-932-9603.

Juditha **Dowd**, 3640 Valley Rd., Liberty Corner, NJ 07938. 908-439-2091.

Sandra **Grundfest,** Ed.D., Princeton Professional Park, 601 Ewing St., Suite C-1, Princeton, NJ 08540. 609-921-8401. Also at 11 Clyde Rd., Suite 103, Somerset, NJ 08873. 908-873-1212.

Susan **Guarneri** Associates, 1101 Lawrence Rd., Lawrenceville, NJ 08648. 609-771-1669. Susan Guarneri, M.S., NCC, NCCC, and Jack Guarneri, M.S., NCC., NCCC. Career and job search counseling.

The Job Club, Princeton Unitarian Church, Cherry Hill Rd., Princeton, NJ 08540. 609-924-1604. The Guarneris (see above listing) are the coordinators. Free service, open to the community.

Job Seekers of Montclair, St. Luke's Episcopal Church, 73 S. Fullerton Ave., Montclair, NJ 07042. 201-783-3442. Meets Thursdays 7:30-9:30 p.m.

Mercer County Community College, Career Services, 1200 Old Trenton Rd., Trenton, NJ 08690. 609-586-4800, ext. 304. Career and job search counseling. Open to non-students (fee).

Lester **Minsuk & Associates**, 29 Exeter Rd., East Windsor, NJ 08520. 609-448-4600.

W.L. **Nikel & Associates**, Career Development and Outplacement, 28 Harper Terrace, Cedar Grove, NJ 07009. 201-239-7460. William L. Nikel, M.B.A., Founder.

Resource Center for Women, 31 Woodland Ave., Summit, NJ 07901. 908-273-7253. Juditha Dowd, Coordinator of the Career Division.

NEW MEXICO

Young Women's Christian Association, YWCA Career Services Center, 7201 Paseo Del Norte NE, Albuquerque, NM 87113. 505-822-9922.

NEW YORK

Carol **Allen**, Consultant. 560 West 43rd St., Suite 5G, New York, NY 10036. 212-268-5182. Career Management/Spirited Worker Seminars.

Alan B. **Bernstein** CSW, PC, 122 East 82nd St., N.Y., NY 10028. 212-288-4881.

Career Development Center, Long Island University, C.W. Post Campus, Brookville, NY 11548. 516-299-2251. Pamela Lennox, Ph.D., Director.

Career Resource Center, Bethlehem Public Library, 451 Delaware Ave., Delmar, NY 12054. 518-439-9314. Denise L. Coblish, Career Resources Librarian.

Career Strategies, Inc., 350 West 24th Street, New York, NY 10011. 212-807-1340. "CB" Bowman, President.

Career 101 Associates, 230 West 55th St., Suite 17F, New York, NY 10019. L. Michelle Tullier, Ph.D., Director. 212-333-4013.

The John C. **Crystal Center**, 152 Madison Ave., 23rd fl., New York, NY 10016. 212-889-8500, or 1-800-333-9003. Nella G. Barkley, President. *(John, the original founder of this center, died ten years ago; Nella, his business partner for many years, now directs the center's work.)*

Hofstra University, Career Counseling Center, Room 120, Saltzman Community Center, 131 Hofstra, Hempstead, NY 11550. 516-463-6788.

Kingsborough Community College, Office of Career Counseling and Placement, 2001 Oriental Blvd., Rm. C102, Brooklyn, NY 11235. 718-368-5115.

Janice **La Rouche** Assoc., 333 Central Park W., New York, NY 10025. 212-663-0970.

Livelyhood Job Search Center, 301 Madison Ave., 3rd Floor, New York, NY 10017. 212-687-2411. John Aigner, Director.

James E. **McPherson**, 101 Ives Hall, Cornell University, Ithaca, NY 14853-3901

New Options, 960 Park Ave., New York, NY 10028. 212-535-1444.

Onondaga County Public Library, The Galleries of Syracuse, 447 South Salina St., Syracuse, NY 13202-2494. 315-435-1900. Karen A. Pitoniak, Librarian, Information Services. Has InfoTrac, a computerized index and directory of over 100,000 companies, plus other job-hunting resources.

Orange County Community College, Counseling Center, 115 South St., Middletown, NY 10940. 914-341-4070.

Celia **Paul Associates**, 1776 Broadway, Suite 1806, New York, NY 10019. 212-397-1020.

Personnel Sciences Center, Inc. 276 Fifth Ave., Suite 704, New York, NY 10001. 212-683-3008. Dr. Jeffrey A. Goldberg.

Leslie B. **Prager**, M.A., The Prager-Bernstein Group, 441 Lexington Avenue, Suite 1404, New York, NY 10017. 212-697-0645.

Psychological Services Center, Career Services Unit, University at Albany, SUNY, Husted 167, 135 Western Ave., Albany, NY 12222. 518-442-4900. George B. Litchford, Ph.D., Director. Individual and group career counseling.

RLS Career Center, 3049 East Genesee St., Suite 211, Syracuse, NY 13224. 315-446-0500. Jerridith Wilson, Executive Director.

Allie **Roth,** 160 East 38th St., New York, NY 10016. 212-490-9158.

Schenectady Public Library, Job Information Center, 99 Clinton St., Schenectady, NY. Has weekly listings, including job search listings of companies nationwide.

Scientific Career Transitions, Stephen Rosen, Science & Technology Advisory Board, 575 Madison Ave., 22nd Fl., New York, NY 10022-2585. 212-891-7609. Works with unemployed and underemployed scientists, specializing in émigrés from the Soviet Union.

VEHICLES, INC., 1832 Madison Ave., Room 202, New York, NY 10035-2707. 212-722-1111. Janet Avery, President.

WIN Workshops (Women in Networking), Emily Koltnow, 1120 Avenue of the Americas, Fourth Floor, New York, NY 10036. 212-333-8788.

NORTH CAROLINA

Career Consulting Associates of Raleigh, P.O. Box 17653, Raleigh, NC 27619. 919-782-3252. Susan W. Simonds, President.

Career, Educational, Psychological Evaluations, 2915 Providence Rd., Suite 300, Charlotte, NC 28211. 704-362-1942.

Career Management Center, 3203 Woman's Club Drive, Suite 100, Raleigh, NC 27612. 919-787-1222, ext. 109. Temple G. Porter, Director.

Sally **Kochendofer,** Ph.D., Northcross Professional Park, 1-77 Exit 25, 9718-A Sam Furr Rd., Huntersville, NC 28078. 704-362-1514. Career change counselor.

Diane E. **Lambeth,** M.S.W., Career Consultant. P.O. Box 18945, Raleigh, NC 27619. 919-571-7423.

Life Management Services, LC, 301 Gregson Dr., Cary, NC 27511. 919-481-4707. Marilyn and Hal Shook. The Shooks originally were trained by John Crystal, though they have evolved their own program since then.

Joyce **Richman & Associates, Ltd.,** 2911 Shady Lawn Dr., Greensboro, NC 27408. 910-288-1799.

Bonnie M. **Truax**, Ed.D., N.C.C.C., Career/Life Planning and Relocation Services, 2102 N. Elm St., Suite K1, Greensboro, NC 27408. 910-271-2050. Free support group.

Women's Center of Raleigh,128 E. Hargett St., Suite 10, Raleigh, NC 27601. 919-829-3711.

NORTH DAKOTA

Business & Life Resources Career Development Center, 112 North University Dr., Suite 3300, Fargo, ND 58103. 1-800-950-0848. Gail Reierson.

OHIO

(There is a new area code in Dayton, 937, which may affect some of the numbers below:)

Adult Resource Center, The University of Akron, Buckingham Center for Continuing Education, Room 55, Akron, OH 44325-3102. 216-972-7448. Sandra B. Edwards, Director.

Career Initiatives Center, 1557 E. 27th St., Cleveland, OH 44114. 216-574-8998. Richard Hanscom, Director.

Career Point, Belden-Whipple Building, 4150 Belden Village Street, N.W., Suite 101, Canton, OH 44718. 216-492-1920. Victor W. Valli, Career Consultant.

Cuyahoga County Public Library InfoPLACE Service, Career, Education & Community Information Service, 5225 Library Lane, Maple Heights, OH 44137-1291. 216-475-2225.

The **Human Touch**, 260 Northland Blvd., Suite 234, Ciincinnati, OH 45246. 513-772-5839. Judy R. Kroger, LPDC, Career and Human Resources Counselor.

J&K Associates, and Success Skills Seminars Inc., 607 Otterbein Ave., Dayton, OH 45406-4507. 937-274-3630, or 937-274-4375. Pat Kenney, Ph.D., President.

New Career, 328 Race St., Dover, OH 44622. 216-364-5557. Marshall Karp, M.A., N.C.C., L.P.C., Owner.

Pyramid Career Services, Inc., 2400 Cleveland Ave., NW, Canton, OH 44709. 216-453-3767. Zandra Bloom, Director.

OKLAHOMA

Career Development Services, Inc., 5555 E. 71st St., Suite 6110, Tulsa, OK 74136-6547. 918-495-1230. William D. Young, EdD, LPC.

OREGON

Career Development, PO Box 850, Forest Grove, OR 97116. 503-357-9233. Edward H. Hosley, Ph.D., Director.

Joseph A. **Dubay,** 425 NW 18th Avenue, Portland, OR 97209. 503-226-2656.

Lansky Career Consultants, 9335 S.W. Capitol Highway, Portland OR 97219. 503-293-0245, 800-498-5247. Judi Lansky, M.A., President.

Marion Bass **Stevens**, Ph.D., 2631 E. Congress Way, Medford, OR 97504. 541-773-3373.

Verk Consultants, Inc., 1190 Olive St., P.O. Box 11277, Eugene, OR 97440. 541-687-9170. Larry H. Malmgren, M.S., C.R.C., President.

PENNSYLVANIA

Career by Design, 1011 Cathill Rd., Sellersville, PA 18960. 215-723-8413. Henry D. Landes, Career Consultant.

Career Development Center, Jewish Family & Children's Center, 5737 Darlington Road, Pittsburgh, PA 15217. 412-422-5627. Linda Ehrenreich, Director.

Career Management Consultants, Inc., 2040 Linglestown Rd., Suite 205, Harrisburg, PA 17110. 717-657-2066. Louis F. Persico, Career Consultant.

Center for Adults in Transition, Bucks County Community College, Newtown, PA 18940. 215-968-8188.

Center for Career Services (CCS), 1845 Walnut Street, 7th floor, Philadelphia, PA 19103-4707. 215-854-1800. William A. Hyman, Director. Lucy Borosh, Aviva Gal, Tracey Tanenbaum, Career Counselors.

The **Creative Living Center,** 1388 Freeport Road, Pittsburgh, PA 15238. 412-963-8765. David R. Johnson, Director.

Carol **Eikleberry,** Ph.D., 1376 Freeport Rd., Suite 3A, Pittsburgh, PA 15238. 412-963-9008.

Lathe **Haynes**, Ph.D., 401 Shady Ave., Suite C107, Pittsburgh, PA 15206. 412-361-6336.

Jack **Kelly**, Career Counselor. Career Pro Resume Services, 251 DeKalb Pike, Suite E608, King of Prussia, PA 19406. 610-337-7187.

Options, Inc., 225 S. 15th St., Philadelphia, PA 19102. 215-735-2202. Marcia P. Kleiman, Director.

Priority Two, P.O. Box 343, Sewickley, PA 15143. 412-935-0252. *Five locations in the Pittsburgh area; call for addresses.* Pat Gottschalk, Administrative Assistant. No one is turned away for lack of funds.

RHODE ISLAND

Career Designs, 104 Rankin Ave., Providence, RI 02908-4216, 401-521-2323. Terence Duniho, Career Consultant.

SOUTH CAROLINA

(There is a new area code in South Carolina, 864, which may affect some of the numbers below:)

Career Counselor Services, Inc., 138 Ingleoak Lane, Greenville, SC 29615. 864-242-4474. Al A. Hafer, Ed.D., N.C.C.C., N.C.C., L.P.C.

Greenville Technical College, Career Advancement Center, P.O. Box 5616, Greenville, SC 29606. 803-250-8281. F.M. Rogers, Director.

SOUTH DAKOTA

Career Concepts Planning Center, Inc., 1602 Mountain View Rd., Suite 102, Rapid City, SD 57702. 605-342-5177, toll free: 1-800-456-0832. Melvin M. Tuggle, Jr., President.

University of Sioux Falls, The Center for Women, 1101 W. 22nd St., Sioux Falls, SD 57105. 605-331-6697. Tami Haug-Davis, Director.

TENNESSEE

(There is a new area code in Tennessee, 423, which may affect some of the numbers below:)

Career Resources, 2323 Hillsboro Rd., Suite 508, Nashville TN 37212. 615-297-0404. Jane C. Hardy, Principal.

Mid-South Career Development Center, 2315 Fisher Place, Knoxville, TN 37920. 615-573-1340. W. Scott Root, President/ Counselor.

Dan **Miller**, The Business Source, 7100 Executive Center Drive, Suite 110, Brentwood, TN 37027. 615-373-7771.

World Career Transition, P.O. Box 1423, Brentwood, TN 37027-1423. 1-800-366-0945. Bill Karlson, Executive Vice-President.

TEXAS

(There are new area codes in Texas, 281 and 972, which may affect some of the numbers below:)

Austin Career Associates, 4501 Spicewood Springs Rd., Suite 1007, Austin, TX 78759. 512-343-0526. Maydelle Fason, Career Consultant.

Career Action Associates, 12655 N. Central Expressway, Suite 821, Dallas, TX 75243. 214-392-7337. Joyce Shoop, L.P.C. Office also at 1325 8th Avenue, Ft. Worth, TX 76112. 817-926-9941. Rebecca Hayes, L.P.C.

Career Management Resources, 222 W. Las Colinas, Suite #2114, Irving, TX 75039. 972-556-0786. Mary Holdcroft, M.Ed., L.P.C., N.C.C., N.C.C.C.

Career and Recovery Resources, Inc., 2525 San Jacinto, Houston, TX 77002, 713-754-7000. Beverley Marks, Director.

Richard S. **Citrin,** Ph.D., Psychologist, Iatreia Institute, 1152 Country Club Ln., Ft. Worth, TX 76112. 817-654-9600.

Counseling Services of Houston, 1964 W. Gray, Suite 204, Houston, TX 77019. 713-521-9391. Rosemary C. Vienot, M.S., Licensed Professional Counselor, Director.

Employment/Career Information Resource Center, Corpus Christi Public Library, 805 Comanche, Corpus Christi, TX 78401. 512-880-7004. Lynda F. Whitton-Henley, Career Information Specialist.

Maydelle **Fason**, Employment Consultant, 1607 Poquonock Road, Austin, TX 78703. 512-474-1185.

New Directions Counseling Center, 8140 North Mopac, Bldg. II, Suite 230, Austin, TX 78759. 512-343-9496. Jeanne Quereau, M.A., Licensed Professional Counselor.

New Life Institute, 1203 Lavaca St., Austin, TX 78701-1831. 512-469-9447. Bob Breihan, Director.

Chuck **Ragland**, Transformational Consultancy, 2504 Briargrove Drive, Austin, TX 78704-2704. 512-440-1200.

San Antonio Psychological Services, 6800 Park Ten Blvd., Suite 208 North, San Antonio, TX 78213. 210-737-2039.

Mary **Stedham**, Counseling/Consulting Services, 2434 S. 10th, Abilene, TX 79605. 915-672-4044.

VGS, Inc. (Vocational Guidance Service), 2600 S.W. Freeway, Suite 800, Houston, TX 77098. 713-535-7104. Beverley K. Finn, Director.

Worklife Institute Consulting, 2650 Fountainview Drive, Suite 444, Houston, TX 77057. 713-266-2456. Diana C. Dale, Director.

UTAH

University of Utah, Center for Adult Development, 1195 Annex Bldg., Salt Lake City, UT 84112. 801-581-3228.

VERMONT

Career Networks, 7 Kilburn St., Burlington, VT 05401. 800-918-WORK. Tim King, President.

VIRGINIA

(There is a new area code in Virginia, 540, which may affect some of the numbers below:)

Tanya **Bodzin**, NCCC, Career Consultant, 9215 Santayana Drive, Fairfax, VA 22031. 703-273-6040.

Change & Growth Consulting, 1334 G Street, Woodbridge, VA 22191. 703-494-8271; also: 2136-A Gallows Road, Dunn Loring (Tyson's Corner area), VA 22027. 703-569-2029. Barbara S. Woods, M.Ed., NCC, LPC, Counselor.

Educational Opportunity Center, 7010-M Auburn Ave., Norfolk, VA 23513. 804-855-7468. Agatha A. Peterson, Director.

Fairfax County Office for Women, The Government Center, 12000 Government Center Pkwy., Suite 38, Fairfax, VA 22035. 703-324-5735. Elizabeth Lee McManus, Program Manager.

Golden Handshakes, Church of the Epiphany, 11000 Smoketree Dr., Richmond, VA 23236. 804-794-0222. Jim Dunn, Chairperson; also at Winfree Memorial Baptist Church, 13617 Midlothian Turnpike, Midlothian, VA 23113. 804-794-5031. Phil Tibbs, Volunteer Coordinator.

Hollins College, Women's Center, P.O. Box 9628, Roanoke, VA 24020. 703-362-6269. Tina Rolen, Career Counselor.

Mary Baldwin College, Rosemarie Sena Center for Career and Life Planning, Kable House, Staunton, VA 24401. 703-887-7221.

McCarthy & Company, Career Transition Management, 3908 Terry Place, Alexandria, VA 22304. 703-823-4018. Peter McCarthy, President.

Office for Women, The Government Center, 12000 Government Center Parkway, Suite 318, Fairfax, VA 22035. 703-324-5730. Betty McManus, Director.

Psychological Consultants, Inc., 6724 Patterson Ave., Richmond, VA 23226. 804-288-4125.

Virginia Commonwealth University, University Career Center, 907 Floyd Ave., Room 2007, Richmond, VA 23284-2007. 804-367-1645.

The **Women's Center,** 133 Park St., NE, Vienna, VA 22180. 703-281-2657. Conda Blackmon.

Working From The Heart, 1309 Merchant Lane, McLean, VA 22101. Jacqueline McMakin and Susan Gardiner, Co-Directors.

WASHINGTON

Career Management Institute, 8404 27th St. West, Tacoma, WA 98466. 206-565-8818. Ruthann Reim, M.A., N.C.C., President.

Center for Life Decisions, 3121 East Madison St., Suite 209, Seattle, WA 98112. 206-325-9093. Larry Gaffin. Career counseling and consulting.

Diane **Churchill**, 508 W. Sixth, Suite 202, Spokane, WA 99204. 509-458-0962.

The **Individual Development Center, Inc. (I.D. Center),** 1020 E. John, Seattle, WA 98102. 206-329-0600. Mary Lou Hunt, N.C.C., M.A., President.

Centerpoint Institute for Life and Career Renewal, Career Consultants, 624 Skinner Bldg., 1326 Fifth Ave., Seattle, WA 98101. 206-622-8070. Carol Vecchio, Career Counselor. *A multifaceted center, with various workshops, lectures, retreats, as well as individual counseling.*

WEST VIRGINIA

Career Insights, 153 Tartan Dr., Follansbee, WV 26037. 304-748-1192. Frank E. Ticich, M.S., LPC. Free initial consultation.

Ed **Jepson**, 2 Hazlett Court, Wheeling, WV 26003. 304-232-2375.

WISCONSIN

Making Alternative Plans, Career Development Center, Alverno College, 3401 S. 39th St., P.O. Box 343922, Milwaukee, WI 53234-3922. 414-382-6010.

David **Swanson,** Career Seminars and Workshops, 7235 West Wells Street, Wauwatosa, WI 53213-3607. 414-774-4755, 414-259-0265.

WYOMING

Barbara W. **Gray**, Career Consultant, P.O. Box 9490, Jackson, WY 83002. 307-733-6544.

University of Wyoming, Career Planning and Placement Center PO Box 3195/Knight Hall 228, Laramie, WY 82071-3195. 307-766-2398.

U.S.A. - - NATIONWIDE

Forty Plus Clubs. A nationwide network of voluntary, autonomous nonprofit clubs, manned by its unemployed members, paying no salaries, supported by initiation fees *(often around $500)* and monthly dues *(often around $60 per month).* Varying reports, as to their helpfulness. However, one reader gave a very good report on them recently: *"I would just like to let you know that 40+, for me, has been a really big help. They provide good job search training . . . But even more importantly, for me, is the professional office environment they provide to work out of, and the fellowship of others who are also looking for work . . . As they say at 40+, 'It's hell to job search alone.'"* At this writing, there are clubs in the following cities (listed alphabetically by States): California: Laguna Hills, Los Angeles, Oakland, San Diego, San Jose; Colorado: Colorado Springs, Fort Collins, Lakewood; District of Columbia: Washington; Hawaii: Honolulu; Illinois: Chicago; Minnesota: St. Paul; New York: New York, Buffalo; Ohio: Columbus; Pennsylvania: Philadelphia; Texas: Houston, Dallas; Utah: Murray, Ogden, Provo; Washington: Bellevue; and in Canada: Toronto. If you live in or near any of these cities, you can check the white pages of your Phone Book for their address and phone number; also you can call Forty Plus of New York, 15 Park Row, New York, NY 10038. 212-233-6086 to get current information about any of the nationwide locations - - to see if the club is still there, or if there is a new club nearer where you live - - and what their current address and phone number are.

CANADA

(These are listed by Provinces, from East Coast to West Coast, rather than in alphabetical order)

Sue **Landry**, Enhancing Your Horizons Consulting, 25 Birchwood Terr., Dartmouth, Nova Scotia B3A 3W2. 902-464-9110.

careerguide, Ryan Bldg., 3rd Floor, 57 Carleton Street, Fredericton, New Brunswick 506-459-4185. Elspeth (Beth) Leroux, B.A., B.Ed., M.Ed.

Kenneth **Des Roches**, André Filion & Associates, Inc., 259 St. Joseph Blvd., Suite 305, Hull, Québec J8Y 6T1. 819-770-8474.

Jewish Vocational Service, Centre Juif D'Orientation et de L'Emploi, 5151, ch. de la CÔte Ste-Catherine, Montréal, Québec, H3W 1M6. 514-345-2625. Alta Abramowitz, Director, Employment Development Services. *Uses both French and English versions of* Parachute.

After Graduation Career Counseling, 73 Roxborough St. West, Toronto, Ontario M5R 1T9. 416-923-8319. Teresa Snelgrove, Ph.D., Director.

Donner & Wheeler and Associates, Career Development Consultants, Health and Social Services Sector, 307 Richview Ave., Toronto, Ontario M5P 3G4. 905-949-5954. Offers workshops particularly for those in the health and social services sector. Mary W. Wheeler.

Hazell & Associates, 60 St. Clair Avenue East, Seventh Floor, Toronto, Ontario M4T 1N5. 416-961-3700.

Mid-Life Transitions, 2 Slade Ave., Toronto, Ontario M6G 3A1, 416-653-0563. Marilyn Melville.

YMCA Career Planning & Development, 15 Breadalbane St., Toronto, Canada M4Y 2V5. 416-324-4121.

Changes by Choice, 190 Burndale Ave., North York, Ontario M2N 1T2. 416-590-9939. Patti Davie.

Susan **Steinberg**, M.Ed., 74 Denlow Blvd., Don Mills, Ontario M3B 1P9. 416-449-6936.

Harold **Harder**, B.Sc.,B.Admin.St. The Precision Group, 400 Matheson Blvd. East, Unit 18, Mississauga, Ontario L4Z 1N8. 905-507-8696.

Human Achievement Associates, 22 Cottonwood Crescent, London, Ontario N6G 2Y8. 519-657-3000. Mr. Kerry A. Hill.

David H. **Wenn**, B.A., M.Ed. Career Counseling. 9 Lindbrook Court, London, Ontario N5X 2L4. 519-660-0622.

Job-Finding Club, 516-294 Portage Ave., Winnipeg, Manitoba R3C 0B9. 204-947-1948.

People Focus, 712 10th St. East, Saskatoon, Saskatchewan S7H OH1. 306-933-4956. Carol Stevenson Seller.

Work from the Heart, 8708 136 St., Edmonton, Alberta T5R 0B9. 403-484-8387. Marguerite Todd

Susan **Curtis,** M.Ed., 4513 West 13th Ave., Vancouver, British Columbia V6R 2V5. 604-228-9618.

Alice **Caldwell**, P.B. #19009, 4th Avenue Postal Outlet, Vancouver, British Columbia V6K 4R8. 604-737-7842.

Conscious Career Choices, 2678 W. Broadway, Suite 203B, Vancouver, British Columbia V6K 2G3. 604-737-3955. Marlene Haley, B.A., M.Ed., Career counselor. Their motto is: Find Work You Love.

OVERSEAS

(Listed by country and city, in bold type.)

Cabinet Daniel Porot, 1, rue Verdaine, CH-1204 **Geneve, Switzerland.** phone 41 22 311 04 38. Daniel Porot, Founder. *Daniel is co-lecturer with me each summer at our international workshop and has been since 1979.*

Kessler-Laufbahnberatung, Alpenblickstr. 33, CH-8645, **Jona b. Rapperswil, Switzerland.** phone 055 210.46.48. Peter Kessler, Counselor.

Peter Baumgartner, Lowen Pfaffikon, Postfach 10, 8808 **Pfaffikon, Switzerland.** phone 055 415 66 22. *Peter is an author as well* (his book is entitled *Lebensunternehmer,* Berufswahlpraxis Schmid & Barmettler, Beratung und Verlag AG, Marktgasse 35, 8180 Bulach.

Madeleine Leitner, Personal- und Karriereberatung, Steinstr. 62, 81667, **Munchen, Germany.** phone 089 48 10 75.

Castle Consultants International, 140 Battersea Park Road, **London, England** SW11 4NB. phone 44-171 798 5688. Walt Hopkins, Founder and Director.

Anne Radford, 303 Bankside Lofts, 65 Hopton St., **London, England** SE1 9JL. phone 7000 077 011.

The Chaney Partnership, Hillier House, 509 Upper Richmond Rd. West, **London, England** SW14 7EE. phone 081 878 3227. Isabel Chaney, B.A.

Jane Bartlett, Bridgeway Associates Ltd., Career Consultants, Bradford Ct., Bradford Street, **Birmingham, England** B12 0NS. phone: 0121-773-8770.

Philip Houghton, Career Development. 10 York Pl., Brandon Hill, **Bristol, England** BS1 5UT. phone: 0117-9254363.

Brian McIvor and Associates, 43 York Rd., **Dun Laoghaire, County Dublin, Ireland.** phone 353 1 280 6504. Brian McIvor, Principal. *Brian has been on staff at my annual two-week workshop.*

Adigo Consultores, Av. Doria 164, **Sao Paulo SP, 04635-070 Brazil.** phone 55 11 530 0330. Alberto M.Barros, Director.

Centre for WorkLife Counselling, Suite 3, 5 Earl St., Mosman, P.O. Box 407, **Spit Junction, (Sydney area) Australia** 2088. phone 61 2 9968 1588. Paul Stevens, Director. Paul has been the dean of career counseling in Australia.

The Growth Connection, Suite 201, 2nd Floor, 56 Berry St., **North Sydney, N.S.W. 2060 Australia.** phone 61 2 9954 3322. Imogen Wareing, Director.

Career Action, 4/58 Park St., **Erskenville, NSW 2043, Australia.** 61 2 319 138, fax: 61 2 316 656. Narelle Milligan.

Judith Bailey, Designing Your Life, 10 Nepean Pl., **Macquarie Australia**, ACT 2614. phone 61 6 253 2231.

Robert J. Bisdee & Associates, 22 Allenby Ave., Malvern E., **Victoria, Australia** 3145. phone 61 3 885 4716. Dr. Bob Bisdee, Director.

New Zealand Creative Career Centre, Ltd., 4th Floor, Braemar House, 32 The Terrace, P.O. Box 3058, **Wellington, New Zealand.** phone 64 4 499 8414. Felicity McLennan,

Max Palmer, Life Work Career Counselling, P.O. Box 2223, **Christchurch, New Zealand.** phone 64 03 379 2781.

Transformation Technologies Pte Ltd, 122 Thomson Green, **Singapore** 574986. phone 65 456 6358. Anthony Tan, Director

Readers often write to ask us which of these overseas counselors are familiar with my approach to job-hunting and career-changing. The answer is: ***everyone of them****, listed above, have attended my two-week workshop, and therefore know my approach well.*

Other overseas counselors not trained by me, but who may still be quite helpful to you, since they are experienced counselors, and are familiar with Parachute, *are:*

Judy Feierstein, M.A., 46/2 Derech Bet Lechem, **Jerusalem 93504, Israel**, phone (02) 71 06 73.

Lori Mendel, 14/3 Zui Bruk, **Tel Aviv 63423, Israel,** phone (03) 29 28 30.

Johan Veeninga, Careers by Design, Business Park "De Molenzoom," P.O. Box 143, NL-3990 DC, **Houten/Utrecht, The Netherlands.** phone 31 (0) 3403-75153

Epilogue

Resources for Career Counselors

The vocational titles in this field are so various, as to boggle the mind. Career counselor, executive career counselor, career development specialist, etc., etc. Recently, a new one has joined the ranks: career coach.

Books of Particular Interest to Career Counselors:

My pathetic attempts, over the past twenty-seven years, to list a decent number of the new job-hunting books that come out each year finally succumbed, under the sheer weight of numbers.

For example, when I first came into this field, there were only 14 books in existence, on the subject of job-hunting and careers. Contrast that with the fact that since 1990, 3,100 books have been published in this field, according to *Fortune* Magazine.[1]

Okay, I give up!

So, from now on I am simply listing *the ten* books published in the past year that I stumbled across, and liked the best -- often for very idiosyncratic reasons. As I looked over my bookshelves for recent candidates, I realized I haven't encountered ten *new* career-counseling books that I especially *love*; so the list of my ten favorite books is mingled with my favorites from last year. I should mention, in passing, that I encountered one great new book this year *outside the career-counseling field* -- and that is a book called *Data Smog*, by David Henk (Harper/Edge, 1997). It's *wonderful*.

1. *Fortune*, 1/15/96.

Okay, here are my ten favorite career counseling books, last year and this:

No One Is Unemployable: Creative Solutions for Overcoming Barriers to Employment. Debra L Angel, and Elisabeth E. Harney. WorkNet Publications, P.O. Box 5582, Hacienda Heights, CA 91745-0082. 1997. Debra is a former student of mine (and of my son, Gary), and -- with Elisabeth -- has written a book of particular urgency and usefulness to counselors working with people on welfare who are about to enter (or re-enter) the work force.

The PIE Method for Career Success: A Unique Way to Find Your Ideal Job, by Daniel Porot. JIST Works, Inc., 720 North Park Avenue, Indianapolis, IN 46202. 1996. Daniel and I have taught together every summer but one, since 1979. He is a Frenchman, who lives in Geneva, Switzerland. This book, like its author, is tremendously helpful. No career counselor should be without it. It is profusely illustrated, and a marvelous 'read.' (For the worried American, it *is* in English.)

The Guide to Internet Job Searching, by Margaret Riley, Frances Roehm, and Steve Oserman. VGM Career Horizons, a division of NTC Publishing Group, 4255 West Touhy Avenue, Lincolnwood (Chicago), IL 60646-1975. 1996. Three wonderful people have put this book together; I know all of them. Margaret Riley is the creator of the thing; so, it is known on the Web as 'the Riley guide.' I like this book the best of all those which have come out thus far, about job-hunting and the Internet. The table of contents includes such topics as "Jobs in Business," "Jobs in the Social Sciences," "International Opportunities," etc. An impressive work, representing hundreds of hours of research on 'the Net.'

Career Satisfaction and Success: A Guide to Job and Personal Freedom, by Bernard Haldane. JIST Works, Inc., 720 North Park Avenue, Indianapolis, IN 46202. 1996. Bernard has been a leading figure in the career field for fifty years now, having begun in 1946. He is now 86 years old. This is a re-issue, revised and enlarged, of his most important book. I always learn something new when I hear or read Bernard's thoughts. (He and I were together at two conferences this past year, as keynoters.) *Incidentally, this is* not *a recommendation of the executive counseling agency which he founded and then sold some years ago, though it still bears his name.*

The Whole Brain Business Book: Unlocking the Power of Whole Brain Thinking in Organizations and Individuals, by Ned Herrmann. McGraw-Hill, 11 West 19th Street, New York, NY 10011. 1996. Ned is an old friend of mine, and one of the world's authorities on the two sides of the brain; and this is his application of his theory about the four 'quadrants' of 'the whole brain' to the subject of careers. Beginning on page 72 in his book, he shows the dominant brain pattern for a number of occupations. The rest of the book is equally fascinating, as it discusses skills, work styles, etc.

7 Kinds of Smart: Identifying and Developing Your Many Intelligences, by Thomas Armstrong. A Plume Book, published by Penguin Books USA Inc., 375 Hudson Street, New York, NY 10014. 1993. Well, sure, it's been out for quite a while. I'm just a little slow. Saw this mentioned on the Internet, went and got it, found it fascinating. A whole different way of looking at skills, based on Howard Gardner's *Frames of Mind.* Daniel Goleman's current best-seller,

Emotional Intelligence: Why it can matter more than IQ, is also based on Gardner's theory. Both books should be extremely useful to career counselors.

The Career Guide for Creative and Unconventional People, by Carol Eikleberry. Ten Speed Press, Box 7123, Berkeley, CA 94707. 1995. Carol here gives a brilliant exposition of the "A" corner in John Holland's hexagon. I learned a tremendous amount by reading this. Chapter Two alone is worth the price of the book. It lists 215 jobs that creative, "A"-type people might consider.

Another book about Holland's theory also was published recently, and is very useful. It's called *Real People, Real Jobs: Reflecting Your Interests in the World of Work,* by David H. Montross, Christopher J. Shinkman, and the late Zandy B. Leibowitz. Davies-Black, a division of Consulting Psychologists Press, 3803 E. Bayshore Road, Palo Alto, CA 94303. 1995. Interviews with real people, illustrating each of the corners in Holland's hexagon.

Give Yourself the Unfair Advantage! by William D. G. Murray, illustrations by Ashleigh Brilliant. Type and Temperament, Inc., PO Box 200, Gladwyne, PA 19035-0200. 1995. The description of the Myers-Brigg Type Indicator that I find the most appealing among all the books about the MBTI that are out there. Plus, Ashleigh Brilliant is my favorite wit; has been for years.

Benchmark Tasks for Job Analysis: A Guide for Functional Job Analysis (FJA) Scales, by Sidney A. Fine and Maury Getkate, of the Royal Canadian Mounted Police. Lawrence Erlbaum Associates, Inc., Publishers, 10 Industrial Avenue, Mahwah, NJ 07430. 1995. Every counselor who is familiar with the *Dictionary of Occupational Titles* knows Sidney's hierarchy of skills, ranked according to those used with Things, Data, and People. Here he explains his skill charts in detail, and gives sample/benchmark tasks for each skill. A tremendously useful work for everyone who helps people analyze their skills.

Catalogs of Job-Hunting Materials

If you want to know what other career books are out there, I recommend you browse a very big book store, *or* write and ask for various publishers' career catalogs.

Here is a *sampling* (only) of *some* of them, which you can write and ask for -- no matter where you are, in the world. Some of these catalogs feature not only books, but also software, film, videotape, audiotape, and assessment instruments. I have tried to indicate the range of the catalog, in the listing:

The Whole Work Catalog: Career Resources: Books, Video, Software. The New Careers Center, Inc., P.O. Box 339, Boulder, CO 80306. From over 175 different sources. A comprehensive listing.

Career Development Resources Catalog. Career Research & Testing, 2005 Hamilton Ave., San Jose, CA 95125. Lists books, reference books, journals, workbooks, assessment instruments, audiotapes, videos, computer software, and workshops. Has the computerized *D.O.T.*

Career Planning and Job Search Catalog. JIST Works, Inc., 720 North Park Avenue, Indianapolis, IN 46202.

Masterco Career Catalog, Masterco, P.O. Box 7382, Ann Arbor, MI 48107. Books.

Catalog, Careers, Inc., 1211 10th St., SW, P.O. Box 135, Largo, FL 34649-0135.

Catalog. Reed Reference Publishing, 121 Chanlon Road, New Providence, NJ 07974. R.R. Bowker and other publishers' reference books, plus CD-ROMs, computer software, and online services.

Catalog. Wintergreen/Orchard House, P.O. Box 15899, New Orleans, LA 70175-5899. Lists many JIST materials, hence is duplicatory of their catalog, above. But also lists other's materials: CD-ROMs, games, maps, videotapes, workbooks and books. Has the computerized *D.O.T.*

Job Quest Catalog, Planning/Communications, 7215 Oak Ave., River Forest, IL 60305.

The Crisp Catalog, Crisp Publications, Inc., 1200 Hamilton Court, Menlo Park, CA 94025-9600. One section on career books. They are famous for their "50-Minute Books."

Gale's Guide to Job Hunting Resources. Gale Research, Inc., 835 Penobscot Bldg., Detroit, MI 48226-4094. Primarily reference books useful to job-hunters.

Jobs & Careers for the 1990s: 2761 Resources to Plan Your Future. From Impact Publications, 9104-N Manassas Drive, Manassas Park, VA 22111. Books.

Job & Career Library. Consultants Bookstore, Templeton Road, Fitzwilliam, NH 03447. Books.

PAR Catalog of Professional Testing Resources, PAR: Psychological Assessment Resources, Inc., P.O. Box 998, Odessa, FL 33556. John Holland's official publisher. Contains 37 pages of career assessment and planning resources. Assessment instruments, books, tapes, journals.

Peterson's Guides, P.O. Box 2123, Princeton, NJ 08543. Books, reference books.

Employee Development Catalog. Pfeiffer & Company, 8517 Production Avenue, San Diego, CA 92121-2280. Books, workbooks, video.

Sunburst Videos for Grades K-12 & Up. Sunburst Communications, P.O. Box 40, Pleasantville, NY 10570-0040.

Ten Speed Press Catalog. Ten Speed Press, Box 7123, Berkeley, CA 94707. Books. They usually publish, separately, a listing of just their career-related books. Ask.

VGM *Career Books.* NTC/Contemporary Publishing Company, 4255 West Touhy Ave., Lincolnwood, IL 60646-1975. 1-708-679-5500. Books, CD-ROMs,

plus an interesting series of books on careers in various fields: physical therapy, masonry, homecare services, desktop publishing, robotics, tool and die, veterinary medicine, etc.

Writer's Digest Catalog. Writer's Digest Books, 1507 Dana Ave., Cincinnati, OH 45207. Books related to specific careers, such as writing, the arts, etc.

Job Search. Cambridge Educational, P.O. Box 2153, Dept. 7, Charleston, WV 25328-2153. Books, video, CD-ROMs, posters.

Hoover's Business Resources Catalog, 1033 La Posada Drive, Suite 250, Austin, TX 78752.

Periodicals or Newsletters for Career Counselors:

Career Planning & Adult Development Newsletter. Published monthly by the Career Planning and Adult Development Network, 4965 Sierra Rd., San Jose, CA 95132. A single issue for non-members of the Network is $4.50. To subscribe to this Newsletter, you must become a member of the Network (no obligation to *do* anything). Membership/subscription costs $49 in U.S., $64 for overseas. Richard L. Knowdell, Editor.

Newsletter about life/work planning. Richard N. Bolles, Editor. This was published for 18 years -- from 1974–1987, and 1994–1997. I have now discontinued it, as I want to devote myself to writing new books, plus enjoying more leisure time with my family (I turned 70 this year). However, many of these newsletters are included in a training manual for counselors that Howard Figler and I are going to publish in mid-1998.

Human Resource Development News, Al A. Hafer, Editor. This newsletter has also been discontinued. (Al turned 73 this year.)

Career Opportunities News. Published six times a year by Ferguson Publishing, 200 W. Madison, Suite 300, Chicago, IL 60606. Robert Calvert, Jr., Editor. Very useful news for counselors (and job-hunters) about employment fields, fellowships, new books, etc. Extremely knowledgeable editor, a veteran in this field. Six issues plus bonuses, $35/yr.

The Damn Good Resume Pro Newsletter, published quarterly. P.O. Box 3289, Berkeley, CA 94703. Yana Parker, Editor and Publisher. A National Newsletter for professionals, exploring and promoting excellence in resume writing. This has become a kind of non-electronic *bulletin-board* where members of this particular profession can meet and exchange ideas. Yana has also published other materials on resumes, which are listed in the section on "Resumes, Agencies & Ads," and on her website: http://www.damngood.com.

Global Career Resources, published four times a year by Career Decisions International, P.O. Box 421730, San Francisco, CA 94142-1730. Mark Pope, and Martha Russell, editors. A newsletter dealing with international meetings, conferences, and resources. They will send you a complimentary issue.

Counselor Educator and Grad Student Networker. For those interested in research, syllabi, and programs related to the training of counselors. A Service of the NCDA/ACES Counselor Educator and Graduate Student Career Development Network. Order from Rich Feller, ED 222, Colorado State University, Ft. Collins, CO 80523. Fax: 303-491-1317. Phone: 303-491-6879.

The Journal of Employment Counseling. A professional journal concerned with research, theory, and new and improved job counseling techniques and tools. It does not deal so much with the job-hunt, as with counseling; and the counseling is pretty much along the traditional job-hunting lines. This is the official publication of the National Employment Counseling Association, a division of the American Counseling Association (ACA)[2], 5999 Stevenson Ave., Alexandria, VA 22304. $20/yr.

Winning Ways, a professional newsletter for entrepreneurial people, with tips and inspiring stories. Winning Ways, P.O. Box 39412, Minneapolis, MN 55439. $29 ($36 foreign) for six issues.

Life's Work, P.O. Box 460371, San Francisco, CA 94146-0371. Phone or fax: 415-282-7976. e-mail: lifeswork@compuserve.com. Tim Finnegan, editor. A newsletter for career counselors, individual job searchers, and career changers. $16/yr. Inspirational stories and a network, particularly for graduates of my annual two-week workshop (though not restricted to them).

Career Savvy: The Career Resources and Media Up-Date Newsletter. A four page newsletter, issued monthly, which informs career counselors of the latest directories, software, online resources, etc. A service of: Developing Executives, Inc., 32580 Grand River, Farmington, MI 48336. 810-615-1811. $24/yr. Kathryn R. Diggs, President.

All the above periodicals or newsletters have a subscription fee, as noted. To be sure the newsletter meets your particular needs or interests, I recommend you ask for a sample issue, prior to putting down your money on a subscription.

Computer Software, Film, Audiotape, Videotape:

For those who wish to explore the *non-print arena,* there are catalogs which you can order, such as:

The Personnel Software Census, Richard B. Frantzreb, Editor. Advanced Personnel Systems, P.O. Box 1438, Roseville, CA 95678. A dictionary of over 1,200 software programs for human resource management.

650 Career Videos: Ratings Reviews and Descriptions. 1994. Rich Feller, Clearinghouse on Video Usage, Colorado State University, School of Occupational and Educational Studies, Fort Collins, CO 80523. 303-491-6879.

Additional Software Programs (not in the catalogs above)

Most of these are for the IBM computer family; rarely, the Macintosh. A listing here is for supplemental information only, and does not constitute a recommendation or endorsement on my part:

---

2. Previously known as the American Association for Counseling and Development (AACD), and -- before that -- as the American Personnel and Guidance Association (APGA).

The Job Finder's Toolkit, Daniel Lauber. Planning/Communications, 7215 Oak Ave., River Forest, IL 60305. 800-829-5220. Features hundreds of job-sources unique to each of the 50 states. For Windows computers.

Jackson, Tom, *The Perfect Resume.* Davidsons. CD-ROM. Assists in preparing resumes, based on Tom's very popular book. Enables the user to prepare customized, target resumes. For Macintosh as well as Windows 95 computers.

Yana Parker, *Ready-To-Go-Resumes* software. 1995. Ten Speed Press, Box 7123, Berkeley, CA 94707. Self-teaching resume templates, with three computer disks for both Macintosh and Windows computers. It is based on Yana Parker's very popular book.

Visual Resume™. Heapsort Software, P.O. Box 324, Holly, MI 48442-0324. 1994. Gives the user who is interested in preparing a chronological resume, the ability to produce such a resume in a very unusual visual layout format (an 8½ × 11″ page, lying on its side, with a time bar at the bottom); also does cover letters, and labels. $19.95 when ordered directly from the publisher (Michigan residents add 6% sales tax). For IBM computers and compatibles.

Easy Working Resume Kit™. Spinnaker Software Corporation, 201 Broadway, Cambridge, MA 02139. 1992. Written only for IBM computers and compatibles. The merits of this software aside, the program has an *excellent* manual, including a long, helpful, and realistic section called *"Beyond Resumes"* -- obviously written by someone who knows what she is talking about, and who is wise and witty to boot. This company also publishes *PFS: Resume and Job Search Pro,* likewise just for IBM computers and compatibles, though a *Windows* version is available.

Patsy B. Edwards, *Adapting to Change: The NVAB Program.* Constructive Leisure, 511 N. La Cienega Blvd., Los Angeles, CA 90048. 310-652-7389. Designed to increase flexibility, this program is aimed at adults and older teenagers. Users learn how to modify conflictive behavior with others, that arises out of their Needs, Values, and Attitudes. For IBM computers and compatibles.

Course Syllabi:

If you are interested in course syllabi from courses in career development, career counseling and/or career planning, there is a clearinghouse for such materials, maintained by Dr. Stan Cramer, Dept. of Counseling & Educational Psychology, Faculty of Educational Studies, 409 Christopher Baldy Hall, SUNY Buffalo, Amherst, NY 14260.

Career Assessment Instruments:

This, of course, is a wide world. There are a *million* assessment instruments out there: the Strong Interest Inventory, the Holland SDS, the Myers-Briggs, and a host of others -- plus some quasi-instruments, such as my own *Quick Job-Hunting Map.*

If you want to know about instruments available to you, see: Kopes, Jerome T., and Mastice, Marjorie Moran, eds., *A Counselor's Guide to Career Assessment Instruments.* 1988 ed. Published by the American Counseling Association, 5999 Stevenson Ave., Alexandria, VA 22304.

Counselor Training:

By Others: There are countless training opportunities for career counselors in the U.S. and abroad. *Career Planning & Adult Development Newsletter,* mentioned earlier (published monthly by the Career Planning and Adult Development Network, 4965 Sierra Rd., San Jose, CA 95132) maintains a *very good* calendar of these events, and anyone interested in further training would be well advised to be receiving this *Newsletter.*

By Me: Whenever the subject of training comes up, I am asked (endlessly) whether or not I do any teaching. We receive hundreds of letters and phone calls each year asking this. Since I would like to cut down on the mail and phone calls, and also save you some trouble, I will give you the desired information, right here.

I spoke ceaselessly around the U.S. in 1996 and 1997, but now I have gone back to my *"let me stay home in the garden with my wife"* mode, and just *think,* write and praise God. I am essentially not doing any speaking or training in the next couple of years -- except for my annual appearance at the California Career Conference in early November of each year, plus my annual workshop every August, up in Bend, Oregon, where I teach nonstop for fourteen days at a resort there, along with my gifted colleague from Geneva, Switzerland, Daniel Porot, whom I much admire, and whose insights you can see frequently throughout *Parachute.*

We call this workshop:

Two Weeks of LIFE/Work Planning at the Inn of the Seventh Mountain

This workshop is not, as its name might suggest, held in the Orient. The Inn of the Seventh Mountain is a beautiful and popular resort on the outskirts of **Bend, Oregon**, *which -- as everyone knows -- is in the center of the United States (Honolulu is 3,000 miles to the West, New York City is 3,000 miles to the East).*

Since two weeks is a long time, and people who attend usually do so in lieu of their regular summer vacation, we have deliberately put this workshop at a first-class vacation resort, which past participants have delighted in -- as they can 'have their cake and eat it, too.' The Inn has two swimming pools, waterslide, hot baths/saunas, hiking trails, tennis, whitewater rafting,

News

Since I endlessly hear from people around the country and around the world who say, *"I've absolutely promised myself that one day I'm going to attend your two week workshop; I've heard so many wonderful things about it,"* I thought I should give you fair warning that this workshop's days are numbered.

I was 47 when I started offering it annually; this year, I turned 70. I am going to continue to offer it, on a year by year basis, *so long as I remain vigorous and in reasonable health.* But these things can change without warning. And when they do, that will be it!

So if you ever want to come, now is the time. *God willing,* I am planning to offer this workshop in 1998, and the dates will be August 7–21. In 1999, the dates will be August 6–20, *if all goes well.* You can always call 1-510-837-3002 to get the latest news (or fax us at: 1-510-837-5120).

R.N.B.

horseback riding, moped rental, bicycle rental, roller-skating, ski-lifts to the top of Mount Bachelor, and other vacation amenities, outdoor eating -- with *wonderful* food -- all in a lovely pine-forest setting near the foot of a large mountain topped with snow even in the summertime. To enjoy all these amenities, you should plan to come early and/or stay late, particularly if you are coming from a long way away.

The total training at this workshop exceeds 100 hours, and is limited to the first 55 people who apply, each year. In age, participants have ranged from 17–74, have embraced all geographical, ethnic groups and sexes, and have come from all parts of the world -- in addition to the U.S., we have had Scandinavia, England, Wales, The Netherlands, France, Switzerland, Germany, Gabon, Zimbabwe, Brazil, Venezuela, Costa Rica, Panama, Canada, New Zealand, Australia, Singapore, and Japan. Year after year people say

For More Than Just Counselors

Our methodology at this workshop is to have you master the principles of life/work planning by rigorously applying them to your own life during the two weeks, rather than discussing the problems of clients or their case histories, etc., as is often the fashion these days.

Because of this methodology, the workshop is useful to anyone, and each year over half the people who attend are not career counselors -- but job-hunters of all ages, career-changers, homemakers, union organizers, CEOs, teachers, people facing a move, people facing retirement, the recently divorced, college students, clergy and so forth.

that this was close to the most enjoyable fourteen days of their entire life. *Be sure to bring your playful self.*

The cost of these fourteen days is $3600, double occupancy, all expenses included (tuition, fourteen days room, fourteen days of meals, and all materials and handouts for the daily sessions).

As this workshop is our one annual fundraiser, to underwrite our worldwide work throughout the rest of the year, there are neither discounts for early registration, nor any kind of scholarships available. However we do have a piece called "How to Find Your Own Scholarship," which you may request.

The workshop is filled strictly on a first come, first served, basis.

How early registration closes, varies from year to year. It closes as soon as we are full. This has ranged from nine days ahead of August to 9 months ahead of August. You never know.

There are usually some last-minute cancellations, in any case, so always write or call to inquire, rather than simply concluding that it is already filled.

For a brochure and registration blank, write to:

Norma Wong, Workshop Registrar
What Color Is Your Parachute?
P.O. Box 379
Walnut Creek, CA 94597-0379

Phone No.: 1-510-837-3002
(10 a.m.–12 noon. Monday thru Friday, Pacific Coast Time)
Fax No.: 1-510-837-5120 (twenty-four hours a day)

Index

(Page numbers that are in red, and *italics*, refer to the *Parachute Workbook and Resource Guide*)

G

H

K

L

Y

"Parachute CD-ROM

YOU DO THE THINKING THE SOFTWARE DOES THE REST

If there's one constant message behind Parachute's legendary success it's "You *must* have alternatives!" Well here's one alternative that will really help you. It's a new interactive software version of this book, *"What Color Is Your Parachute?"* An easy-to-use software program that walks you, hand-in-hand with author Richard Bolles, through the exercises in the book. If you've already read the book -- even if you've just skimmed through it -- you already know it gives you the necessary tools to make a good job or career decision. You also know that it takes time and work. A complete personal journey that reveals what your life's work should be, it is an in-depth inventory of your skills, goals, and dreams. For some, the traditional pen-and-paper approach to this in-depth inventory will work just fine. For others, (and you may be one of them) there's now an alternative pen and paper that many may find a faster and easier way of completing these exercises. You can now do them on your *computer.* Thus, a process that once took many hours of writing, cutting, and pasting can now be automated -- in about half the time.

SEE & HEAR RICHARD BOLLES WHO USES INTERACTIVE VIDEO AND AUDIO TO GUIDE YOU THROUGH THE CREATE JOB HUNTING METHOD

It's like having the Author sit by your side as you work your way the the "Flower." You'll be inspired. You'll be supported. You'll get the most out of this incredible job-hunting method!

INCLUDES DIRECT ACCESS TO THE BEST JOB AND CAREER LINKS ON THE INTERNET!

Once you've completed the parachute exercises, it's time to actually FIND the ideal job. Today, the Internet is playing a bigger and bigger role in hooking up employers and potential employees. This software provides direct access to such contacts, including descriptions of each site and what you can expect to find there!

YOU'LL GET HELP EVERY STEP OF THE WAY.

This isn't merely a replica of the book on CD-ROM. This new software version comes loaded with all sorts of additional help to make the book's tasks easier. For example, you'll see video clips where Richard Bolles will explain exactly what he wants you to do in each of the "Flower" exercises. You'll listen to audio clips where he'll give you direction and encouragement to complete the next task. There are even suggestions to help you get started whenever you get blocked. And examples to show you what others have said when confronted with the same questions you have. In short, the software does everything you can possibly imagine

Notes

Notes

Notes

Notes

Notes